WIDE
AWAKE

WIDE AWAKE

THE FORGOTTEN FORCE
THAT ELECTED LINCOLN AND SPURRED
THE CIVIL WAR

JON GRINSPAN

BLOOMSBURY PUBLISHING
NEW YORK · LONDON · OXFORD · NEW DELHI · SYDNEY

BLOOMSBURY PUBLISHING
Bloomsbury Publishing Inc.
1385 Broadway, New York, NY 10018, USA

BLOOMSBURY, BLOOMSBURY PUBLISHING, and the Diana logo are trademarks of
Bloomsbury Publishing Plc

First published in the United States 2024

Bloomsbury Publishing Plc does not have any control over, or responsibility for, any
third-party websites referred to or in this book. All internet addresses given in this book
were correct at the time of going to press. The author and publisher regret any
inconvenience caused if addresses have changed or sites have ceased to exist, but can
accept no responsibility for any such changes.

ISBN: HB: 978-1-63973-064-3; EBOOK: 978-1-63973-065-0

LIBRARY OF CONGRESS CATALOGING-IN-PUBLICATION DATA IS AVAILABLE

2 4 6 8 10 9 7 5 3 1

Typeset by Westchester Publishing Services
Printed and bound in the U.S.A.

To find out more about our authors and books visit www.bloomsbury.com and sign up
for our newsletters.

Bloomsbury books may be purchased for business or promotional use. For information on
bulk purchases please contact Macmillan Corporate and Premium Sales Department at
specialmarkets@macmillan.com.

What a filthy Presidentiad! (O South, your torrid suns!
O North, your arctic freezings!)
Are those really Congressmen? are those the great
Judges? is that the President?
Then I will sleep awhile yet, for I see that these
States sleep, for reasons;
(With gathering murk, with muttering thunder and
lambent shoots we all duly awake,
South, North, East, West, inland and seaboard, we will
surely awake.)

—WALT WHITMAN, "TO THE STATES, TO IDENTIFY THE 16TH, 17TH,
OR 18TH PRESIDENTIAD," 1860

CONTENTS

PREFACE

We Shall All Be Wide-Awakes

"The speakers!"

"The speakers!"

"The northern dogs!"

"Let us have them!"

James Sanks Brisbin could hear the hollering and the hissing all around him. Shouts of "Abolitionists!" and "Stone them!" shuddered through the crowds outside his rattling carriage. Inside, Brisbin tried to go unnoticed, tucking his white hat low over big green eyes. His only hope was to get out of Wheeling, Virginia, before they discovered him, back over the bridge to the far side of the Ohio River.[1]

The rain poured, and the carriage jostled. Across from Brisbin sat a rare antislavery White Virginian, who had invited the Pennsylvania Republicans to come make a "modest and moderate presentation of the claims of Abraham Lincoln," one week before the 1860 election. The speeches had not lasted long. An angry throng had mustered outside the lecture hall. Many were armed. They demanded—Brisbin was told while speaking onstage—that the northern speakers be handed over to the crowd.[2]

His hosts snuck him out through a side door, but knew they had to keep him out of sight. In a world where every clothing choice made a partisan declaration, the twenty-three-year-old newspaper editor's long brown hair, his white hat, and his shawl all marked him "distinctly as being a northern abolitionist."[3]

As Brisbin's carriage reached the plaza before the bridge leading off Wheeling Island, "a mass of struggling human beings" blocked its path. Many more furious locals leaned out over balconies. Rumor had it that men were searching the city's hotels for him. The miserable rain pounded the vehicle's roof. Through the darkness, Brisbin could make out the gaslights of the bridge, and beyond it scores of strange golden glimmers, his fellow Republicans disappearing over the span toward Pennsylvania.[4]

He had no choice. He would have to run for it.

Then Brisbin was out of the carriage, trying to move briskly but inconspicuously through the crowds. But his outfit gave him away. Just as he neared the great bridge's iron toll gate, a hand yanked him by his long hair. Another grasped at his shawl. Brisbin sprang forward, losing a fistful of hair and breaking his shawl's fastener. He wheeled halfway around and struck one of his pursuers in the face. Then, certain he was about to die, he dashed for the bridge.[5]

The structure before him was no shabby crossing. Wheeling's famous suspension bridge was the most sophisticated in the world, an inspiration for the future Brooklyn Bridge: a thousand feet long, with tall towers of mottled stone shaped like huge archways, and taut wires that stretched like fingers onto the river bluffs on either side. And now Brisbin was scrambling onto its well-lit span. As he began his sprint, he heard gunshots behind him.[6]

A strange tableau emerged before Brisbin as he pounded down the slick wooden boards. At the very focal point of his panicked vision, between the gray bluffs, the muddy river, the converging suspension wires, and the stone arch, stood a squadron of men in black. Eighty of them, looking statuesque in flared dark capes, dark greatcoats, dark trousers, and dark boots. Many held torches on long wooden staffs. Others clutched blued-steel revolvers, flashing in the gloom. Their young faces were framed by black soldiers' caps, tucked low against the rain. Torchlight flickered off their shining capes, catching broad shoulders, stern stares, and full beards. At their head, a veteran officer kept them in a tight martial column. Some held banners with their stark symbol: an open, unblinking eye.[7]

They looked like soldiers, they looked like monuments, they looked like nothing that had been seen before in American politics. To a panting James Sanks Brisbin, closing his thousand-foot dash, they looked like salvation.

The force assembled on that rain-racked bridge is foreign to us today, but in the heat of the 1860 election, it was famous. Brisbin certainly knew it well. He told his Virginian hosts that he had marched into Wheeling with these "Wide Awakes and I would return with them dead or alive." Others, like a doctor in Lincoln's adopted hometown, considered the group the "most soul-inspiring organization the country had ever seen." Diverse communities saw the movement as an army rising to crush slavery, or a fun night out, or as "Modern Huns" organizing "an invasion of the South for murder, rape, lust, and similar unamiable intentions." A few screamed "Kill the damn Wide Awakes!" as they launched guerrilla attacks on the companies.[8] Millions hailed the Wide Awakes as saviors in a nation on the brink, even as others swore they were the very force pushing democracy into war.

Whether friendly or hostile, most Americans in 1860 would agree with the *New York Tribune*'s summary: "The most imposing, influential, and potent political organization which ever existed in this country is the Wide-Awakes."[9]

Over 160 years later, this history can feel distant, made irrelevant by the immediacy of our times. But the Wide Awakes of 1860 wrestled with the same forces—mass democracy, public protest, free speech, political violence, slavery, and race—that we grapple with today. And because they helped march their nation from an election into a war, we should listen to their story. Once we appreciate the Wide Awakes' full size, scale, and diversity, their role in electing Lincoln, in sparking secession, in fighting for the Union, and in redefining democratic behavior, it becomes hard to think of any partisan organization in American history as "imposing, influential, and potent."

The Wide Awakes were a militaristic youth movement. They marched to protest against slavery's death grip on democracy. Though not all abolitionists, most were antislavery in one way or another. They united around a fear that a small minority of enslavers, aided by northern allies, were perverting America's fragile politics. After watching their elders slumber for decades, a rising generation was eager to wake up. A culminating clash was coming. Wide Awakes would form companies and elect officers, don uniforms and organize rallies, vote for Lincoln and then fight for him, driven by this militarized grievance.

"How long must the South kick us," shouted a stump speaker to a crowd of black-caped, torch-bearing Wisconsinites, "before we shall all be Wide-Awakes?"[10]

Plenty were eager to enlist. White working-class Northerners in their early twenties made up the core, but a surprising swath of Americans became Wide Awakes. Fugitive slaves formed companies in northern cities, lighting a path toward Black public partisanship and military service. Radical new immigrants enlisted, mixing awkwardly with xenophobic ex–Know Nothings. Thousands of Southerners braved furious crowds to march on slavery's front porch. A few bold women even formed female clubs; many more attended mass rallies. Prominent entertainers, musicians, boxers—even the notorious showman P. T. Barnum—backed the movement. At their peak in November 1860, there were Wide Awakes in every northern and western state, and in the major cities of the Upper South. We'll never know exactly how many Americans joined, but the nation *believed* the movement had half a million members.[11] Adjusted for today's population, that would be the equivalent of five million Wide Awakes, dwarfing any mass movement in recent memory.[12]

How—in a tribal, fractured, distrustful age—did a movement of novices get so many to march in the same direction? How did they build this unlikely coalition? And how did they convince people who mostly saw themselves as bystanders on the slavery issue to take to the streets?

Started by five obscure young textile clerks in Hartford, Connecticut, the Wide Awakes would come to include railroad guards and blacksmiths' apprentices and telegraph boys, with the support of seamstresses and barmaids and factory girls. They mobilized much of the bustling North's "laboring classes." The story of this era is usually told through presidents and generals, but the Wide Awakes were a grassroots force pushing elite leaders into action. Some politicians, awoken by torchlight and brass bands outside their windows late at night, ordered the young marchers back to sleep. Even Abraham Lincoln sometimes seemed to quietly, diplomatically sigh as he struggled to manage this confrontational fraternity mustering around him.

For a lot of these laboring, striving youths, joining the Wide Awakes felt like *doing something* in an age of political gridlock, dread, and fear. Put on a cape, light a torch, march at night. There had been other mass movements in American political history, but none offered the Wide Awakes' simple method of action, or their clarity. The uniforms, the marches, the iconography—even the name—made them comprehensible to all. No political movement had ever been so expertly branded, promoted by Yankee salesmen as a nationwide political franchise.

The clubs' political goals were murkier. They first formed "to act as a political police"—muscle fighting back against frequent attacks on antislavery speakers. As they spread, it became hard to tell if they were paramilitaries or party planners, sometimes plotting war on slavery, sometimes meeting to design uniforms or organize spectacular rallies. But it would be a mistake to dismiss the movement as a game of political dress-up. After Lincoln's election, the word many commentators chose when describing Wide Awakes' contribution was *embody*: they embodied their cause. Their uniforms, torches, and parades declared their defense of democracy, a public, combative, disciplined uprising in a system being dragged down by suppression, compromise, and chaos. The movement's physical presence enunciated an ideology as legible as any policy plank.[13]

To twenty-first-century readers, it can feel obtuse to call this electorate—in which only a fifth of the total population could vote—a "democracy." Before women's suffrage, before the Voting Rights Act, this political system might not merit the term. But democracy is both a question of *who* gets to participate, and *how*. The Wide Awakes did alter the *who*, introducing young people to leadership and mobilizing Black men for partisan and military participation. But more profound were the questions the companies posed about the *how* of democracy. How should a movement mobilize and motivate? How should it build a coalition? How does its rhetoric, iconography, and behavior impact various audiences? And, most important: How far is too far, in a dangerously unstable political system? At bottom, the movement posed enduring questions about the processes of democracy—exploring three challenges that still devil us today: free speech, majority rule, and political violence.

Wide Awakes formed to defend antislavery speech in a world where critics often faced mobs wielding bricks, bowie knives, and pistols. They built a diverse coalition against the minority rule of a small cohort of enslavers. And they chose militaristic symbols to excite their supporters (and terrify their rivals). That final element was ultimately the most consequential. The clubs' rhetorical militarism somehow segued into the real thing. It remains a strange, gnawing fact that a year *before* America's Civil War, hundreds of thousands of campaigners started dressing up like soldiers. Did the Wide Awakes anticipate that conflict, or precipitate it?

When Americans think of the start of the Civil War, we tend to imagine a jump cut from the 1860 election, to cannon fire on Fort Sumter, to men in blue and gray arrayed on a field in Virginia. As some point, politics stops and fighting starts. But the Wide Awakes help tell this story contiguously, from an electoral campaign to a military one. Their clubhouses became paramilitary headquarters became army recruiting stations. Their members disproportionately made up the first Union volunteers. The machine they built to win votes was hastily, tentatively repurposed to fight a war. And everywhere the conflict began—in a partisan Washington, a secessionist Charleston, or the streets of Baltimore and St. Louis where blood was first shed—members of the movement were either present as fighters or invoked as a justification by their rivals.

The Wide Awakes never quite appreciated the impact of their militarism. They failed to consider how others might perceive columns of partisan marchers streaming through their streets at night. Supporters dismissed others' fears, stating that "there is no warlike intention whatever in the movement." But the critics were not wrong to worry. "If all men who do not agree in politics are to don uniforms," warned an irate New Yorker, "then partisanship will soon degenerate into hostility, hostility into tyranny, and tyranny into treason." The proslavery political militias formed to "offset" the Wide Awakes in the South prove this point. Southern secessionists caused the war, but they did so with a wary eye on the Republican army rising to their north. The Wide Awakes demand that we ask: Where, exactly, is the line between symbol and meaning, free speech and public menace, politics and violence?[14]

Democracy exists to restrain such violence. Open, managed competition is supposed to safely channel the aggressive energies that usually snatched power for most of human history. Political campaigns turn war into sport. But democracies also need to draw out participation from their citizens. And in 1860, Wide Awake Republicans discovered militarism's unparalleled ability to excite the public, pantomiming the aggressive energies their system was meant to restrain. It worked, electing a bold new president and drawing out one of the highest voter turnouts in U.S. history. And yet, it all looked like coercion to their opponents, beginning a spiral that would end in war. Democracy's contradictory imperatives—pacifying and mobilizing—crashed into each other, as the Wide Awakes and their rivals rewilded the forces that their system was meant to tame.

The nineteenth-century Prussian general Carl von Clausewitz is often misquoted as having written that "war is politics by other means." A closer translation of his original writing has it as "war is the continuation of policy," with the two existing on a single spectrum. This view better fits the Wide Awakes' story. War extends from politics, and politics borrows from war. The young Americans who put on Wide Awake uniforms in 1860 soon found that democracy's faith in a clean separation between politics and violence meant little to those teetering between the two.[15]

I'VE BEEN CHASING these guys for seventeen years.

When I started, it was the Wide Awakes' distinctiveness, their unlikely *did-that-actually-happen-in-American-history?* vibe, that attracted me. In 2007 I was a new graduate student at the University of Virginia, wondering how to add anything to the towering stack of work on the Civil War. Then I began finding, in older history books, stray references to the Wide Awakes. Most were brief campaign color, a glancing paragraph between drawn-out descriptions of Lincoln's 1860 nomination fight and the 1861 secession conventions. I was intrigued by how distant their midnight marches felt from the usual depictions of nineteenth-century American politics as genteel, restrained, or hokey. The Wide Awakes looked more like what you would expect from a nation on the brink of a civil war. And yet historians' references to the companies often had a whiff of disdain, relying on old-timey terms like *hoopla, hullabaloo,* and *folderol.* They made the movement seem almost meaningless, far from the Big Questions that brought on the war. But I started to wonder if the Wide Awakes' spectacle contained a larger meaning, a debate about the functioning of democracy at the very heart of the conflict.[16]

I mentioned my curiosity about the Wide Awakes to my thesis advisor. Given his tweed jacket and blue-and-orange bow tie, his office fragrant with pipe tobacco, I expected more talk of hoopla and folderol. But he swiveled to his desktop and fired up one of the keyword-searchable newspaper databases that were revolutionizing historical research. Typing in "Wide Awakes," for the year 1860, he got fifteen thousand hits. "Wide-Awakes" got another twelve thousand.

"I do believe"—he smiled generously—"we have something here." It was one of those moments as a historian when you feel like you can grasp at the ephemeral past.

The Wide Awakes became my fixation. I spent long hours with my eyes trained on a computer monitor, reading digitized old newspapers. I neglected my other classes, propelled by a contrarian hunch that the Wide Awakes were more fertile soil. On a research trip to the Connecticut Historical Society,

I mentioned to a cardiganed archivist that I was chasing the Wide Awakes. It was like he was spring-loaded. He had been waiting years for somebody to come ask just this question, and this very still man popped into action, pulling box after box of letters, pamphlets, and song sheets. In 2009 I published an article on the Wide Awakes in the *Journal of American History*, and thought I was done.[17]

Just because you think you are done with a history does not mean it is done with you. Every few years, the Wide Awakes would come marching back into my life. I could almost hear their brass bands coming. As a curator of political history at the Smithsonian, I've had the pleasure of meeting diverse Americans who were also enticed by the forgotten movement. People contacted me with references in ancestors' letters, or striking banners they'd found at auction, or to share their enthusiasm and sport their WIDE AWAKE tattoos, complete with the open eye symbol. In 2015 volunteers at the tiny Milford Historical Society in New Hampshire went digging through an old attic. A retired school principal found a beat-up cardboard box. Pulling out costumes and wigs, he glimpsed some crinkly, battered beige material at the bottom. Unfolding the ungainly shape on the floor, the volunteers discovered an off-white cape, six feet wide, bearing the dark-violet words "1860 WIDE-AWAKES," and a large drawing of an open eye. Here was a creature from this forgotten past, hibernating in a New Hampshire attic.

Still, most audiences I spoke to about the Wide Awakes expressed a halting sense that this story did not fit with what they expected from American history. Someone would always comment that the slides of uniformed men marching in lockstep reminded them more of Nazi Germany than of Honest Abe.

That changed after the 2016 election upended our thinking about appropriate political behavior. It became clearer that in a democracy, how we behave while getting power is as important as how we use it. The year after that, neo-Nazis marched with tiki torches in Charlottesville, Virginia. They stomped right past the elegant brick building where my professor and I had first searched "Wide Awakes" in the newspaper databases, ten years before. New cultures of public protest exploded over those years, ranging from peaceable gatherings like the Women's March to the dire summer nights of 2020's Black Lives Matter protests to far-right militias whose ballistic vests and AR-15s pointed back, unknowingly, to a past movement of performative militarism.

No one called any of this "hullabaloo."

People started, here and there, to invoke the Wide Awakes. The activist arts organization For Freedoms launched a new Wide Awake social justice movement, aiming to reawaken the spirit of the old association. They used the same open eye insignia, but shared little else with the original club. The Fox News host Ben Domenech lectured on the Wide Awake Republicans of 1860 and told his viewers to be "Wide Awake, not woke"—whatever that meant. "Woke" survived as a political football, highlighting the recurring power of the metaphor of awakening. Commentators contorted the knotty movement, trying to cast the Wide Awakes as earnest abolitionist heroes. Tweets and memes played with the club's striking iconography and enigmatic toughness, calling for a revival today.

These days, fewer people see Nuremberg when I show slides of the Wide Awakes. More see Charlottesville. They comment on how "relevant" the Wide Awakes seem, in our democracy of torch-waving protests and norm-breaking elections, testing the line between politics and violence. The delicious obscurity that attracted me in 2007 now has a dreadful relevance.[18]

There is a duality in the Wide Awakes' story. It's both hard to believe they ever marched down the humdrum streets of Hartford or Wheeling or Kenosha and easy to imagine reposting GIFs of them battling counterprotestors in messy melees. This twoness shows in their legacy as well. It can be tempting to squint and see the Wide Awakes as a long-awaited army of abolitionist caped crusaders finally rallying to crush slavery. But the same organization that mobilized against the Slave Power also unleashed the scariest energies of mass politics. Its members held plenty of nasty beliefs of their own. Most consequentially, the Wide Awakes helped spur the nation into a bloody civil war, which brought both unimaginable human suffering and the ultimate end of slavery. Refusing easy satisfaction, the movement reminds us how jumbled and conflicted the past can be, even as it looks more and more like the present.

How could it be, that in the sprawling canon of Civil War history, this crucial element has been neglected? Few have written about the movement. At the time, the *New York Tribune* predicted that "the future historian" studying "the political revolution of 1860," would "devote one of his most glowing chapters to the achievements of the Wide-Awakes." That historian never came; most people haven't heard of them.[19]

Maybe it's because its members were young, laboring nobodies, neglected by historians mostly interested in powerful elites. Maybe it's because the titanic war that followed the Wide Awakes swamped out much of what came before. Or maybe it's because historians tell stories from the past that feel applicable to the present, and an ambiguous tale about the motivating power of the darkest forces in our democracy was not one that Americans were eager to tell. Looking back on the 1860 election, it was usually easier to appreciate Abraham Lincoln's woodsy rail-splitter charm than to think too deeply about the army of partisans marching in the night.[20]

But the logic that made the Wide Awakes a footnote now makes their story urgent. They grew out of the fight over slavery, stoked by party politics, racial and ethnic hatreds, new communications technologies, a fixation on conspiracy, a habit of vigilantism, a nation's love of spectacle, and the immense power of martial metaphors. Of these factors, only slavery has ended. The rest worry us still.

The movement—so earnest in its intentions, so justified in its aims, so ingeniously crafted and well promoted, so motivating—inadvertently made political use of the most dangerous elements in American society. The result was both inspiring and catastrophic. The fact that America's most creative political campaign preceded America's most destructive war should tell us something about the dangerous relationship between the two. The question the Wide Awakes asked in 1860, one with renewed salience today, is what our democracy is capable of.

PART ONE

The Systematic Organization of Hatreds

CHAPTER ONE

Don't Care

EDDIE YERGASON WATCHED and waited. Downtown Hartford came alive around him, across the bleary blue February afternoon. Main Street began to buzz. Barkers announced the evening's big event in drawn New England accents. Top-hatted and bonneted Republicans mingled and chatted. A stained worker from Hank's Illuminating Store piled kerosene-stinking torches atop an old wagon.

No one paid much attention to the gawky, foppish nineteen-year-old on his perch outside the textile shop where he worked, ate, and boarded. With his big dark eyes and his buzzard's profile, his natty new coat and a loud plaid shirt, Eddie looked the part of the puckish young clerks busily swooping around Hartford's downtown. But even as the hubbub picked up and crowds filled out, Eddie kept his eyes on his prize.

In a few hours the brawling Kentucky abolitionist Cassius M. Clay was due to speak, to kick off Connecticut's spring gubernatorial race. It would be the first significant race of the 1860 presidential election cycle, closely watched nationwide in an age before polling. To cap off the evening, Hartford's Republicans planned a procession back to Clay's rooms at the Allyn House Hotel. Through pestering reminders in the newspapers, local leaders had gathered up torches used for previous marches, recovered from closets and attics. Hank's Illuminating Store trimmed them, filled them, and prepared to distribute them for the march after Clay's lecture.

Eddie Yergason worried that the torches might disappear just as fast, snatched up by multitudes waiting for the main event. And though two years too young to vote, he wanted in on what was coming. So he watched for the moment when Hank's wagon driver was distracted. Then he darted forward, yanked a metal torch top off its wooden staff, and stuffed it under his coat, disappearing into Talcott & Post's textile shop.

Inside that dim, rambling building—past rows piled with Persian rugs, past hoop skirt frames and rolls of French velour, past the taxidermied crocodile that old Mr. Talcott kept to scare children—Eddie found his fellow clerks. Opening his coat, he displayed his prize, the stolen torch, but also a nasty slick of oil staining his new garment. The five young clerks chuckled at Eddie's luck. The crocodile grinned. Grumbling, Eddie marched to the rolls of fabrics and cut himself a yard and a half of treated black cambric, shiny and crinkly on its waterproofed side. Working carefully, he threaded a cord onto a long steel needle and got to sewing "something very novel for a political campaign."[1]

Thirty years later, in practically another lifetime, Edgar S. Yergason would be celebrated as one of America's finest designers. With studios in Hartford and New York, the older man would curate interiors for Theodore Roosevelt and Thomas Edison. He made his name renovating the White House in the 1890s, discussing decor with presidents and first ladies. He installed the Executive Mansion's first electrical lighting system, and enlivened its stodgy Victorian walls and draperies with bold color schemes. Can it be a coincidence that the boy who launched American democracy's most striking, most visually composed political movement grew up to be a celebrated designer, always dressed in sharply tailored suits? The man who lit and draped the White House in the 1890s got his start three decades before, working with torches and capes.[2]

And while his later palette favored the pale blues, lemon yellows, and sunrise pinks of the Gilded Age, when Eddie Yergason created the Wide Awakes in 1860, he was working in the starker hues of that earlier era.

IN THE DREARY late winter of early 1860, no one could predict what would happen over the next few years. Not that they didn't try. At the start of a presidential campaign, in a culture enthralled by technological progress, among people who were often devout believers in an imminently arriving Messiah, and in a nation that muttered anxiously about civil war, it was tempting to try to guess what was coming. The era's funniest humorist used that anticipation in a routine in which he awoke a few centuries into the future to see what insanities America's schoolhouses were teaching about the 1860s.[3]

People usually predicted the future they wanted. Those with visions of disruptive change were often the young, the radical, those wanting a better place for themselves or eager for a fight, hoping to bring the change they augured. James Garfield, then a handsome young schoolteacher with bright-blue eyes and brighter ambitions, was certain that "the old race of leaders and lights, religious and social and political, are fast fossilizing and fast becoming extinct." Those who had already grown stout with power forecast more stability. The eminent editor and poet William Cullen Bryant wrote that while many liked to debate the possibility of disunion, "Nobody but silly people expect it will happen."[4]

One thing almost no one predicted was the end of slavery. Few institutions in American life seemed more permanent. The economy might sour, political parties might crumble, construction on the Washington Monument might stall, but even the most hopeful abolitionists could not lay out a likely path to ending slavery any time soon. In 1860, slavery was well into its third century on the U.S. mainland, exacting an incalculable toll of murder, rape, torture, family separation, and ceaseless theft. That year the census would count 3,953,762 humans trapped in slavery, in a nation of 31 million. Generation upon generation had lived their entire lives enslaved. And unlike many previous manifestations across world history, American slavery followed the principle of *partus sequitur ventrem* ("that which is born follows the womb"), an inheritance passed down from mothers to children, making it a perpetual state, an unending claim on the future itself.[5]

The New England sage Ralph Waldo Emerson hoped for abolition as the 1860s began—but, he sighed, "We shall not live to see it."[6]

In fact, across that three-century history, slavery had rarely looked stronger. While the abolitionist mathematician Elizur Wright considered slavery a "pitiful little ogre cub" at the time of the nation's founding, by the mid-nineteenth century it had grown into what Frederick Douglass called "the pet monster of the American people." The beast just kept swelling, demanding more and more of America's physical and political map. By the 1850s slavery claimed more territory than ever before. The humans it imprisoned fetched higher prices. Most of the wealthiest states in the Union, per capita, were in the South, and all of the poorest states were in the North. Slave owners and their allies controlled the presidency and skewed the majority of votes in Congress. The Supreme Court had just declared that the Constitution simply did not apply to Black people. Some proslavery radicals were talking about reopening the slave trade with Africa, banned for fifty years.[7]

Yet while America's "pet monster" grasped ever more wealth and power, it increasingly fell behind in sheer numbers of supporters. There were dire predictions, coming from proslavery corners, about the demographic wave that would crush them. The North was growing at an astounding rate, outpacing a stagnating South. In the first census, in 1790, Virginia had been the most populous state, nearly twice the size of New York. Now New York had three times Virginia's numbers. After that came Pennsylvania, then Ohio. Even newcomers like Illinois had more people that any southern state. Of the nation's hundred largest cities, seventy-eight were outside the South. By 1860 White Southerners made up roughly a fifth of the total population, down from one third in 1790. Actual slave owners made up just under 2 percent. More people walked the streets of Manhattan or Philadelphia than "owned" slaves nationwide. Of course, the 393,975 enslavers were protected by widening circles of family, neighbors, and allies, but nationwide, slavery seemed to be losing a demographic test.[8]

On paper it looked so clear, wrote William Tecumseh Sherman. The unsentimental Ohioan, working as an instructor at a Louisiana military academy, was no radical; in fact his politics ran pretty close to the middle of the American spectrum. But "majority has passed to the North," Sherman summarized. "Power," he predicted, "must follow."[9]

This shrinking club of enslavers had no plans to give up the reins of the federal government. Instead, as political majority moved north, proslavery voices found a new justification for the tyranny of their minority. The problem, they argued, was not slavery but democracy. Every society needed a lowest level, a "mudsill" under the foundation of its national house, declared the South Carolina senator James Henry Hammond. The trick for an aristocracy, Hammond explained, was simply to make sure that the lowest class was totally enslaved, as in the South, not enfranchised, as northern states had done with their large working-class White populations. Northerners, hissed the brash, goateed South Carolina congressman Laurence Keitt, had made a crucial mistake when they armed their mudsills with the ballot, initiating "the wildest democracy ever seen on this earth." The ballot box itself, in the words of the Texas senator Louis Wigfall, was "an instrument and means of oppression." Demography put these aristocrats on a collision course with democracy.[10]

The logic of enslavement, with its constant demand for mastery, did not exactly train these men to peacefully surrender power. The three politicians quoted above enslaved many hundreds of people among them. Keitt brawled and waved a revolver on the floor of Congress. Wigfall had murdered unarmed men. And Hammond was known to have raped four of his nieces. It should be no surprise that men like these struggled with notions of majority rule, human equality, or fair play.[11]

Their only option, then, was to keep that northern majority from taking power. As early as 1839, abolitionists had started to talk about a "Slave Power conspiracy" suppressing the voice of the majority. Usually in history, when movements warn of cabals and conspiracies, they are scapegoating bogeymen. But the Slave Power was an exception. The Slave Power was *real*. It amounted to a pyramid scheme disfiguring American democracy, in which 393,975 slave owners led 7 million White Southerners in control of the national Democratic Party, the federal government, and the destiny of 31 million. The 87 percent of the population who were neither enslavers nor enslaved had to pick a side. But, penned in by self-interest, patriotism, White supremacy, electoral tricks, financial entanglements, and open intimidation, they often let the Slave Power lead.

The first pillar of the Slave Power's rule was to appeal to the warm feelings White Americans still felt for each other, often invoking a shared love of the concept of Union that held them all together. Union meant fealty to the nation's revolutionary heritage, an appreciation of the interstate trade that was making Americans rich, and a willingness to turn a blind eye on ugly behavior elsewhere. But it could also be a bludgeon. The Democratic Party, founded in the 1820s to deter "sectional prejudices," brandished the ideal of Union against anyone who threatened the proslavery status quo. Even in the North, Democrats wielded it against local dissent. When the Pennsylvania legislature banned Black men from voting in 1838—a prerogative they had long enjoyed—Democrats argued that "the right of the negroes to vote was to be put in the scale against the union of these states." Union beat free speech across the North.[12]

Even those who personally disliked slavery were expected to shut up about it. A onetime congressman named Abraham Lincoln wrote to a friend from Kentucky, in 1855, asking him to appreciate how "the great body of the Northern people do crucify their feelings, in order to maintain their loyalty to the constitution and the Union." Three years later, in the midst of a heated campaign for U.S. Senate, a more confident Lincoln denounced what he succinctly summed up as the "don't care" attitude toward slavery that many Northerners pretended to take. His rival, the wily Stephen A. Douglas, claimed that it wasn't the job of a senator from Illinois to care about slavery in Georgia. With probing questions and lightning strikes of morality, Lincoln denounced this notion. "No man," he argued, "can logically say he don't care whether a wrong is voted up or voted down."[13]

The Slave Power also gamed the political system, relying on the antidemocratic elements of the Constitution, especially the Three-Fifths Clause. This clause allowed slave-owning states to count three fifths of their enslaved people when apportioning congressional seats and electoral votes. It meant that a shrinking population of White Southerners could exaggerate their numbers with every additional human they enslaved. The result distorted everything.[14] By the 1850s, the South had gained thirty additional congressional seats because of it, deciding the majority of roll-call votes.[15]

And when things got even uglier, and southern and northern congressmen fought brawls in the late 1850s, the Three-Fifths Clause meant thirty extra mouths, and sixty extra fists, on the southern side of the aisle.

With this added boost, the Slave Power and its northern allies were able to compound their advantage. They led the invasion of Mexico, conquering even more land for slavery. As the northern majority grew in the 1850s, the shrinking proslavery minority pushed harder. In 1854 a coalition of southern and northern Democrats threw open to slavery vast tracts of what would become Kansas and Nebraska, which Congress had long agreed to keep free. The move unleashed a bloody war for Kansas. Armed gangs barged into the state to swing elections and kill rivals. Between fifty and two hundred died. In 1856 a Democratic president and Congress supported a proslavery Kansas constitution that had been won only with massive fraud and violence. That new constitution made it a felony to write or speak against slavery.[16]

Finally, the Supreme Court's 1857 *Dred Scott* ruling found that African Americans could not be citizens of the United States, and questioned the federal government's power to limit the spread of slavery. Of the nine justices on the court, the seven who supported this view were all Democrats—even though Democrats had won just 45 percent of the popular vote in the most recent presidential election. Five of the nine were slave owners, like just 2 percent of the nation. Minority rule found its greatest ally in a partisan court.

What Union and electoral tricks could not suppress, force could. In the South, this meant the brutal regime of slavery. Nationwide, it meant that violence against critics became a normal part of political life. As the Georgia congressman (and future vice president of the Confederacy) Alexander Stephens smirked, "I have no objection to the liberty of speech, when the liberty of the cudgel is left free to combat it."[17]

This was no metaphor. Cudgels were a regular part of American public discourse in this antebellum era. So were bricks, and bottles, and boiling tar, and shoemakers' awls, and revolvers, and even the occasional cannon. Antebellum America faced an epidemic of "mobbings"—riotous attacks on one group or another for a perceived violation of public order. A historian of such mobbings counted 1,218 separate incidents between 1828 and 1861. These assaults persecuted diverse victims: African Americans and immigrants, Catholics and Mormons, labor organizers and brothel owners. Partisan rivals were a common foe. Newspapers were popular targets, their offices torched, their cast-iron presses hurled into rivers. Schoolteachers were easy to bully too. Most mobs made a humiliating racket, but plenty tortured or lynched. As a mob advanced down a typical American city street—pistols and placards waving, crazed boys and barking dogs darting about—a bystander would have to pause and really listen to determine who was preparing to mob whom.[18]

This was not just a case of the bad old days, when people were wilder. Mobbings were not as common in America's early years. They spiked precipitously after 1835—around the same time that partisanship, slavery, and a mass newspaper culture all shook the national conversation. Sensing a violent new irritability in the American character in the 1830s, one observer in South Carolina wrote, "The whole country seems ready to take fire on the most trivial occasion." Aggression became a tactic in public discourse, a specific vernacular of bricks and bottles used to make a point when other forms failed. And in a censorious society, many assumed that the victim of a mobbing had to be to blame somehow. Abolitionists must be truly awful, if people kept throwing their presses in rivers.[19]

Mobbings peaked again in the 1850s, their collective violence now justified as "vigilance." This was another element of Americans' zeal for predictions: a watchful belligerence toward threats to come. Looking at the spiraling conflicts of those years, Walt Whitman proposed that the whole nation needed "one grand vigilance committee." Even the "grannies of New England," William Tecumseh Sherman groaned, seemed to be taking the law into their own hands. "Men have ceased to look to constitutions and law books for their guides," Sherman grumbled. "Popular opinion in bar rooms and village newspapers" took their place. It was dangerously easy to get up a riot, promising to crush disorder by mobbing it away. In gold-rush California—filling with armed young men who drove the homicide rates sky-high—the forces of order formed "Committees of Vigilance" to terrorize purported criminals. In Boston, fugitive slaves organized their own vigilance committees, doing battle with slave hunters and federal marshals trying to drag people back into bondage. But no matter the purpose, such "vigilance" indicated a civic dysfunction, pushing many to take the law into their own hands.[20]

A new movement injected this vigilante tone into politics during the 1850s. On the ballot they went by the American Party, but the press dubbed them "Know Nothings," sworn to secrecy about their shady doings. Know Nothings are remembered as all-purpose xenophobes, but usually they were more specific. Though free-floating nativism infused American culture in the 1850s, as an organized movement the Know Nothings expressed little concern with Protestant immigrants. Many ignored Jews. It was Catholic immigrants they really hated. Preaching conspiracy theories about a Vatican plot to control American democracy, they won about a million members, and elected mayors, congressmen, and governors across the nation.[21]

The Know Nothings sprouted up wherever the old Whig Party was dying. The paranoid movement fit the mood of the 1850s better than the optimistic rising-tide-lifts-all-boats economic theories of the Whigs. The resulting organization was a crazy quilt of factions—urban gangs, old blue bloods, progressive reformers, even some African American activists—all seeking a new vehicle to fight the Democrats. Tragically, impoverished Irish Catholic immigrants often became the easily persecuted face of the larger Democratic Party, especially among the young, urban, native-born Protestant laborers who saw them as competition for work. As these conspiratorial young voters gravitated to politics for the first time, they brought an unprecedented bloodthirstiness.

In cities stretching down the mid-Atlantic coast and along the Ohio River, polling places turned into battlefields. In Washington, in 1857, Know Nothing election rioting grew so bad that the president called out U.S. marines to put them down, killing eight not far from the Capitol.[22]

Too bad these Know Nothings blamed the wrong conspiracy. They correctly diagnosed that some minority was perverting the democratic process, but neither immigrants nor Catholics were the true culprit. The Slave Power was. Sensing a malfunction somewhere, they traced the leak to the wrong source. But beneath all their bigotry, the Know Nothings tapped into powerful energies driving midcentury public life. A young Rutherford B. Hayes, denouncing the movement in Ohio, acknowledged their appeal among voters who felt "a general disgust with the powers that be." "*We are* determined," swore Know Nothings in Pittsburgh, to give the "old party hacks a glorious drubbing."[23]

And then, in October 1859, the high priest of American vigilantes struck. John Brown was no granny of New England; he was an American on fire, convinced that "constitutions and law books" could not resolve the evils around them. "Talk," Brown dismissed, "is a national institution, but it does no good for the slave." "The crimes of this guilty land will never be purged," he predicted in his final note, "but with blood." Rallying twenty-two followers, he launched an assault on the federal armory at Harpers Ferry, Virginia, hoping to spark a wider slave revolt. They quickly bungled the plot, and John Brown's body swung from a Virginia gibbet just eleven months before the 1860 presidential election. The whole incident left many Americans wondering when the next attack might come.[24]

There was a sense, in the late 1850s, that chaos was spreading. Most Americans still lived peaceful, rural, settled lives. Read their diaries, and the great majority write about weather and work, crops and courtships. Most rarely saw a mobbing, a lynching, or an election riot. But their shared, virtual nation—held together by the ideal of Union, by political parties, and by newsprint—seemed more dire. Rustle open a newspaper, and the flashpoints on the nation's map all seemed to bleed together. In California and in Kansas, at Harpers Ferry's arsenal and at Washington polling places, disorder menaced. It all amounted to a test of the "domestic tranquility" the Constitution had promised. If the spiraling democracy could not maintain public order in its streets, the *Sun* wrote in mob-prone Baltimore, "our boasted experiment will be to the world an example to be shunned."[25]

The "boasted experiment" was at its worst on the floor of the U.S. Capitol. It was a rough environment: a huge, bustling complex with a crude, aggressive air. "Bad manners were conspicuously in evidence," complained a young Charles Francis Adams Jr., "whiskey, expectoration and bowie-knives were the order of that day. They were, indeed, the only kind of 'order' observed in the House." For decades, this shadow "order" supplemented parliamentary procedure with the Slave Power's elaborate dueling codes and performative bullying. Between 1830 and 1860, congressmen were involved in at least seventy violent incidents in and around the august building. Petty squabbles devolved into insults and threats, nose-tweakings and cane-smackings, elected officials egging their colleagues on while the Clerk of the House begged, "Gentleman, for God's sake come to order." The uglier feuds found their way to the "Dueling Creek" in Bladensburg, Maryland.[26]

"Are those really Congressmen?" mused Walt Whitman, wandering antebellum Washington, amid the cane-waving, name-calling, pistol-loading representatives of the people. "Are those the great Judges? is that the President?"[27]

America's divided voters made it all worse. Southerners often rewarded a representative who dueled, while Northerners shunned politicians who engaged in such barbarism. This set up an ugly dynamic, over the years, where northern "noncombatants" became easy prey for Slave Power bullies. For a southern culture powered by a belligerent code of honor, it became an easy taunt: Northerners won't fight.[28]

It all came to an ugly peak in 1856, when the Massachusetts senator Charles Sumner gave a strident antislavery speech, calling out South Carolinians in particular. Pacing in the back of the room, Stephen Douglas muttered, "That damn fool will get himself killed by some other damn fool." Sure enough, a damn fool named Preston Brooks, congressman from South Carolina, pounced upon the seated Sumner in the Senate chamber two days later, beating him with a gold-headed cane. Fellow South Carolina congressman Laurence Keitt held off intervening senators at gunpoint. Remembered as "the caning of Sumner," that name is a little polite for a brutal beating that left its victim debilitated for years.[29]

As Alexander Stephens had promised, "the liberty of the cudgel" had answered "liberty of speech."

Seen from today, the Slave Power's thefts and threats looks like a zero-sum war between slavery and freedom, in which all had to pick a side. But people in the past rarely view the evidence the way historians think they should. The Slave Power's minority rule camouflaged itself among the other aspects of busy nineteenth-century lives. The northern White majority disliked slavery, sure, but many also disliked Catholic immigrants or preachy evangelicals, European monarchs or holier-than-thou abolitionists, African Americans or Mexicans or bankers or saloonkeepers. The constant churn of a big, booming society, in which people were trying to live their lives and make their fortunes, kept most people from seeing their politics as starkly as they look from our time.

"Politics," as the sharp, funny, cruel chronicler Henry Adams observed, is really the art of the "systematic organization of hatreds." A century later Kevin Phillips, the architect of the "emerging Republican majority," made the same point, stating that the secret of politics came down to knowing "who hates who." In 1860, Americans had plenty of people to hate. Add their love of Union, their weighted Constitution, their fear of mobs, their caustic racism, and their otherwise busy lives, and a shrugging "Don't care" seemed to be the safest stance on slavery.[30]

And yet that same "systematic organization of hatreds" was assembling a coalition of the majority. Mobbing in the streets and bullying in the capital reigned from the 1830s on, but by the mid-1850s a movement was coalescing to push back. The further the Slave Power overreached, the more they smushed together otherwise feuding elements of society against them. Teetotaling Yankee abolitionists disliked beer-drinking German radicals, who hated Know Nothing gang members, who shunned formerly enslaved African American fugitives, who distrusted the odd antislavery Southerner. But if they could all be made to see a common enemy, many of antebellum America's vigilantes might march in the same direction, against the same conspiracy.

The key would be to re-slice the pie of America's dislikes. The portion of Americans who wanted to end slavery tomorrow was small. Certainly, four million slaves felt this way, but among the White majority only a sliver could be considered true abolitionists. The number who hoped to stop slavery from expanding further was bigger. But the largest slice merely wanted the Slave Power to stop imposing on their lives. That sense of imposition could unite forces who had spent the previous decade at war with each other. As the White

Kansas activist Charles Robinson put it in 1855, the best reason to fight slavery—from the tribal perspective of the fractured 1850s—was "to be free ourselves."[31]

Drawing together ex-Whigs, reformed Know Nothings, disenchanted Democrats, and unchurched abolitionists, this biggest slice of the pie called themselves the Republican Party.

At its head was a "wise macaw" of a man, with wire-brush hair, untamable eyebrows, and a big, insistent nose. William Henry Seward had been in politics for decades, as a New York governor and senator. He was a talented diplomat, at once a populist reformer friendly with Harriet Tubman and a working politico happy to swig brandy and smoke cigars with who-knows-who down in Washington. And Seward had suffered for the cause. At least twice, beloved dogs on Seward's New York estate had turned up poisoned, most likely by some Democratic ruffian. After helplessly watching the death of their big, bounding Newfoundland mix, Seward's daughter Fanny concluded that their family should adopt no new canines. "It seems certain death," the fourteen-year-old wrote in a pained diary entry, for "a dog to belong to our family."[32]

But burying his pets himself only seemed to sharpen the senator's resolve. Seward's greatest talent was his intellectual clarity, the way he focused the Republicans on a pointed, defensible, lawyerly attack. "The single and only issue," Seward explained, "is the extension or non-extension of slavery."[33]

This was wise policy, but a hard slogan for canvassing in saloons. For most Americans, the Western territories were a crucial, but distant, concept, what William Tecumseh Sherman called "a mere abstraction." The Republicans also argued a kind of thesis, a belief in northern economic, social, and cultural superiority they called "free labor." It united the party and bridged the many critiques of the slave South, but everyday voters often needed a blunter weapon in their arsenal. Along with free labor, free soil, and free men, Republicans called for free speech. The latter was the simplest way to dramatize the Slave Power's constant impositions. A White majority might be unreliable on rights for African Americans, or on distant Kansas, or on abstract theories of labor. But bloodied senators and burned-out newspapers offices were the kind of concrete offense you could build a campaign around, proof of a national conspiracy creeping northward. This was the most widely shared hatred, a humiliated majority tired of being shut up and trampled on.[34]

Republicans started to select "fighting men" to stand up for their embattled speech. In Congress, there was Galusha Grow—six feet of lean muscle from Western Pennsylvania who famously knocked Laurence Keitt on his butt on the House floor; a squad of northern senators who publicly swore a pact to "fight to the coffin" together if threatened; and the six-foot-three-inch Roscoe Conkling, sent to Congress for his skill as a bare-knuckle boxer. African American abolitionists in cities like Boston began to confront slave catchers and federal marshals enforcing the new Fugitive Slave Act, battling in streets and besieging courthouses to free captured escapees. The abolitionist magazine the *Liberator* ticked off a list of Black Bostonians known to carry revolvers, and asked whether the Slave Power realized that "this arming and fighting was a game that *two* could play at?" A diverse coalition was exploring the possibility of a more aggressive stance, "noncombatants" no longer. Sensing a new confidence, the Republican *New York Times* exulted: "There *is* a North, thank God."[35]

Of course, to really take on the Slave Power, the Republicans would have to control the presidency. The Democratic Party had won six of the last eight presidential elections, most recently in 1856. But that last contest was instructive. The Republican Party, barely two years old, ran the explorer John C. Fremont. They performed well in the Yankee stretches of the Upper North, but wobbled in the middle states, swamped in a three-way race against both the Democrats and the Know Nothings. The dull, tired, slavery-accommodating Democrat James Buchanan squeaked into power. If the Republican Party was going to win nationwide, it needed to recruit the Lower North—Pennsylvania, Illinois, Indiana, and New Jersey, keystones with strong ties to the South, deep skepticism of New England radicals, and a fear of threatening the union of states. For the next presidential election, in 1860, the party had to convince a majority to see itself as one.

One Republican strategy was to force northern bystanders to pick a side by making the clash seem inevitable. William Henry Seward turned that premonition into a talking point in an 1858 speech, in which he declared that an unstoppable conflict was hurtling America's way. Moderates who considered the fight between slavery and freedom to be "accidental, unnecessary, the work of interested or fanatical agitators, and therefore ephemeral" were kidding themselves. "An irrepressible conflict" was coming, a final reckoning that would end with "either entirely a slaveholding nation, or entirely a free-labor one." "Irrepressible" became another political catchphrase, as motivating for Seward's admirers as it was terrifying for his opponents. The question—How bad would this election year get?—worried Americans going into 1860.[36]

Over the 1850s, Americans introduced another old phrase to new use. People said that populations that had shaken off their stupor and were finally alert, aware, and assertive were "wide awake." Usually it referred to a discrete identity group, a portion of the diverse nation announcing new vigilance. Newspapers reported that "the Mormons are wide awake" in Utah, that slave owners were "wide awake to the rights and honor of the South," or that the "Church of Rome was wide awake" in its alleged conspiracies. Before key elections, the Democratic Party warned: "DEMOCRATS, BE WIDE AWAKE against all sorts of devices to deceive you on Election Day." Yet the biggest slice of American demography rarely seemed to merit the term. If anyone was asleep, it was the don't-care caucus, the noncombatants, the Union savers, who had to work harder and harder to claim that they were merely bystanders.[37]

Watching armed Missouri settlers board steamboats toward Kansas, intent on seizing the state for slavery, a correspondent for a Pittsburgh paper worried: "We fear that the people of the North are not as wide awake as they should be."[38]

NOW THE 1860 campaign was beginning, not with a mobbing, but with a sewing circle. Eddie Yergason had all the Talcott & Post clerks stitching away. Five gleaming needles. Five black garments. Five stolen torches, jammed on curtain rods as makeshift torch-staffs. Cassius Clay was taking the stage as the Talcott clerks threw flashing black capes over skinny shoulders and stepped out into the February darkness.[39]

If anyone needed a sign of what was to come in that presidential election year, Republican Hartford's choice of opening speaker offered a noisy hint. "Cash" Clay had become a kind of southern mascot for many Northerners, admired for his bloody fight against slavery. Born into a large Kentucky family—he was cousin to the senator Henry Clay—Cash renounced slavery and spent twenty years facing down its thugs. A big bowie knife helped. That famous knife actually deflected an assassin's bullet fired at him during a political rally in Lexington. Another time, when he debated a proslavery opponent, the candidate's six sons came at him with guns, daggers, and cudgels. Clay fought them all, killing one with his knife, refusing to join "that long list of *tame* victims, who have been murdered in the South, for exercising the liberty of speech." So when men and women lined up to hear him on February 25, 1860, they were making a declaration of what they expected from the coming campaign.[40]

Clay spoke for two and a half hours in Touro Hall, Hartford's largest venue. He came onstage fittingly broad and handsome, with chubby cheeks, arching eyebrows, and a thick mop of slicked black hair. He began by reminiscing about his first arrival in Connecticut, as a Yale student fresh from the South. "Why," he had wondered, marveling at Connecticut's relative income equality, could not "the laboring men and mechanics in Kentucky thrive as well as here?" The answer was slavery, dragging everyone in the South down.[41]

Then Clay dove into the coming campaign's themes of free speech and majority rule, slavery's ceaseless assault on democracy itself. If the Slave Power went unchecked, Clay announced, he would rather "leave my country for Russia, France, Italy—I would live under *any* despotism but the despotism of a slaveholding oligarchy." But there was hope, he predicted. An "insurrection" was coming. One day soon, people would stand up against the censorship of speech and mails, the silencing of the pulpit and the press. Perhaps it would start in 1860. If not, if the Republicans could not unite the nation's antislavery majority, from Connecticut to Kentucky, the country would continue to be "ruled by a minority composed of a miserable, rotten, corrupt Democracy."[42]

When he was done, fifteen hundred men and women filed out into the night. At their head stood thirty-two-year-old George P. Bissell, trying to organize the motley, gossiping crowd into a march back to Clay's hotel. Republican volunteers and Hank's Illuminating Store workers handed out torches. Bissell climbed atop a wagon and shouted orders into the night. And he was a shouter, a brash young banker with a bulldog face and wild gestures. He had proved himself on sea voyages to China and filled the local paper with combative, all-caps announcements of his new business partners and dissolved alliances. Bissell was also famous from the 1856 campaign, known for waving a big, floppy white hat and loudly campaigning for John C. Fremont and his vivacious wife, Jessie.[43]

Now Bissell was waving his "old white hat" in the moonlight, hollering directions, craning his neck over the sea of peacoats and shawls. He spied five young clerks, standing to attention, with lit torches on long poles, wearing . . . shimmering black capes? Bissell hollered his compliments to the Talcott boys, waved his white hat, and ordered them to lead the march.[44]

Looking down from above, through the bare lindens and elms of Main Street, it's easy to understand the weird costume's chromatic power. Between two parallel lines of dirty late-winter snowbanks pinballed fifteen hundred bodies wrapped in dull grays and mouse browns. A single shouting dot, waving a white hat, and five flashing black forms began to lead, each holding pinpoints of golden light aloft. Then five hundred other torchlights pulled behind those capes, followed by another thousand bodies marching in something like order. In the center, a carriage, some horses, and an honored guest, Cassius Clay's big head shining like his escort's cloaks. Edgar Yergason and his fellows led off into the darkness, only dimly aware of what they were starting.

Even such a march could not safely command the antebellum streets. "Certain dirty-mouthed runners of the Democratic Party" dogged the procession, shouting the usual slurs from the sidewalks. At one point they made a rush on the crowd, grabbing for torches. A young marcher was knocked down, lost his torch, and came up with a "severely lacerated forehead." Other Republicans dove into the fray, knocking down the Democrats and recapturing their torches. One short but solid fellow seemed to be in the center of the fight immediately, ferociously fighting back on instinct. It was a minor fracas, by nineteenth-century standards. But the combative *Hartford Courant* would not let that insult slide, seizing on it as exactly the kind of mobbing that Republicans had to resist, proof of everything Clay had just warned against.[45]

The *Courant*'s assistant editor pointed out that this little brawl had taken place at the same site where, during the 1856 election, Hartford Republicans tried to hold a rally for presidential candidate John C. Fremont. Back then, troublemakers had launched a carefully plotted ambush. Turning campaign fireworks into makeshift artillery, Hartford Democrats had angled them like howitzers into the Republican ranks, firing volleys of skyrockets and Roman candles into the crowds of men, women, and terrified horses. Rockets crashed through the windows of Hartford's *Religious Herald*, blasting the group of ladies assembled to view the demonstration. The Slave Power's mobbing could still command public political space, even as far north as Hartford.[46]

Four years later, after the brawl for the torches during Clay's parade, the *Courant* snarled that if the coming contest "is to be conducted upon the principles shadowed forth last night," and if every march was to be attacked as ruthlessly as the Fremont procession had been, "it is well we know it now."[47]

Eventually the crowd melted into the night. Cassius Clay made it safely back to his bed in the Allyn House Hotel. George Bissell collected torches. And the five clerks locked up Talcott & Post's and went back to their boardinghouse cots. Eddie Yergason carefully folded his makeshift cape, a bit of drapery on its way to becoming a relic.[48]

CHAPTER TWO

America's Armory

HARTFORD'S CLERKS WOKE up exhilarated. Elite Republicans mostly stroked their beards and wondered what might come in 1860, but the youths who arranged their merchandise and did their bookkeeping were chattering. Over quick lunches at Cooley's Coffee Room, or five-cent whiskeys (with a free side of kippered eels) at the Marble Pillar, they discussed Eddie Yergason's novel invention. Ideas were percolating. The Talcott boys had friends in shops up and down Main Street, in the Allyn House Hotel, over at the railroad station, and down by the river. As their political discussions widened, the boys who worked downtown did what Yankees do over a long winter. They planned a meeting. Next Saturday night, a crew of young fellows who usually got together for music and gossip would convene to plot a movement.[1]

NO ONE WILL tell you that the Civil War began in Hartford, Connecticut. Usually historians point to Charleston Harbor, or the tobacco-stained floor of the U.S. Capitol, or Harpers Ferry, or Bleeding Kansas. But if you want to explain how ordinary democratic practices led to fratricidal war, how political conflicts became military ones, and why the war came in 1861 rather than 1850, or 1820, or 1619, Hartford may be a wise place to start.

Connecticut's placid, prosperous capital has sometimes been called "America's filing cabinet," as it was the home of the decidedly unsexy insurance industry. But in the years before the Civil War, Hartford was "America's armory," manufacturing the firearms bristling at sectional flashpoints. More than 80 percent of America's small arms were made in the Connecticut River Valley, with Hartford as its high-tech hub. So when congressmen waved their Colt revolvers on the House floor, or when fugitive slaves sat shotgun in carriages secreting escapees away from slave catchers, or when guerrillas brought Sharps carbines to Kansas polling places, the products of prim Hartford played their part in the widening violence of more chaotic locales.[2]

Firearms technology had exploded in the previous decade, jumping from single-shot pistols and precarious multibarrel contraptions to consistent, unfailing six-shot revolvers. The pistols of that era look like steampunk birds of prey—swooping muzzles, beaklike hammers, clicking and snapping levers poised for action. The Connecticut factories that produced them were equally astounding, considered the most advanced in the world. Samuel Colt's Hartford armory stood first among them, cranking out tens of thousands of pistols—trim Navys, cheeky little Sidehammers, monstrous cavalry Dragoons. It's no coincidence that widespread revolver ownership increased along with civil discord over the 1850s. Each pistol symbolized the barely controlled havoc of the era. Like the nation itself, Hartford's revolvers seemed to ask what could be repressed, and what would inevitably explode.[3]

Proud locals dragged visitors to Colt's plant to witness the heights of nineteenth-century technology. Moving to Hartford in those years, Mark Twain wondered at how "one can stumble over a bar of iron as he goes in at one end of the establishment, and find it transformed into a burnished, symmetrical, deadly 'Navy' as he passes out at the other." The armory itself was awe-inspiring, a huge building in the shape of a giant H. You could walk down a yawning hall—"a dense wilderness of strange iron machines that stretches away into remote distances and confusing perspectives," wrote Twain—turn a corner, walk down a second hall just the same, turn another corner, and find yet more cranking machines. Everywhere, belts whirred down from the ceiling on systems of pulleys, powering the devices operated by skilled craftsmen. The giant hall resounded with the sound of metal scraping metal, metal piercing metal, metal buffing metal, set to the nonstop thrum of enormous steam engines powering it all. Regular gunfire punctuated the din, as veteran inspectors fired each revolver at an in-house testing range. Owing to a clever ventilation system, the entire factory was eerily odorless.[4]

"It must have required more brains to invent all those things," Twain joked, "than would serve to stock fifty Senates like ours."[5]

Leaving Colt's armory, a visitor could stroll down "Rifle Avenue" to the Sharps Rifle Manufacturing Company, makers of equally sophisticated breech-loading rifles and carbines. While Sam Colt was a conservative Democrat who preached Union and sold pistols north and south, Christian Sharps's guns were favored by abolitionists. John Brown chose one for his Harpers Ferry raid. Politics invested the Sharps carbine with a larger, symbolic meaning.[6] But Colt, Sharps, and many others fit into the same Connecticut scene, along with designers of sewing machines, Yale locks, and other sophisticated devices. This was the genius of Hartford—inventing machines to make more machines, an industry that could build itself.[7]

Meanwhile, Hartford's insurance industry was reaping huge profits by gaming out likely outcomes for shipping, or fires, or harvests. Equidistant between New York and Boston, well placed to analyze both (slavery-sustained) Atlantic shipping and inland farming, Hartford was becoming the center of that booming industry. This city, which specialized in making guns and guessing the future, would play a key role in the long-predicted conflict to come.[8]

It all helped to make Hartford a singularly prosperous place, distant from the slave cabins, frontier settlements, and Dickensian slums many associate with the age. Hartford cuts against that cliché, this city of swept streets, carefully parked carriages, and bustling businessmen. It was, in the view of one English visitor, "the most orderly of communities." Few wild hogs or gangs of boys terrorized the locals; the newspaper ads are most noteworthy for their frequent announcements of new business ventures. Connecticut was the wealthiest state in the Union per capita, even richer than the slave states that held the other spots at the top of that list. In addition to the wealth flowing in from insurance and firearms, Connecticut became a hub for publishing. All those books pointed at another key fact about the region: in 1860 Connecticut registered the highest literacy rate in the nation, at 99.7 percent. An old Puritan culture of Bible-reading, robust schools, and greater gender equality helped drive up the zeal for the printed word. At a time when America's reading rates surpassed the rest of the world, Connecticut justly claimed to be the most literate place on earth.[9]

The state's unique charms appealed to Mark Twain, who left us sparkling accounts of how the place looked to a Missouri "border ruffian" like himself.

Twain joked that Connecticut's "Puritans are mighty straight-laced and they won't let me smoke in the parlor." It almost seems like the humorist moved to Hartford specifically for the material, the jokey Twain riffing on the "absurdly proper" Yankees. But Twain chose to settle in the wealthiest, most literate, most technologically advanced corner of the nation for a reason, admiring Hartford as "the best built and the handsomest town I have ever seen." He was not alone. Visitors remarked on Hartford's broad streets, neat brick buildings, and eight church spires planted in a row down Main Street.[10]

Yet straitlaced Connecticut had always produced rebels and outliers. John Brown, P. T. Barnum, and Harriet Beecher Stowe all came from Connecticut. The famous Yankee coldness had long generated a powerful frisson, a tension between the conservative elite families like the Talcotts, Trumbulls, and Walcotts and everyone else. The state had been the last to maintain an officially established state religion, and it even banned theaters for the first half of the 1800s. Outsiders often felt compelled to push back against this conservative ethos. P. T. Barnum got his training in the humbug business growing up in a Connecticut family of practical jokers. And he made his start publishing a newspaper devoted to fighting against the religion in politics, attacking "the desires of certain fanatics," and doing jail time for his libels. Religious freethinkers pushed against puritan Calvinism and preached heterodox beliefs. Previously the northern state with the highest proportion of enslaved people, Connecticut saw its Black communities fight for space in a state that still traded deeply with the enslaved South and Caribbean.[11]

Perhaps most of all, in a tiny state where an old, unmoving elite controlled so many resources, young people struggled for a way forward in life, frustrated by what the popular newspaperman Joseph R. Hawley called the "awful, awful, awful fogyism of Connecticut."[12]

And those young people were, more and more, looking west in the 1850s. For centuries, cities like Hartford had seen themselves as part of the broad Atlantic world of seafaring and trade. The hard logic of travel drove this orientation. Owing to open seas and poor roads, it took nearly as long to travel across the state as it did to sail from Hartford to the Caribbean. But over the last generation, a blossoming network of canals, railroads, and telegraph lines pointed young Connecticuters toward the vast expanse to their west. By 1857 nearly all of the North could be reached in three days of travel, but reaching much of the American South could take far longer. A new generation of young strivers looked to Detroit or Des Moines, more than Savannah or Havana, for partners, economic or political.[13]

As Connecticut Yankees looked west, new arrivals came from the East. Famine immigrants from Ireland made homes in a state that was previously mostly native-born. Hartford grew 53 percent over the 1850s, almost entirely from overseas immigration. By 1860, one third of the population was either Irish-born or children of Irish immigrants. And whereas much of the rest of the nation received a diverse mixture of immigrants from the British Isles, continental Europe, and beyond, Connecticut's arrivals were overwhelmingly Irish Catholic. They met a frosty Puritan welcome. Settling along the Connecticut River wards, barred from the high-paying skilled jobs in firearms factories, many took work as domestics or at the lowest levels of the building trades. Irish "hoddies" hauled the millions of bricks that built Colt's plant, but few found jobs there. And the Know Nothings launched a nasty backlash, winning every seat in Connecticut's congressional delegation in 1855 and electing a governor who passed a raft of spiteful culture war restrictions on immigrants.[14]

The state where the very word *Yankee* had been coined—by cosmopolitan Dutch New Yorkers grumbling about the flinty Johns ("Yans") of New England—was not a welcome home to new, impoverished migrants practicing a hated faith.[15]

By the late 1850s the land of steady habits was wobbling. Politics were not quite as brutal as elsewhere, but still showed the dangerous tensions over slavery, Union, immigration, class, and democracy itself. Hartford sat uneasily between the antislavery bastion of Boston and the Democratic metropolis of New York City. A line dividing the solidly Republican Upper North from the contested Lower North would slice right through Hartford. And even as the Republican Party grew, Democrats were still strong in Hartford, winning five of six recent mayoral elections. Conservative, business-minded, Union-invoking Democrats like Sam Colt held sway, buoyed by new numbers of Irish Catholic voters.

So it was with nervous anticipation that Connecticut Republicans launched their 1860 gubernatorial campaign. It would be the first significant vote of the presidential election year, set in what nineteenth-century Americans considered a "doubtful" swing state, and the first campaign since John Brown's earth-shaking raid. And though the party held the governor's office, their dull incumbent, William Alfred Buckingham, faced a significant challenger. Tom Seymour was a big, sneering, bearded four-term Democratic governor and Mexican War hero, whose ancestors had practically ruled Hartford for much of the previous century. Even Republican campaigners whispered that it might be "a hopeless task to beat Tom Seymour."[16]

A win for the Democratic Seymour would, to many observers, confirm the Slave Power's hold, even in this northern locale. "A vote this spring in Connecticut for Thomas H. Seymour," the *Hartford Courant* warned, "is a vote for slave labor." Nor should the Democrat be viewed as merely a local rival; he would do the bidding of the maximalist Slave Power. A Democratic victory in Connecticut could set the stage for an avalanche of state-level losses across 1860, culminating in yet another Democratic presidential win in November. "Slavery will be established as the national law of the country," the *Courant* practically shrieked, and the young Republican Party would crumble like so many antislavery coalitions before it. The paper's writers knew how to wield the conspiratorial, catastrophizing rhetoric of their age, predicting a future in which "the slave-holding aristocracy will govern us with the rod of iron."[17]

AND SO THE next Saturday night, one week after the Clay rally, thirty-six young men squeezed into the shabby third-floor apartment of J. Allen Francis. Francis was a teller at City Bank, over which his rooms sat. Decades later it would come out that he had been stealing thousands from the bank all along. But that night Francis welcomed in a crew of young men he knew from downtown. There was the sharp-dressed, sharp-faced Edgar Yergason. The jokey assistant druggist at the Allyn House Hotel's pharmacy, Julius Rathbun. The mouthy, self-assured young tailor Henry P. Hitchcock. Henry T. Sperry, the tall, grave railroad ticket agent who quietly nursed literary aspirations, stooped his way into Francis's cramped rooms as well.[18]

They were all so young that most of what we know of their lives comes from after 1860. These thirty-six "Hartford Originals" would become almost archetypal northern men of the nineteenth century. They would go on to fight in the war, then build a Gilded Age empire after, hunting buffalo and sperm whales. Given their roles in finance, textiles, technology, and whaling, their populist politics, and the fact that more than a few of them later ended up in prison, they were almost perfect embodiments of southern stereotypes of busy, "go-ahead," plotting Yankees.

Time would tell about another stereotype, the commonly held southern belief that Northerners were "a race of traders too cowardly to fight."[19]

Most nights, the clerks gathered in J. Allen Francis's apartment to talk politics and sing together, accompanied by Francis's jaunty, wheezing melodeon. But on March 3 they came together to form an organization. Feelings were high. Sitting on Francis's bed or his few scattered chairs, leaning in doorframes or pacing the floorboards, they began to build off Yergason's uniform idea, forming a plan for a club. Instead of the foot-stomping sea shanties and old Yankee melodies they usually sang, "numerous impromptu speeches were made by young men who never before spoke in public." One of the boys, reminiscing from 1884, captured the tone of that night, writing, "It was felt that there was real danger ahead." Reflecting on that moment while floating on a whaling vessel in the South Atlantic eight years later, Silliman B. Ives kept repeating that it was "the will of the majority" that brought them together.[20]

Why was it Hartford's clerks, and not its pistol makers, seafarers, or dockworkers, who got the new movement going? They were certainly not the model of laboring masculinity many associate with antebellum urban politics, not the blood-splattered butchers or yeast-stinking saloonkeepers who built America's political machines. But butchers and bartenders built empires not because they were brawny archetypes but because they knew a lot of people. And downtown clerks did too, the Talcott boys especially. Consider the sheer volume of upholstery in a typical Victorian home. Yergason and his mates would have sold curtains or tablecloths to much of Hartford. It was fitting that a movement more interested in presentation than violence got its start in that textile shop, rather than Colt's armory.[21]

Radiating out from the original five Talcott boys, there were plenty of other young men working downtown, growing their first beards and wearing their only good shirt collars. They lived in the same boardinghouses and shared the same chowder suppers at Mrs. McClaffin's or Mrs. Spencer's tables, talking politics all the while. Many were hurting from the "hidden depression" that hit northern cities in the years after the financial panic of 1857. These young clerks had hazy futures. Some might make incredible profits in insurance or manufacturing; some might find themselves back on the rocky New England farms where they were born.[22]

Two factors especially pointed these boys to their future political organization: their boring jobs, and Connecticut's incredible literacy rates. Low-level white-collar work in a store or office involved a lot of downtime between customers and paperwork. Many of these clerks were farm boys recently come to the city, brimming with energy. Consider what office work was like without the internet, radios, or telephones. While Nathaniel Hawthorne joked about older clerks who lazed away their days dreaming about what to eat for dinner, these young clerks spent their time reading and arguing about the news. As Silliman B. Ives reflected years later on his whaling vessel, "All Yankees are given to talking politics."[23]

They floated in a vast watershed of partisan ink. Since the invention of the electric telegraph in 1844, America's already robust newspaper network had doubled, to four thousand different outlets in 1860. These publications distributed hundreds of millions of pages a year. Nearly everyone seemed reliant on newspapers. Even some enslaved people—though legally forbidden to read—surreptitiously learned from the papers left lying about. As inventors built the telegraph network from Maine all the way to Texas, Henry David Thoreau famously quipped that "Maine and Texas, it may be, have nothing important to communicate." What they had to communicate, it turned out, was endless political debate, our first truly national conversation. The nationalizing of the newspaper network coincided, between the mid-1840s and 1860, with a darkening of the long-running debate over slavery. Things got uglier when Maine and Texas could really have at each other.[24]

In some ways, it amounted to a changing of the guard of information's gatekeepers. National news had once been spread by a narrow cohort of merchants and politicians who—in private letters, visits to the capital, and college educations in other regions—built the bonds of stability, compromise, and Union. Now that elite was swamped out by the hollering thousands, who prized conflict above all. Behemoths like the snarky, Democratic-leaning *New York Herald* and the utopian, antislavery *New York Tribune* circulated far outside their hometowns, while many fly-by-night papers wended smaller routes. Small-town editors worked their own presses and collected subscriptions, often borrowing liberally from the bigger guys' reporting. The busy, aggressive, sarcastic trade did not take much education, or much money (the parties paid to keep favorable papers in business). What it did take was a wordy, pushy, snarky verve, and an eagerness to joust with rivals in print. In a world of unprecedented but fleeting connections, hard news and wild disinformation floated together, reproduced and altered ad infinitum, like a national game of telephone. It was easy to spread a myth, and hard to check a fact.[25]

The young, bored, argumentative clerks of Hartford were the news junkies of their day, keeping up a constant commentary on the many papers they read. The state with the highest literacy rate in the nation boasted forty-five different political papers, fourteen of them dailies, printing over nine million pages for the 460,000 people in the state. Though Cassius Clay's Kentucky had more than twice the population, Connecticut had three times as many dailies. New York and Boston papers were easy to come by too. Hartford's Republican clerks read and cursed the Democratic *Hartford Times*, and admired the new, earnestly antislavery *Hartford Press*. The latter's editor—Joseph Hawley—had been mobbed out of North Carolina as a child by locals who suspected his father held antislavery views. Joseph swore to fight slavery in revenge. He set up shop in Hartford with his wife, Harriet, attacking "slavery fanatics in Washington and obliging doughfaces of the North."[26]

But most clerks preferred the more pugnacious *Hartford Courant* (still in business today as the oldest continuously in-print newspaper in America). At the time, it was four pages of dense print defined by its hatreds. Antisouthern, anti-Democratic, antislavery, anti-immigrant, anti-Catholic, and anti-Black, the *Courant* was not an easy paper to like. Even in 1850s America, it was rare to pick all of these fights at once. But when bored clerks rustled open its pages on store counters, or shopgirls pored over its frequent appeals to Hartford's ladies at lunch, they found voice for all the anxieties of nervous, nativist young working Yankees. Often the overwhelming ethos of these readers was the suspicion that some small group—slave owners, Washington politicos, the pope and his bishops, immigrant laborers, or African Americans—was scheming against their majority. Many took note of a heated article by the *Courant*'s assistant editor, the young William P. Fuller, announcing that the Cassius Clay rally left Hartford's Republicans feeling "Wide Awake!"[27]

That Saturday night, the boys in Francis's rooms remembered that article when it came time to choose a name for their organization. Political clubs from the era often opted for dry fare, like the Young Men's Republican Association. Hartford already had one of those, drawn from the wealthiest families in town, which mostly wrote resolutions, adopted platforms, and took lunches with older leaders. Openly violent street gangs selected gorier titles, like the

Dead Rabbits, Blood Tubs, Plug Uglies, or Roach Guards. To suit Yergason's stark design, this new company needed something stronger than a Young Men's Association, but more upright than the blood-and-guts monikers favored in Manhattan or Baltimore slums. Mentioning William P. Fuller's excited article in the *Courant*, twenty-three-year-old Henry P. Hitchcock—always known for his creativity—suggested, "Why not name it 'Republican Wide Awakes'?"[28]

A roomful of goatees and muttonchops nodded in assent.

The choice of name seems obvious, affirming that even steady old Connecticut was finally stirring, joining all the other combative vigilant groups of the era. "This is no time to sleep!" hollered the *Courant*. The metaphor stretches through nearly all of human civilization. Think of the ancient Egyptians' Eye of Horus; the Buddhist concept of Bodhi, the Awakened; Maimonides's "Awake, you sleepers from your slumber"; Milton's "Arise, Awake, or be for ever fall'n"; Washington Irving's Rip Van Winkle; even the "Wokeness" that cable news squabbles over today. It hardly needs explaining.[29]

But the term also had darker associations. Across the 1850s, *wide awake* did not mean merely "vigilant" or "enlightened." As early as 1854, newspapers were announcing the formation of a "secret order of Americans . . . comprised exclusively of persons who can boast purely American ancestors for the latest three generations." These violent, anti-immigrant, anti-Catholic clubs might be called Uncle Sam, the Order of the Star-Spangled Banner, or simply Know Nothings, but others referred to them as "Wide Awakes."[30]

Soon the name had gotten mixed up with the term for an old hat—the broad, floppy white hat called a wideawake, seen on the heads of countless riverboat captains.[31] Useful for shielding one's eyes for a nap or waving at embers to stoke a fire, the wideawake had working-class associations. In England, "the young man who wore a wide-awake" was often suspected of socialist politics, but in America, white wideawakes marked "the peculiar badge of the Know Nothings." Especially in the rougher cities of the Mid-Atlantic, where men and women gathered to listen to street preachers scream against the pope, men wearing broad, floppy, white hats sent an immediate message to immigrants. And soon those immigrants fought back, smacking the wideawakes off nativists' heads in Irish corners of Brooklyn, often sparking a flurry of shoves and punches, and eventually pistols drawn and mobs assembled. "It is as much as a man's life is worth now," one nativist paper whined, "to wear a 'wide awake' hat in any street tenanted by these arrogant refugees."[32]

It must have been awfully tempting to knock one of those broad-brimmed hats into the gutter.

The nativist furor was dying down by 1860, but the fact that the new club chose this name can be no accident. Just five years before, gangs had been killing each other merely over a style of hat associated with the term. The men forming the new club in Hartford were mostly too young to have been active Wide Awakes of the 1850s, but they did have suspicious associations with the old movement. Their preferred newspaper, the furiously anti-immigrant *Hartford Courant*, had backed the American Party before switching to the Republicans, plotted "to Americanize this country," advocated a twenty-one-year waiting period before voting for new immigrants, and referred to the Irish part of Hartford as "Pigville."[33] Each of the thirty-six young men present had an Anglo last name, with the sole exception of Edgar Yergason. He was descended from Norwegian immigrants who had been in the country for centuries, and would fly into a sputtering rage if it was implied that he was not "an American." He zealously attended Protestant Sunday schools, courted the devout daughter of the editor of the Congregationalist *Religious Herald*, and testily reminded all who would listen that he was "a thorough Yankee, even if my name is Yergason."[34]

Finally, when George P. Bissell steered Yergason and the Talcott boys to the front of Clay's march on February 25, he had been waving his famous "old white hat"—a big, floppy wideawake.

To be fair, many other Republicans were working hard to crush out this nativism. Joseph Hawley, at the abolitionist *Hartford Press*, blamed the Know Nothings both for nasty bigotry and for sapping valuable energy away from fighting slavery. "The Devil did himself credit," Hawley wrote, in inventing nativism "to distract Northern sentiment," instead of uniting against the Slave Power. Within industrial New England, a cohort of ex–Know Nothing party leaders worked to "blow the whole thing to hell" for failing to tackle slavery. Many—like the former cobbler's apprentice Senator Henry Wilson and the mill boy turned Speaker of the House Nathaniel P. Banks—became heroes for young, laboring Republicans like the Hartford Originals. On a national scale, leaders like William Henry Seward and Abraham Lincoln were eager to disentangle antislavery from anti-immigrant politics. Yet they still borrowed from the momentum of the 1850s Know Nothings, particularly the antiestablishment movement's mobilizing sense that *someone* was stealing American democracy away from its rightful inheritors.[35]

Considering that the club being founded in J. Allen Francis's rooms would have such a formative impact on the struggle to end slavery and affirm human freedom, its roots in violent anti-immigrant street gangs stand out. As would often be the case with the Wide Awakes of 1860, the highest promises of democracy and the lowest politics of who-hates-who resentment swirled together.

The young men in Hartford took a few more votes that night. Their club needed a captain. As soon as the question was broached, almost all agreed. It would have to be James S. Chalker.[36]

Chalker was not even present at that first meeting. Why did so many choose him? Even staid photographs and engravings of the era offer a hint. Chalker always looked ferocious, short but solid, with rearing eyebrows and a jutting goatee. Years later he would go into law enforcement, though his career catching smugglers in New York Harbor would end in scandal when he was caught taking bribes. At twenty-eight, with a wife, two kids, and a tidy business as a tailor, he was slightly older than the rest, of the same generation as George Bissell and Joseph Hawley. Often big brothers and older cousins helped pull younger men into politics. And the younger men knew that James Chalker would fight. When those "dirty-mouthed" Democrats had attacked the Clay march a week before, it was Chalker who led a counter-rush, knocking down one especially "sturdy Democrat" in the melee and wrestling back stolen torches. He would captain their ship, with the help of an elected secretary, treasurer, and various other officers.[37]

Two more votes loomed. For their uniform, they unanimously adopted a spiffed-up, even shinier oil cloth version of Edgar Yergason's cape, adding a glazed martial cap and another new innovation. Yergason's cape was a stroke of genius, but those leaky old torches needed work. Before the Saturday-night session, Silliman B. Ives, the nineteen-year-old future whaler, had met up with his friend Henry P. Hitchcock. Together they visited Horatio P. Blair at the metal shop where he was assistant blacksmith. Like good Connecticut Yankees, they tinkered and tested, designing a better torch. They came up with a device that contained the entire torch apparatus and oil can within a swiveling metal frame. You could hold its staff at any angle, and the flame would still burn straight and bright and vertical.[38]

It was no Colt revolver, but their modest invention would illuminate a movement. On that Saturday night, the Originals voted to add it to their uniform.

Then the Wide Awakes took their last vote of the evening, just as telling as all the others. After exhausting themselves discussing their name, their leadership, and their outfit, all agreed to save the political issues for another time. No shouting over the exact latitude where the line between free and slave states should be drawn; no debates over immigrant naturalization periods, or the long-awaited Homestead Bill, or any of the knotty issues of the day. No platforms, no resolutions. It was a fitting end for the first meeting of a movement that would become known for acute imagery and oblique ideals.[39]

THE NEXT DAY, Eddie Yergason wrote to his mother. With genuine pride, but questionable spelling, he boasted about the new club. Hartford was "haveing exciting times about Election now days." And he was at the heart of it, a member of a unique new movement. Ever the budding designer, Eddie described their club's uniforms: "Each one that joyns has to have a rig like the rest, it is a Black Oil Cloth Cape to go over the Shoulders, A Black Shiny Cap & torch, all alike." His stress on each man having an outfit "like the rest" hints at the power that came with uniformity, the element that most appealed to the young designer. Just one day after their first meeting, Edgar wrote, fifty young men had joined, up from the thirty-six of the night before. Eventually, he imagined, "there will be 2 or 3 hundred in it I presume."[40]

Eddie's note illustrates something else: these club members were kids. Yergason wrote homesick letters back to his family in rural Windham, Connecticut. His mom still mended his clothes. His dad bought a pen and ink just to write to his boy, away from home for the first time. A series of childlike sketches Eddie drew from this era show crude figures firing cartoonish shotguns (although the lines on a house display the careful draftsmanship of a future designer). And nineteen-year-old Yergason was not unusual. People matured both faster and slower in those days. On the one hand, kids started working far younger. Often by ten or eleven they were plowing fields or chopping wood or doing the washing or raising their little siblings. But biologically, Americans reached puberty later than they do today. Eddie may have been closer to a contemporary teen physically. He lived a life that later scholars would call "semi-dependence," common among nineteenth-century youths, venturing out into the world but still relying periodically on his family back home. The other Hartford Originals were similar.[41] This only makes their skyrocketing political influence more astonishing.

Just one day after Eddie wrote to his mom about "exciting times," Abraham Lincoln came to town.

Lincoln was not exactly a household name yet. Elsewhere in Connecticut he was being introduced as "the next Vice President of the United States." But newspaper readers were aware of the rising Illinoisian, admired for his bold fight against Stephen Douglas for one of Illinois' seats in the U.S. Senate. Lincoln traveled east in the late winter of 1860 to check on his son Robert at the Phillips Academy in Exeter, New Hampshire (the boy kept flunking Harvard entrance exams). It was all a nice pretext for the long-shot presidential aspirant to introduce himself to the Eastern wing of the Republican party. While in New York, Lincoln gave an electrifying speech at Cooper Union, introduced by Cash Clay himself. That address established Lincoln's bona fides as a national Republican presence, and a moderate but moral voice on slavery. He seemed at once folksy and lawyerly, with clear lines on what was acceptable. Then Lincoln headed north to speak throughout New England, though he worried that zealous readers would have already "seen all my ideas in print."[42]

Lincoln got off the train in Hartford's Italianate castle of a railroad station, shaking the coal grime from what had been a brand-new suit when he left Illinois. Perhaps he walked past the twenty-three-year-old ticket agent and Wide Awake recruit Henry T. Sperry. That evening Lincoln arrived at Hartford's city hall for his sixth speech in a little over a week. He wowed the thousand listeners present. The *Hartford Press* gave his speech the headline "THE 'DON'T CARE' POLICY, EXPOSED," admiring Lincoln's forceful reminder of the impossibility of remaining a bystander to slavery. Comparing it to "a venomous snake lying on the open prairie," Lincoln called on his audience not to "put it in bed with the children"—that is, extend slavery into new territories. Whether Republicans should kill the snake where it already lay was a harder question that Lincoln did not answer.[43]

Reporting on the speech, the *Courant* cheered his directness, and concluded: "There could not have been even a ten year old boy in that crowd at City Hall who did not leave the room satisfied that Mr. Lincoln was right."[44]

And then they were outside, in another bracing Connecticut night, perhaps a thousand spectators drawn up around the tall and ungainly speaker. Lincoln joined Mayor Allyn in his carriage for a short procession back to his hotel. Hartford's Cornet Band was warming up as the Illinois visitor got settled for another bumpy ride. Young men began to emerge from the crowd. Each wore a black cap and a black cape and held a lit torch on a long staff. The corps silently encircled Lincoln's carriage.[45]

See Lincoln seeing the Wide Awakes. Imagine the torchlight flickering on his bemused, craggy face as he assesses the uniformed boys around him. Watch the young men begin to march, keeping in formation with conscious effort as Mayor Allyn's horses pull his carriage down Main Street. Lincoln had a long history of recruiting young activists, prizing the energies of "shrewd wild boys" in campaign organizations. But now, in Hartford on March 5, the shrewd wild boys were recruiting him, folding Lincoln into their movement. Maybe Mayor Allyn explained that the boys were a new local club, or perhaps he still had no idea who they were. As the horses' hooves clomped and the cornets honked, the young marchers and established politicians moved uncertainly in the same direction together, in an illuminated circle of torchlight marching through the darkness.[46]

Was there ever a political movement that had the simple good luck of debuting before the next president of the United States at its first event, just two days after its official organization? Ten days earlier, Eddie Yergason had been cutting and sewing himself a makeshift cape. Now he and his fellow clerks were escorting Lincoln through Hartford's downtown. Of course, in March 1860, both Lincoln and the Wide Awakes were minor factors in American politics, with little hint of their future import. It was not possible to know how dramatically Lincoln would mold the future of the nation, and even less apparent that those boys in strange costumes would reshape their democracy.

Certainly, no one watching the handful of young men in capes escorting a second-tier political speaker could guess that in 364 days, hundreds of members of the same movement would be escorting Lincoln down Pennsylvania Avenue to his inauguration. Nor could they predict that—showing the difference that a year, and a campaign, could make—the Wide Awakes of March 1861 would be wearing plainclothes and concealing revolvers.

CHAPTER THREE

Quiet Men Are Dangerous

THE BLOOD WAS already drying in Adelbert Seeley's hair as the crowd filtered past. Edwin Couch's three wounds were still fresh, though, and Will Bradley's eye looked ghastly. At least their capes kept most of the blood off their jackets, though plenty dripped down their trouser legs and pooled on the New Haven stage. The eleven young Wide Awakes did their best to sit still. They made an awful tableau, all blacks and reds, matted brown hair and purpling bruises, for the crowd to take in.[1]

The fifteen hundred New Haven Republicans present did not expect anything so grisly. They had been promised "a season of pleasure and enjoyment"—tables loaded with food and drink, warming late-March weather, the chatter of men and women separated over the long winter, maybe a few rousing speeches. The famed Hartford Originals would be there, having organized a railroad excursion from forty miles north. Captain James S. Chalker sold tickets from his tailor shop; Julius Rathbun dispensed more from his drugstore with a joke and a smile. Meeting the new Wide Awake club in New Haven was meant to be a celebration, and a passing of the torch. In the weeks since Edgar Yergason sewed his first cape, the Hartford Wide Awakes had assiduously cultivated their movement, which was now bubbling across the state.[2]

The eleven Wide Awakes on stage had intended to enjoy those same refreshments, not end up on display. Earlier that morning, they'd set out from the neighboring village of Fair Haven, part of a company of seventy-four oystermen, carriage makers, and shipbuilders in their early twenties. The Fair Haven Wide Awakes planned to march over the Barnesville Bridge and into New Haven. It was the most direct path to the Republican rally, but meant heading down busy Grand Street, through a neighborhood inhabited "almost exclusively by Democrats."[3]

In these early days, it's hard to say whether this was a deliberate provocation, or just poor planning.

Grand Street's Democrats knew the drill. As Fair Haven's Wide Awakes moved through the neighborhood, "a mob of rowdies" launched a coordinated ambush. Hidden behind fences, leaning from windows, and assembled in empty yards, they heaved "a perfect shower of stones and broken bricks." Such attacks had a tidy division of labor in those days. Women gathered spare bricks in baskets. Boys cracked them against the paving stones into easily handled missiles. And men chucked them at peoples' heads. In an economy where many immigrants were consigned to a life as hod carriers, beasts of burden who spent their days schlepping the bricks that built nineteenth-century cities, there was a joyful release in pulling back and lobbing a red shard into the dismal March sky.[4]

At least three chunks came down on Edwin Couch, an eighteen-year-old carriage trimmer's apprentice and new Wide Awake. Four more hit N. M. Catlin's cap and cape. A hefty one crashed into poor Will Bradley's eye and cheek. As of reporting time, two days later, it was feared that Will's eye would be permanently disabled.[5]

The fusillade stopped after about twenty Wide Awakes had been hit. The rest hurried off Grand Street, making their way to the Republican rally. The wounded found a doctor before staggering, bandaged, into the Republican hall to spread the news of what had just happened. There, some New Haven Wide Awake had the political savvy to seat the eleven injured Wide Awakes onstage behind the speaker's rostrum, as a material embodiment of the stakes of the coming fight.[6]

Getting bricks lobbed at you was not an uncommon part of nineteenth-century political life. At least no one had been blasted with fireworks. What was unique was the Wide Awakes' decision to put their injured on display. Usually the victims of mobbings slunk away in shame, but these young Republicans were making their humiliation a rallying point. Edwin Couch's bleeding head and Will Bradley's purpled eye were what Frederick Douglass would call "tolerable endorsements of the anti-slavery tendencies of the Republican party," physical proof that they were marching in the right direction.[7]

The crowd got the point. Antislavery movements were forever having to endure such demeaning assaults, but the new Republican party was organizing to be "*tame* victims" no longer. Speakers pacing the stage called upon everyone present to swear "never to submit to such outrages peaceably again, and to revenge themselves most terribly, not upon the miserable scoundrels who blindly acted after the custom and natural tendency of their party, but upon the party and its leaders." Swear to it now, the orator demanded. Fifteen hundred men and women answered with a resounding "AYE!"[8]

Revenge on the brick throwers of Grand Street would not be enough. For too long, respectable Democrats had explained away the party's worst actors as outliers, drunks, or rowdy boys who could not be expected to behave better. Now Republicans were working, through Wide Awake symbols, to make the case that a single cohesive Slave Power held sway, as much on Grand Street as on Pennsylvania Avenue. The Republican press thrilled to the resounding energy in the room, the way the words "revenge" and "never submit" made the crowd vibrate. Papers spread the news, happy to see "a throng of men thoroughly and truly 'WIDE AWAKE.' " Others welcomed rumors that young Republicans were "taking steps to protect themselves in future."[9]

The Wide Awakes were certainly taking steps. In the weeks after their first meeting in J. Francis Allen's cramped rooms, the Hartford Originals learned to manufacture and distribute their new club as if it were a product of Colt or Sharps factories. First, the founding club grew until it split into multiple companies, then Waterbury launched a club, then New Haven, then New London, then Bristol. This growth relied on the Originals' cultivation of two forms of uniformity. First, their physical uniform, simple and striking, helped build a compelling sense of membership and militarism. Second, they were able to throw a metaphorical uniform over their many rivals, uniting all enemies of the Republican Party. Blending local elections and Kansas thefts, mob assaults and hated legislation, Wide Awake Republicans clumped their rivals into a single threat to democracy itself, demanding a united solution.[10]

In its first month of existence, the new movement addressed the problem many Republicans had long struggled with: how to group a big, messy society into a majority "us" and a minority "them." How to connect popular ideas (like antipathy to the Slave Power) with more radical ones (like abolition). How to pose as both rightful heirs and embattled victims.

And nothing, they learned, clarified the "systematic organization of hatreds" better than matching outfits.

THE THIRTY-SIX ORIGINAL Wide Awakes got to work right after their first meetings in early March, building out the idea among likely and surprising demographics. They were able to add dozens of young clerks and apprentices every day, circulating in Cooley's Coffee Room, Touro Hall lecture crowds, and the Pearl Street Congregational Church's Sunday school. Meeting multiple nights a week, they built the movement by word of mouth. In their diaries and letters, these early adopters make clear the appeal of a fraternity, a uniform, a clubhouse, and regular meetings to boys hungry for structure and belonging. Especially if you were twenty-two, lowly at work, bored in your boardinghouse, and looking for something to fill your evenings as winter turned to spring.[11]

But James Chalker and the other leaders of the Originals were also quick to branch out. Their most useful allies were a bit older, well-off, well-known thirtysomethings like George P. Bissell and Joseph R. Hawley—individuals who were still called "young men" by Republicans in their sixties, but who were old enough to look down the ladder and hoist up a rising younger generation.

On Friday, March 10, the "Young Men's Republican Union" organized a meeting in Hartford's Union Hall, "CROWDED TO OVERFLOWING!" in the Courant's breathless announcement. About a thousand turned out, "Armed and Enlisted for the War!!" the Courant declared, adding "Buckingham and Victory!!" almost as an afterthought, an elbow in the side reminding foot soldiers of the name of their candidate. Caped Wide Awakes were present, their uniforms always the best advertisement for the movement. Young men from Hartford's banking and publishing elite led the meeting, but shared the stage with cloth cutters and ticket takers like James S. Chalker, Henry T. Sperry, and Julius Rathbun. No one had to articulate the difference between the Young Men's Republican Union and the Wide Awakes, however. The former would canvass, lobby, and assist the older politicians in running the official gubernatorial campaign. The latter would march and fight.[12]

Along with Hartford's "best men" and its Wide Awake clerks, the March 10 meeting drew in another fertile crop. Gunmakers from Sharps's and Colt's armories crowded in, led by an athletic twenty-six-year-old named William H. Banks. Banks worked in the Sharps factory but was known for his public speaking skills, and for being the fastest sprinter at the factory's annual foot-races. He took the stage, introduced with more than a little condescension by the lawyer George Gilman as a "young mechanic." But the factory worker and the prominent attorney were both Republicans, joined by shared antipathy. Banks hit the main Republican talking point, forcefully arguing that the entire Democratic Party was "a supple and willing tool" of the Slave Power. Skilled workers, downtown professionals, and lowly clerks were coalescing into a move-ment, hailed by the *Courant* as "coming from the counting-room and the workshop to talk of the principles of freedom."[13]

The factions intoxicated each other. The gunmakers and Wide Awakes inspired tough posturing from the bankers and lawyers. When the meeting wrapped up and the chairman proposed that Wide Awakes escort club pres-ident Rowland Swift home, Swift puffed up his chest and bellowed: "The Presi-dent isn't afraid to go home alone!"[14]

After the bankers had left, the Wide Awakes stayed behind for a separate purpose. Gathering together, the growing company of old friends and new comrades were introduced to thirty-year-old Arthur T. Hinckley. Hinckley worked with firearms too, as the armorer of the State Arsenal, and was well known as an award-winning marksman. He was also lieutenant of Hartford's Light Guards, the ceremonial local militia. Organizing the Wide Awakes into columns, Hinckley opened his copy of Lieutenant Colonel William J. Hard-ee's *Rifle and Light Infantry Tactics*. Then he began to drill the men, shouting commands, teaching them how to march in line, how to break into two flanking forces, and how to briskly re-form into a single "line of battle." There were few veterans in town—most of the men who fought in the Mexican War a decade earlier came from farther south and west, and no Indian Wars simmered within a thousand miles. So the Wide Awakes had to learn everything fresh, an educa-tion in combat rehearsed in the streets of America's most orderly city.[15]

No one recorded it, but James Chalker seems to have added an additional code word to Major Hardee's maneuvers. Somehow, the men all learned what was expected of them if their captain shouted: "Do Your Duty!"[16]

Finally, the club gathered for one last lesson. Henry T. Sperry, the tall ticket agent with a grave and sensitive face, drew the new recruits in close. Sperry was the original company's secretary, and an aspiring poet who later worked with Mark Twain. It is easy to imagine him cracking a thin, knowing grin as he instructed the boys on the "Wide Awakes cheer" he'd been drafting, as if he was proffering an incantation of great power. Soon the caped men were all throwing their heads back and hollering Sperry's invention into the night, bellowing: "Hurrah, Huzzah! Hurrah, Huzzah!! Hurrah, Huzzah!!!"[17]

Like so much else about the Wide Awakes, Sperry's cheer feels at once cryptic and comprehensible today. Composed of nonsense words, it made no explicit political arguments, endorsed no candidates, and articulated no statement of what the Wide Awakes wanted.[18] And yet anyone who has heard a crowd of energetic young people chanting in unison, be they protestors or athletes or cadets, can imagine the power it had in reverberating through Hartford's dark streets. Something about the escalating rhythm of Hs, Rs, and Zs, bellowed by a few hundred deep-voiced young men, worked to pump up the adrenaline and camaraderie of the group. As the Hartford Originals built a movement over the coming months, they always insisted on teaching new companies Sperry's "Wide Awakes cheer."

On the evening of the Cassius Clay rally on February 25, Yergason's cape had been an inarticulate gesture, owing mostly to a leaky torch and his fussy personal style. George P. Bissell, waving his white hat, saw something promising in the five caped torchbearers. Now, captained by Chalker, drilled by Hinckley, and scripted by Sperry, the club was coalescing from a few gestures into a package of symbols. After the March 10 rally, all the key elements of the Wide Awakes—wearing capes and caps, lighting torches, organizing companies, electing officers, militaristic drilling, and cheering in unison—were firmly in place. Now the real marching could begin.

But why did these young Republicans—almost none of them veterans or interested in joining the lowly U.S. Army—choose militarism in 1860? Ever since, the lazy answer has been that the Wide Awakes were preparing for the military conflict coming in their future. But that's not the direction history moves, and most of the Wide Awakes in 1860 insisted that war was not on the horizon. One typical New Haven Wide Awake overconfidently assured his girlfriend that "I watch things pretty close but do not expect anything serious." The tensions with the South would "play out in time and be for the best in the end." Most of the claims that their movement saw the war coming were made decades after the conflict.[19]

The other obvious explanation is that military metaphors have always enliv-ened politics, from use of the term *campaign* down to the shared Latin deriva-tion of the words *bullet* and *ballot*. But this too falls short—most campaigns used some military metaphors in the decades before 1860, but this one was the first to have its members dress up, form ranks, and drill in the night.[20]

The better explanation is that military symbolism answered the problem Republicans, and all Americans, faced in the 1850s. Martial rigor could face down the disorder of mobbings and lynchings, stolen elections and vigilante chaos. Militarism had been gaining cachet in American society across the decade, part of an international "militia fever" in the midcentury West. Connecticut, like all states, had long maintained a state militia, a holdover from colonial days when such companies fought wars against Indigenous people and rival empires, as well as suppressed slave revolts, and served as riot control. By the 1850s, state militias mostly gathered on "Muster Days" to drink ale, smoke cigars, and sing old songs. But a new crop of volunteer militias was popping up in the 1850s, exciting young men with the promise of donning uniforms and marching in parades. America long lacked European states' grand standing armies and ostentatiously uniformed officer-aristocrats, relying instead on a culture of humble citizen soldiers stretching back to the Revolution. But in the 1850s, increasingly showy "Stay-at-Home Rangers" preened and marched across the nation.[21]

Such militias were also coming to serve an interesting function in northern Black communities, where African American men in uniforms marching in the streets made a more radical declaration. The same activists who fomented resistance to fugitive slave hunters organized at least two dozen militia compa-nies from Rhode Island to Ohio. West Boston's Massasoit Guards were the most prominent, but even in Massachusetts they were forced to fight for the right to march. Henry Wilson, the state's Republican senator, made their case, lobbying to allow Black militias "a little of the fun and pleasure of a military display."[22]

But this new militia fever grew from more than just "fun and pleasure." In an age of upheaval, military aesthetics were shedding their old association with conservative aristocracy. In Europe—riven by the thrilling but ultimately failed revolutions of 1848, the ongoing battle to unite Italy, nascent socialism and anarchism, and burgeoning nationalist causes—a bold new martial style was emerging. Figures like Italy's Giuseppe Garibaldi and Giuseppe Mazzini and Hungary's Lajos Kossuth stood out as bearded, caped, bayonet-wielding icons in progressive circles. Their struggles against conservative autocracies in Austria, Prussia, Russia, and the Papal States easily synced with the American North's hostility to the Slave Power. A young generation of Americans looked across the Atlantic and saw militarism as romantic, dynamic, and proud.[23]

Nineteenth-century Europe offered two competing military styles, each loaded with meanings. The old militarism of elaborate uniforms and glinting sabers, epaulets and insignias, intricate braiding and chests of medals, all connoted the regressive aristocracy that brutally controlled much of the continent. Imagine the uniform of a Prussian or Austrian officer from this time. It broadcast restraint and tightness, tucked and cinched at boots, stockings, belts, waistcoats, chinstraps, and elaborately plumed hat. On the other hand, the revolutionaries favored bold, stark colors—red and black most of all—and loose and flowing capes, greatcoats, or simple matching outfits, like those of Italy's Red Shirts. Garibaldi, a kind of superhero of international revolution, was famous for the billowing poncho he picked up while fighting in South America. Mazzini, the movement's intellectual architect, wore only black, a priest of revolution. Zouave units borrowed from the robes of North African tribesmen. A column of men in flowing, unadorned matching uniforms hit notes of equality and uniformity—itself a political goal for liberals struggling against the hierarchal empires built on the ranks, privileges, and animosities of a fractured Europe. Even facial hair sent conflicting messages. Waxed and manicured mustaches symbolized the aristocratic classes who made up cavalry corps and led conservative regimes; Garibaldi, Mazzini, Kossuth, Karl Marx, and many other revolutionaries favored full, flowing beards.[24]

Young Americans followed these revolutionaries with rapt fascination. Newspapers reported daily on Garibaldi's campaigns across Italy. When Lajos Kossuth toured America, he spoke to massive crowds, made famous for his romantic style and what later historians have identified as his "extraordinary sex appeal." A generation of boys bought "Kossuth hats," proudly sporting Magyar headgear in Ohio or Missouri. Thousands of German revolutionaries, the "Forty-Eighters" exiled after the failure of their uprisings across the German states, settled in St. Louis, Cincinnati, Chicago, and

Philadelphia, bringing with them a mix of radical antiautocratic and antislavery politics. They organized Turnverein clubs, where German American "Turners" gathered in white uniforms to practice gymnastics and marksmanship, talk politics, drink beer, and fight Know Nothings. Many came to see America as inheritor of the torch of democratic militarism, extinguished by the conservative regimes in Europe. Few Americans wanted revolution at home, of course, but it was fun and thrilling to support it for Vienna or Rome. And the wounded glamour of liberal revolution in Europe strengthened its appeal in America, playing to the combination of chauvinism and grievance on which Republicans were betting.[25]

A generation before, the Jacksonian Democratic Party had claimed the cause of international revolution, building a Young America movement in concert with Young Ireland, Young Italy, and other youthful romantic European causes. But the Democrats had ceded so much over the years, in thrall to the Slave Power. In 1860 the Republicans seized the mantle of international democratic revolution, and the boys in Connecticut led the way.

The Wide Awake founders knew all this—Garibaldi was mentioned 134 times in the *Courant* in 1860 alone—and chose their symbols accordingly. Their black capes sent the right message politically, borrowing what worked in Italy for use in Connecticut. Uniform and billowing, the Wide Awakes' capes combined a sense of modern martial order with an exotic romanticism drawing from North Africa, South America, and beyond. In one early article explaining the club, the *New York Tribune* noted how the long capes obscured the clothing of individual members underneath, all subsumed in a company of equals. The symbolic power of those capes would only grow, as the movement spread and each company set out to design its own uniform.[26]

Wide Awake militarism drew from European models, but fit into a specifically American political context. This is why all that drilling mattered: it set the movement apart from the usual chaos of American street-level politics. The original Hartford company made clear in its constitution that the Wide Awakes would follow orders and maintain decorum. "No boisterous or disorderly conduct" was permitted. Cigar smoking while marching was forbidden, and Wide Awakes generally drank less than many members of the whiskey-soaked movements of the day. Soon companies decided to march in absolute silence, when not hurrahing.[27]

None of this sounds very fun, but the Wide Awakes were deliberately dialing down the "fun" of public politics. What made ordinary nineteenth-century street politics enjoyable could also make them noisy, messy, and downright scary. Partisan marches were usually confused affairs, huge clumps of men and boys waving various torches, banners, and hats, stomping along, children at their feet, halloing friends in the crowd, throwing their hats, lighting firecrackers, shouting "stupid utterances." An English correspondent for Charles Dickens's London magazine *All the Year Round* reported that many American processions often started at whiskey barrels and ended in "a grog shop, where endless glasses of 'Lager beer,' 'brandy cocktail,' and 'Jersey lightning' are drunk."[28] Some of this messiness built on the old British tradition of shivarees or skimmingtons—wild, disorderly events that subverted usual decorum and class boundaries—and some on the uniquely American approach to unrestrained public life.[29] It all could get a little offputting, especially when amped up with alcohol and partisanship. One young woman in Wisconsin later recalled being raised to believe that it was "unwomanly" even to attend a political event; her elders told her to avoid that "drunken, fighting, smoking outfit."[30]

In contrast, the Hartford Wide Awakes organized squads of uniformed men, marching in columns, usually silent but occasionally letting loose with a coordinated "Hurrah, Huzzah! Hurrah, Huzzah!! Hurrah, Huzzah!!!" Looking back on black-and-white newspaper engravings of political marches, it can be hard to tell just how *different* Wide Awake processions were from the usual muddy parade. The Wide Awakes weren't selling fun; they were selling order, in a political context where it felt like disorder was all American democracy could produce anymore.

And though twenty-first-century readers may look back on the whole era as drab, the black-clad Wide Awakes emerged at the height of variety and color in Victorian fashion. The rise of sewing-machine-manufactured clothing in the 1850s saw men embrace a galaxy of checkered pants and flashy cravats, while women's wear reached peak hoop skirt. Rich, jewel-tone (often toxic) green and mauve dyes enlivened everything from gowns to gum drops. In this vibrant context, a thousand silent men in black sent a message.

If not conventionally enjoyable, it was thrilling. Trying to explain what was happening up in Connecticut, the *New York Tribune* admired the Wide Awakes' "obedience to the word of command," "their strict discipline," and "the regularity of their movements," concluding, "in this lies the great beauty and efficiency of the organization." The *Tribune's* rival, the *New York Herald*, also noted the way the Wide Awakes marched "as if one power was moving it," but preferred the traditional "gay, romping crowd of 'devil-may-care' fellows who have hitherto composed our political clubs, and infused a life into our politics by their wit and song." The anti-Republican *Herald* warned: "Quiet men are dangerous."[31]

By mid-March 1860, the Hartford Originals had assembled a package of symbols, and won a few hundred members. It could all still fade away. Yet there was something in the sternness of their marching, the fluttering romance of their capes, even in Sperry's silly chant, that felt like an answer to the problem that hung over American democracy. Especially as Republicans struggled to prove that "there *is* a North" worth standing up for, Wide Awakes provide a model for the majority to rally round. The Slave Power, prone to viewing itself as a kind of national cavalry, had its own culture of (purported) chivalry, dueling, horsemanship, and honor codes. Urban Democrats and Know Nothings had established themselves as mob-prone brick-throwing guerrillas. But up in orderly Connecticut, the Wide Awakes were training a stoic northern infantry.

DRILLED AND UNIFORMED, the Wide Awakes hit the road. The industrious Captain Chalker got the Hartford company on the move, collecting seventy-five cents each for a special excursion to Waterbury. On March 15, they set out in a twelve-car train for the industrial town thirty miles from Hartford. Arriving in Waterbury around nine P.M., one hundred black-caped Hartford boys climbed out to meet three thousand local Republicans, eager to see the movement they had read so much about in the *Courant*. The Hartford club had been billed as "active, enthusiastic working young men," promoted in Waterbury's brass foundries to "all those opposed to the National Administration."[32]

Welcomed by Waterbury's "Republican Campaign Club," the crowd marched through town. Many waved banners stressing their youthful free-labor ideology: WORK, WORK, WORK; THE YOUNG MEN WHO ARE NOT GOING TO VOTE FOR SEYMOUR; UNION FOREVER; and, from the new Wide Awakes enlisted in Hartford's rifle factories, REPUBLICAN SHARPSHOOTERS. Youth, working-class identity, pro-Union assurances, and masculinity seemed to be the driving engines. Mixed into the crowd was also a large contingent of "the fair women of Waterbury," in a town known for its workforce of young, single ladies, waving their handkerchiefs in fervid support.[33]

But as usual, rock-throwing Democrats turned out too. As the procession gathered in front of Brown's Hotel for speeches, "a howling mob" shouted down every attempt to communicate. Earnest Henry Sperry tried to invite the Waterbury Republicans to visit Hartford in a few weeks, but much of what he had to say was lost in the hooting of about two hundred Democrats who had "put their noodles together to break up the meeting." Some even tried to roll a burning barrel of tar into the square where the Republicans had gathered. It was a familiar scene, with one new addition. Captain Chalker, perhaps sensing an opportunity to test his club's new trick, looked to his men, standing to attention on the edge of the Republican crowd. Lifting his head, flaring those ferocious eyebrows, James Chalker commanded:

"About face!"

"Wide Awakes: Do your duty . . ."

"*Charge!*"

On those orders, one hundred black-uniformed men shot out of the larger mass of Republicans, crashing into the bewildered Democratic hecklers. Looking at the formal photograph of the Hartford Originals, it's hard to imagine their composed faces—Rathbun's grin, Sperry's grimace, Chalker's scowl, Yergason's eager smile—contorted with rage as they bore down upon the surprised Democratic rowdies in Waterbury. Yet that was the sight on March 15, as this Republican fighting force closed the distance, torch-staffs and fists raised. Striking left and right, the Hartford boys sent the "crowd of dirty headed Locofocos" sprinting back away from the rally. The Wide Awakes were learning a lesson of urban political warfare: a smaller squad of organized men could scatter a much larger mob of muddled loafers. Then the Hartford boys promptly reassembled in an orderly column, and the speaking resumed.[34]

"What is the excuse," the *Courant* reporter demanded to know the next day, for the Democrats' constant mobbing and heckling. Wielding an old anti-Democratic nickname, now a meaningless slur, the paper's headlines shouted: "Locofocoism the Same Everywhere! WIDE-AWAKES: DO YOUR DUTY!" In the face of such barbarities, the *Courant* predicted that all respectable men would leave the Democrats by the time the spring campaign was over. After each outrage, the Democrats blamed a few "rum-swilling rowdies" in their ranks, but was that any better? In laughably Victorian phrasing, the *Courant* fumed: "They admit the drunkenness for the sake of palliating the rascality!"[35]

For the young leader of Waterbury's Republican Campaign Club, the Wide Awakes' ability to clear the square of local knuckleheads made a big impression. He converted his organization into a Wide Awake club at their next meeting. It was the first outside of Hartford. Soon they were drilling in black capes trimmed with white leather bands in that same square by Brown's Hotel. In a little innovation on the unarmed Hartford club, Waterbury's officers carried stout batons. "We introduce just enough military to preserve good order," a Waterbury club member explained, eliciting "the fancy which military display always calls forth, using *torches* instead of *muskets*."[36]

After Waterbury, New Haven organized a club. Then New Britain. The whole Connecticut Valley seemed to be joining up. Edgar Yergason wrote home to his mother again, shocked at the growth of the club he had accidentally started. Hartford alone had at least five hundred members now, and "they have sprung up all over the State patterned after us . . . & every time we Come out We make New Republicans of the Democrats." Yergason bragged that he'd converted his brother Henry. To counter the Wide Awakes, the Democrats had organized "Seymour Clubs," named for their candidate, but they did not even have uniforms, the future designer scoffed.[37]

Charles O'Neill was another new Wide Awake with a proud grin. The young carriage trimmer from New Haven wrote of the movement in his love letters to Caroline Bartholomew, a seamstress in New London. Usually he signed them with her pet name for him: "Ducksy." Elected to the rank of sergeant, he asked Carrie to "imagine me in a silver and green cape, blue lantern in one hand, a yellow cane in the other, trooping through the mud giving orders, file left, march, shoulder arms, &c. &c." He bragged about his garish uniform—New Haven's Wide Awakes were experimenting with their own color scheme—which sat in his closet next to a blue-and-scarlet overcoat from the National Blues volunteer militia. There was a new swagger in his writing. Ducksy was busy with nights of drilling, hanging out in the clubroom, reading newspapers and arguing politics. There was even talk of promoting him to captain of a club; he was "raising a side whisker" to look the part. He asked

Carrie: "How would you like to see your Ducksy's name in print as the Captain of the Washington Wide A Wakes?"[38]

But the uniform—whether the standard black or Ducksy's silver and green—brought risks too. One day in March, William L. Speare walked briskly through daytime Hartford, his black Wide Awake cape fluttering around him. Usually Wide Awakes only put on their uniforms for nighttime rallies, but here was a lone club member, the captain of the second Wide Awake club of Hartford, alone in broad daylight. An angry Democrat caught up with the thirty-one-year-old tailor, fists balled, shouting, "You are one of those damned Wide Awakes, are you?" and took a swing. Speare dodged and knocked the man down, but he came up for a second try and landed a hard blow on Speare's caped torso, breaking one of his ribs. The *Courant* was sure to detail the fight, adding, "These assaults upon the Wide Awakes have been carried on long enough."[39]

Every time the movement faced violence, its promotors gave its tussles and scrapes top billing, with goading headlines like: "OH, NO!" As the Connecticut gubernatorial race picked up, and nationally known speakers filtered into Touro Hall, Wide Awake bodyguards frequently clashed with Democrats while escorting Republican leaders back to the Allyn House Hotel. There was even a sense of satisfaction in the *Courant* reporting, treating fights as the narrative climax of each rally, proof that the Democrats really were as awful as speakers had just said they were. The assault on the Fair Haven Wide Awakes—and the placement of injured men onstage at the following rally— showed the leadership's skill at broadcasting their opponents' worst behavior. Wide Awakes often threatened to respond in kind, and occasionally "did their duty," but more often they shouted about the latest attack in Republican papers, right next to announcements of future meetings and ads for black capes. When the noisily Democratic Sam Colt's factory started firing Republican workers just before the election, it played into the same narrative.[40]

Democratic assaults proved extremely helpful to the Wide Awakes. The Republican appeal turned on the Slave Power conspiracy, the idea of a cohesive assault on democracy. Though no one in the South had done a thing against the Wide Awakes, or even heard of them yet, partisan warfare in Hartford's streets helped fit Connecticut politics into the larger national narrative. Republicans could make the case that Democrats threatened free speech in Congress, in Kansas, on Georgia plantations, and also in the streets of Hartford, New Haven, and Waterbury. Their party had long struggled to convince voters that the northern Democrats were guilty of the same atrocities that the southern wing clearly perpetrated. Now the *Courant* could point to assaults on the Wide Awakes and hiss "Locofocoism the Same Everywhere!" Of course, mobbing was endemic in nineteenth-century American politics, but the Wide Awakes seemed to insist upon making their public events a target, and then broadcasting it when they were attacked. It made it harder to shrug "Don't care" about fights on Main Street, and easier to argue that minority rule imposed on the North. The new movement was learning how to throw a single uniform over all their enemies.[41]

The Wide Awakes spent nearly as much time declaring who their movement excluded as whom it was fighting against. And while they opposed slavery expansion, the early organizers were brutally clear: African Americans were not invited. In fact, the new movement used White supremacy as a campaign tool, making their Republican campaign in Connecticut that spring among the mostly nastily racist in the North.

At Wide Awake rallies, an atrocious but telling slogan started appearing on banners. In Waterbury, Hartford, and elsewhere, sign makers stenciled: LAND FOR THE LANDLESS—NOT NIGGERS FOR THE NIGGERLESS. The first half of the slogan referred to the Republican hopes for a Homestead Bill, the promise of free western land that especially appealed to young men and women. But in the second half, Republicans twisted the knife. Often, Republicans pushed the idea that the Slave Power was foisting "the pestilential presence of the black race" on the North. In a region that was 98 percent White before the Great Migration of the twentieth century, many Yankees viewed southern slave owners as racially tainted by their contact with African Americans. In this context, White supremacy could be antislavery, because expanding slavery threatened to expand Blackness. Of course, the Republican Party had a big faction that found these views repellant, but the gubernatorial race was not worried about swinging those voters. Electing a Republican governor would help "confine the negroes where they belong," snarled the *Courant*. On the other hand, "a vote for Seymour, is a vote for MORE NEGROES." "The territories," the Wide Awakes' friends at the *Courant* opined, "must be preserved for the SONS OF WHITE MEN. That's the whole point of the issue."[42]

It was all part of a maneuver to distance the Republican Party from old associations with abolitionists. An insecure new organization and nascent youth movement tried to claim the mantle of laboring White men, peeling away some Democrats in the process. The moderately Republican *New York Times* correspondent informed Manhattan readers that he had "been most impressed with the expression of much conservatism on both sides" of the gubernatorial race. He described a modest lecture by a Republican to Wide Awake clubs as "a queer speech for a Connecticut Republican, wasn't it? It was hardly the John Brown, insurrectionist, disunion platform that your one-eyed neighbor undertakes to fasten on the Republicans."[43]

To the region's African Americans, it confirmed what many already suspected about the Republican Party. Hartford's small Black community of seven hundred mostly kept out of politics, anchored by a few prominent churches and still scarred by racist rioting in 1838. The city had seen important moments in Black history, including the Amistad trials and the writing of the first history of American Americans by Minister James W. C. Pennington. But Connecticut had long maintained New England's weakest abolitionist movement. William Lloyd Garrison's *Liberator* called the state "the Georgia of New England." And despite its close proximity to Massachusetts, noticeably few Boston abolitionists came down to campaign.[44]

Many Black Northerners simply did not see Republican momentum as anything that might benefit them. The sharp *Anglo-African* magazine in New York argued that of all the parties in 1860, the Republicans were actually "the more dangerous enemy." The Democrats were at least plain about their intentions. But the Republicans opposed expanding slavery into the territories or reopening the African slave trade "under the guise of humanity." Really, the magazine argued with stark clarity, they just wanted to keep Black people away from the White North. "Their opposition to slavery means opposition," it summarized, "to the black man—nothing else."[45]

The *Hartford Courant* confirmed this suspicion, grotesquely boasting that "The great aim of Republicanism, is, to DRIVE THE NIGGER OUT OF NATIONAL POLITICS."[46]

Yet like the Wide Awakes' nativist roots, the scalding racism of its early days would be jettisoned as the cause grew and diversified. The bigoted *Courant* could not speak for the surprising diversity that the party would soon attain. Dogma was never iron-bound for the Wide Awakes. Only symbols and behavior were, and the movement was building to a heady finish to the spring campaign.

THE THUMP OF hammering resounded around downtown Hartford. Saws gnawed through fresh lumber. Dust-coated men took breaks to swig ale, while others—Edgar Yergason among them—planned the decorations. Hundreds of Republicans worked to erect a massive wooden structure, rough and unfinished, but capable of holding four thousand or so. Democrats mocked the edifice as "John Brown's Tombstone."[47] Republicans called it simply "the Camp." The old Whig party had a long history of woodsy retro appeals, stretching back to the Log Cabin and Hard Cider campaign of 1840, and their Republican inheritors were constructing a suitable venue for the last few big events of the race. They dedicated it with a huge rally. At least eleven hundred Wide Awakes marched around the structure, including four hundred up from New Haven. Senator Henry Wilson—the cobbler turned Massachusetts senator who never seemed to stay in one place long—zipped down from Massachusetts to help dedicate it.[48]

In the last few days before the April 2 election, Connecticut echoed with the sounds of campaigning, from the Camp's hasty construction to Henry Sperry's "Wide Awakes cheer." Locals—at least those who were not intoxicated with the unusually exciting race—were complaining about the constant cheering, hurrahing, and fireworks. The *New York Times* reported that the whole race was making "noise enough for the intense disgust of the population of the Nutmeg state." Yet many marchers, spectators, and businesses hoping to cash in had clearly caught Wide Awake fever. The Essman & Haas tobacconist was selling "Wide Awake Cigars"—whatever those were—while Smith, Gross & Co.'s advertisements peddled: "SHIRTS! FOR THE REPUBLICANS. SHIRTS FOR THE DEMOCRATS. SHIRTS FOR THE WIDE AWAKES. SHIRTS FOR THE ADOPTED CITIZEN. SHIRTS FOR THE GERMAN CITIZEN. SHIRTS FOR THE COLORED CITIZENS." The editors of the *Courant* seemed to be overheating, finally having some gripping news in their tidy town. A single page of the paper on March 27 contained eleven separate articles mentioning the Wide Awakes.[49]

Mixed in among the Wide Awakes were "a goodly number of ladies." The movement was specifically courting young women, encouraging them to turn out for rallies at "the Camp." The structure's designers even built a special

"Ladies Gallery." Published notes assured women that "the Republicans want their wives, sisters, or friends, to take advantage of these accommodations, and will work with the more enthusiasm when receiving the countenance of the fair sex." This summed up the role expected of most women in politics: not entirely discounted, but mostly looked to for encouragement, smiling faces, and fluttering handkerchiefs. Still, in a sexist society, the Wide Awakes were doing more than most to, in Henry T. Sperry's words, "respectfully solicit . . . Republican Wide Awake Ladies." The movement's reputation for orderly marches probably made their events more welcoming to women than the usual "drunken, fighting, smoking outfit" so often found at rallies. And plenty showed up. A correspondent from New York later joked that the Ladies' Gallery "was perfectly filled with ladies—probably not one more could have got in and lived; such a jamfull place I never saw, not even a Bowery omnibus on Saturday evening."[50]

Kezia Peck jammed her way in. The twenty-five-year-old schoolteacher was as excited about the Wide Awakes as any man. Her older brother hung around the Bristol Wide Awakes' headquarters, helping to sell uniforms. Kezia was thrilled to turn out for the dedication of "the Camp." One can imagine how making the seventeen-mile journey into Hartford, packing into the Ladies' Gallery for speeches, then filtering out into the April night to behold a thousand torchlit marchers felt. But she seemed to maintain a bit of irony about her historical moment. In a letter to a male cousin, Kezia asked sardonically: "Will you vote this year—this Spring? If so please do notice the sensation produced by thus deciding the destiny of the nation."[51]

It's hard to express just how monumental this off-season, state-level election somehow felt, even though both candidates had already been governors. Reporters from New York remarked on the knots of men filling the streets, campaign headquarters, clubrooms, and saloons, talking politics. Much of it had to do with the strange new movement marching in the night. There were, reportedly, three thousand Wide Awakes in Connecticut by early April. A month earlier there had been thirty-six. Newspaper numbers are never to be taken literally, but the movement was growing, inspiring allies and infuriating enemies. A rare emotionalism crept into the politics of the land of steady habits. The day before the vote, the *Buffalo Morning Express* joked that not even "large capital letters in newspapers" could capture the enthusiasm. The little race "arouses the energies of every man, and stirs the sympathies of every woman and child. . . . There are many staid and firm men who can hardly talk politics without weeping."[52]

National correspondents from both sides set the stakes. The *New York Herald* warned Connecticut readers that Republican victories could spark southern disunion. And besides, the *Herald* snarled, why were Connecticut voters even talking about slavery? Instead, they should take a breath, "before they disturb the existing order of things for any visionary Utopian ideas." The status of enslaved people in the South was no more the business of people in Hartford than "the condition of the inhabitants of Kamtschatka or Hindostan." Yet the *Courant* argued back that the national context was exactly why Connecticut *must* vote Republican. A victory in the small state would inspire victories next month in Rhode Island, in Maine and Vermont in September, in Pennsylvania, Ohio, and Indiana in October, and then, in November, a Republican president would send a message to all "the minions of slavery in the whole country."[53]

On Election Day, Captain Chalker and his Wide Awakes were out early, awaking Hartford with an earsplitting fireworks salute at three A.M. Morning dawned, clear and cold for April, and Connecticut's voters started to head to the polls. Over the course of the day, ten thousand more voters would participate than in the previous year's gubernatorial race, in a state with just eighty thousand voters. Republicans were electrified, but so were Democrats. Men turned up, "wild with excitement," at busy polling places, impatient to place their paper ballots in the box. In Hartford the Wide Awakes stationed fifty members at each polling place, usually in plainclothes, who "did noble service in challenging, sending for voters, suppressing rowdyism, and attempts to brow-beat those who had recently left the Loco-Foco party."[54]

From the Democratic perspective, the presence of a militaristic club, throwing out voters—many of them naturalized Irish immigrants—looked like a purge. But Republicans insisted that Seymour voters were arriving "full of whiskey and fight," looking for scuffles with known Wide Awakes. Elsewhere, like in Waterbury, the clubs were more methodical, sending out teams of well-known Wide Awakes to canvass specific blocks around each polling place. They left behind a battle plan in carefully calligraphed script, listing exactly which Wide Awakes should canvass where.[55]

By the end of the day, the Republican William Alfred Buckingham came away with 538 more votes, or just 0.7 percent of the count. For all the talk of "deciding the destiny of the nation," the Republicans squeaked by with a tight win. The Wide Awakes' ability to motivate their supporters, and their rivals, would become a key element of their legacy.

Getting Buckingham reelected was no great feat. He already was governor, after all. Had he won again, without the creation of the Wide Awakes, it would not have changed very much. You can tell the whole story of the 1860 election without remembering his name. The real victory was the creation and dissemination of the Wide Awakes. They helped Republicans claim the public square, face down mobs, and win the nighttime. They proved that neither chaos nor suppression, neither John Brown raid nor Dred Scott decision, would shut them up. They offered a physical symbol and a thrilling ethos for Northerners to rally around. More than deciding who sat in the State House in Hartford, the Wide Awakes waved a flashing black flag, noticed by Republicans throughout the North.

The news spread out from Connecticut in a flurry of national and even international coverage. Reporters were primed for the presidential race but looking for content, without too much else to discuss before the party conventions a month away. The movement, named by a newspaper, was spreading through that winding watershed of ink. Four hundred miles from Hartford, a Buffalo reporter explained the club's style: "This is the initial note, it would seem, of the presidential tune. The wide-awake clubs will spread over the whole Republican fighting ground of the nation." In London, British readers learned of the movement from the *Morning Post*'s correspondent. He was less supportive, glad that the Connecticut election was over, and "not a day too soon for the preservation of the peace of the State." The weird new companies seemed to inspire a lot of violence, and the Wide Awakes "were fast converting one of the most orderly of communities into a Donnybrook fair." Living in London, the young American Ellen Dwight Cabot wrote to her sister Elizabeth in Massachusetts, asking what was going on in Connecticut. The two had a bit of a spat through the mails, the abolitionist Elizabeth admonishing her conservative sister overseas about the importance of the Republican Party. Shortly after, Elizabeth started attending Wide Awake rallies.[56]

Back in Hartford, the Originals were busy doing interviews, handling inquiries. Captain Chalker led the way, and got most of the credit. Edgar Yergason, just nineteen years old, neither well connected nor elected to any leadership role, was forgotten by the national press. The movement's origins were already getting murky. The Buffalo correspondent shrugged—infuriatingly—"who invented the name we do not know."[57]

But its value in fighting Democrats was obvious. The Hartford Originals publicized a "sarcastic vote of thanks" to Alfred E. Burr, the Democratic editor of the *Hartford Times*, who gave them so much free press in his hateful publication. "The Shams," the *New York Tribune* smiled (using the slangy slur for the Democratic Party, a sham of its previous glory), "are terribly annoyed by this Wide-Awake movement." Wasn't that endorsement enough?[58]

Yet a small but telling feud was brewing, even among the celebrants. Rumors circulated that Captain Chalker and the Originals would march, in uniform, in the traditional postelection victory parade held after each governor's race. Democrats, and even some Republicans, cautioned that the age-old celebration was "not a party affair." Each year, the election done, citizens marched together, signaling a healthy truce in the campaign warfare. A partisan club, marching in those ominous uniforms, broke the promise of such a truce. Democrats swore they would not march alongside Wide Awakes in uniform.[59]

Newspapers weighed in from around the state. The Democratic *Bridgeport Farmer* denounced the idea as "contrary to all custom and precedent." It was one thing for a few young nobodies to play dress-up in the furious midnight of a campaign. But could they do so in broad daylight, once the race was run and the elected governor was in the procession? The Hartford Originals insisted there was nothing partisan about the Wide Awakes parading in uniform, and argued that their march would technically take place *after* the official parade. But they were kidding themselves. It was just one example of the symbolic and unexpected power of those shiny black capes. There would be more questions like this, about the line between partisan victory and official power, about the eroding of established norms, about when a campaign was truly over, about a defeated minority's frustration with a gloating majority. Were the Wide Awakes in the wrong for wanting to march, or the Democrats, for abandoning the old tradition?[60]

The little postelection feud—to march in capes or street clothes—hinted at the challenges that the new movement would bring, even as information about it was zipping along telegraph wires across the broad nation.

CHAPTER FOUR

If I Want to Go to Chicago

W AS IT THE pettiest fight in the history of the U.S. Capitol? Just days after the Connecticut election, the "most remarkable man in congress" tried to tackle the dire issues facing the country, only to be dragged down in an avalanche of name-calling, fist-shaking, and childish threats. All fought over who was encroaching on whose "side" of the House of Representatives. As the Wide Awakes were getting their act together in Connecticut, forces at the center of American politics were affirming just how much danger democracy was in.[1]

The speaker was Owen Lovejoy, one of those rare figures in the era who was both admirable and likable. Unless, of course, you had a problem with abolitionists. Lovejoy was a "good-natured, sleepy-eyed lion," seen at Republican events grinning broadly, his hands rested on his capacious belly. He sat ringside at the Lincoln-Douglas debates, whispering advice in Abraham's big ear. For thirty years Lovejoy had preached antislavery, ever since his brother Elijah was shot dead while defending his Alton, Illinois, printing press. In an abolitionist movement often criticized for its sniffy self-righteousness, Owen spoke with an endearing "off-the-cuff, up-front western style." He was particularly beloved by female audiences, with whom he playfully made himself an "irresistible target for teasing." His skills as a speaker were matched by his bravery in the face of the enemies who had murdered his brother. Lovejoy famously took out jokey ads in newspapers inviting "ladies and gentlemen of color of the South, who wish to travel North to benefit their condition or any excursion of pleasure to the falls of Niagara" to visit his Princeton, Illinois, home. And he printed his actual address. Lovejoy publicly made his unassuming cottage a stop on the Underground Railroad, facing threats of imprisonment with puckish good humor.[2]

As the Republicans coalesced in the 1850s into a viable but moderate antislavery movement, Lovejoy took the controversial step of joining a mainstream party. Though criticized by more doctrinaire abolitionists, he explained: "Personally, I may, in my opinions go further than the Republicans, but . . . if I want to go to Chicago and you offer me a ride half way, I go with you as far as you go." Such pragmatism won him a seat in Congress in 1856. Once in Washington, though, the devout Lovejoy found the city's proslavery White churches disgusting—so he became the sole White member of the African Methodist Episcopal Church on E Street. The appearance of this portly western White man humming hymns to himself must have been a strange sight for a congregation of free African Americans. But after "laughing with him for a couple hours," as the *New York Times* put it, just about any crowd could be won over.[3]

Except the combative slave-state Democrats in the thirty-sixth U.S. Congress. Lovejoy—a Congregationalist minister—chose to deliver a bold sermon titled "The Barbarism of Slavery" in April 1860, in the midst of an already ugly session of Congress. Stepping to the front of the hall, with that knowing twinkle in his eyes, he began striking out against slavery as "the sum of all villainy," an unholy assault on the Christian values of marriage, home, and family. Worse still, it was perverting democracy. Lovejoy boiled down the entire conflict to "this question: Whether these twenty-eight million people shall be accommodated or two million people be accommodated." Slavery was a zero-sum proposition. Its presence wrecked freedom for everyone. Americans had to choose. The next census would prove his numbers were slightly off, but his fundamental premise was accurate. A shrinking minority was demanding special treatment by a growing majority. How long would Chicago accommodate Charleston?[4]

The congressional minutes recorded "Laughter" or "Great Laughter" fourteen times in Lovejoy's short speech, but little of it came from the Democratic side of the House. As he got caught up in his preaching, Lovejoy strayed over an invisible boundary into Democratic territory, shaking his fists with rage.

Democrats did not stay seated for long. Soon a whole gaggle were on their feet, clucking and cursing and threatening. At the lead was Roger Pryor, a thirty-two-year-old freshman congressman from Virginia, and nearly a caricature of a preening Slave Power aristocrat. Charles Francis Adams Jr.—channeling his presidential ancestors' gift for apt and devastating description—wrote that Pryor was "as ugly as a stone fence, with tallowy, close-shaven features, and prominent high cheek-bones, his eyes had a hard, venomous look, while his flowing locks, brushed carefully back behind his ears, fell down over his coat collar." Photographs of the greasy congressman confirm Adams's observation.[5]

Now Pryor was in Lovejoy's face, shouting. Theoretically addressing the Speaker of the House (but leaving little flecks of spit on Lovejoy), Pryor yelled: "He shall not, sir, come upon this side of the House, shaking his fist in our faces." Lovejoy was a godly man and not a brawler, but the entire crew of Republican fighters were behind him now, shouting back at Pryor. Somewhere in the tumult, the muscular Wisconsin congressman John Fox Potter squared up with Pryor. The Republican had the good humor to point out, as Pryor fumed about fist shaking, "You are doing the same thing sir." What ensued was a long, childish debate about where in the House Owen Lovejoy could stand while denouncing slavery, the petty parliamentarism of it interspersed with Democrats craning their necks over Pryor's shoulder to squawk that they would hang Lovejoy if he ever visited Virginia.[6]

The confrontation was ultimately settled with the speaker's gavel, but now Roger Pryor and John Fox Potter nursed their own feud. Over the next few days the rivalry hardened, until Pryor gathered his seconds and issued a dueling challenge to the Wisconsin Republican.

Poor, greasy Pryor. In an earlier Congress, a northern noncombatant would have fustily declined, offering an easy victory for a Slave Power bully. Reelection campaigns were once built on such coups. But, channeling the newly belligerent mood, Potter accepted the challenge. Claiming his right to stipulate the time, place, and weapons, the Wisconsin congressman selected bowie knives, of equal size, at four feet. It is a shame we can't see Pryor's face when he heard the news, the way his "venomous" eyes must have bulged as he nervously tucked his hair behind his ears. Congress was stunned. Most expected an artful pistol duel at twenty paces along Bladensburg Creek, not a slashfest in a Washington broom closet. There was no way to conduct such a duel without atrocious bloodshed all around. And Potter, though eleven years older and a bit shorter than his Virginian challenger, had a powerful boxer's build. Also, he was starting to seem creepily serious about the whole prospect. Observers noticed that he now wore a belt with a revolver and a bowie knife to Congress each morning. The Wisconsin friend later claimed he knew Pryor would never accept his challenge, but it is difficult to tell whether, in April 1860, he was spoofing the whole notion of dueling, or as crazy as he seemed.[7]

In any case, Roger Pryor wriggled out of the duel, sniffing that it was a "vulgar, barbarous, and inhuman" choice of weapons, below the dignity of a gentleman. Newspapers reported in rapt fascination. The Republican press let out "a guffaw all over the North" at Pryor's humiliation, thrilled to finally have a cast of fighting men of their own. For the rest of his life, stretching into the 1890s, John Fox Potter would be known as "Bowie Knife" Potter.[8]

But while partisans cheered, the Lovejoy-Pryor-Potter feud represented a new low. The whole affair was just so deflating—the bickering, the turf claiming, the threats, each faction calling the other barbarians. Even the appearance of Republican fighting men, heartening as it may have been to many Northerners, looked less admirable when it involved two congressmen clutching bowie knives at four feet apart. Owen Lovejoy had tried to tackle the real issues of the day, of slavery, of minority rule, but the newspapers mostly focused on who would cut whose throat. The way out of America's political mess was not going to come from either flock of yelling, fist-waving congressmen. Something new was needed in 1860, coming from outside the increasingly distrustful Capitol.

Potter and Pryor were acting out in preparation for their parties' conventions, coming over the next month. It was always a good time for freshman politicians to gin up some favorable coverage. But while that could be good news for individual careers, conventions rarely left their parties, or democracy, much better off. Often the early-summer gatherings meant "profanity and pugilism, disorder and deception," in the view of an Ohio Republican who would become Lincoln's bodyguard. Frequently parties came away with an unsatisfying and unfamiliar nominee to canvass for back home. In this regard, 1860 would be an unusual year. Over the next month the parties would host both the most disastrous convention in American history, and the most exciting. Two entirely new parties would appear on the scene. And the nation would meet the Wide Awakes.[9]

Salvation was certainly not coming from the Democrats. Though attacked by Republicans as a national Slave Power conspiracy—"the same everywhere"—the organization was in dire internal trouble. Outsiders overlooked how much stress minority rule was putting on its creaky machinery, the way a tiny faction of "fire-eating" Deep South Democrats kept pushing the already conservative organization into indefensible stances. Much of the left wing of the party, made up of Northerners once attracted by the party's working-class roots, abandoned the movement over the 1850s in disgust. Centrist Democrats willfully ignored the party's drift, hoping that a Democratic ticket might squeeze between fire-eating "Ultras" on one side and what they mocked as the "Black Republicans" on the other. The goal would be to capture the votes of moderates who hated abolition and disunion and just wanted to stop talking about slavery. They placed their hopes on one very strange individual.

Stephen A. Douglas was so colossal in his time that his disappearance from our memory leaves an awkward absence. In the 1850s, certainly, he was the most written about politician in America, both for his bold maneuvers and for the seething hatred he inspired. Practically every political observer left delicious descriptions. Jefferson Davis—a fellow Democrat—called him "our little grog-drinking, electioneering demagogue." Charles Francis Adams Jr. sneered that Douglas was "a squat, vulgar little man with an immense frowsy head." Adams captured the physical weirdness of "the Little Giant," the way Douglas was at the same time barely five four and also a menacing physical presence. An immigrant familiar with the workings of diverse European assemblies marveled, "I have never seen a more formidable parliamentary pugilist."[10]

For a time, Douglas seemed to draw power from making people hate him. The Illinois senator surfed the waves of 1850s politics, engineering titanic moves like the Compromise of 1850, the Kansas-Nebraska Act, and plans for a transcontinental railroad, all designed to placate southern fire-eaters without alienating his northern Democratic base. He continued to be "the idol of the rough element of his party," who appreciated his combative zeal. But the problem was that Douglas could not merely feed scraps to the Slave Power monster. Each of his compromises made the fire-eating wing of the Democratic Party hungrier. Too self-impressed, too convinced that he could manipulate everyone else, Douglas helped drive many northern Democrats into Republican arms with his stunts, while encouraging the most dangerous forces in his own party.[11]

"There is in our history no more striking example," the Republican Carl Schurz summarized, "of a political leader falling victim to his own contrivances."[12]

The bigger problem for the Little Giant, in April 1860, was the upcoming Democratic convention, "strangely and ominously" located in Charleston. Douglas expected the nomination, but he faced fire-eaters intent on blocking the Illinois candidate. More than that, a minority within this minority hoped to blow up the entire organization, viewing the Democratic Party as an obstacle to southern secession. This group of burn-it-down disunionists was led by William Lowndes Yancey, an agitator as skilled as Douglas, though his goal was wild division, not artful addition. Yancey was an Alabamian, but had been raised by an abusive abolitionist New York reverend stepfather, from whom he may have developed an oedipal hatred for Yankees, abolitionists, and the Union itself. In an elaborate preconvention campaign, Yancey rallied Deep South Democrats to "stop Douglas," though they could supply no more popular candidate. Douglas believed that Yancey's real goal was "to destroy the only political party in existence that might hold the country together."[13]

The Charleston convention unfolded as one might have predicted. Even on the trains rattling south, northern Democratic delegates were grumbling. Murat Halstead, the great chronicler of conventions, sat next to an Ohio Democrat who complained that Southerners had been ruling over slaves for so long that they thought they could "rule white men just the same." As the train steamed southward, the delegate added darkly that if it came down to "a fight between sections," this Democrat would defend his "own side of the Ohio."[14]

Few in the country understood just how bad things would get at the convention. Although Douglas won 60 percent of delegates in vote after vote, he never cleared the unreachably high bar that Democrats had set for their nominee. Intransigent fire-eaters had been whispering antimajoritarian schemes in each others' ears for so long that even Douglas's broad support was not enough to convince them to compromise. Fifty southern delegates simply walked out, forming their own rival convention. Using the same kind of high-handed tactics they had long deployed in Congress, the southern Democratic minority ensured that the convention had to adjourn with no nominee selected.

As with Connecticut's postelection parade, it was easier to walk away than accept a loss. Democrats agreed to meet again in Baltimore in June, but there was no reason to assume that would go any better. It looked, in the words of the New York diarist George Templeton Strong, as if "the National Democratic

Party is disintegrated and dead," replaced by separate southern and northern organizations. The nation's oldest party, so closely associated with the rise of popular politics that many simply called it "the Democracy," was crumbling. And what would replace it? Breaking up that venerable old organization was like splitting the atom of American self-government. It contained within it powerful, fissionable energies, restrained by partisanship's demand that coalitions find a way to get along. As the party fractured, it was unlocking forces Americans had kept in check for decades. If there was any one point when it became fair to talk about conflict as *irrepressible*, it was probably this freeing of a southern minority in the Democratic Party to go their own way. "It is a bad sign," wrote Strong.[15]

Even as the Democrats divvied up their heritage, the nation still had more voters who didn't want to see a Republican victory than did. The problem was that each of the splintered options seemed increasingly unable to fit together. The mainstream Douglas wing of the Democratic Party had spent the last decade alienating many Northerners, while the fire-eating southern element would not accept Douglas, or compromise, or defeat. Many of them seemed to actively want to lose the election. Hardliners in this emerging Southern Democratic Party were already dreaming about a new enslavers' republic that might conquer Cuba and import African slaves again. Northern Democrats were whispering about defending their "side of the Ohio." There were, of course, the Republicans, but millions in the South and border states would never vote for that party, and daily consumed wild propaganda about them. That left a big chunk in the middle.

The result was a fourth contender in 1860, one of the weirdest alliances in American political history. On May 9, the Constitutional Union Party met in Baltimore and nominated a sour-faced Tennessean named John Bell. Though the movement preached compromise and old-fashioned avoidance of slavery, it drew together a dog's breakfast of everyone left in the center of American politics. Its voters hated the Democrats, but also hated the Republicans. Its leadership came from elite old Whig families in the Upper South, like the ancient John Crittenden, who had been born before the U.S. Constitution was even signed. But on the ground, its base contained elements of the disintegrating Know Nothing movement. Baltimore's street gangs, Washington cops, and nativist mobbers from Louisville to St. Louis now called themselves Bell Men. In those Upper South strongholds, young native-born working-class White men (the same boys who fed the Wide Awakes in Hartford) staked out turf against immigrants, enslaved people and free Blacks, Republicans, and Democratic elites. Many were joining their third party in eight years. A movement that tried to join mob-prone youngbloods with "conservative fogies and fossils," all on a platform of pretending it was not 1860, had little room to grow.[16]

Frederick Douglass dismissed the movement's amoral moderation, writing, "I say nothing here and now about the Bell and Everett party. A party without any opinion need have no opinion expressed of it."[17]

So 1860 was shaping up to be a four-horse race. There had been multicandidate elections before, races like the one in 1836 when five politicians scrambled for control in Andrew Jackson's wake. But usually those elections were personality-driven, with some prominent senator organizing a regional push among his allies. The election in 1860 was something more concerning: a four-*party* race. As of early May, only one of these factions had anyone of note to lead them, and a lot of people spat on the floor when they heard Stephen Douglas's name. This was not a few leaders in Washington angling for their chance. This was a political crisis, in which the American people could not figure out how to fit together.

It signaled a potential future of endless fracture. How long would it take for the Southern Democrats to secede from themselves? Or for the Whig–Know Nothing–Constitutional Unionists to start up their *fourth* organization of the decade? In such a crumbling edifice, the fight might no longer be between majority and minority, as Republicans wanted it, but among endlessly dividing factions. Americans might look back wistfully on the days when there was only one boundary line in Congress to duel over.

In the face of this endless division, only the Republicans seemed to be good at addition. And they had a new device, capable of throwing a wide, embracing cape over the fast-fracturing land.

IN HIS QUIET corner of the Hartford Republican headquarters, Henry T. Sperry was hard at work. The brick edifice sat bathed in soft spring light, exuding a sleepy smugness now that the governor's race was won. Many of the older partisans had gone home, or were at least taking long lunches at the Honiss Oyster House. But Sperry was putting in hectic hours, stooped over his desk, his sloppy cravat loosened, a look of anxious focus on his face. He sat at the nerve center of an exploding movement. Ever since the nation had watched the Wide

Awakes help Governor Buckingham win reelection, the inquiries had been flooding in, first from New York and Massachusetts, and lately from Wisconsin, Iowa, and Illinois most of all. Sperry spent much of April and May fielding inquiries, writing replies, drafting promotional pamphlets. Though merely a twenty-three-year-old ticket agent for the Hartford, Providence and Fishkill Railroad—with little experience and too young to have ever voted in a presidential election before—Henry Sperry was running a movement.[18]

Many Republicans had questions about these "Wide Awake clubs." Especially after their victory in the "hand-to-hand political fight" for Connecticut's governor, news was spreading. From Troy, New York, Trenton, New Jersey, and Philadelphia, eager inquiries were arriving. One Philadelphia Republican confused his Connecticut cities and sent his questions to the New Haven Wide Awakes, causing the *Courant* to grumble about his mistake, jealously guarding Hartford's role as originators. But Sperry chuckled that the club had received questions from "nearly half the States in the Union." There was curiosity to spare.[19]

The Originals had a new role. They still met at city hall for evening drills, but now they ran something more modern, a long-distance promotional organization, more like a newspaper or advertising business than a militia. Henry T. Sperry, as corresponding secretary, was now the chief voice, with a broader reach than even Captain Chalker. Tired of answering hundreds of letters by hand, Sperry printed up fill-in-the-blank pamphlets explaining the movement and how to start a club of your own. Sperry's pamphlet detailed the club's history, command structure, even the finer points of the uniforms (Inverness overcoats for the captains, blue lanterns for the lieutenants, special positions for the two tallest men in each company). He listed their drilling techniques, helpfully citing page numbers from William J. Hardee's *Rifle and Light Infantry Tactics*. And still proud of his "Wide Awakes cheer," Sperry spelled out the appropriate huzzahs and hurrahs using the big, bold Gothic Fraktur font. Perhaps its wild angles might capture the chant's ineffable verve. But most important, Sperry explained the Wide Awakes' role as marchers, bodyguards, and Election Day patrol. Summing up the movement's motive, Sperry swaggered: "Wherever the fight is hottest, there is their post of duty, and there the Wide-Awakes are found."[20]

And in the spirit of good Connecticut bookkeeping, Sperry requested that anyone who formed a club send copies of their constitution, bylaws, and officer's roster back to Hartford, America's filing cabinet.

James S. Chalker was busy as well. No longer needed leading charges, he began aggressively promoting the Wide Awake capes out of his Main Street tailor shop. When inquiries about the movement came in, Chalker would send a folded uniform through the mails. Soon he was selling capes to much of the region. In fact a large number of early Wide Awakes, including the Talcott boys as well as Chalker and Henry Hitchcock, were in the textile industry. As the movement spread, textile shops from Massachusetts to Illinois served as key local nodes. The clothing industry was, in 1860, the nation's fifth biggest, after flour, cotton, lumber, and footwear, providing both a cast of promoters and easy replication of Yergason's design. Soon Chalker was shipping tens of thousands of capes, sold, along with a torch, for about $2.25. It is unclear what he was doing with the profits.[21]

Ideally, those profits were not coming from the pockets of eighteen-year-olds. As the movement grew, the *Courant* admonished: "We trust that the older and richer part of the community will perceive the importance of giving their countenance to the boys, and of encouraging them in their useful labors." Their hint to the "richer part of the community" was obvious. Elders should pay, youths should march.[22]

Yet the *Courant* had a "word of caution" for those youths. "There exists, (rightly or wrongly is nothing to the question,) a degree of jealousy of this organization," warned its editors, "among the more illiterate of the supporters of the administration." Democrats *hated* the Wide Awakes, and were looking for any excuse to punish the Republicans for the new movement. Every Wide Awake, therefore, should "do nothing, and write nothing, to exasperate this jealousy. Some of the wise heads among our own friends, are somewhat afraid that the Wide Awakes will do our cause more harm than good." It was wonderful to see young men donning uniforms and forming clubs. But there was still plenty of finger-shaking coming from veteran Republicans, worried about the harm a mass youth movement might do. *Don't make us look bad.*[23]

The *Courant*, however, was overestimating how much control they, or anyone back in Connecticut, had over the hurtling movement.

The Wide Awakes first jumped out of state to Williams College in western Massachusetts. Some of its Connecticut-born students went home to vote for Governor Buckingham on April 2, and brought the movement back with them like a bad case of mono. Soon 150 students were wearing uniforms, building bonfires, firing salutes into the Williamstown night. Professors spoke to the clubs, led by seniors who preemptively endorsed William Henry Seward for president. From there the movement hopped to other northern locales with Connecticut connections. Buffalo editors admired "the Connecticut plan" and asked, "What say our Republican young men to a 'cape and cap' uniformed society for torch light parades and demonstrations?" Newark, New Jersey, launched an especially fervent company, which built a friendship with the Hartford Originals. In a way, Newark was a mirror image of Hartford, another midsize industrializing city filling with migrants, in a contested state on the other side of the New York region. The clubs also showed up among Connecticut's cousins in Ohio's Western Reserve, once owned by the extended Colony of Connecticut. There it was hailed as "A GOOD INSTITUTION—YE WIDE-AWAKES." Ohio editors praised the movement's nativist undercurrents, proud to see "men from the hills and the valleys, the good old yeoman stock of Connecticut" (i.e., Protestant Yankees) defeat "naturalized voters" (i.e., Irish Catholic immigrants).[24]

While Henry Sperry, James Chalker, and the *Courant* were pushing their club out from Connecticut, interested forces pulled it into distant regions. Chicago yanked the company into their city in early May, in the run-up to the Republican convention there, scheduled for May 16. No one from Chicago seems to have met a Wide Awake, but by assiduously reading the eastern papers, they built their own clubs with astounding speed. A handful of well-connected East Coast transplants led the way, amplified by the *Chicago Tribune* and its unusually pushy editor Joseph Medill. The Republican *Tribune* took over the role served by the *Hartford Courant* (like the *Courant*, it was also a nativist formerly Know Nothing paper). The newspapers leaned heavily on local readers, writing, "There should be company of them in every considerable town in the Western States." *Should* is a word Joseph Medill used a lot, not merely reporting the news of the movement but actively dictating future growth. Recognizing how powerful the reports of mob violence had been back in Connecticut, the *Tribune* raged against the attack on the Fair Haven Wide Awakes too. Reporting the attack in March as if it were breaking news, Chicago newspapermen goaded Republicans into joining. The bricks heaved by Connecticut Democrats, nine hundred miles away and weeks earlier, came down hard in Illinois.[25]

Chicago organized its first Wide Awake club on May 9, drawing together fifty members to meet by city hall. Those who gathered differed, in key ways, from the Hartford Originals. The bedrock of the movement seemed to come from slightly older, better-established young men in their late twenties and thirties—grocers, merchants, and small businessmen. Very few were born in Illinois; many hailed from Connecticut, New York, Massachusetts. And though most of the leadership had English names—Johnston, Ladd, Howland, Ward—the club loudly announced in *Tribune* ads that "young men of all nationalities are cordially invited to become members." Chicago, in 1860, was 52 percent foreign born—second in the nation at the time, and far more than any modern U.S. city—and the transplanted Wide Awakes wanted the Germans, Scandinavians, and Bohemians drawn to the new metropolis. Chicago's Wide Awakes were not the very young, jealously nativist, laboring local boys who formed the Hartford club. Instead they seemed to be energetic, up-and-coming, cosmopolitan capitalists, eager to promote their new town.

In a booming city—whose population was five hundred times larger than it had been at its 1832 founding—a different cast of marchers was needed. If Hartford boys formed the Wide Awakes because they felt trapped in the past, blocked by "awful, awful, awful fogyism," Chicago youths wanted the club to announce their future, especially as the Republican Convention neared. They were already selling Wide Awake capes from their own textile shops. A visitor from Lancaster, Pennsylvania, noted that "The Chicagoans, with their peculiar spirit of velocity, have already adopted the institution," well before Lancaster would organize its own Wide Awake club.[26]

As the movement stretched out from Connecticut, it was showing an impressive adaptability. In an age of fracture, with deep ethnic, religious, and class hostilities, the Republicans had stumbled on a tool that could appeal to Hartford clerks, Connecticut pistol makers, Massachusetts college students, Ohio farmers, and Chicago entrepreneurs. With simplicity and uniformity, eager promoters and a modular structure, the Wide Awakes were spreading to surprising places.

Working with their trademark velocity, the Chicago Wide Awakes caught the Hartford model with one hand and passed it out to their hinterlands with the other. Chicago was, famously, a city with a huge geographic reach. At a point in early May when most of the Northeast lacked Wide Awake clubs, companies were spreading from Chicago onto the Great Plains, down the Mississippi, and up into the Great Lakes woods. Clinton, Illinois, Muscatine, Iowa, and Janesville, Wisconsin, were all forming clubs in a roughly 150-mile radius around Chicago. In each town a local newspaper reprinted the *Tribune*'s heated coverage, and added their own exhortations: "Similar Clubs should be organized in every Town and Ward in the State. YOUNG MEN! You must put your shoulder to the wheel." Stretching into regions with healthy Democratic presences where many loved Stephen Douglas, local Republicans announced that they were forming Wide Awake companies "to Act as a political police." The less exciting goal—to have an impressive turnout of Wide Awake clubs at Chicago's Republican convention—went unsaid.[27]

In mid-May, Republicans began their great pilgrimage to Chicago. It took considerable effort to drag twenty-five thousand people to a city of just over a hundred thousand. Some floated in by steamboat, others bounced up on strutless carriages, many chugged from the east by railroad. Generally, they were a cheerier bunch than the grumbling Democrats riding down to Charleston and muttering about fighting for "their own side of the Ohio."[28]

A smirking *New York Herald* correspondent tagged along with the New York delegation. Simon Hanscom's reports of the train ride to Chicago add to the great tradition of sardonic accounts of American party conventions, from Murat Halstead to H. L. Mencken to Hunter S. Thompson. Hanscom satirized the self-impressed politicians aboard: the New York governor Edwin Morgan, "who always looks as if he accidentally became a great man, and did not exactly know how"; the enormous bare-knuckle boxing champion Tom Hyer in his towering silk top hat and "Seward" badge; the wisecracking president of the New York police, James W. Nye, whose "animal spirits nothing can dampen." Along the never-ending ride, the worthies lost some of their pretentions, mobbed at every small-town junction by excited Republicans playing strains "more or less dulcet," firing celebratory cannons distressingly close to the trains, and sharing "no little quantity of whiskey."[29]

Everyone on board his train, Hanscom wrote sarcastically, "ate the same luxuriant sandwich, swallowed the same quart of dust, were singed with the same cinders, enjoyed the same festive doughnut, gnawed the same juicy railway station beef, hung in epicurean delight over the delicious pie, and exerted their imaginative faculties upon the rural coffee and the provincial whiskey. It was a touching and dusty scene. All your famous equalizers—dirt and politics, hunger and thirst—did the work of fraternization."[30]

After a wearying day of alternately blasting along at *forty miles an hour*, then stopping to admire some small town's SEWARD banner, the delegation arrived in Chicago. It was around nine in the evening, and the trains were coming in along the lakefront. At an agreed-upon distance, the engineer let out six screams from his steam whistle. All along the lake, houses illuminated on command, lighting thousands of twinkling candles in windows. This meant hundreds of Chicagoans heard those six blasts and scrambled from room to room with matches and candles, putting in physical effort to pull off the effect. In a world before electric lighting, such nighttime illuminations took labor and resources. Partisan banners flapped against new construction as the train slowed at the station. Suddenly "numerous enthusiastic individuals who call themselves Wide-awakes" stepped forward, casting a wall of torchlight that shimmered along the glassy surfaces of the lake, bounced off their black capes, flooded the bleary train windows. Hundreds of tired politicians—"at no period especially attractive objects" to begin with—stepped down, only to be mobbed by Chicago citizens, while a double line of Wide Awakes stood stoically behind them.[31]

"The cannons began to boom," Hanscom wrote, "the rockets to soar, the small boys to hurrah, the police to get in everybody's way, and the dense crowd which filled the great railway station and all the streets adjacent, to push and elbow and general annoy each other." Most aboard had already sat through plenty of political demonstrations on their way to Chicago, "and have been bored to death with them." But these "Wide Awakes" were something different.[32]

The papers claimed that Chicago Republicans had mustered two thousand Wide Awakes for the reception. This was nearly as many as Connecticut had recruited between their February 25 formation and the April 2 election. The midwestern clubs had accomplished almost the same feat in just ten days. Maybe it was Chicago's unique "velocity." Maybe it was the clever way Henry Sperry and James Chalker had packaged and promoted their movement. Whatever the case, Republican politicians met something striking and new as they stepped down from dusty trains, faced with a silent Republican army standing to attention in the illuminated city.[33]

IT SEEMED LIKE half of the North was in Chicago: eastern worthies, western boosters, emissaries from the South, recent immigrants, foreign correspondents, and thousands upon thousands of curious locals. Omnibuses filled with state delegations rolled through packed and muddy streets. Chicago in those days was both descending into the swampy lakeside and beginning a massive municipal project to raise the whole town. Some streets were slimy with muck, while others were suddenly four feet higher. It was a nice metaphor for the country in 1860, simultaneously rising and sinking.[34]

The hotels packed in as many Republicans as they could. Even in a culture used to sleeping a few strangers to a bed, the "rush and crush and jam" felt extreme. Simon Hanscom, the *Herald*'s dusty reporter, chuckled at "the vigorous, earnest, bustling way in which everybody rushed about to do nothing in particular." Everyone was talking politics, all pretending they knew some secret about the nomination. Looking for adventure, Hanscom sought out Chicago's ladies, enjoying the crowds in large numbers. But he found that "the ladies here are all violent politicians," and he could not "commence the smallest hint of a flirtation without defining his position upon the question of the power of Congress over slavery in the Territories."[35]

Party conventions always have the air of an unsatisfying night out, everyone convinced that someone more powerful knows better, sits closer to the action. For his Democratic readers, Hanscom satirized the typical small-town politician, stalking about "as if the fate of the nation rested on his shoulders." Or even worse, the local newspapermen—"the more obscure his paper, the more ornate his behavior, the more expansive and superb his dignity." Really, Hanscom believed, "two or three quiet, pleasant fellows behind the scenes work matters as they please." This may have once been true, but even the powerful were at a loss in 1860. Horace Greeley—the antislavery editor of the *New York Tribune*—was a good example. The odd shrew of a man, with his fluffy white chin beard, little round spectacles, bald head, and bloodless pallor, was busily campaigning against William Henry Seward's nomination. Some wag pinned a "Seward" badge to his swishing coattails, which the preoccupied editor carried through hotel lobbies for hours.[36]

The hubbub orbited around "the Wigwam," an immense, temporary building thrown up like Hartford's Camp. It was the biggest venue in America at the time, capable of holding ten thousand people, with six hundred on the stage alone. Constructed in rough western style, it was no beauty. Its "hasty and irregular construction" reminded Hanscom of the entire Republican Party.

Outside the Wigwam, Chicago's streets filled with thousands of uniformed Wide Awakes making their national debut. Many delegates had never heard of the movement; others had read a stray mention, and were suddenly faced with the strange organization. Chicago-based Wide Awakes who originally hailed from the East met their home states' delegations at the train station and escorted them through uneven streets to their hotels. Visiting Republicans joined up, instructed to visit J. A. Smith & Co.'s Lake Street store and buy the proper Wide Awake gear to " 'fall in' for drill this evening." Why not give the new club a try while in town? Among those drilling, one delegation hoisted a six-foot-long bowie knife, dedicated to John Fox Potter, inscribed with the silly pun "Always Meet a Pryor Engagement." More seriously, in a town with a significant Democratic population, corps of Wide Awakes stood guard outside the Wigwam, "always on duty to 'see that things go right.' " Once again, "duty" was code for something rougher.[37]

But the surging crowds were not there to try on capes. They had a candidate to nominate. The obvious choice was William Henry Seward. That "wise macaw" had spent thirty years in politics, first rising to national fame as the young, energetic, Whig governor of New York. He had spent the last half decade ruddering the Republican ship in the Senate. He had huge reservoirs of support from across the Yankee North, helped along by his Whig bona fides, antislavery wife, and concise political messaging. And Seward really had suffered for the cause, burying his dogs and facing innumerable threats for his stand against slavery extension. Yet he was well liked in Washington, living in a perennial cloud of cigar smoke, easy with the brandy, a pleasantly odd figure, "bluntly original" in his conversation.[38]

In addition, Seward boasted a professional campaign organization. Though he stayed back in Auburn, New York, honoring the tradition of campaigning via proxy, his ally Thurlow Weed went in his place. Weed was one of those "quiet, pleasant fellows behind the scenes" who seemed to run everything, a "political wizard" acknowledged as one of American history's greatest managers. The tall, dark, and mysterious fixer had brought several thousand Seward supporters from New York to Chicago, rented out huge offices, and organized marchers with the famous boxer Tom Hyer at their head. From Albany to Chicago, the campaign had already left a trail of banners and badges bearing the candidate's name.[39]

But everything that made Seward a strong politician made him an unlikely nominee. That immense campaign organization, for instance, annoyed the other delegates. There was a sense that an occupying army of New Yorkers had stomped into town. One Chicago correspondent groused, "The Seward pressure is tremendous . . . their impudence is amazing. Your New Yorker 'knows it all.' He can't be taught anything." The biggest state in the Union, the California of its day, had a way of ostracizing everyone else. In addition, Seward had made a lot of enemies. Since his famous warnings about an "irrepressible conflict," Seward had been cast as a wild antislavery radical. He was truly hated by many in the South. But tacking to the center to try to reassure voters, Seward had ostracized abolitionists like Cassius Clay, who wrote of one moderate speech, "*it killed Seward with me forever.*" At the same time, Seward had taken an admirable stand against xenophobia in the Republican Party, offending former Know Nothings in key states like Pennsylvania and Indiana.[40]

Worst of all, Seward had been in politics for decades, with a long record and a familiar face. He was a poor match for his antiestablishment era, when Washington politicos looked like fist-shaking duelers or out-of-touch fogies.

But who else could the party nominate? The peripatetic Henry Wilson was everywhere. Collections of letters of key Republicans contain his hasty notes scribbled in monstrous handwriting, demanding "Give me your views" on alternative nominees. Some were arguing for an actual abolitionist for once, pushing forward the eminent and uncompromising Ohio governor Salmon P. Chase. But most felt the party was not ready to tackle slavery that directly. In a Chicago hotel, Horace Greeley explained to a gaggle of delegates that antislavery feeling was not as robust as it seemed. The editor asked the crowd a simple question: Imagine if your average Republican received news that they had just inherited a southern plantation, "stocked with slaves," from some distant relation. Would they set the slaves free? After a moment of silence, someone in the crowd muttered, "I fear I could not stand that test myself." "Then it is not yet time," Greeley summarized, rhetorical finger in the air, "to nominate an Abolitionist."[41]

In a nation where enslaved people still represented the second greatest sources of wealth, after land, even many Republicans could not be sure how antislavery they really were. No wonder few Black activists attended the Chicago convention.

If Seward's candidacy faltered because too many people knew too much about him, maybe the best choice was someone with adequate name recognition but few concrete associations. One man seemed to be known, vaguely, and liked, vaguely, by all. Abraham Lincoln was not present in Chicago, but his friends in the state were building a strong movement to nominate him as everyone's second-favorite choice. In a democracy run by the "systematic organization of hatreds," Lincoln was at the top of no one's list.

What people knew of Lincoln, they liked—his admirable battle for the Senate seat against Stephen Douglas; his balance of legal, logical, and moral opposition to slavery expansion; his rootsy western ways. Even those who could be witheringly critical of Republican politicians, like Frederick Douglass, admired Lincoln as "a man of unblemished private character," "one of the most frank, honest men in political life." People could be cruel about his humble origins and "grotesque" appearance, but even that added to his charm, as an outsider, as an alternative, distant from Seward, Washington, and the collapsing center of American politics. In an era attuned to political symbols, Lincoln's ugliness was one of his most useful tools.[42]

Few realized how much like Seward Lincoln actually was. Both were moderate antislavery men, devout ex-Whigs, strongly opposed to nativism. Both were (or would prove to be) cunning politicians, gifted with language, with generous senses of humor. Both were genuinely likable in their own ways. In fact, Lincoln was more radical than Seward and less willing to back down from a fight. The abolitionist editor James Sanks Brisbin wrote to his father that while Seward was hurt by "the hoodoo kicked up over his 'irrepressible doctrine,' " Lincoln was actually "even more advanced" on slavery issues.[43]

Lincoln had two key strengths over his rival. The first, which most would only realize in time, was what Frederick Douglass called his "great firmness of will." The next few years revealed an iron disposition in a crisis. The second was his newness. Modern Americans know Abraham Lincoln so deeply that it can be hard to accept that the thing which gave him greatest cachet in 1860 was how little people knew about him.[44]

The twists and turns of convention nomination battles are usually most interesting to historians writing books about them. Suffice it to say that after a fair amount of horse-trading in Chicago hotel lobbies, Seward's lead fell away. Crucial Lower North delegates threw in for Lincoln, and after three rounds of voting, the Republicans had their nominee. Party leaders tried to certify the vote and offer some final remarks, but were drowned out by thousands of hoarse, cheering voices, filling the Wigwam "with the energy of insanity." Cannons fired from the roof, and the news went out over the wires.[45]

Back in Auburn, Fanny Seward watched her father's friends roll the celebratory cannons away unfired when they heard of his defeat. Her father could be heard "cursing and swearing" in their house. Down in Springfield, in the offices of the *Illinois State Journal*, Lincoln's face spread into a quiet grin as he received the news from a messenger boy. He sat in silence, staring at the cable he held, for a few long moments before rising to shake hands.[46]

Lincoln's nomination did complement those Wide Awakes marching in Chicago. Republicans chose to promote Lincoln's humble origins as a rural rail-splitter. Never mind that he was now a talented and sophisticated lawyer and ex-congressman. Selective as the rail-splitter image may have been, it synced nicely with the free-labor values of the Republican Party and the class and age politics of the Wide Awakes. Lincoln's backstory was perfect for a movement led by young laboring men, hostile to elite pretentions and old fogies. Soon after his nomination, the *Evansville Daily Journal* called on the Indiana town's young men to form a "Lincoln Wide Awake" club, to honor Lincoln as a figure who "by his perseverance and indomitable spirit, has ascended from rail-splitting and working in old fashioned saw pits, to be candidate for the Presidency." "Cannot our young men," the paper demanded, "who admire that kind of grit, organize a 'Wide Awake Club' in this city?"[47]

Lincoln and the Wide Awakes fit together in another way. The Lincoln campaign hardly existed outside of a few close friends in Illinois. While Seward had been ready with banners and badges and celebrity endorsements, everyone's second-favorite candidate had little infrastructure. This was the downside of a dark horse nomination. It was to Lincoln's benefit that the nation teemed with small newspapers and local printers, ready to start churning out campaign stuff. But even more important were two guys in their twenties back in Hartford. While Lincoln may have lacked a national campaign infrastructure, James S. Chalker and Henry T. Sperry had a branded movement ready to go, pamphlets printed, uniform samples packed. So the two new forces in 1860—Lincoln and the Wide Awakes—twinned together as news spread across the North. It was easy to talk up the Wide Awakes as Republicans prepared to promote Abe Lincoln. The young movement had even escorted the new nominee already.

Chicago was a vector, drawing in all those small-town politicians and editors, exposing them to Wide Awakes, then dispersing them to their communities to spread the contagion. Ratification rallies started to break out across the North, with bonfires and fireworks and august speeches certifying the nomination. Celebrating crowds also formed Wide Awake companies, based on the thrilled reports of returning delegates. Soon after the convention, Wide Awake companies emerged in Bangor and Brooklyn, Cambridge and Columbus, St. Paul and San Francisco, and hundreds of cities and towns in between. Burlington, Vermont, got a club going. So did Burlington, Iowa. And Burlington, Wisconsin. And Burlington, New Jersey. Out in tiny Littleton, Iowa, nineteen locals formed a Wide Awake company so small that half its members were officers. One thousand miles from Hartford, in a settlement just five years old (and literally called "Littleton"), young Republican men were drafting their company's constitution. And it was a fighting one. The Littleton Wide Awakes denounced Democrats as pawns of the Slave Power, made up of "timid children—not men."[48]

"While professed politicians *talk*," the Littleton Wide Awakes bragged, "let the People *work*."[49]

The people were working, against incredible odds. In the most contested corners of America, Republicans' postconvention momentum crashed into the chaos of mob politics. Returning to St. Louis from Chicago, Francis Preston Blair Jr. tried to hold a ratification rally for Lincoln. Blair was a scion of an elite, formerly slave-owning southern family. His father had been shot by, then befriended, Andrew Jackson. But the Blairs had broken with southern Democrats, convinced that slavery was killing their region. Frank Blair Jr. was the dynasty's most aggressive son, a handsome, iron-jawed athlete with a gruff personal manner. He spoke in a "snappy, flowing, fiery way," one of the great cursers of the age, pouring out profanity at slavery, Know Nothingism, and the "whole damn pack of old Fogys" who ran Missouri. And he was skilled at the systematic organization of hatreds, building a tight alliance with St. Louis's German community. The northern Republicans who admired him as a southern mascot tended to overlook the searing racism that powered his antislavery politics.[50]

Frank Blair gathered Missouri Republicans outside of St. Louis's Lucas Market to endorse Lincoln's nomination. But they had to fight to be heard over the "yells and blasphemies" coming from a huge crowd of Democratic ruffians. The cold-eyed, mustachioed Blair glared angrily into the noisy crowd. Other speakers were treated far worse, pelted with stones and scraps from the market. Great gangs of rowdies crashed through the Republican ranks again and again.[51]

The whole meeting ended in a "grand row," with partisans fighting their way out of the claustrophobic market stalls and dispersing in disappointment. A group gathered in private, nursing their wounds. Frank Blair was fuming. Joining him were a number of the same type who formed the Chicago Wide Awakes—youngish northern businessmen settling in the West, along with German Forty-Eighters, restaurateurs, and brewers. Together they formed an organization, "which, in ability for self-defense . . . has never been surpassed by any political club in America. Thus originated the celebrated club of 'St. Louis Wide Awakes.' " Among all the Wide Awake clubs in the nation, none would prove to be the more committed to "self-defense." From the start, the new club ordered torches that were "attached to particularly heavy sticks" filled with lead weights.[52]

Across the river, the town of Belleville, Illinois, prepared too. Instead of a blustering southern aristocrat, a courtly German refugee led the way there. Gustav Koerner grew up in Bavaria but ended up on the wrong side of the authorities by drunkenly pelting soldiers with snowballs while a student in Munich in 1830. Forced to flee Europe, Koerner settled outside St. Louis and worked hard to convert its refugee community to Republican principles. For his Wide Awake company, Koerner chose a delightful ensemble of white caps and black capes, with red, white, and blue ribbons for their hats. In the same region where Owen Lovejoy's brother had been shot dead in 1837, Republicans were forming a movement that could draw together old southern elites like Blair, refugees like Koerner, devout abolitionists like Lovejoy, and buzzing young Yankee businessmen. At a time when news from Washington mostly reported scuffles, when the venerable Democratic Party was splitting in two, and the Constitutional Union Party looked abortive from the start, the Republicans alone came away with two good reasons for momentum and optimism: Lincoln and the Wide Awakes.[53]

"And now commenced," Koerner wrote decades years later, "a campaign such as I never witnessed before or after."[54]

PART TWO

Let the People *Work*

CHAPTER FIVE

A Spontaneous Outburst
of the People

H AS ANY BODY told you"—Susan B. Anthony inquired in a letter to Elizabeth Cady Stanton's teen boys—"of the grand affair that came off here at your Castle last Monday evening?"[1]

It began as a quiet summer night at the Stantons' wooded property outside Seneca Falls. Elizabeth Cady Stanton was holding court, verbose and pouncing, along with her drier, wittier friend Susan. Sitting with the pair were Stanton's husband, Henry, an abolitionist speaker with a bushy salt-and-pepper Hulihee beard; "the most beautiful & lovely" twenty-eight-year-old Nellie Eaton, and the Stantons' son Theodore. All were chatting softly when they first heard the music.[2]

There was only one explanation for the cornets, trombones, and drums wafting through the upstate woods. The Wide Awakes were on their way. Quickly, the Stantons scrambled to illuminate their home. Soon lamps and candles flickered from windows, and they all assembled outside, holding torches. Little Theodore watched in awe from the side.

Out of the woods marched young men in flashing black, moving in word-less order, passing through the Stantons' gate and assembling around the four surprised adults. "Our Quartette," Anthony wrote in a letter to Stanton's boys, was "completely encircled with the caped, capped, torch lighted host." Their captain—a local painter named William Failing—shouted: "Halt."[3]

In the torchlight, the group studied their visitors: the dozens of young men, their flapping uniforms, their scraggly mutton chops, some still boys, others full grown. All were younger, and mostly lower-class, than the prosperous, middle-aged Stantons. All were male. Had they considered the strangeness of a crowd of young men emerging at night, in black, uninvited, at a quiet home occupied mostly by women and children? Did they weigh, in the best case, the obligations they were putting upon their surprised hosts? It was exactly the way a group of twenty-year-olds might try to do something grand: at once impressive, imposing, and ridiculous.

"And then a silence, for a space of half a minute passed," Anthony relayed to the boys, her smirk palpable. Captain Failing stared at the Stantons. Elizabeth stared at Henry. Henry stared at Captain Failing. All stood in a confused hush. Finally Henry Stanton doffed his hat, bowed gracefully, and introduced his wife to speak.

But she had already said her piece. A few days earlier Stanton had led Seneca Falls' "Female Auxiliary to the Wide Awakes" in presenting a fine silk Lincoln banner to the club. Standing with the assembled young ladies behind her on stage, Stanton had accompanied the gift with an unusual speech. She actually welcomed the "discord, division + confusion" in American politics, hoping the Wide Awakes would catalyze some kind of mass awakening. And Stanton had not shied away from listing the Republican Party's shortcomings, warning its members that they "by no means come up to my highest idea of true republican."[4]

For his part, the Wide Awakes' captain had acknowledged that their movement "may fall short of what you and perhaps many others may feel to be the Correct position for a political party to occupy." But together, he hoped that the young men of the movement and female activists of Seneca Falls could unite under the shared battle cry of "freedom of speech, freedom of the press, and freedom of the person!"

Now those same Wide Awakes stood blinking on the Stantons' lawn. Captain Failing called for "Three cheers for Mrs. Stanton." Then another round of hip-hips for Mr. Stanton. Then someone called, "Three cheers for the little Stantons," and asked how many children the Stantons had. A voice answered glumly, "Seven."[5]

"For mercy sake take them *all* in a *lump*," Henry Stanton begged.

More hip-hips followed. Then the crowd called for "Susan B. Anthone" to make a speech. Anthony was in a speechifying mood, telling the men "she hoped they'd not only keep *Wide awake* to inaugurate Abram Lincoln—but also to go to the aid of the *Slaves*, in case of an insurrection, or another John Brown invasion in Virginia." This was pretty strong stuff; Republican surrogates in the summer of 1860 rarely called for invasion of the South.[6]

The Wide Awakes enjoyed some more cheering: hip-hips for Anthony, hip-hips for the beautiful Miss Eaton, hip-hips for Old Abe. Racking their brains for other gestures of hospitality, the Stantons offered up some pears and melons, the moist fruit split and shared by the men in black. Then the company was off again, marching back into the woods. "We had but fairly got settled," Anthony went on in her letter, when the Stantons realized that nine-year-old Theodore had marched off with the club. Around eleven he came sheepishly back, escorted by an older boy. In that summer of 1860, Americans learned just how irresistible a Wide Awake march could be to a youngster.[7]

Anthony played it cool in her letter to the Stantons, relishing the awkward comedy of the "grand affair." But on the evening of the march, standing before the men in their uniforms, she had felt called to give a speech on slavery, John Brown, and insurrection. Something in the rally moved her, despite all the silliness. And from the perspective of a torch-bearing Wide Awake, or nine-year-old Theodore, or his brothers reading about the incredible event they had missed, the evening seemed even more compelling. It all captured perfectly the tone of the summer of 1860—by turns thrilling and awkward, full of promise and menace, at once devoted to interminable hip-hips and preparing to fight an insurrection.

The incredible proliferation of Wide Awake clubs in the months after the Chicago convention also presented political elites with an unusual challenge. Wide Awakes just showed up at their homes, at rallies, at hotels and restaurants, seventeen- and twenty-three-year-olds traipsing through their gardens, calling for speeches, shouting hurrahs, dragging cannons, assembling bonfires on their property. William Seward frequently found himself pleading with Wide Awake companies to "allow me to go to sleep." Never before had a grassroots movement taken on such momentum, so free from the guidance of elites, or even elders.[8]

This was a mixed blessing, at least for the party's leaders. Republicans finally had the support that antislavery parties had long desired. But how to control this surging tide, now that they had it flowing? The Hartford Originals could feed the movement, sending out uniforms and pamphlets and fielding interviews, but they could no longer guide it. Bystanders—women, African Americans, and Democrats especially—all had to figure out how to interpret its impositions, waking their communities and clogging their streets.

By the summer of 1860, Wide Awake companies seem to have formed "in every village, town and city" in Connecticut. In New Hampshire, a nineteen-year-old Wide Awake recruit wore through his boots marching to "every town, village and city" nearby. Even in London, it was being reported that America's Wide Awake clubs had been "found in almost every ward, village, borough, and four corners in every state north of Mason and Dixons line." The repeated stress on the Wide Awake presence in "villages" is key, as the originally urban movement exploded across the rural north. In a nation that was still 80 percent rural, and for a Republican Party that was strongest outside of cities, this was promising news. And while Wide Awake clubs were expanding into every northern state, they were especially popular in Republican-leaning but still contested regions. The states that had given pluralities or slim majorities to the Republican Party in the 1856 presidential election—Pennsylvania, Indiana, Illinois, New York, Ohio, Iowa, Connecticut, New Hampshire, and Wisconsin—saw incredible Wide Awake growth. Those that gave over 55 percent of their votes to the Republicans in 1856—Vermont, Massachusetts, Maine, Rhode Island, and Michigan—went a little less crazy.[9]

"Wherever the fight is hottest," Henry T. Sperry had explained, "there the Wide-Awakes are found."[10]

It did not necessarily feel like a fight in the summer of 1860. This was the most interior part of the Wide Awakes' story, a northern celebration, less focused on the "irrepressible conflict," more interested in enjoying the new movement and the nice weather. This makes sense for northern culture, with its seasonality of public life. Summer was the time of celebrations and late-night gatherings; winter was the season for indoor discussions, lyceums, and self-education. Summer meant church picnics; winter meant prayer groups huddled by a stove. People living in New Hampshire or Wisconsin, where the winters could be so cold and so dark, made the most of their July nights. And so, all across the blueberry belt, from Maine to Minnesota, towns hosted rallies, drills, "collations" with pies and cider, excursions drawing dozens of companies together, bonfires licking the evening sky. Wherever the fight was hottest, there Wide Awakes entertained, filling local calendars with activities that were as social as they were political.

While there was less "fight" in the summer of 1860, it sure was hot. The nation sweltered through one of the worst heat waves of the century, causing devastating droughts and wildfires from Iowa to Texas. All the more reason, in the gentler northern climates, to get outside, even if it meant throwing on "a heavy cape and carrying a vile-smelling torch on a hot, sultry night," as the *New York Times* complained. The mass excitement of a Wide Awake rally provided a kind of political air-conditioning.[11]

It was all driven by young men joining up, in such numbers that it is impossible to do them all justice. There was George Kimball, the nineteen-year-old junior newspaperman from Saco, Maine, and Abram Dittenhoefer, a twenty-four-year-old New Yorker, frustrated with his German Jewish Democratic parents. John Meredith Read Jr., the twenty-three-year-old scion of Philadelphia aristocrats, joined up, as did William Dansberry, the orphaned railroad guard living across the Delaware River. Clubs of German Wide Awakes formed in Illinois, French Wide Awakes in Detroit, and an Italian "Garibaldi Wide Awake Club" in Brooklyn. One twenty-eight-year-old Swedish immigrant wrote that he first took "a lively interest in political discussions" when he was made captain of the Red Wing, Minnesota, Wide Awakes. Towns rarely mentioned in the papers—Tiffin, Ohio; Littleton, Iowa; even Healdsburg and Folsom, California—proudly announced their Wide Awake clubs.[12]

At this point, all known Wide Awakes were White, and all were male, but within these confines the movement showed other forms of diversity. Its greatest power was its ability to bridge class divides. The Republican Party's free-labor rhetoric mobilized various categories of workingmen, all convinced it was *their* labor that the movement was trumpeting.

Wide Awake club rosters display a movement capable of joining men of varied backgrounds. Cleveland's Wide Awake companies published rolls, ranging from swells like the youthful mayor George B. Senter to carpenters, masons, police officers, and clerks. Some were fifteen, a few were over fifty, but most were in their twenties, averaging around twenty-four years old. Noticeably few had been born in Ohio. Young, mobile, employed-but-not-quite-established men seem to have gravitated to the rising movement.[13]

The press pushed the Wide Awakes with astounding speed, and like the *Hartford Courant* before them, Republican reporters refused to maintain even a veneer of journalistic disinterest. A correspondent for the *Chicago Tribune* who went by "J.C.M." began his account of a rally in Clinton, Illinois, enthusing: "I am hoarse this morning with shouting, and wearied with laughing; but I must begin my letter with, Hurrah for DeWitt County!" It sounds like he had a good time; the summer of 1860 was the phase in which the sometimes creepy movement could be the most fun. Another journalist detailed a rally of eight thousand in John Fox Potter's southeast Wisconsin district—after Connecticut and Illinois the hottest Wide Awake corner of the country. The reporter complimented the banners praising "Bowie Knife" Potter, but apologized that he could not recount any of the speeches. He had been "on duty as a Wide Awake," and his "attention was called off so much." It was hard to take notes while wearing a cape, waving a torch, and hurrahing into the night.[14]

Newspapers needled and pushed, filled with pointed suggestions like: "Cannot such an organization be gotten up in this town?" The reporting could be saturating. A single page of the *New York Tribune* announced seven different Republican club meetings in Brooklyn on one evening. Another paper reported on twelve new clubs being formed in Suffolk County, Long Island. In central Illinois, the *Tribune* correspondent J.C.M. attended at least eleven rallies between July 27 and August 8 alone. He jumped from Pekin to Mackinaw to Urbana to Clinton to Monticello to Tuscola to Sullivan to Pana, counting thousands of Wide Awakes and tens of thousands of spectators. In addition to the men in capes, J.C.M. witnessed "Railsplitters" toting giant novelty axes, "Rocky Mountain clubs" in climbing outfits, brass bands of varying ability, and floats bearing thirty-three young women costumed as the different states. But for all this variety, the Wide Awakes formed a core, and the newspapers never let readers forget about the burgeoning movement.[15]

This was not merely a story of the press ordering clubs into existence. Newspapers were community products with low bar for entry, town-bulletin boards, and businesses that needed news to win subscriptions. There was a give-and-take; newspapers courted the clubs as often as they lectured them. The *Muscatine Evening Journal* in Iowa solicited its far-flung region, begging: "By-the-way, what are our other township clubs doing? Let us hear from you now and then, young Wide Awakes." The *Racine Journal*—in heated southeastern Wisconsin—complained that Wide Awakes favored the rival *Racine Advocate*, perhaps because the local club members gathered in the *Advocate*'s kitchen to drink London dry gin with its editors. Arcane feuds often worried Wide Awakes. George W. Rives, of Edgar, Illinois, wrote to Abraham Lincoln with pride about his local Wide Awake company. "We have every thing in order," George bragged, then darkened, "except our damn editor."[16]

The Originals in Hartford struggled to keep up with this postconvention boom. Henry Sperry and James Chalker worked harder than ever to monitor, let alone supply and guide, the movement as it spread. In July, Sperry told the *Hartford Courant* that he had received four hundred letters of inquiry. By August, James Chalker said they had been informed about a total of nine hundred clubs nationwide. Club size swung wildly—from 19 members in Littleton to 250 in one Chicago company—but averaged around 100. Those nine hundred clubs could easily have represented 100,000 men by August, with many other companies uncounted. Soon Americans would decide, based on no reliable information, that there were half a million Wide Awakes in the nation. That number stuck.[17]

Perhaps a better way to track the Wide Awakes' spread was the disappearance of waterproofed cloth from marketplaces as clubs bought it all up. The *Wheeling Intelligencer* tried to calculate sales of Wide Awake capes in the North, and concluded (probably erroneously) that New York City merchants alone were selling six thousand capes daily. In San Francisco, it was clear that agents selling uniforms were "making a great deal of money," especially if they had something for "all parties and latitudes." Supplies of mill-produced materials were drying up that summer. Much of what New York merchants sold was sewn by a network of women doing piecework in their homes, "stitching away for dear life" to keep up with demand. Companies posted newspaper ads searching for more enameled cloth. Recent chemical analysis of the Wide Awake cape discovered in the New Hampshire attic found that it had been painted with a zinc-based paint, better suited for a house or a barn than textile work. Clearly, people were rushing out these things in a hurry.[18]

And yet the materials that built so many companies were available almost everywhere. Most towns could get or make capes and caps, torches and oil, space for a clubhouse and a book of military drills. The Wide Awake model seemed to hit a sweet spot: simplistic enough to be reproducible from Saco,

Maine, to Healdsburg, California, but full of symbols and gestures with greater depth. It was almost like a child's game, in which a few token toys could transport its players into another world. Wide Awakes saw themselves linked to the war against the Slave Power, the international struggle for democracy, laborers battling aristocracy, and the future of the American empire, all pieced together by materials sitting in the average crossroads general store.

For those who had been lobbying against the Slave Power for decades, the summer of 1860 felt like a long-deferred dream. On July 30 a former Democrat from Somerville, Maine, wrote to the *Bangor Daily Whig*, "The people here are all wide awake, and impatient for the time to come, and do not calculate to be deceived any longer by the old fogies of democracy." On that same day, thirteen hundred miles west in Muscatine, Iowa, a sixteen-year-old letter writer agreed. Though he was too young to vote, "I am 'Wide Awake' in one sense—I am wide awake to the fact that three-fourths of the rising generation will be Republicans." It's no accident that, if the average Wide Awake was about twenty-four years old, they had been born around 1836, just as the new culture of mobbing was shutting down American public discourse. Raised for their whole lives in an environment of suppression, watching compromises break, parties crumble, and America's "pet monster" grow ever greedier, they found that finally rising up felt revelatory.[19]

Elizur Wright hailed this great northern rising. Wright had been a vocal Connecticut abolitionist for decades. An eccentric, bushy-bearded inventor who pioneered the mathematics of life insurance, Wright hailed the new movement with a pamphlet titled *An Eye Opener for the Wide Awakes*. In it he described himself as a "union-saving, constitutional, conservative, law-and-order, right-side-up-with-care, unblushing, unquivering, unsectional, Zouave-Drill, Garibaldian, Up-to-the-Times Abolitionist." The book reads like the work of someone's flinty, cranky, funny Yankee uncle, full of political wisdom, strange puns, rambling asides, and inexplicable slights against the Dalai Llama. Welcoming the Wide Awakes, Wright begins with the lines: "Bless your young hearts—you of the fresh, new generation, the blossoming future American—the America which is to decide whether Liberty or Slavery shall be universal,—you are 'waked up.' Good!" Hoping that the movement would lead moderates to full abolition, Wright urged: "You are wide awake, you say, keep rubbing your eyes, for it is early in the morning with some of you, and perhaps they will open wider."[20]

Wright tried to use his insurance industry skills to forecast just how much more "waked up" the movement might get. Gaming out the options for the North and South, Wright assured radicals that the Republican Party "creeps sneakingly along toward the grandest victory in the annals of time"—complete abolition. Looking even further into the future, the white-bearded time traveler explained that he had written his pamphlet "so that when the world comes to laugh at and pity the adult Republicans of 1860, some descendant of mine or yours, rummaging an old closet, may discover this little brown brochure." Wright hoped to leave proof for future generations that not all Americans were Slave Power–accommodating cowards. And he predicted, darkly and accurately: "Wo to the Slave Power under a Republican President if it strikes the first blow."[21]

To many others, the movement seemed like it came out of nowhere. Republicans had long worried that "the people of the North are not as wide awake as they should be," and the sudden emergence of uniformed marchers surprised bystanders. Formed from young and obscure men, and with their unique habits of silent marching punctuated by deafening shouts, the clubs often seemed to come hurrahing out of the wilderness. When Wide Awakes assembled "the largest mass of humanity that the oldest inhabitant had seen gathered" in tiny Hennepin, Illinois, locals had to wonder "where all the people came from." To Benjamin F. Thompson—a nineteen-year-old farm laborer in New Hampshire who joined the Keene Wide Awakes—the excitement of that summer felt like "a spontaneous outburst of the people from one end of the North to the other." Nineteenth-century farming communities were not known for crowds or excitement. The new movement supplied both.[22]

And Thompson was on the inside, attending drills, hanging out in clubhouses, planning rallies. To those outside the movement, its emergence could stir strong emotions. First and foremost, nineteenth-century America was filled with animals—draft horses and sheepdogs and stray cats—whose lives could be made miserable by the Wide Awakes' sudden bombardment of fireworks, drums, and "Huzzahs." Among the humans, even in the thickest Wide Awake regions of Connecticut, Illinois, and Wisconsin, there were always more bystanders than members. Often, the ratio was something like one to ten: fifty Wide Awakes might march before five hundred spectators, or five thousand marchers could entertain fifty thousand. Of course, clubs needed those audiences. Each procession enacted an exchange between club members performing and audiences observing.

Many of their observers were young women, and the Wide Awakes continued to provide a welcoming, if limited, opportunity for female political agency. Their rallies offered novel forms of involvement, advocated sympathetic causes, and established safe and enjoyable public environments. At many Wide Awake events in the summer of 1860, young ladies seemed to outnumber any other demographic. A visitor at a rally in Clyde, Ohio, counting bonnets and top hats, found that three hundred of the seven hundred people crammed into Clyde's wigwam were female, compared to just one hundred Wide Awakes marching around. Other women turned out to enjoy the spectacle, cheer on their husbands, or meet potential beaus in the ranks. When the Newark Wide Awakes visited Hartford for a grand celebration, reporters noted that the streets were "filled with bright-eyed ladies who enthusiastically waved their handkerchiefs, eloquently signalizing their lovers." Those bright-eyed ladies saw bright-eyed young men, proudly marching in uniforms for a valiant cause. In a Victorian culture averse to flirtation among strangers, sudden eye contact or a suggestive smile could turn a public political rally into something more intimate.[23]

Other women contributed by preparing collations of food, banquets, or tables piled with pies and cakes. One Iowa paper called on female Republicans to "bake and roast, and boil and fry" in preparation for a big rally. A mean-spirited Democratic paper in Milwaukee suggested that all the free "gingerbread, water melons, green apple pies, and canal water lemonade" were "furnished by young ladies that could not get boys near them in any other way." But women's presence and labor symbolized a moral endorsement, useful for a movement that could look scary in the wrong light. At a huge banquet in Independence, Iowa, the club president thanked the "Wide Awakes ladies of Independence," toasting "Heaven is with the right—the right is with the ladies— the ladies are with us!"[24]

Many young women stepped up as more than observers. Women sewed banners, decorated bandstands, threw bouquets, waved handkerchiefs, and filled other traditionally female roles. In a culture where musical proficiency was part of a respectable woman's education, many marching bands featured female horn players or drumbeaters. Penobscot, Maine's finest singer, a nineteen-year-old weaver named Ada Wingate, gave a rare speech, hoping the

Wide Awake rising would mean that "the deeprooted system of slavery shall soon be abolished." Often, individual young women marched along with Wide Awakes, not in militaristic capes but dressed as goddesses or symbols of the states. In the Midwest, Republicans liked to pair female riders on horseback, in flowing robes and sashes, with male Wide Awakes riding in long black capes. The women were almost always costumed as some allegorical figure, a Victorian dodge to avoid acknowledging them as full citizens with individual views. Yet they were still present, still active, still picking sides and aiding in the fight for their nation.

All this handkerchief-waving can feel unsatisfying to modern audiences, expecting women's suffrage and benefiting from long and hard-fought feminist campaigns. But that perception is more ours, in the twenty-first century, than theirs, in the nineteenth. The women who joined Wide Awake rallies, even in patriarchal ways, felt like they were *participating*. Most expected that participation to be gendered. Many bragged in their diaries and letters about their role in the events.[25]

Some did go further. As the campaign excitement grew in the fall, East Chatham, New York, did take that final step. Some of the most prominent young ladies in town came together to form their own "Female Wide-Awake Club." They chose sand-colored capes and dresses, with the word "ABE" spelled out in red, white, and blue letters. Their presence made national news, reported as far away as Louisiana.[26]

All the ladies flocking to Wide Awake rallies gave political rivals extra reason to hate the movement. A proslavery Missouri judge looked North and denounced "the tendency of society in the free states to discard modesty from the list of female virtues." He blamed the associations and clubs so common in the North. The South, he reassured himself, "is untouched by such disastrous monomaniacs. To slavery we owe this distinction." He was probably right. The corners of the country most comfortable with female political agency were the abolitionist Yankees and German Forty-Eighters now at the forefront of the Wide Awake movement.[27]

But what *did* slavery have to do with the crowds marching and rallying across the North? In the summer of 1860, with the new movement spreading but the election still far off, many Republican campaigners were comfortably vague. Some White abolitionists, like Elizur Wright, were heartily endorsing the movement. Owen Lovejoy spent that summer crisscrossing the North and working to widen the ranks of the antislavery army. Lovejoy even had a routine onstage in which he would wiggle his feet above a crowd and ask whether he truly had hooves like the abolitionist devil he was accused of being. His easy humor made antislavery seem less threatening. And yet the banners at rallies— even in Lincoln's Springfield—still contained that noxious slogan: LAND FOR THE LANDLESS VS. NIGGERS FOR THE NIGGERLESS. Some were less nasty, but simply concise, like the Boston Wide Awakes whose banner articulated: WE ARE REPUBLICANS BUT NOT ABOLITIONISTS.[28]

Wide Awake companies were all over the place on the issue. In Ohio, the abolition-inclined West View Wide Awakes wrote to Lincoln, "We here have a little John Brown Sperrit in us." Yet the nearby Tiffin Wide Awakes declared in their company's constitution that the club existed "to promote the interests of White Men" alone. George P. Holt—the Wide Awake whose cape was found in the Milford Historical Society's attic—had actually worked as an overseer on a Columbus, Georgia, plantation before coming North to join the Wide Awakes.[29]

Such paradoxes abounded within the movement. Republicans were united about the Wide Awakes, yet so scattered on slavery and race, because the movement had always cared more about the processes of democracy than its outcomes.

The movement presented Black Northerners with a particular challenge. On the one hand, the Republican Party was far and away the most popular anti–Slave Power political organization the nation had ever seen. Never before had antislavery produced a movement that could *win*. The purer Liberty Party never won the majority of a single county anywhere in a presidential election. Frederick Douglass took some heart watching the North's most prominent speakers giving anti–Slave Power speeches to masses of ordinary White men and women. And yet their promises were so partial and dilatory, proposing "a cautious siege" of the Slave Power rather than the "storming party" Douglass craved. While he hoped that the White masses might continue on their journey toward a wider vision of human rights, Douglass could not imagine himself joining in with that crowd.[30]

Watching thousands of young, uniformed White men march against slave owners must have held out an exhilarating possibility to Black bystanders in 1860—the dangerous and capricious White majority expressing a shared hatred, for once. But every Black Northerner knew that hating the Slave Power did not preclude hating Black people. Could they join in this campaign? Could they, for once, be part of this majority?

One powerful voice warned African Americans not to get caught up in all the enthusiasm. H. Ford Douglas had been born into slavery in Virginia, but escaped in his late teens and settled in Illinois, finding work as a barber while educating himself in abolition, history, and literature. In 1860 he offered a powerful warning at a Fourth of July event in Framingham, Massachusetts. Douglas argued that in this four-way election, "so far as principle so freedom and the hopes of the black men are concerned, all the parties are barren." In a stirring, erudite, funny speech, Douglas told his audience, "I know Abraham Lincoln, and I know something about his anti-slavery." Their shared state of Illinois maintained some of the most racist laws in the North, making Black migration difficult, banning African Americans from testifying against Whites, and preventing Black children from attending White public schools, even as their tax dollars paid for them. Douglas had been petitioning against these laws for years, specifically soliciting Lincoln's help, and getting nowhere.[31]

Lincoln, H. Ford Douglas declared, famously held up the late Kentucky Whig senator Henry Clay as his political hero. As did many of the Wide Awakes—Henry T. Sperry's pamphlets quoted Henry Clay on their cover, to link their anti-slavery-extension views to this symbol of good old-fashioned American compromise. Admiring Clay was a way of signaling a conservative, Whig pedigree. But Clay had enslaved at least sixty people, buying and selling and severing families along the way. "I want to know if any man can tell me the difference between the antislavery of Abraham Lincoln," Douglas asked, and "the antislavery of Henry Clay? Why, there is no difference between them. Abraham Lincoln is simply a Henry Clay Whig."[32] This was an exaggeration— Lincoln was far more opposed to slavery than Clay—but it raised a valid critique. How distinct were Lincoln's proposed policies from Clay's?

H. Ford Douglas pointed to the discomfort he could see in Republicans' faces, who "do not like this kind of talk," and "say that they cannot go as fast as you anti-slavery men go in this matter; that they cannot afford to be uncompromisingly honest." It was true that going further might lose voters, but White Republicans just seemed so smugly satisfied with their baby steps. Constantly stressing the limitations voters put upon them, Republicans nonetheless patted themselves on the back about their antislavery stand. It was this play-acting, congratulating themselves for rhetorical bravery while avoiding the real thing, that most irked Douglas.[33]

But there were African Americans who ventured beyond this cautious skepticism. In the abolition hotbed of Oberlin, Ohio, John Mercer Langston liked what he saw in the Wide Awakes. Langston was the only Black lawyer in Ohio, making his home in the city famous for its large population of educated African Americans and its collective resistance to slave catchers. The bearded, light-skinned, long-faced speaker of mixed African, Native American, and European descent gave hair-raising antislavery addresses throughout the state. Though never enslaved himself, Langston had seen the ugliness of the Slave Power without leaving the North. He had watched in terror as racist mobs burned down the Black section of Cincinnati in 1841, forcing eleven-year-old Langston to flee for his life. Like many others, he found solace in the Wide Awakes' militaristic response.[34]

As chairman of the Oberlin Republican Party caucus, Langston organized the local Wide Awakes. He did the daily work of tracking down capes, procuring torch oil, coordinating with the brass band, and assembling a towering bonfire to celebrate Lincoln's nomination. Though he preferred Seward or Chase, and worried about Lincoln's insufficient "humanity toward the oppressed," Langston campaigned hard across the summer of 1860. He gave speeches to Wide Awake audiences and led marches. When clubs from across the state joined with the Oberlin company for rallies, the otherwise entirely White corps of young men saw Langston, and a few other Black Oberlinites, marching with the club. Democratic papers mocked the "Oberlin Afrikan Linkun Guards." Such participants were a rarity, but they hinted at the influence Black voices might have on the Republican Party. Langston hoped to push from the inside to make it "the great party of freedom." His efforts were an act of hope, at a time when other Wide Awakes were openly racist, and Ohio only permitted Black men to vote if they "visibly" were predominantly of "Saxon blood." But despite these discouragements, John Mercer Langston made himself the first Black Wide Awake in America.[35]

By late summer of 1860, the Wide Awakes included Ohio's only Black lawyer and a White former plantation overseer, the nativists of the Hartford Originals and new immigrants—Protestant, Jewish, Atheist, and even a sprinkling of Catholics. Cleveland's mayor marched in a black cape, as did Wisconsin's "Greasey Fisted Mechanics and Mud Sills." The movement's admirers included the white-bearded time traveler Elizur Wright and nine-year-old Theodore Stanton, the arch Susan B. Anthony and the sweet-voiced singer Ada Wingate. It was tempting not to look too far South, or too deep into the future, but to enjoy the warmth and the fun of that Wide Awake summer, sip their lemonade or dry gin, and lose themselves in the thousands of bonfires flickering across the North.

ANNA RIDGELY WAS growing to hate the 1860 campaign. When Republicans first nominated Abraham Lincoln in May, the eighteen-year-old Springfield girl went out to celebrate with all her friends. The fact that her family members were strict southern Democrats did not seem to matter then. Her father played cards with the sociable Lincoln. Besides, half the young men she courted—including the future president's secretary John Hay—were ardent supporters. She enjoyed the nomination rally, and even exclaimed, "Hurrah for Lincoln!" in her diary. But Anna was also a devout Presbyterian, and the blaring Republican campaign that summer was fast reminding her of her Democratic roots. She sat in quiet church services while Wide Awakes and brass bands stomped past. When she ran into a Republican boy she was fond of, he was so hoarse from hurrahing that he couldn't speak to her. People always seemed to be shouting that summer. Eventually the local Republicans got hold of an enormous Mexican War cannon, firing it just outside Anna's church during prayer meetings, making "such a deafening noise I never heard," shaking the building until "I thought I should go crazy."[36]

On the other side of those bonfires flickering across the North sat Democrats, glaring back through the flames. They were not having a good summer. By mid-June it was official: the venerable old party had split in two, its northern wing nominating Stephen A. Douglas, and a southern faction choosing John C. Breckenridge. Vice President Breckenridge was not actually all that radical himself, but the thirty-nine-year-old had become a symbol of the Deep South fire-eaters' intransigence. The Democratic Party's historic strength had always been its ability to line up Southerners and Northerners behind one ticket; now that was gone. And in its place, they saw a North teeming with uniformed Republicans, elated and confident. It was all extremely annoying. And as Anna Ridgely demonstrated, Wide Awakes were no distant phenomenon. They marched past her door, fired cannons outside her church, distracted the boys she liked, lit up the town square, filled the night sky with fireworks, and sang songs "very trying to musical ears." It was not just stray dogs that winced when the Wide Awakes came to town.[37]

Few political devices in the history of American democracy seemed to have elicited as much sputtering fury as the Wide Awakes of 1860. "The Shams are terribly annoyed by this Wide-Awake movement," the Hartford Originals bragged when promoting their club. A huge Wide Awake rally in Madison, Wisconsin, enjoyed teasing the Democrats, "who looked on with blanched countenances, declaring that when they got a candidate, if they should happen to get one, they too would have a Wide-Awake Club, with torches." Republicans scoffed: "Well, let them imitate us—who cares!"[38]

Democrats had newspapers too. As their editors floundered, cut loose from trying to make a convincing case for a single nominee, many attacked the Wide Awakes' "dumb show." Their insults ranged from petty mockery to bubbling wrath. But they occasionally stepped beyond mean-spirited partisanship to an apt criticism of the ways the Wide Awakes really were defying democratic norms. It could be hard to notice, amid the giddy Wide Awakes and grumbling Democrats, but those Republican marchers were introducing some dangerous new precedents.[39]

In newspaper printing shops across the North, Democratic editors searched for language harsh enough to condemn the new movement. Many started with insults. When the clubs first emerged, the *Detroit Free Press* homed in on their physical silliness, describing caped marchers as having "the appearance of a disheartened Shanghae chicken in a rain storm. It is all legs and cape, legs predominating." From there, editors often targeted the youth of the marchers, in an age when the voting age was twenty-one and much of society was still dominated by rigid hierarchies. Papers called Wide Awakes "beardless boys," "infantile politicians," "the little Lincoln boys," and "foolish virgins." Reporters in Lancaster, Pennsylvania, claimed parents hated the movement that was stealing their sons' attentions. The snide *Rock Island Argus* joked that Wide Awakes' mothers made the companies wear those oilcloth capes, "to be used by their sons in cases of necessity as diapers."[40]

Hiding behind all this sniping was the very real fact that the Republican Party was stoking incredible enthusiasm among a young generation, many of whom grew up hating Democrats. Much of this cohort had come of political age over the last decade, watching Stephen Douglas and James Buchanan make atrocious concessions to the Slave Power's "pet monster." No wonder sixteen-year-olds were predicting that "three-fourths of the rising generation will be Republicans."

Democrats tried another tack, slightly stronger, targeting the Wide Awakes' growth among immigrants. Republican agents were organizing companies among the Welsh, Cornish, and Ulster Irish coal mining camps in northeastern Pennsylvania. Across the Midwest, rural German and Scandinavian communities were joining up. Over 70 percent of Illinois Germans had been Democrats in 1852; now it seemed like every other German settlement had a Wide Awake company, especially among Forty-Eighters and Protestants from northern Germany. This frustrated Democrats. Their party simply could not survive in much of the North if Republicans could poach immigrants. Nor could it rely on Irish Catholics alone, as the famine migrations ebbed and the German tide flowed in. Irate Democrats tried to remind foreign-born voters about the Wide Awakes' roots. A German-language paper in Illinois wondered if those "who are now so zealously blowing their horns" for the movement could not "remember the outrages which those white-hatted lot who called themselves 'Wide Awakes' repeatedly committed upon the Germans of New York, Brooklyn and Williamsburg. For the sake of decency, the Republican battalions should have adopted a different cognomen."[41]

Democrats were on to something here—the Hartford Originals did have worrying nativist origins. It was a legitimate question: Why didn't the Republicans adopt "a different cognomen"? Some Democrats felt legitimately frustrated, as if Republicans expected them to just forget the last decade of Know Nothing persecution.

Often, though, Democrats seemed to be clinging to the past. The Republicans had worked hard to quiet the nativist voices in their Wigwam. The Wide Awakes simply were not what the *Rock Island Argus* said they were, a "secret order, an offshoot of know nothingism, the object of which is said to be to prevent naturalized citizens from voting." For one thing, unlike the Know Nothings, the Wide Awakes were not at all secret. In fact they were exasperatingly public.[42]

A free-floating irritability settled over Democrats, who accused the burgeoning Wide Awakes of being "a sort of cross between Know Nothingism and Abolitionism"—the two chief Democratic villains of the age. The tiny central Pennsylvania *Clinton Democrat* cursed: "If the cutest Yankee on earth had had his wits at work for a century he could not have invented a more thorough machinery to destroy the morals of our youth," promoting "debauchery, drunkenness, profaneness, violence, and riot." Really, Wide Awake rallies were notoriously less debauched, less drunken, and less profane than any other campaign organization. The stronger argument was that the Wide Awakes were threatening some unspoken limits on campaigning. "When will these disgraceful exhibitions cease?" the Pennsylvanian cried. "When will political partizans learn to discard those rude appliances which only appeal to the ungoverned passions and appetites of mankind."[43]

And yet envious Democrats began to experiment with their own "rude appliances." Rarely, in American history, does one party develop a successful campaign technique that the other side doesn't quickly copy. By the second half of the summer of 1860, northern Democrats were organizing their own clubs—"Douglas Invincibles," "Little Giants," "Hickory Clubs," "Ever-Readies." At the corner of Court and Sackett Streets in Brooklyn, local Democrats rallied a "CHLOROFORM CLUB," organized for the purpose of "putting the black republican 'Wide Awakes' to sleep.'" But the Democratic clubs were messy, sometimes wearing militaristic capes, sometimes brandishing brooms to sweep away the opposition, often just turning out in the usual hat-waving, cigar-smoking, fire-cracker-throwing lot. A Democratic club organizer who bought up a big supply of uniforms bemoaned, "I have not succeeded in giving half of them away."[44]

The Wide Awake model worked for Republicans because it articulated a material thesis, tailored to the problems Republicans faced. Stressing uniformity, order, and militarism, Wide Awakes offered Republican voters a physical solution to the threats they diagnosed in their era—a divided majority in need of unity, the chaos of mobbing, a muscular defense of free speech and public politics. Their capes *fit*. But for a Democratic Party that had just split, that seemed comfortable with violent suppression of public speech, it made little sense to go marching around in military uniforms. Instead, the hodgepodge of outfits only amplified their disorder.

Democratic clubs often seemed to bring chaos in their wake. Gustav Koerner, the dignified German who had organized three hundred Wide Awakes in Belleville, Illinois, took in a Democratic "Broom Brigade" rally that summer. He had to admit that the marchers were "handsomely uniformed and carrying large brooms." "But how different was their conduct from that of the

'Wide Awakes'!" Koerner noted. The Broom Brigades quickly got drunk, forced their way into respectable saloons, "insulted everyone," and got into a fight in which "some of them were very badly handled." Koerner was biased, of course, but many complained about the rowdiness of Democrat clubs, contrasted to the strict order of Wide Awakes.[45]

The *Chicago Tribune* correspondent identified as J.C.M. listened in when a modest Douglas march, equipped with "drums and banners, fire-crackers and whisky," happened upon a huge Republican procession, looking out at column after column of silent Wide Awake marchers, ladies on horseback, color-coordinated floats, and young women in white-and-blue gowns. J.C.M. overheard an old Democrat admit: "This meeting beats ours all to hell."[46]

And when Charles Dickens's American correspondent for *All the Year Round* attended a Democratic ox roast in a grove at what is now Third Avenue and Sixty-Sixth Street in Manhattan, he found a similarly undignified scene. The Democrats had invited four thousand guests and laid out neat tables with bread and maple sugar cakes, cheap cigars and "fresh, light, frothy, pleasant" lager beer. But as soon as the roasted meat appeared, the crowds started climbing over each other to snatch at the "Douglas beef." The meat carvers backed away in disgust, and the English journalist and the New York cops looked on as "half savage, half mischievous" mobs tore the meat apart with knives, axes, and bare hands, scrambling away with fistfuls of "oily, oozing pig," then entertained themselves pelting each other with the leftover bones.[47]

Many Republicans saw the rowdy and riven Democratic clubs as a sign that the party truly was dying. Republicans constantly referred to the splintered party not as legitimate rivals but as "the bogus Democracy," "the spurious Democracy," "the Shams," or "the Shamocracy." The flip side of the great northern rising of 1860 was a belief that the Democratic Party would completely die away. The *Hartford Courant* predicted that if defeated, Democrats "will never rally again in the Northern states." Iowa Wide Awakes promised that their "prairie fires will utterly destroy that hydra headed reptile, Democracy." And the snide New York diarist George Templeton Strong, no fan of Republicans, mused about the Democrats: "I half expect that Republicanism and Abe Lincoln will sweep every vestige of that party out of existence."[48]

Parties do die. The Democratic-Republicans smothered the Federalists, the Jacksonian Democrats ultimately outlived their Whig rivals, and the Republicans had made the Know Nothings redundant throughout most of the North.

It was not far-fetched, in 1860, to imagine that the Democratic Party really could be killed off, at least north of the Mason-Dixon Line.

The northern Democrats were split, their clubs were sloppy, young people seemed to hate them, even some immigrants were turning their backs, and they were awkwardly beholden to a Slave Power that openly scorned them. But they were not entirely wrong about the Wide Awakes. Slowly, over the summer of 1860, ordinary Democrats articulated a more grounded concern about the youth movement. Rumors—entirely baseless—began to spread that the Wide Awakes were "literally arming for battle in November," carrying Connecticut revolvers under Connecticut capes.

The notoriously shoddy *New York Express* spread this misinformation, but added a better-justified apprehension. The Wide Awakes' appearance "has a look, nevertheless, so sectional, for there are no such organizations out of the Free States, so unfraternal, for they exist with no other parties, so belligerent, for they have the appearance of an armed force of open enemies to all who are not Republicans." They were scaring people. What would happen, the paper asked in a widely reprinted article, "if all men who do not agree in politics are to don uniforms and carry muskets"? Weren't America's elections bloody enough already?[49]

A letter writer going by "ZADICAL" took up the same point in the pages of the *Detroit Free Press*. While watching Wide Awakes drill a few nights before, ZADICAL came to "a few plain and common-sense reflections." Interpreting the Wide Awakes as a club organized for Election Day bullying, he wondered: "Have we arrived at that point that we will permit, without rebuke, the organization in our midst of a trained military band, designed to surround the polls and over-awe, by the force of numbers and discipline, citizens assembled at the ballot-box?" Were the Republicans bored with being "rail-splitters," ready to become "head-splitters"? The presence of militarism in campaigning was, in ZADICAL's eyes, "anti-republican, anti-democratic," signaling the start of a "wide-spread system of 'plug-ugly-ism.' " Political violence had often been associated with the Plug Uglies and Blood Tubs in rough towns like Baltimore or Philadelphia, but the Wide Awakes seemed to be spreading thuggish behavior into peaceful Michigan and beyond. And, ZADICAL asked, what would stop every party from uniforming and arming its young men? A political system like that would "need but a spark, one rash word, one injudicious act of a single foolish and hot-headed partisan of either side, to explode in riot and bloodshed."[50]

ZADICAL's careful concern about a partisan arms race was undermined by a big ad, on the very same page of the *Free Press*, for Wide Awake uniforms, "made to order from the recent styles adopted by eastern clubs," at S. A. Fuller's textile shop.[51]

By August, small Democratic newspapers across the Lower North were spreading worries about the "half military and half bullying" Wide Awakes, mixed in with silly insults and baseless rumors. There were, at this point, very few actual violent incidents, but the movement's appearance worried many. For the first time, Democrats began to spread the rumor that Republicans were actually plotting a "sort of body guard" to defend Lincoln "when he shall come to approach the White House, and the Southerners begin to kick up their heels." This view of the movement as an army of inauguration would only grow. Almost no one, from the Hartford headquarters on down, was planning that far ahead. But the Democrats were not wrong; in fact they were thinking more deeply than the Republicans, in worrying that militaristic partisanship would march beyond the usual political boundaries, toward a day when "our elections will become pitched battles."[52]

Wasn't this what Susan B. Anthony had told the Seneca Falls Wide Awakes, standing at awkward attention by the Stantons' front gate? Anthony was a radical and an outlier, but perhaps she was more honest about the capabilities and consequences of the army of uniformed young partisans that had just stomped out of the night. Years later, when Henry Adams would consider the "systematic organization of hatreds," he mentioned witnessing a Wide Awake march. "Pretend what they liked," he wrote, "their air was not that of innocence."[53]

Few Republicans wanted to think this way during the spontaneous fun of the Wide Awake summer. Their militarism was a symbol, nothing more. Their goals—free speech, majority rule, and ending the extension of slavery—were defensive, conservative. All that talk about dying Democrats was just campaign rhetoric. The *San Francisco Bulletin* attempted to offer some reassurance to the many Democrats in their state, concerned about the Wide Awake clubs forming on Montgomery Street. The companies were "composed generally of clumsy Dutchmen, who have no fiercer purpose than to enjoy the fun and beer of a campaign." Their outfits might look martial, but they were merely the invention of "some shrewd Yankee, who invented a cheap uniform" (this was actually pretty close to the truth). "There is no warlike intention whatever in the movement," the *Bulletin* assured Democrats.[54]

If the Wide Awakes were guilty of one thing, in the summer of 1860, it was not carrying rifles, or being secret Know Nothings, or using their capes as diapers. It was not appreciating how revolutionary, how destabilizing, their political entertainment that summer truly was. Caught up in a campaign like none other, they seem to have lost track of the stakes of the contest and all those predictions about the "irrepressible conflict," looming just a few months away.

CHAPTER SIX

They Get Me Out When I'm Sleepy

C ARL SCHURZ HOPED for a quiet supper and a good sleep. Deep in the July campaign, in a small town in southern Indiana, the famous German Republican needed a night off. Sick of the usual canvasser's dinner of "sour bread and horrible coffee," Schurz was eagerly tucking into a large meal in his hotel's dining room when the local Republican committee appeared at his tableside.[1]

The theater was full. They were ready for him. "How was this?" Schurz stammered in his clipped Rhenish accent. He had been spied coming into town, the Wide Awakes alerted, the brass band assembled, the townsfolk rushed to the theater. "What could I do," Schurz reflected, "but surrender."[2]

Outside, Wide Awakes were lined up in martial order, torches flickering. "With a tremendous hurrah," the company "took me like a captive to the theater, brass bands ahead." The small town hall was "crowded to suffocation," packed with men and women. This was the summer of that great midwestern heat wave. Schurz estimated the temperature was in the nineties inside the theater, an unventilated box holding the heat of hundreds of bodies, all wrapped in jackets or dresses to their ankles. It was like nothing Schurz had experienced growing up in Erftstadt, Germany.[3]

Schurz had been born in a castle, and the course that took him from that Rhineland fortress to an Indiana theater wound through the nineteenth century's boldest causes and bravest revolutions. Raised from a long line of caretakers who managed a medieval *Schloss*, Schurz catapulted into the democratic movement challenging the old aristocratic order, which expected him to spend his life cleaning castle floors. He joined the revolutions breaking out across Europe in 1848 as a young student, fighting Prussian troops and breaking a friend out of a Berlin prison, all while drinking copious quantities of good Rhenish wine. He was not the most romantic hero to look at—with his turkey eyes, scarecrow frame, and angry turtle's jaw. But he was always pushing to the forefront, fighting for every liberal democratic cause of the age. Even after the German revolutions failed and he relocated to America, Schurz's greatest strength (and most irritating characteristic) was his compulsion to be in the vanguard, dragging those behind him along. His most enduring phrase, though tragically misremembered, was his declaration as a new American: "My country right or wrong, if right to be kept right; and if wrong to be set right."

In Wisconsin, Carl Schurz and his dynamic wife, the educational activist Margarethe, made war on slavery. Yet he noted that the antislavery population, though thoughtful and steady and well read, lacked the kind of verve it took to launch a revolution. Native-born "American farmers," Schurz complained, "follow politics with a great deal of conscientiousness but with little zeal." And far too little wine. These Yankees were just too uptight, too cold-blooded for the crusade Schurz envisioned. The Republicans would have "to wage a bit of a war" to get them moving.[4]

In the baking summer of 1860, that finally seemed to be happening. Schurz followed his Wide Awake escort into the Indiana theater and took the stage. There he launched into one of his pyrotechnic addresses, his gangling limbs dancing, his beady eyes bulging, his black mustache waggling as he cut into the Slave Power. But as he spoke, men were taking off their coats. Then their vests. Finally their collars, all while trying to maintain eye contact. Women were fanning themselves desperately while nodding in assent. Sweat dripped from Schurz's face, down his back, under his arms. No one could accuse Schurz of not giving a speech his all. Finally an old Hoosier stood up, and "pronouncing my name in an indescribable way," offered: " 'Now, I am sure, the ladies here won't mind if you take off your coat and whatever else you like." The hall exploded with applause. Ladies waved their handkerchiefs in assent. "My coat went off first, then, after a while, my vest, my necktie, and my collar." Now practically in shirtsleeves, Schurz finished up an hour-long speech, eager for the open air. The audience, Schurz recalled, cried, "Go on; go on!" until he gave them more of his mind, his mustache flinging sweat for another hour.[5]

That night was not unusual for Schurz. Between June and November, he gave at least one campaign speech a day, aside from a short break demanded by his wife. He was, along with William Seward, Frank Blair, and Owen Lovejoy, among the most popular Republican speakers in America. Pennsylvania's Republican leaders considered him their "ablest disputant." Schurz spoke from Milwaukee to Hartford, then looped back across the lower Midwest to St. Louis. And he was a Wide Awake favorite. He saw more companies, looking down from stages, across Wigwams, and in sweat-lodge theaters, than probably any other American.[6]

He was struck by what he saw. After about a decade in America, awed by the potential of the place but frustrated by the deadened malaise in its Slave Power–dominated politics, Schurz felt 1860 was a renewal. He said as much in his widely reprinted speech ratifying Lincoln's nomination in Milwaukee. America's founding made a democratic promise to the world, but slavery was dragging that down, and "the hope of humanity sinks with it." Schurz feared that the age of revolution was ending—stymied by conservative empires in Europe and thwarted by the Slave Power (and apathetic Yankees) in America.[7]

But in the summer of 1860 "the popular conscience wakes up," Schurz exulted, "the people of the North rise in a great effort." This rising felt physical to him, watching as Wide Awake companies "sprang up all over the land as by magic," accompanied everywhere by brass bands that "seemed to grow out of the earth." For ten years, he had wondered what it would take to get "Don't care" Yankees moving. Now it felt as if the people "had little else to do than to attend meetings, listen to speeches, march in processions, and carry torches."[8]

Carl Schurz was an egoist, prone to envisioning himself at the center of grand historical events. But he was also an idealist, compelled to be on the right side of history. And no cause ever felt more right than the 1860 campaign, which he remembered ever after as America's Good Election. "We were all lifted up by the inspiring consciousness of being, for once, wholly right," he recalled. "There was nothing to apologize for, nothing to defend, nothing to explain, nothing to conceal."[9]

But even idealists grumbled about those insatiable Wide Awakes. Margarethe Schurz received dozens of letters that summer from her husband, his peppy handwriting bragging about the receptions he received, while bemoaning every time he was forced to speak. Really, the Wide Awakes served less as bodyguards for Schurz and more like a raiding party. Cutting across the same burning region in central Illinois where the *Tribune* correspondent J.C.M. had tirelessly reported, Schurz was pressed to speak again and again. In Peoria, he told Margarethe, he was "surrounded by a multitude of people who almost smother me with their friendliness . . . cheered, drummed and trumpeted to deafness" by local Wide Awakes. The next morning, he griped, "Everything would be well if it were not for the serenades" of Wide Awakes who spent the night singing and marching back and forth under his hotel window. In Beardstown, Schurz took a rare break to write to Margarethe, but in the midst of his letter, he noted, "I hear music again; the discouraging Bum! Bum!" of the Wide Awakes coming for him. Even on a ride down the Ohio, Wide Awakes gathered along a wharf, eager to hear Schurz speak from the swaying steamboat deck. Though always on the verge of spontaneous oratory, Schurz was stunned by the demand for his voice.[10]

A sense of historic urgency kept Schurz moving. It was also what made him so appealing to the Wide Awakes. Both felt that their time had come, that an awakening was not just a good idea but a historical necessity. In St. Louis, Schurz spoke to a crowd of thousands, including large numbers of the town's brawling Wide Awakes. Reminding Missouri's slaveholders that "this is the Nineteenth century," Schurz asked, "Are you really in earnest when you speak of perpetuating slavery? Shall it never cease? Never?" The moment to finally end the atrocity was here. Schurz really had little interest in slaveholders' views; usually he preferred to battle "The Slave Power" as a symbol of international despotism, and he seemed to care less about actual enslaved people. But he was outraged by the idea that Americans might miss their destiny.[11]

The Baptist preacher and Wide Awake Galusha Anderson would always remember seeing Schurz's St. Louis speech. At one point, the orator addressed Missouri's slaveholders (though surely few were in his audience). "Imagine a future generation," Schurz suggested, "standing around the tombstone of the bravest of you, and reading the inscription, 'here lies a gallant man, who fought and died for the cause—of human slavery.' What will the verdict be? His very progeny will disown him."[12]

If the giddy clubs of the summer of 1860 seemed at risk of forgetting the stakes of the election, Carl Schurz was there to remind them.

But meeting one's moment also means surrendering control. Again and again, Wide Awakes made plans for Carl Schurz of which he was only dimly aware. During that Wide Awake summer of 1860, a movement of young men finally inspired antislavery zeal, if little conscientiousness. For all his grumbling to his wife, Schurz was a man who loved being hoisted up to a rostrum, from Berlin to Beardstown. Of course 1860 felt like the perfect campaign.[13]

THE WIDE AWAKES were a gift to Republican politicians, but one in an awkward black wrapping. After years of political defeat, losing elections, leaving parties, and facing mobs, it was thrilling to witness an army of foot soldiers "grow out of the earth." Almost all Republican politicians—except for those very young men leading the Wide Awakes—had previously been members of a failed political movement, be they Whigs, Democrats, Know Nothings, Free Soilers, or abolitionists. They had all witnessed a beloved organization die, or become untenable, or never have a chance. Now the men who ran the Republican Party saw a political organization arise around them, almost independent of their efforts. At its head was, if anyone, an anxious-looking ticket agent in Hartford who had never voted in a presidential election before. And even Henry Sperry had little control over them. Now Republicans had not just voters but a mass movement, stretching from Burlington, Vermont, to Burlington, Iowa.[14]

But this movement, with more zeal than conscientiousness, presented unexpected challenges. The Wide Awakes were hard to manage, the way they ruined Carl Schurz's or Susan B. Anthony's quiet evenings. Many leaders felt trapped atop something running away under them. Politicians, groused William Tecumseh Sherman, "may agitate, but cannot control," and the Wide Awakes were proving his point. Yet they had no choice but to try. Democratic leaders could denounce the movement, mock it as a bunch of babies, or worry about the meaning of their militarism. But Republicans had to figure out how to benefit from, live with, pay for, and make use of their strange new gift.[15]

Many had concerns. Politicos were not used to accommodating the whims of nineteen-year-old clerks or farmhands. Carl Schurz, for all his complaining to his wife, was actually an incredible sport, beloved by the Wide Awakes for good reason. Other leaders were less obliging. Many worried, first and foremost, that the companies would harm their chances among moderate

Democrats, especially through violence. The *Hartford Courant* had warned, back in April, that the "wise heads" among the Republicans leadership feared that the Wide Awakes "will do our cause more harm than good." On that front, the companies had behaved well. They may be scaring Democrats, but there had been little violence. The fretful letters to editors were, to that point, mostly hypothetical.[16]

Republican politicians felt a second concern, more grounded in how campaigns really worked. Many leaders feared that the Wide Awakes would waste their promise, burn out their energies with silly rallies, and forget the hard work of canvassing voters that won races. It was an article of faith among nineteenth-century wirepullers—one mostly borne out by modern political science—that campaigns were won by systematic face-to-face canvassing of individuals. Quiet conversations in barrooms, in drugstores, or at church picnics were thought to be more decisive than shouting processions.

Thurlow Weed made this point. The New York state boss, regarded as "a man of mysterious powers" who had orchestrated decades of Republican and Whig victories, published a letter of warning on this topic. Weed offered his professional view of the election, now that his man Seward was not the nominee. With the Democratic Party split, Weed worried that Republicans might get overconfident, and "we may neglect the systematic organization" and lose to a better Democratic ground game. He cheered the new movement, writing, "let our Wide Awakes by hundreds and thousands organize and equip themselves. The more the merrier." But Weed also cautioned: "But above them all, and before them all, and better than them all, let us have our school district committees, our canvassers, and our poll lists." Veteran campaigners worried that a bunch of merry Wide Awakes might distract from the real race, which came down to quietly counting individual voters.[17]

Carl Schurz argued back against Weed, whom he hated. At a speaking event in Weed's Brooklyn backyard, Schurz insisted that a movement in the streets mattered more than a party's machinations behind the scenes. "I wish every true Republican would join" the Wide Awakes, Schurz shouted, or would at least become "wide awake to the problem to be solved, wide awake to the necessity of placing a reformed Administration in office, wide awake to the necessity of seeing Abraham Lincoln inaugurated and last, wide awake to the responsibility that will devolve upon a victorious party when in power."[18] Weed was plotting a campaign; Schurz was envisioning a crusade.

Lincoln himself wondered whether to believe Schurz or Weed. He spent that summer writing to state Republican Committee chairmen, like the brash Aleck McClure of Pennsylvania, making sure they were "counting noses"— systematically organizing at the most intimate level. Lincoln worried that those monster Wide Awake rallies were misguided. In a letter to Henry Wilson—who was busily attending as many Wide Awake rallies as the rail network could get him to—Abe noted that most of "our friends" prefer "parades, and shows, and monster meetings" to the "dry, and irksome labor" of canvassing individual voters. Perhaps Republicans were having too much fun that summer. But, well aware of human nature, Lincoln added, "I know not how this can be helped."[19]

Lincoln's concerns challenge the myth that he had a central role in the Wide Awakes' story. Because they seem to have emerged together in early 1860, he is often too closely associated with the clubs. Really, the Wide Awakes acted on their own, in ways that were not always pleasing to the man whose name their companies often bore. Lincoln wrote noticeably little about the movement, perhaps keeping his skepticism to himself, and much of what he did write was ambivalent.

Maybe he was jealous. The Republican nominee spent the campaign laying low in Springfield, honoring the tradition that a candidate ought not campaign for himself, lest he seem desperate. Instead he read joke books, wrote letters, and devoured newspapers. This was not easy for the sociable natural canvasser, however. "I will be entirely frank," Lincoln wrote to Senator Lyman Trumbull, "the taste *is* in my mouth a little."[20]

The tide of letters from Wide Awakes pouring into Springfield could not have made Lincoln's abstinence easier. Wide Awakes wrote him from all over: inviting him to rallies in Buffalo, offering him honorary membership in Chicago, alerting him to a secretive company in Washington, D.C., informing him that, in the view of one Pennsylvanian, "those Wide Awakes are the greatest Political Institution ever started." Even the fifteen-year-old boy who cleaned his office joined a club. Lincoln had given that "lovable rascal" a drum as a Christmas present, and now he was banging away in a Wide Awake fife and drum corps. It must have been astonishing for Lincoln to see that novel club he had first witnessed back in March, in Hartford, bubble all the way across the nation to his Illinois front door. But excited young Wide Awakes buried Lincoln in so much mail that he had little time to savor the surprise. "You cannot conceive the enthusiasm & furor," cheered George W. Rives of

Illinois. "But oh those damn lies they tell, I know are hard to endure in Silence." That Wide Awake's suggestion: "Don't write much, or to many— Keep cool & bear up & on the 6th of Nov. you will be out of the woods, & prepare for the White House."[21]

Who were all these boys in capes, offering the Republican nominee advice? Their letters would only get stranger from there.

Wide Awakes would physically drag Lincoln into the fight, just as they had captured Carl Schurz. On August 8 they planned a tremendous "Political Carnival at Springfield." Much of the heavy lifting was done by Louis D. Rosette, the corresponding secretary of the Springfield Wide Awakes—their Henry T. Sperry. Rosette was a mopey, self-doubting young lawyer who never quite seemed to grasp success. But suddenly, in the summer of 1860, his notes to his sister Ann begin to crackle with agency and energy, as he worked to coordinate one of the largest Wide Awake rallies of the campaign. Rosette wrote Ann that he had become so caught up in the electrifying campaign that "it is difficult for me to sit down and attempt to write a letter without getting it full of politics." He sent those letters to Wide Awake companies across Illinois, Indiana, Wisconsin, and Missouri, inviting them to the Springfield rally. Wide Awakes wrote back encouragingly. The captain of the Alton Wide Awakes promised to send at least 280 marchers and 800 spectators by special trains. An officer from the Beardstown Wide Awakes told Rosette that his men would be there too, ready to "strike terror to the hearts of all opponents."[22]

Beardstown was the Illinois village whose Wide Awake drummers had commandeered Carl Schurz mid-letter to his wife. Now that "Bum! Bum! Bum!" was coming for Lincoln.

Working with Lincoln's friends in the Illinois Republican leadership, Rosette helped orchestrate what one farmer called the "most magnificent torch light procession ever witnessed in our state." "Monster excursion trains" packed with Wide Awakes and spectators rolled into Springfield: nine cars from Indiana, fourteen from Chicago, seventy-five from eastern Illinois, forty-five from western, a total of a hundred and twenty from the General Western Railroad, and another sixty from the St. Louis, Alton, and Chicago line. The logistics were daunting—not just getting the thousands of Wide Awakes to Springfield, but housing and feeding them. On the night before the rally, Wide Awakes slept under their capes, in barns and back rooms, filling "every imaginable and unimaginable covert" in the bemused view of the *Tribune* correspondent. Rosette commandeered the law office where he worked, spreading mattresses and blankets across the floor for visiting Wide Awakes. Struggling to feed them all, Springfield's ladies slapped together thousands of sandwiches. Some were awfully thin, boasting "only a faded smell of ham." But it was all worth it, packing astounding crowds—estimated to be anywhere from nineteen thousand to eighty thousand—into a city of just nine thousand residents.[23]

On August 8 they poured through Springfield, putting Lincoln in a bind. Company after company marched through his town, calling his name, begging for his attentions, yet the candidate had sworn not to campaign. Given the stakes of the election, he was trying to be especially inoffensive. Lincoln chose to join the crowd but insisted: "It has been my purpose . . . to make no speeches." Viewing the rally from inside a carriage, Lincoln soon became stuck in the mud churned up by so many thousands of marchers. Unable to move his vehicle, a lake of Wide Awakes pooled around the carriage and "came near smothering Lincoln." Finally a crew of locals, helped by some German Wide Awakes from Chicago, picked up the lanky nominee and plopped him onto a horse, then "led the horse to town." In gratitude, Abe invited the Wide Awakes "to come down to my house to-night," smiling that he wanted to "shake hands with 'em." The Republican nominee greeted the Wide Awakes who milled around outside his home, while lesser politicians speechified from five different bandstands.[24]

When the Democrats swore that they too would hold a rally in the Illinois capitol, the *Chicago Tribune* smirked: "Let Mr. Douglas come! Let us see whether his presence will induce 500 men in Champaign County to harness their teams, and drive a hundred miles, camping out two nights as they have just now done to greet Abraham Lincoln. Let us see whether his presence induces a Wide Awake company or any other company to march from Beardstown on foot (forty miles)." And this was central Illinois's fourteenth Wide Awake rally that month. Behind the scenes of each, a secretary like Louis D. Rosette was working furiously.[25]

Those five buzzing bandstands hinted at the role political leaders could play. Young Wide Awakes may have sent out the invitations to Springfield, but party leaders dispatched the speakers. The most beloved headliners—the visionary Carl Schurz, the hilarious Owen Lovejoy, the gruff Frank Blair, and William Henry Seward most of all—gave hundreds of speeches. Each shared rostrums with regional celebrities, down-ballot candidates, and "boy orators" giving their first talk. Most were elected politicians, beholden to the official party structure and the dictates of its leaders. A few men, the "quiet, pleasant fellows behind the scenes," spent their time shipping popular orators across the North like dry goods.

The chief architect of the Republican's crucial Pennsylvania campaign, Aleck McClure, was a hulking, no-nonsense newspaperman with a stern brow and glowering dark eyes. Just after the Chicago convention, McClure kitted out makeshift Philadelphia offices on Chestnut Street with battered desks, bottles of liquor, ice, and cigars, and began to build a speakers' network that reached every district in his state. Building a coherent organization "from our disjointed and often jarring opposition elements" was, he later wrote, "an appalling task." But usually, when an orator was asked to help, he "cheerfully gave his time to speak wherever ordered by the State committee, and paid his own expenses." McClure was an intimidating force, and hundreds of orators had to surrender some of their autonomy to his orders, enduring a hot, grueling summer on rural Pennsylvania's bumpy roads.[26]

And each northern state had a McClure. This campaign was not yet a "machine," the political metaphor preferred later in that industrializing century. Instead, top Republicans worked more like newspaper editors (which many of them were), pasting together hurried editions of disparate articles, or panicked switchmen, trying to keep rail cars circulating in complex permutations. Carl Schurz was right: this *was* the nineteenth century, and campaigning meant more than counting noses. It meant a dizzying jumble of railroad schedules and telegraphed updates, an exhausting scramble to feed the Wide Awakes a steady stream of free speech.

From the outside, it looked so calm. Frederick Douglass, temporarily warming to the Republicans, admitted that "the canvass has sent all over the North most learned and eloquent men." But on the ground it was sloppier, more fly-by-night, and far more grueling. The New Hampshire Wide Awake Benjamin F. Thompson recalled watching Henry Wilson climb down from one train in Keene, give his speech at the station, and hop back on another train as it chugged past to another event. Chuckling as Owen Lovejoy entertained a sea of Wide Awakes in Hennepin, Illinois, the event's organizers wondered how they had managed to get up "the whole affair" with just the four days' notice that Lovejoy was coming through. Organizers worked hard to match speakers of foreign languages with immigrant settlements. They were pleased to find the slim, dapper Austrian immigrant Friedrich Hassuarek, who demonstrated an incredible skill. He could give a two-hour lecture in fluent English to native-born speakers, turn 180 degrees to an audience of Germans seated behind him, and do the same speech over in Deutsch.[27]

Looking back, we might wonder why the throngs didn't find this all a little repetitive, but crowds of Republicans loved and admired these speakers. Many kept track of who they saw, and in what combinations. Like later rock fans who saw Jimi Hendrix play with the Rolling Stones, or Carlos Santana open for the Grateful Dead, Republicans of 1860 would recall the rally that featured Owen Lovejoy *and* Charles Sumner, or Cassius Clay followed by William Seward.

But keeping it all going was a tremendous burden. A Michigan newspaper complained that Wide Awakes' demands for rallies, speakers, and coverage "have been a constant drain upon our time and purses." And those purses were already light. The Republican Party was new, and it was not wealthy. The richest men in the nation—southern slaveholders, Cornelius Vanderbilt, Sam Colt, and August Belmont—all voted Democratic. With James Buchanan in the White House, most of the federal postmasters who could offer free support to a campaign were Democrats. Aleck McClure achieved incredible feats that summer on a total budget of just ten thousand dollars, paying expenses out of his own pocket. Most orators spoke for free. Only Carl Schurz, typically, barnstormed across the Keystone State, then sent McClure a five-hundred-dollar bill for his services. And this was in Pennsylvania, the most important state in the race. Abram Dittenhoefer in New York estimated that the entire campaign was run with less than one hundred thousand dollars from the Republican National Convention.[28]

Of course, the Wide Awakes worked for free, as did the ladies making sandwiches and most of the orators shouting themselves hoarse. Incredible amounts of voluntary labor ran this campaign. But the Wide Awakes' uniquely material model did require cash. Someone had to pay for all those capes, torches, and oil. A Wide Awake's gear cost between $1 and $3, depending on the region, not counting the fuel. The *Hartford Courant* estimated that if there were five hundred thousand Wide Awakes (the unlikely but universally believed statistic) who all needed uniforms and torches, a pint of oil per parade, and paraded an average of eight times over the course of the campaign, the movement cost $1,650,000. Even if these calculations exaggerated the number of Wide Awakes by a magnitude of five, a campaign of one hundred thousand Wide Awakes would still have cost $330,000—three times what the RNC had in its piggybank.[29]

This sum was more than what most young Wide Awakes could afford. The *Courant* estimated that Wide Awaking cost an average of $3.30 per person; an Upstate New York paper's breakdown came to $4.10. Surely it varied from region to region, but these prices would stretch the budgets of many of the laboring men who joined up. In 1860, the average carpenter earned $1.65 a day, and the average farm laborer made just $0.88. And that was across all ages; average salaries were usually lower among those young workers who composed the bulk of the Wide Awakes. Edgar Yergason made a paltry $50 (plus room, board, and washing) clerking in Talcott & Post in 1860. Those who joined the movement would have had to spend nearly a week's wages on their cape, cap, torch, and oil. And this left out the cost of train or steamboat tickets for excursions, not to mention food and lodgings, booze and cigars. Such marginal laborers would have to scrounge up the cash for their capes somehow.[30]

Here, again, political leaders and local elites could step up. Wide Awakes might seem to emerge from the ground, organized by twentysomethings, but they grew out of communities with parents, bosses, and benefactors. The St. Louis Wide Awakes, for instance, found incredible financial support from the local German restaurateur Anton Niederwieser and the brewer Julius Winkelmeyer, who kept the companies in beer, pretzels, and cigars, while the inventor August Loehner paid to rent the company's Seventh Street headquarters. The New Haven Wide Awake Charles "Ducksy" O'Neill wrote to his girlfriend that his whole company was paid for by a John Scranton, who "foots all the bills" and periodically stopped by the clubhouse with bottles of champagne. "He has plenty of money and likes to spend it," Ducksy grinned, "and the boys are willing he should."[31]

This philanthropy explains why so many clubs were founded and captained by textile merchants, who could provide uniforms from their own supplies. "The older and richer part of the community" paid for the political labor of the boys in the ranks.[32]

John Meredith Read Jr. was not above asking his father for money. Albany's Wide Awakes clubs elected this twenty-three-year-old military school graduate as their president in June. He had campaigned in 1856, knew something about marching, and loved wearing uniforms and giving orders. Read Jr. had a long, somber face that somehow always looked dismayed, and a right hand that had been mangled in a shooting accident when he was a teen. Despite his support for the free-labor Republican Party, he nurtured an image of himself as a kind of American aristocrat, a natural leader of men. He also had a dad—John Meredith Read Sr.—who could pay. Read Sr. descended from a wealthy old Pennsylvania family. Both his grandfathers had been in the Continental Congress, and owned land across the state. And, unlike many other wealthy men in 1860, Read was a devout Republican. Read Sr. had been Pennsylvania's attorney general and Supreme Court chief justice, but since denouncing slavery, he had been blocked from further political jobs by "the interests of the Slave Power." Instead, Read Sr. devoted his time and resources to Republicans. He corresponded with everyone from Aleck McClure to Mary Todd Lincoln. And he wrote daily to his princely son in Albany, his letters bringing political wisdom and generous checks.[33]

Read Sr. balanced fatherly advice and offers of cash. Read Jr. responded with a son's combination of appreciation and manipulation. Father pushed son to take care of himself, to get more rest, and to smoke less, writing, "Everybody says you smoke more segars than almost any one they ever knew." Read Jr. wrote back about his success as the leader of Albany's Wide Awakes, bragging that "when I make up my mind to succeed politically I always do." And he asked for his father's support for the clubs, again and again. His letters rarely mentioned the South, or slavery, or what would come after the election. Mostly he focused on the Wide Awakes, their uniforms, their numbers, their expenses, and how supplying his companies would increase his status. Son asked father for funds to buy barrels of whiskey for his Wide Awakes in early August. After the whiskey money, Read Jr. needed more cash for uniforms, for torches and oil, for travel expenses. It all added up. Between August and October, John Meredith Read Sr. sent his son over $1,500 to pay for companies in Albany's ten wards.[34]

The money did not come cheap. Father lectured son and questioned his math. He read Albany newspapers and complained that Read Jr. was unappreciated. He shopped around for better deals on uniforms, concluding that the Philadelphia Invincibles club got all their gear for less than Read Jr. had spent. He also used letters to give his son little fatherly nudges, hinting:

"Upwards of a week ago Mrs. Read sent a new dress to our grandson, but we have never heard of its receipt."[35]

Junior showed the same passive-aggressive strain. In one letter he casually mused that he needed to raise an additional $1,500, then mentioned that his father-in-law (whom he knew John Meredith Read Sr. detested) was thinking about donating. The younger Read abruptly concluded his note: "Do write me at once to let me know your views."[36]

Surely not all, or most, Wide Awake companies were paid for by rich parents. Most clubs were made up of laboring men without dynasties to draw from. But John Meredith Read Sr. mentioned sending an additional five hundred dollars to the Philadelphia Invincibles. This one wealthy man seems to have spent at least two thousand dollars on the Wide Awakes, probably more. That was one fifth of Aleck McClure's total budget. Add together donors like Read Sr., textile merchants like James Chalker, and millions of women who sewed banners and capes for free, and it accumulates to clothe a movement. It also helps depict an awkward relationship slowly syncing up, party leaders and boys in black learning to help each other.[37]

But this money, it should be noted, did not pay young men to *be* Wide Awakes, only to help them do what they were already doing. Hundreds of thousands of young men put in incredible amounts of voluntary labor, and there is little evidence of them profiting personally from doing so. The best that wealthy leaders could do was encourage and enable their existing ambitions. Like Carl Schurz or Abe Lincoln, Republican leadership was surfing atop a surging movement, hoping to help guide its runaway direction.

MORE THAN ANY other politician, it was William Henry Seward who figured out how to ride the Wide Awake tide.

They never really gave him a choice. After his surprise defeat for the Republican nomination, after filling his mansion with curses and watching the Auburn Wide Awakes roll their celebratory cannons away unfired, he tried to disappear on a quiet New England vacation. Wide Awakes ambushed him at every turn. In Boston, Seward joked "I have committed a great blunder" in thinking he might sneak through the region unnoticed. In many towns, local Wide Awakes who had been "fast asleep" when his train arrived suddenly "woke up quite too soon for the convenience of a quiet traveler." Companies in Massachusetts, Vermont, and Maine marched for Seward, serenaded Seward, roused Seward. He met these marchers with self-deprecating humor, teasing them and himself. At one rally on the New York border, Seward warned the crowds that if "all this rejoicing around him was because he was leaving the State," he had bad news. He would be coming back.[38]

Seward matched this warm humor with the sharpest political speeches of the campaign. They are also the most legible to a twenty-first-century reader. Carl Schurz disliked Seward, but nonetheless considered him the most apt Republican speaker, admiring his ability to "compress into a single sentence, a single word, the whole issue of a controversy; and those words became the inscriptions on our banners." In an age when newspapers could blast a headline across the nation, this was a crucial skill. And losing the Republican nomination had set him free. Instead of the nominee's summer of seclusion and silence, Seward could really strike out. He returned in the summer of 1860 to the theme of the irrepressible conflict. Like Schurz, Seward was always good at thinking in grand historical terms. And he predicted that Americans "have arrived at the last stage of this conflict." He told the Boston Wide Awakes as much, standing on the high balustrade outside the Revere House hotel, a rumpled parrot with floppy hair and twitching eyebrows, looking down on Bowdoin Square coursing with men in shining black. The end of the Slave Power would come with the end of the campaign. "The last democrat in the United States," Seward winked knowingly, "has been already born."[39]

With that, Seward set out on a "great Western peregrination." Niagara, Detroit, Kalamazoo, Madison, St. Paul, St. Louis, Lawrence, Chicago, Cleveland: a campaign loop through the northern tier of Yankeedom, where he was most popular, where there were fewer Democrats, and fewer people talking about the actual nominee. It was an easier place to predict the future of an all-Republican nation. For the trip, Seward assembled a jolly party. He recruited the beloved James W. Nye, a "coarse, genial, humorous" fixture of New York politics, a heavy-drinking, heavyset jester with an aptitude for "making people happy wherever he goes." Charles Francis Adams Sr., the Massachusetts congressman and son of President John Quincy Adams, would come as well, to make sure that Seward and Nye did not have too much fun.[40]

Seward's traveling party also included members of that new Wide Awake generation. James W. Nye's sharp seventeen-year-old daughter Mary came along, as did twenty-five-year-old Charles Francis Adams Jr., eager for an

adventure. The young lawyer had grown bored with his "unmeaning and friv-
olous" Boston society life, having "summered it and wintered it, tried it drunk
and tried it sober." When Seward proposed the trip to Charles Francis
Adams Sr., Adams's son "eagerly caught at the idea, and prevailed on my father
to fall into it. We went, and it proved a considerable episode in my life."[41] To
round out the youthful crew, William Seward asked his fifteen-year-old
daughter Fanny to come. She adored her father's attentions and, as a voracious
reader of history, witnessing the 1860 campaign in action seemed tempting.
Fanny agreed, bringing her best friend, Ellen Perry, and the entourage of old-
guard Republicans and wide-eyed teens began to pack for their journey.[42]

To send them off, two hundred and twenty Auburn Wide Awakes arrived
at Seward's sprawling estate for one last rally. They promptly got lost in its
groves and gardens, to the absolute amusement of Seward, Nye, and the
reporters gathered for a send-off dinner. One newspaperman recorded—like
Susan B. Anthony—the sight of disoriented companies trying to remain serious
while their torchlights bobbed "here and there through the branches of trees
and shrubbery." Young voices shouted, "Where's Ward Four?" and "Here's
Ward Four—who the deuce are you?" Seward himself could be seen "through
the interstices of the shrubbery, with segar in mouth, cheering the boys on
this way and that." The goofiness enlivened Nye as well, and he began "dancing
through those sylvan grottoes by torchlight, and over and under this bramble
and that bush, through the bouquet of Michigan roses, and athwart that bed
of daises like an irrepressibly funny character of the fat Cupid." Seward shook
with laughter, while Nye's sides "were bursting with jolly guffaws."[43]

The party set forth by train on September 1, first rattling up toward Niagara
Falls. Sleeping arrangements were "singularly crude," with built-in, curtained
compartments, three to a wall, and the toilets were ghastly. The gang played
games to pass the time. Fanny Seward joined General Nye to challenge her
father and Mary Nye at whist, or Fanny and Ellen tucked themselves away
with a blanket and a backgammon board. The older men let loose. Adams Jr.
recalled that "consumption of liquors and cigars during that trip was out of all
cess." Seward smoked and drank brandy-and-water nonstop. Yet he was always
"a very considerate, delightful traveling companion." Despite his appearance—
"small, rusty in aspect, dressed in a coat and trousers made apparently twenty
years ago and by a bad tailor at that"—he struck young Adams as the greatest
statesman of the age. Many mornings, Adams watched the sun rise over

Seward, already up and puffing a cigar in the baggage car, his shoulders wrapped in an ornate Syrian cloak from his travels overseas.[44]

Most important, Adams marveled, "I never could understand where, when or how he then prepared the really remarkable speeches he delivered in rapid succession."[45]

Stopped at Niagara, Seward addressed Wide Awakes, lectured to local leaders, and shook the hand of a formerly enslaved man who ran a prosperous grocery. Seward sat near the grocer's former enslaver, Senator Robert Toombs of Georgia, in the Senate. Here was a man Toombs claimed to own, a flesh-and-blood reminder of the evil they were fighting. Fanny kept track of her father's addresses, noting a constant succession: "Splendid torch light procession," "Father brought up soon after by a long procession of Wide Awakes columns," and "Procession more than mile long—Wide awakes—Sister States—etc—Father in midst—Cheering of each company at house." Outside the International Hotel in Niagara, Seward joked with the Wide Awakes that the racket they were making was merely the sound of "the effort of the country to turn over. . . . For forty years it has been lying on its South side, now it is going to try its North side. That's all."[46]

His speeches came to a peak, almost a thesis, in Detroit. Fifty companies of Wide Awakes met Seward's party there, perhaps five thousand Wide Awakes and another twenty thousand spectators, in a city of just forty-five thousand, including "several hundred ladies and quite a few colored people." The night before, Seward had begged the Wide Awakes outside his hotel window to "allow me to go to sleep, whatever they may do for the rest of the night." The next day, Seward gave them his best speech. First, he acknowledged the awful state of the nation's politics. A Congress torn by "popular commotion," a Senate that "listens unsurprised, and almost without excitement, to menace of violence, secession and disunion," "frauds and violence in the Territories," a northern majority that felt continuously undermined. Though he claimed that he did not believe that "the country is, as so many extravagant persons say, on the high road to civil war," he did warn "that disorder and confusion are more flagrant among ourselves now than ever before."[47]

But there was a solution to all this disorder, Seward claimed. "The end of a great national debate is at hand . . . the people have become at last attentive, willing to be convinced, and satisfied of the soundness of the Republican faith." It was not an easy task. "I have never expected my own age and generation to relinquish the prejudices in which they and I were born. I have expected, as has been the case heretofore in the history of mankind, that the old would remain unconverted." As long as those older generations ruled, the young could not rise. "Ten years ago, and twenty years ago, the young men were incapable of being organized," Seward explained.

But now, in 1860, as he looked out on a sea of young faces in black capes, "the first generation of the young men of the country educated in the Republican faith has appeared in your presence, by a strong and bold demonstrative representation to-night. It is the young men who constitute the wide-awake force." They heralded a future in which "none but Republicans will be born in the United States." Shouting, "Go on, then, and do your work," Seward watched as five thousand marchers began their stoic, steady, orderly tread through town.[48]

Fanny kept track. She sent detailed letters to her mother, as well as recording cursory notes in her diary. But her letters have since been lost. With them, we lose the feelings of a fifteen-year-old girl, watching an army arise at her father's command. A girl who had seen her beloved dog poisoned "for spite of us," less than a year before. A girl who had played at the feet of her family friend, Harriet Tubman. How did it feel to see men in uniform, nearly everywhere she looked, rallying to defend her family, to stand "on the side of freedom against slavery"? How did it feel to stand next to her father as he hailed Wide Awake marchers and horsemen, as cannons and fireworks lit the night, as her father promised, "The end of a great national debate is at hand"?[49]

History hides her feelings. But not what she saw. She noted at least twenty-one huge processions in her diary as the party crossed though Lansing, Kalamazoo, Madison, La Crosse, St. Paul, Dubuque. Everywhere, the Wide Awakes were "the great feature of this campaign," according to a newspaperman with the Sewards. "Every town and village has its companies." Deep in the North woods, silent Wide Awakes on horseback emerged to escort Fanny and her traveling companions. Awaking in a country hotel, Fanny pulled open the curtains to find a "band of little boys, fifty in number, as wide awakes, called 'Little Giant Killers,'" who "saluted us with cheers and drum & fifes." Staring out the windows of the rattling train cars, at magnificent prairies so different from her Auburn home, she saw torches bobbing along riverbanks and flickering in the Mississippi.[50]

Charles Francis Adams Jr. stepped up to greet his generation. His father and Seward put him on rostrums, asked him speak to his peers. Adams Jr. had a perpetual glare on his face, dashing in youth, that would harden into mean-ness with age. But he wrote and spoke with verve, like a typical Adams, in a cutting style that was at once superior and self-deprecatory. As with his brother Henry, reading his reflections feels like sitting next to the funniest, meanest person at a party. Nevertheless, Adams seemed to know how to woo a crowd, proudly telling audiences that he was a member of the Wide Awakes in Massachusetts.[51]

Seward tried a similar tack, declaring that the Wide Awakes "have done me the compliment of electing me as a member." Adams Jr. and Seward were among a growing number of prominent figures who not only learned to joke with the Wide Awakes but also joined the movement. Chicago Wide Awakes made Lincoln an honorary member, and his son Robert enlisted in the company at Exeter. New York governor Edwin G. Morgan, Massachusetts governor John A. Andrew, even vice presidential nominee Hannibal Hamlin started to march at the head of Wide Awake companies. In St. Louis, Frank Blair attended Wide Awake meetings, and showed up at speaking events with a burly Wide Awake entourage. As summer turned to fall, Republican leaders stopped shaking their fingers at the movement and started to tag along.[52]

Charles Francis Adams Jr. saw a weird scene as their trains headed back from Kansas to New York at the end of their journey. Crossing Ohio one evening, "I was suddenly waked up by a sound of loud cheering." Pulling open the curtain to his cramped bunk, expecting to find more Wide Awakes surrounding the train, he saw a strange figure instead, truncated but sturdy, climb aboard. The satyr was shouting, "Where's Seward?" It dawned on Adams that he was looking at that "squat, vulgar little man with an immense frowsy head"—Stephen A. Douglas. And "he had a bottle of whiskey with him." The Little Giant was then actively campaigning as the Democratic nominee, despite the taboo on running for oneself. He claimed to only be traveling to visit his mother, but that visit was taking an awfully strange route to his mom's house in Upstate New York. And Douglas was drinking more than ever. Thrusting open the curtains behind which Seward slept, Douglas cajoled, "Come, Governor, they want to see you; come out and speak to the boys!" Roused awake, Seward replied flatly, "How are you, Judge? No; I can't go out. I'm sleepy." Always protective of his rest, Seward would not get up for the crum-bling nominee of a crumbling party. Douglas muttered, "Well, what of that. They get me out when I'm sleepy," and stormed out of the shadowy train car, pausing to swig from his bottle in the doorway, illuminated by the torchlight from outside.[53]

Politicians like Seward did drag themselves out of bed when the Wide Awakes came calling. Charles Francis Adams Jr., reflecting decades later, recalled that the whole race felt like "essentially a midnight demonstration—it was the 'Wide-awake' canvass of rockets, illuminations and torch-light processions. Every night was marked by its tumult, shouting, marching and countermarching, the reverberation of explosives and the rush of rockets and Roman candles. The future was reflected on the skies."[54]

At the same time, however, Adams Jr. saw in those skies the "ominous gathering of heavy lowering clouds." For all the future-predicting being done, no one accurately read the menace in those gathering clouds. "We all dwelt in a fool's Paradise," Adams reflected. "It is a source of amazement now to realize our own short-sightedness." All that talk of knowing what was coming was "pure self-deception."[55]

As Adams recalled, Republicans—like Carl Schurz, like John Meredith Read Jr., like the Hartford boys—focused mostly on their campaign, their marching and countermarching, their uniforms, their awakening. They thought dangerously little about the opponent they faced. "We knew nothing of the South, had no realizing sense of the intensity of feeling which there prevailed," Adams Jr. lamented. "We fully believed it would all end in gasconade. We fell into the rather serious error of under-estimating our antagonist."[56]

CHAPTER SEVEN

Wide Awakes! Charge!

F OR NEW YORK City reporters in the fall of 1860, there was no easier way to drum up a story than to visit one of the town's grand hotels, order a mint julep, and eavesdrop on visiting Southerners. Many considered the city "virtually an annex of the South" in those years. During the months when Savannah and Natchez were just too stifling, whole families would decamp for Gotham's grand hotels, lavish theaters, and sprawling department stores. As September came, the capering children would return home, replaced by businessmen who shipped millions of dollars in cotton from New York wharves each year. And in September 1860, those men sipping minty bourbon from little silver cups offered choice words on the coming election.[1]

At the Lafarge Hotel, a reporter heard a guest from Georgia talk about shooting Wide Awake marchers out of his window with a rifle, especially the portly ones. "The thing that most troubled the Georgian," a *New York Times* reporter related, "was the perfection of military drill which they exhibited." The Wide Awakes' "air of bayonet determination" rankled. At the St. Nicholas Hotel, another guest from Georgia was asked to stop talking about fighting Wide Awakes. He responded "I won't shut up; I'm in a free country"—to which a droll bystander quipped: "You are in a free country, because you are not in Georgia." And at the Metropolitan, two guests were heard to mutter that they were tired of the whole election, one adding: "Give us the benefit of civil war and put an end to it."[2]

But nowhere was the eavesdropping richer than in the mirrored lobby of the New York Hotel.

That "severely conservative" locale was among the grandest on the earth, at a time when American hotels were surpassing European ones as stunning palaces for travelers. For four dollars a day, guests got a room at its prime location, at 721 Broadway, just east of Washington Square, with floor-to-ceiling mirrors, a private parlor, and courteous servants. The food, served in the French style, was known for southern favorites, especially heaping platters of the hotel's famous fried sweet potatoes.[3]

And the guests made for incredible eavesdropping. More than anywhere else in Gotham, the New York Hotel was known as "a staying place for southerners and those who sympathize with them." There was the famous Mrs. Hayward of South Carolina, loudly telling anyone who would listen that she had moved into the hotel because abolitionists were trying to poison her. There were "cotton lords" wearing gleaming gold watch chains three inches thick, who "cherish an angry hatred of Lincoln" from the lobby's easy chairs. The hotel was also a favorite of New York's Democratic Party. Tammany Hall bosses enjoyed the restaurant, and quietly fought out internal feuds—sometimes with revolvers—in its secluded hallways and parlors. The place was infamous enough that one guidebook observed, "The politics of a man who registers his name at that house almost ceases to be a matter of doubt."[4]

No one doubted the politics of its owner, either. Hiram Cranston was a famous and vocal Democrat. Born in New York's Hudson Valley, he had nonetheless thrown in his fortunes with the South. Much like Samuel Colt, Cranston was a northern Democrat who "advertises his business by constantly proclaiming his devotion to the Union." Though adored by his southern guests, the mutton-chopped, dark-eyed hosteller had a way of making enemies. Over the years, two staff members had separately tried to kill him—one stabbing him in the gut, another beating him with a champagne bottle—after he treated them harshly. But in September 1860 he saved his capacity to infuriate for his neighbors. He was getting louder about the election, and "those horrid fellows, the Wide Awakes." Which was unfortunate, because one of the things that made eavesdropping so profitable for reporters was that just outside the hotel's broad windows stood the movement's central headquarters in New York City.[5]

Step out of the hotel's guarded front doors, slip through sidewalks dense with shoppers and b'hoys, and dodge the omnibuses and phaetons in the street, and directly across from 721 Broadway stood 722 Broadway—the Wide Awake Central Committee headquarters. That organization coordinated the efforts of Manhattan's twenty-eight separate Wide Awake companies. Anyone glaring out the windows of the New York Hotel would see young men bustling in and out, often in black capes, or drilling on Broadway at night. Hotel guests might mutter at the sight of the Central Committee's twenty-nine-year-old president, Silas Dutcher, or its "strict, impartial, brave, fearless and uncompromising" grand marshal, the towering J. H. (John Henry) Hobart Ward. And they certainly could not have enjoyed the late-night salutes by the cannons of the Wide Awakes' "Knickerbocker Artillery" club.[6]

Making everything worse, these Wide Awakes hatched a truly ridiculous idea. They wanted to string a "remarkably fine banner" with Lincoln's face on it across Broadway, from their chimney to the New York Hotel's, across the street. They asked again and again, writing to Cranston that if his hotel was not a political institution, he would not mind letting Wide Awakes tie Republican banners to the top of it. Cranston published their letter, and his response, in the *New York Herald*, swatting down the idea. His hotel was "as directly opposite to you in politics" as it was in address, Cranston scoffed, and everyone knew it. His letter was reprinted approvingly across the South. Were these Wide Awakes crazy? Did they really think that the *New York Hotel* would fly a Lincoln banner from its rooftop?[7]

Meanwhile, Cranston's guests were having trouble with the boys in black capes. Local Democrats were congregating outside and jeering the clubs. Rumors spread that one South Carolinian was trying to pick fights with the men going in and out of 722 Broadway. Wide Awake sympathizers complained that his attitude was "entirely too Southernish for this latitude."[8]

It was not just the 700 block of Broadway that was reevaluating its latitude that fall. Before 1860, the South used to reach farther north. Certainly, regions that twenty-first century Americans scarcely consider southern, like Delaware, Maryland, Washington, D.C., or northern Virginia, were indisputably southern (and slave-owning). Big chunks of the free Lower North looked South as well. Much of the population of southern Ohio, Indiana, and Illinois had ancestors who hailed from Virginia or Kentucky. You wouldn't call them Yankees. There were those who said that the South began at the Harlem River, claiming Manhattan. This was especially true in urban, Democratic areas. Of the ten largest cities in America, three were in the far North (Boston, Chicago, and

Buffalo), three in the South (Baltimore, St. Louis, and New Orleans), and the majority, and the biggest ones (New York, Brooklyn, Philadelphia, and Cincinnati) were in the North but of mixed sympathies. If you add Baltimore and St. Louis to this club, most of America's big urban areas were in the transitional middle. This was where the tensions were growing fastest. After a summer of Wide Awakes cavorting across the rural North, forgetting their antagonists and focusing on the internal life of their new movement, in September 1860 many remembered who their neighbors were.[9]

Hiram Cranston, at least, was in a position to reject the Wide Awakes' banner. Poor Bettie Ann Graham—a fifteen-year-old Virginian attending finishing school in Philadelphia—seemed haunted by the Wide Awakes that fall. She adored their style, admitting in her diary that "I always experience a peculiar sensation when I see a military company." But the dawning sense that the Pennsylvanians in uniforms were somehow arrayed against her family made their presence ominous. She scowled down at the Wide Awake processions stomping under her Spruce Street windows, which she "would have enjoyed very much, had it not been in honor of Lincoln." Philadelphia's Wide Awakes made a point of marching past the popular Continental Hotel, not far from Bettie's rooms, late at night, "making infernal and diabolical noises, intermingled with cheers for John Brown and groans for the Southerners." She grew afraid to go out at times of heated politicking. Fifteen-year-old Fanny Seward looked out of her train-car window and saw an army rising to defend her family; Bettie Ann Graham saw the same army rising against hers.[10]

Newspapers spread the fear. Even as politics divided and parties crumbled, America's vibrant press was still engaged in a heated national conversation. News and rumor bounced back and forth, agitating everyone. Northern Democratic papers scared their southern readers with stories about the awful Wide Awakes in their regions. Feeling targeted, southern editors amped up the panic about this distant threat. Back North, Democratic newspapers then felt called upon to oppose the Wide Awakes in defense of their southern allies (whom they had scared to begin with). Twenty-first-century Americans talk about living in a media bubble, but discrete, isolated bubbles would have been safer than the media landscape in 1860. Agitating each other, each bubble rubbed up against those around them, working the country into a froth.

Increasingly panicked southern newspapermen printed claims that qualify, at best, as confused misinformation, and at worst as deliberate disinformation.

Some fears are so outlandish that a clear reading of the moderate Republican press would disprove them. Others remind us just how distant Dallas, or even Richmond, felt from Hartford or Kalamazoo. Charles Francis Adams Jr. had warned, after all, that Northerners had "no realizing sense" of the feelings in the South. That went both ways. Many Southerners believed, erroneously, that the Wide Awakes were a secret movement, like the Know Nothings. The *Charleston Mercury* reasoned that, "if not of a surreptitious character, how was it possible for you to enroll four hundred thousand names on your black lists unknown to the public?" A movement that was so irritatingly loud in the North that it ruined church meetings and scared dogs could legitimately seem "surreptitious" when read about in Charleston.[11]

Often northern Democrats were to blame for growing misinformation. In an article titled simply "STOP LYING," the Republican *Chicago Tribune* identified the three "most atrocious falsehoods" of the campaign: that Abraham Lincoln was an abolitionist, that vice presidential nominee Hannibal Hamlin was of mixed race, and that "the Wide Awakes are a semi-military organization, ready at any moment to put pikes instead of torches on their poles, and march upon the South, for the overthrow of slavery and subjugation of slaveholders." Many blamed the widely circulated *New York Herald*, a publication that, in the view of Charles Dickens's correspondent in America, "seems to have gone mad."[12]

The fear snowballed. In July the *Richmond Dispatch* predicted that "the Republicans are literally arming for battle in November." By September, southern papers spread the story that William Henry Seward was traveling the Midwest, plotting to replace the U.S. Army with an abolitionist Wide Awake force. October saw real panic, as papers spread the false rumor that John Brown's men in Kansas had called themselves "Wide Awakes," and the Republicans had chosen the name as an homage (the clubs were really named after a *different* crew of murderous conspirators). The *Georgia Chronicle* outdid all other papers, warning that the Wide Awakes could soon "commence a drunken bacchanal, to end in the wild orgies of blood, of carnage, lust, and rapine." "The time may come," the paper shrieked, "that these semi military organizations, the sport of the hour, shall erect the guillotine, tear down the temples of justice, sack the city and the plain, and overturn society." If only these Georgians could read the minutes of the Hartford or Littleton Wide Awakes, debating what color sash to wear, or how many "Hurrahs" should precede each "Huzzah," they might have stopped predicting "orgies of blood."[13]

The Wide Awakes marched right into this. The whole ethos of the militaristic companies sent minds racing. They just were not very careful about how it all might look from a thousand miles away, in a nation already whispering about war. For years, conspiratorial habits of mind had been floating around the nation, warning of nefarious cabals, demanding constant vigilance. Now, looking North, many Southerners saw a secretive, militaristic movement of half a million Northerners drilling in the streets. The Wide Awakes played into the same paranoid style that they grew out of. The usually unreasonable *Charleston Mercury* asked of Republicans, with some fairness, "By what custom or precedent are you authorized as a mere political party to form a politico-military organization?"[14]

The clubs were altering what many in the South thought about their northern countrymen. A lengthy assessment in the *Richmond Enquirer* warned that Southerners "who are disposed to sneer at Puritan courage, will find themselves mistaken when they have to encounter these 'Wide Awakes.' " A Mississippi editor cautioned, "Our Northern friends are men of action, not words; they organize, drill, march and file, while we speak and talk." Old stereotypes of Southerners as fiery but lazy, and Northerners as cold and methodical, fed fears about what the Wide Awakes were preparing. The sections knew each other just well enough to scare each other, and all that stoic drilling did not help.[15]

Extremist leaders stoked the panic. Virginia's former governor Henry A. Wise, who had run the state when John Brown was executed the previous December, warned that the Wide Awakes were an extension of Brown's revolution. The next invasion, however, would not be led by one "poor old fanatic" but by "thousands—perhaps tens of thousands—of trained 'Wide Awakes." Wise predicted that the invading army would take away both the South's "personal property in Negro slaves" and their "political property" in the Union. Again and again in September and October he hit that theme, predicting defeat in November by an "exultant, blatant, domineering majority at the North," which would leave "a poor, pitiful, subdued minority in the South, submitting and succumbing."[16]

"Submission" was a frequent theme in southern fears that fall; defeat in the election was viewed not just as a question of having fewer votes but as an illegitimate and emasculating theft. By setting this tone, a small core of leaders like Wise primed the region to reject the results of the election barely a month away.

No one did more harm than William Lowndes Yancey. He was the fire-eating Alabamian who had worked to block Stephen A. Douglas's nomination and break up the Democratic Party, the one with serious issues with his Yankee stepdaddy. Now Yancey headed north on a speaking tour. In Washington he appeared at the Southern Democratic Party headquarters, warning that the North "is arming itself and training its midnight bands for the purpose of forcing the Union of a mere majority upon the South." Like Wise, he equated the South's shrinking political numbers with a dark future, warning that the southern "minority will be placed as a 'lamb that is led to the slaughter.' " Speaking in New York, taking the same Cooper Union stage where Lincoln had stood in February, he told Northerners that the best solution was for them to enforce the Fugitive Slave Act. "Enlarge your jails and penitentiaries, re-enforce and strengthen your police force, and keep the irrepressible conflict fellows from stealing our negroes."[17]

The message was clear: submit to the Slave Power, because it will not submit to you.

The other option was a Republican victory, Yancey predicted, which would commence a plot by Lincoln to build an abolitionist movement in the South, induce slaves to poison their masters, and culminate with a Wide Awake invasion "in the darkness of the night, with torch to burn and destroy."[18]

Talk of control by "a mere majority" grew in concert with the work on the 1860 census. This election fought over minority rule was coinciding, for the first time in twenty years, with the decennial federal head count. The statisticians were still collecting data, but each census pushes Americans to consider their demographics in political terms. Owen Lovejoy announced—with better statistics than back in April—that "there are only four hundred thousand slaveholders. There are thirty million people in this country . . . and this is the question." Ulysses S. Grant, helping to train Wide Awake marchers in Illinois, considered the whole election a contest between "minority rule and rule by the majority." And George Templeton Strong, though friendly with many southern guests at the New York Hotel, including the paranoid Mrs. Hayward, came to believe that the fundamental issue of the election was whether a few hundred thousand slave owners "have or have not a veto on the popular choice."

Even two southern guests of the Metropolitan Hotel who had wished a civil war would finally put an end to the whole issue were overheard to worry that the North was "getting foreigners faster than South" and "musn't be allowed to go ahead so."[19]

But Governor Wise and William Lowndes Yancey had an easy answer for that problem. It didn't matter if the North was getting ahead in population if the entire premise of majority rule was an insult.

Yancey and Wise cannot be allowed to speak for all Southerners. There were more than eleven million people in the South, including about seven million White Southerners and four million enslaved Black people, and they nurtured a real diversity of opinions. Among enslaved people, rumors were flying. Despite brutal suppressions of speech, slaves were watching the campaign. Masters talked loudly with each other, often venting about abolitionists and "Black Republicans," well within earshot of enslaved people skilled at subtly gleaning information. Later, during Reconstruction, northern educators would be struck by formerly enslaved and illiterate peoples' incredible ability to absorb and retain huge amounts of spoken material. Eavesdropping slaves in 1860 surely picked up a lot. Though most states banned teaching slaves to read, 5 to 10 percent knew how, and newspapers brimmed with hysterical election predictions. One enslaved woman in Missouri had the courage to cut a print of Abraham Lincoln's face out of a newspaper and hang it on the wall of her room—a "crime" for which she was "knocked down" three times, and punished with a month in the slave yard. How many more like her were quietly watching the unfolding campaign? Perhaps more tantalizing, how many were whispering about the army of "Wide Awakes" that was preparing to march south?[20]

Among White Southerners, factions and rivals fought out a confusing multiparty race. Most southern voters were picking between the Southern Democratic and the Constitutional Union Parties. But in the cities of the Upper South, some were quietly building a small Republican movement. These towns mixed Southerners and Northerners, enslaved and free African Americans, German and Irish immigrants, Protestants, Catholics, and Jews, industrial laborers, rising merchants, and old families. They witnessed the collision of all the forces shaping nineteenth-century American life. Many were—like a southern equivalent of the Hartford Originals—young, urban, native-born laborers, hostile to nearly everyone around them. Some had spent the 1850s in the Know Nothings' American party, making Baltimore a stronghold for nativist gangs like the Blood Tubs and Plug Uglies.[21]

But in 1860, they were reranking their hatreds. Some had come to see elite Democratic slave owners as their greatest enemy. They began to espouse free-labor views, pointing to the ways the Slave Power imposed on their lives, robbed them of work, silenced their speech, gerrymandered their elections, controlled state legislatures, and harmed their economies. Others were, as in Washington and St. Louis, quietly building strong, covert, abolitionist movements.[22]

This was the fire-eaters' greatest fear. Far more than a defeat by voters in Connecticut or Michigan, the idea of Republican infiltration across the Mason-Dixon Line fed nightmare scenarios. Republican control of southern states might enable a genuine assault on slavery in ways the federal government could not achieve. And a Republican president could appoint Republican postmasters, Republican customs officers, and Republican judges to positions of power across the South. They could build a local campaign machine out of this patronage, perhaps among the aggrieved White lower classes, who were also harmed by slavery. The Slave Power had long relied on a quiescent White lower class, and the Republican Party threatened to activate them. What had been the most effective way to control southern political speech—"the liberty of the cudgel" that Alexander Stephens had smirked about—was facing something new in 1860: southern Wide Awakes with cudgels of their own.[23]

In the late summer of 1860, they started marching. Boys in black capes bravely showed themselves in the streets of St. Louis, St. Joseph, Wilmington, Wheeling, Washington, and even Baltimore, about two to three thousand southern Wide Awakes in all. But it was rough going. The mobbing of Wide Awakes in Hartford was nothing compared to the sensation of marching through southern cities, already the scene of years of low-level political violence, packed with a broad majority of inhabitants who thought the movement wanted to burn down their society. In Wilmington, Delaware, about as northern a southern town as you could find, the Wide Awakes wrote to the Hartford Originals, "It is an easy matter for you in Yankee land to be Republicans, but with us it is a different affair." And down in Baltimore, the Wide Awakes seem to never have marched without facing "groans, jeers, brickbats and cudgels." Suppression was the expectation. After one march in which the Maryland Wide Awakes were pelted with eggs, garbage, and only a few stones, the

Baltimore American found it "wonderful to relate" that "no one killed, and no one badly beaten." Standards were low for reporters working the Blood Tubs beat.[24]

Farther south, Washington's Wide Awakes showed how the constant assaults on free speech pushed some young Southerners into the movement. That outfit's president, Lewis Clephane, was the southern-born clerk and manager of the abolitionist *National Era*. He came from printing royalty—his father published Walter Scott's works in Scotland; his brother would help invent the typewriter. Lewis printed the first editions of *Uncle Tom's Cabin* and schemed with its author, Harriet Beecher Stowe, about how to circulate copies of her bestseller in the South. With narrow gray eyes, looking out through steel-rimmed glasses framed by a full chin-beard, he looked the part of a stern Presbyterian minister, but he had faced down howling mobs over the years. Clephane watched rioters try to trash his paper's offices; at one point he even used the oversize key to trick men into thinking he brandished a revolver. In the summer of 1860, he graduated to real pistols. When attackers stormed into Senator Charles Sumner's Washington rooms, it was Clephane who turned up with armed bodyguards to protect him. Looking back, several decades later, Clephane recalled that "in those days it was a crime to be called a Republican," sighing, "We have fought the battle."[25]

Yet Clephane never stopped considering himself a Southerner. He spelled out his identity in a note to Lincoln, accompanying a box of Virginia-grown grapes sent "as a slight testimonial of respect from a resident of the South." Clephane's letter assured Lincoln that the strange box did not contain an "infernal machine" designed to blow up the nominee, as some threatened. Instead, Clephane wrote that "as a native of the South it is particularly gratifying to me to witness the rapid progress our cause is making in the South." As president of the 250-man Washington Wide Awakes, and the 1,000-member Washington Republican Association, Clephane informed Lincoln that his black-cloaked Republicans were regularly drilling in the national capital, coordinating with other local supporters, and printing ballots for use in Maryland and Virginia in November.[26]

None of this made southern Wide Awaking any safer. The Washington companies set up a Wigwam at Indiana Avenue and Third Street Northwest, but were often forced to defend it. Rumors spread that they all wore pistols under their capes. At times their processions turned into hurried retreats to the safety of that Wigwam. On one occasion, Democratic roughs entertained themselves by smashing the drums and trumpets left behind by the Wide Awake brass band as they fled an assault. The squeaks and pops made by instruments as they splintered against cobblestones were as much the music of democracy as the proud marches Wide Awakes preferred.[27]

But more and more, Washington's Wide Awakes claimed public space, often accompanied by ladies waving handkerchiefs and onlookers "almost persuaded" to join. Washington was an inverse of New York City—a southern town frequented by large numbers of Northerners. A regular tide of Yankee federal appointees offered fertile ground to grow a movement, especially in the face of violent suppressions. Often, their banners read simply FREE SPEECH. Orators made the Wide Awakes' embattled presence their key talking point. It had only been three years since election rioting broke out in Washington's streets, suppressed by the U.S. Marines, leaving eight dead. Congressman David Kilgore promised Washington's Wide Awakes he would tell his constituents in Indiana that in a national capital "where but a few years ago riot seemed to have run mad, and tumult and strife and murders were committed day in and day out; where the very name of black Republican stunk in the nostrils," there were now men in uniform marching to defend "liberty of speech."[28]

But a few southern Wide Awakes could not rehabilitate the name Republican in most of their section. The panic was too intense. Many Southerners sympathized with the proposal of the *Richmond Enquirer*: "What we have to do now is simply what our enemies are doing. We must organize, arm, drill and discipline with all our might." A common turn of phrase, used hundreds of times, called for southern political militias "as an offset to the terrible Wide Awakes of the North." Again and again, "offsets" cropped up: Minutemen and Palmetto Clubs in South Carolina, Breck Clubs and Bell Ringers in New Orleans, National Volunteers in Washington and Baltimore. Of course, Wide Awakes would claim that *they* were the offset to Slave Power's mobs, but that was the nature of a spiraling conflict.[29]

John Dimitry of New Orleans, a squarely built twenty-five-year-old with a horseshoe mustache, recalled learning about the Wide Awakes: "The news felt like a breath of war from the Hudson." Among young Southerners like Dimitry, "Instant was the antagonism to this veiled threat: 'Wide awake to what?'" He argued with the older members of his family, a large Greek American Creole clan, who tried to calm their aggressive son. But the more intimidating the Wide Awakes looked, the more they confirmed the sense that youthful hotspurs "had looked more clearly into the future" than their moderate elders. The darker the political climate got, the more vindicated the hotheads felt. Dimitry joined "an offset," New Orleans' Southern Democratic Young Men's Breckenridge and Lane Club, riding through town on horseback in a black uniform with gold buttons and a cap with a gold band.[30]

Offsets were fair game—the Wide Awakes could not complain about anyone dressing up in uniforms. But others were going further. Senator Toombs of Georgia told the *New York Herald* that he would "resist" Lincoln if he was elected, promising to "commence the revolution . . . if I have enough to back me to make treason respectable." Toombs's son-in-law was already recruiting another offset to the Wide Awakes: "Five hundred men can be enlisted in Atlanta to-morrow under the disunion flag."[31]

Militias in Georgia or Louisiana felt distant, theoretical. Closer still was the shadowy network calling themselves National Volunteers, growing among Washington and Baltimore's Southern Democrats, street gangs, and even—rumor had it—the police guarding the U.S. Capitol. Reporters snuck into the National Volunteers' private meetings in Washington ("the first noticeable thing was the all-pervading smell of whiskey") and heard talk about offsetting the Wide Awakes, not in the November election but for a March inauguration. The national Capitol was seventy miles into southern territory, after all, and the path to the White House led through Baltimore and Washington. Young men in the way were coordinating something that looked more like a resistance movement than a campaign club. The Wide Awakes bear some responsibility for making it so difficult to tell which was which.[32]

By early October, reporters felt certain that "there will be hot work in Washington when Lincoln is inaugurated, there is no doubt."[33]

THE UNNAMED ENGLISH correspondent for Charles Dickens's magazine also haunted Manhattan's hotels that fall, enamored with the mint juleps. He noted the differences between New York and London, finding Gotham cheerier ("nobody looks poor or hopeless") and with a bolder swagger, especially at election time. And he found himself unexpectedly saturated with political stuff, informing Londoners about the ubiquitous partisan trinkets sold everywhere during that four-way race. In the great hotels, boys hocked cigar boxes full of them. In train cars, weather-beaten men brandished more, and shops along the broad avenues packed their windows with so many trays of partisan medals, ribbons, and buttons that you could guess a neighborhood's politics "by the majority of medals you meet." On the omnibuses, men and women hummed tunes from campaign song sheets (including those of *The Wide-Awake Songster*, written by John Hutchinson, front man of America's most famous singing group, the Hutchinson Family Singers). The very walls of New York's buildings fluttered with campaign banners and advertisements, a great political canopy rustling and rippling "all the way up Broadway."[34]

Except for the contested cobblestones between 721 and 722 Broadway, a no-man's-land devoid of campaign paraphernalia. But the New York Wide Awakes' Central Committee still had its eyes on that valuable real estate.

On the night of Wednesday, September 26, club members gathered to plot a grand rally set for October 3. The New York Republican Central Campaign Committee's president, Simeon Draper, was there, as was Wide Awake president Silas B. Dutcher, and the towering, stone-faced Mexican War veteran J. H. Hobart Ward. The building was "crowded full of enthusiastic Republicans." Among the five separate companies present were the Fifteenth Ward Wide Awakes—sons of elite Washington Square families—and the Sixteenth Ward Wide Awakes, drawn from the young clerks of middle-class, Republican Chelsea. Sandwiches were served. And plenty of ale. The Knickerbocker Artillery company fired a salute. Speeches were made. The boys engaged in a heated discussion about the situation with Hiram Cranston across Broadway, complaining that his public intransigence about their banner was an attempt "to make capital out of this act, through the newspapers." Then, after more ale, the Sixteenth Ward Wide Awakes headed out for their late-night march up Broadway toward Chelsea.[35]

There had been hundreds of Wide Awakes in 722 that night, drinking, shouting over each other, and firing cannons. The guests across the street took notice. As the Sixteenth Ward boys assembled on the east side of Broadway, New York Hotel guests gathered on the west, leaning out on balconies and crowding out of the front doors, all "engaged in the laudable business of hissing the Wide-Awakes." The boys in black tensely watched the growing crowd on the opposite sidewalk. Then one "rather tall and heavy man" (reputedly a South Carolinian) stepped out from the hotel throng and marched onto Broadway,

shouting, "You damn sons of bitches, I will whip any one of you." A Knickerbocker club member stepped to him and replied: "What's that?" It's hard to
tell if this was fighting talk, or simply trouble hearing among the jeering and
the hissing.[36]

The South Carolinian struck the Wide Awake in the ear. He wobbled back-
ward, then sprang forward, throwing his own punch. Marshal Ward saw the
blows. He had fought his way through Monterrey and Veracruz during the
Mexican War; now urban warfare had come to Manhattan's streets. Reacting
instantaneously, Ward bellowed: "Wide Awakes! Charge!" With that, the wary
Sixteenth Ward boys "shot across the street as from one electric impulse." They
crashed into the jumbled ranks of the hotel guests, a blur of flashing black capes
and thrashing torch staves. Sweeping through the unorganized crowd, they
beat the startled men back into the hotel. The guests scrambling into its graceful
lobby, the *New York Tribune* later boasted, bore the bruises and bloodied noses
that proved it was unwise "to interfere in this latitude with an orderly assembly
of freemen."[37]

Order restored and hotel guests scattered, the company reassembled on their
side of Broadway. The Sixteenth Ward boys gave three "lusty Wide-Awake
cheers," their hurrahs and huzzahs amplified by the adrenaline pulsating
through their veins. For months the Wide Awakes had drilled and practiced,
but rarely fought. They had threatened, they had "passed some very pertinent
resolutions," but little more. The militaristic movement had long posed the
dangling question: Would they fight? On the west side of Broadway, in front
of the New York Hotel's windows and gaslights, they supplied their answer.[38]

Police arrived. Hotel guests streamed out again, dabbing bloodied faces
and pointing at the Wide Awakes on the other side of Broadway. It became
clear that the Metropolitan Police had no intention of arresting club members,
even the ones holding bloodied torch-staffs. This is no surprise. Wide Awakes
often found friends and members in police departments. In this era before the
stereotype of the Irish cop, many officers came from the same native-born
Protestant laboring classes—hostile to Democrats—that joined the Wide
Awakes. Some of New York's metropolitan police captains were even embroiled
in a scandal, accused of making their officers contribute five dollars each to
the clubs.[39]

Guests started to shout at the officers, and an older and younger man among
them got into a scrape with four policemen. Another dozen police flooded the

street and arrested the duo. They were neither South Carolinians nor Georgians, nor were they the Irish Catholics too often blamed for urban violence. Edward L. Corlies and Joseph Corlies ran a prosperous father-son auction house in the Gramercy Park area. They were native New Yorkers, from an old line of northern Democrats. Arresting southern guests at the New York Hotel would have made for a more comprehensible narrative, an early clash between North and South. But really the fight grew, as so much else did in 1860, from internal partisan divisions, the clash between North and North that came first.[40]

News spread hysterically. New York was the center of the newspaper world; its chief publications reached everywhere. Papers in at least twenty-seven states printed articles about the fight. "SERVED 'EM RIGHT" was the headline in the *Long Island Farmer*. The morbidly elated *New York Herald* screamed "FIRST BLOOD OF THE IRREPRESSIBLE CONFLICT." Philadelphia Republicans reported that New York Wide Awakes were quietly asking their members to come to 722 Broadway, "armed and equipped." Really, the fight was not particularly noteworthy, but the characters involved—Wide Awakes, southern visitors, New York Democrats—made it a perfect encapsulation of the fracturing system. Everyone interpreted the news exactly as expected. The moderately Republican *New York Times* came the closest to evenhandedness. They smirked that the New York Hotel guests "were finally thrashed according to, and perhaps a trifle beyond, their deserts." But they shook a finger at Republicans who seemed to be encouraging Wide Awakes to "invade, assail and overthrow the NY Hotel, its host, guests and furniture." And the *Times* printed a warning for Hiram Cranston himself: the Wide Awakes "are a very thoroughly organized body of young men filled with the vigor and the excitability of youth. Is it quite a prudent thing to risk a collision with such a body?"[41]

It was a question many were asking. After a basically peaceful summer, fights like those at the New York Hotel were spreading across the North. At a Wide Awake rally in Wisconsin, U.S. marshals attempted to arrest an abolitionist, wanted for aiding fugitive slaves, as he lectured. The orator threw a marshal down a flight of stairs and drew a Colt revolver. Armed Wide Awakes came running, and faced down the officers. In Indiana, a Democratic candidate for coroner opened fire on a club's procession, only to be chased off in a hail of bricks. In Philly, the Invincibles club poured out of a saloon to shoot up a Constitutional Union Party march. In St. Louis, German Wide Awakes crashed into a saloon, shouting, "Vide-Avakes tu your tudy," in thickly accented English, beating the Democratic drinkers inside. Alcohol—whether frothy lager or dewy mint juleps—played a role in many of these confrontations. Colt revolvers and Sharps derringers showed up more and more as well.[42]

In perhaps the ugliest fighting, Democrats in Troy, New York, ambushed a procession of four hundred Republicans, screaming, "Kill the damn Wide Awakes!" from the rooftops. Men and boys rained down bricks, then set upon the felled marchers with clubs, leaving broken torch-staffs and cracked teeth amid the cobblestones.[43]

Wide Awakes lost about as many fights as they won. Though "a very thoroughly organized body of young men," their style brought tactical advantages and disadvantages in the urban warfare of nineteenth-century politics. Clubs usually won face-to-face confrontations, like the scuffle at the New York Hotel. Even a small company of organized, drilled, and coordinated men could rout a huge but uncertain mob. Yet their nighttime marches made them extremely vulnerable. A few b'hoys with bricks, and knowledge of local rooftops, could terrorize tightly grouped companies of marchers. The Wide Awakes' torches brought an unexpected weakness as well. Marching through dark cities clutching flaring lights made them visually striking, but also blinded then to opponents lurking in the darkness. The glare of their lights was useful for political theater, but unhelpful for street fighting, a further indication of their movement's intent.[44]

But winning fights was not the point. Dramatizing their battle for free speech was. It had been a useful appeal back when the New Haven Wide Awakes were brutally stoned in March, now it returned as a theme as things got uglier in October. In meetings, speeches, and in newspapers, Wide Awakes spent far more time on the fights they lost than on the ones they won. It had been satisfying to clear Broadway of the New York Hotel's Democrats in "one electric impulse," but clubs found that their membership rosters increased more when Wide Awakes were the victims. Newspapers relished fresh reports on the condition of the members who had been shot in Indiana, or lost teeth left in Troy. This fixation on their defeats made the Wide Awakes unique: a militaristic movement that drew strength from its losses, organized both to showcase its power and to broadcast its weakness.[45]

The movement dramatized this fixation in an odd proto–comic book called *Pipps Among the Wide Awakes*. Written by the editor of the satirical magazine

Vanity Fair, Charles Godfrey Leland, the book told the tale of a young voter's decision to join the Wide Awakes. But Leland chose a surprising narrative. On succeeding pages, Pipps grows out his first mustache, decides it's time to cast his "virgin vote," joins a Wide Awake club, and learns a silly spoof of Henry Sperry's "Wide Awakes cheer." Yet instead of making his protagonist a partisan action hero, Leland has Pipps beaten by a gang of Irish stereotypes, who leave the "powerful arguments of McGinnis and Booley being observable on Pipps' left eye." His conservative parents admonish him: "You've been out Wide Awaking when you ought to have been fast asleeping." Neither Democratic violence nor parental condescension stops Pipps. Motivated by an orator's speech full of barely comprehensible slang ("Go it lemons," "Show the world you're pumpkins"), he turns out to vote. Pipps doesn't break a torch over anyone's head, but he does face down a " *ferocious Irishman*," and proudly votes for Lincoln. Pipp's initiation into manhood takes place at that rough polling place, where he is "is sworn in a little, and sworn at considerably."[46]

Pipps is a strange little book, full of unkind stereotypes and fruit-based 1860s slang. But Leland's message is clear. He does not mention slavery, or the South, instead focusing on the violent suppression of young Pipps's views, and his maturity-affirming struggle to overcome those forces at the ballot box. The fight for free, public, political speech provided the frisson that had so many real Pipps stomping through dark neighborhoods by torchlight in September and October 1860.[47]

Just as news of the 1860 census rekindled frustrations with minority rule, the surge in street fighting amplified focus on free speech. The last two months of the campaign loudly reprised those two chief themes, defining the 1860 election by debates over democratic behavior. The Slave Power might not impose slavery on northern states, but the suppression that sustained it seemed to be trickling north. The young Ohio Republican (and future Lincoln bodyguard) William T. Coggeshall told an assembly of Tiffin Wide Awakes that wherever the Democratic Party held sway, it "forbids free discussion, violates public mails, burns independent newspapers, and imprisons schoolmasters." When the Alabama firebrand William Lowndes Yancey complained that the North was hostile to his speaking tour, Henry Raymond, editor of the *New York Times*, responded with venom. "Of all men," Raymond lectured, Yancey "should be the last" to talk of incivility. "You spoke in nearly all our principal cities, to large audiences, two thirds of whom had not the slightest sympathy with your views, or the least respect for the object you sought to accomplish. But you were heard with the most respectful attention. In no instance was there the slightest indication of personal disrespect." Imagine, Raymond asked, a Republican antislavery man "who should attempt to address the people of your own section on the same subject, you will find no ground for claiming superiority over us."[48]

It was not even the scale of the violence that rankled—American politics had seen worse over the last decade, as had revolution-prone European cities. But the violence in the streets synced perfectly with the rhetorical war for antislavery free speech that the Republicans were fighting. Every brawl argued the Wide Awakes' case.

The threat to free speech really was changing minds. George Templeton Strong kept a good account. A northern conservative who whined in his diary, "I for one am tired of talk about niggers and feel much inclined to vote for anybody who promises to ignore that subject," his politics in early 1860 were shortsighted and bigoted. But the free-speech issue wore on him. By September, he concluded that "freedom of speech and of thought is extinct south of the Potomac." Though hostile to abolitionists, by the fall of 1860 Strong was scribbling in his diary that "while Toombs speechifies and Wise writes letters, it's hard for any Northern man to keep himself from Abolitionism and refrain from buying a photograph of John Brown."[49]

Putting it bluntly, Strong wrote in his diary that the "grisly antics of insane Southern mobs and the idiotic sanguinary babblings of Southern editors and orators tempt me to become a disunion man." Yet even here, he still associated voting Republican with disunion.[50]

Strong was musing over all of this one evening, leaving dinner at the New York Club near 722 Broadway, when he happened upon a Wide Awake march. His dining companions inspected the movement, "intended (as people say) to keep order at Lincoln's inauguration (he will certainly be elected) in case Governor Wise or Mr. Yancey or other foolish Southern demagogues try to make a disturbance." But despite this dangerous reputation, Strong liked what he saw. The companies were "imposing and splendid," they "marched in good order," and obeyed their captain's commands. He had "never seen so beautiful a spectacle" fill Manhattan's streets. "Everyone," he later wrote, "speaks of the good order and earnest aspect of the 'Wide-Awakes.' " He repeatedly stressed the "order" of the movement—much as Eddie Yergason saw uniformity as its key feature.[51]

George Templeton Strong hated southern barbarism. He hated abolitionist radicalism. But in the Wide Awake companies marching through Astor Place, Strong saw a rejoinder to both, an orderly army of the moderate majority. No fan of Lincoln, but a great admirer of the Wide Awakes, he mused, "I've nearly made up my mind to deposit a lukewarm Republican vote next month."[52]

THIRTY-FIVE YEARS BEFORE the Wide Awakes started marching, Lewis Hayden sat on a fence rail in Lexington, Kentucky, observing a different parade. He was fourteen years old, small, with "jet black" skin and clear, honest eyes. He was also enslaved. That year, 1825, the Marquis de Lafayette had returned to America on a grand reunion tour. He rode into Lexington escorted by cavalry officers and local professors. Young Hayden snuck away from his labors to watch from a lonely post, apart from the cheering crowds of White people. He was stunned when the marquis caught his eye and offered him a slow and deliberate bow. Hayden looked to either side of him: the aged revolutionary hero was clearly bowing to him alone. He did not know about Lafayette's labors for French abolition and the "Société des Amis des Noirs." But he knew respect when he saw it, and the power of public political statements. It would take many hard years before Hayden was orchestrating marches of his own, but looking back, he always felt that "I date my hatred of slavery to that day."[53]

The years in between were excruciating. Hayden's mother was sold away from him. He was traded for a carriage and two horses, some china thrown into the deal on his side of the bargain. Growing into adulthood, he married a woman named Esther, enslaved by a different master, and fathered a son. Soon Esther and his young son were sold to slave traders by an unsympathetic enslaver, who simply shrugged that "he had bought them, and he had sold them." Losing that son was the greatest pain in Hayden's long life. Years later he would reflect that it hurt more than any other loss, having loved a son who was sold "nobody knows where." It was a pain "I can never bear to think of."[54]

In time, Hayden remarried and adopted a stepson. He worked at a Lexington restaurant, leased out by his enslaver. He showed, early, a quiet, convincing manner that could have great influence over others. He befriended a Vermont preacher at the restaurant, who surreptitiously inquired about helping Hayden escape. Hayden agreed. Lewis, his wife, Harriet, and their eight-year-old son Joseph orchestrated a daring escape across the Ohio, pursued by slave catchers all the way to Canada. From Canada, from safety, Hayden wrote a letter to his old enslaver. He explained that he wanted to see "how it will seam to be my own master." "Robbing and crushing slavery" would not steal another child from him, Hayden wrote; "my little son is going to school."[55]

Hayden and Harriet made their way to Boston, opened a clothing store at 66 Southac Street, and dove deeper into antislavery politics. In the 1850s they made their store the headquarters of the Underground Railroad, harboring an estimated three quarters of the fugitives coming through town. They could easily change a fugitive's identifying clothing, and feed and house someone laying low in the mostly African American West End. Over the 1850s the Haydens grew more militant. Lewis led bold missions to rescue recaptured slaves, confronting slave catchers and federal officials, once using a battering ram to smash the door of a courthouse, and firing his revolver at federal marshals in a melee. John Brown stayed with them for a while. Harriet turned their home into a fugitive-slave fortress, with tunnels in the basement and (supposedly) bombs set to blow the whole place up if it came to that. Slave catchers, the *Liberator* wrote, "knew that the road to hell lay over Lewis Hayden's threshold."[56]

Lewis Hayden emerged as "the undisputed leader of the Negro community." He wielded an unusual power—small, quiet, a poor public speaker, he could nonetheless command and inspire. Hayden was, one friend later reflected, "a man of compelling qualities and of a nature which would not brook opposition. With the Negroes he held a position almost of dictator." Pictures show him finely dressed, in a crushed velvet vest with a cream cravat, but with a face lined by years of hardship. He was also a joiner, a believer in organizations, and a member of a half dozen associations working against slavery and racism, including the African American Massasoit Guards militia.[57]

Hayden was gravitating to the strongest association he could join, the Republican Party. With his friend Mark DeMortie, he dipped cautious toes into mainstream White politics. The two men's goals were concrete and local: desegregation in Boston, protecting Black voters, and integrating education. Hayden was working to ensure that his "little son" could go to school. In the confused mid-1850s, they first found allies among the Know Nothings, whom they embraced as a local anti-Democratic force with some progressive ideas. But soon Hayden threw in with the more palatable Republicans. The rising star John A. Andrew—a kind-eyed and curly-haired White Republican—became Hayden's good friend. It was Hayden who advised him to run for governor. In 1860, Hayden was considering a new way to bring his organizational skills and love of associations to the aid of the Republican Party.[58]

On Friday, October 5, 1860, it all came together: Hayden's love of organizations, his background in textiles, his membership in the Massasoit Guards, even Lafayette's parade thirty-five years earlier. One hundred forty-four African American men stepped out into the Boston night, in shiny black capes and caps, holding torches, standing to attention. The first all-Black company, calling themselves the West Boston Wide Awakes, organized "to parade and arouse an enthusiasm among all voters in securing the election of our much beloved Abraham Lincoln." Hayden was the kind of man who planned processions, but he did not lead them. For that he asked John P. Coburn, one of the West End's richest Black men, a burly, light-skinned clothier (and gambler) who had proved his martial skills as commander of the Massasoit Guards militia. Coburn was a good man to march at the front of a parade, and may have paid for the uniforms, including his own flowing black cloak and commander's baton.[59]

Many of the members were, like Hayden, former slaves. Others, like Coburn, were born in Boston. They were all taking the bold step of forming their own club and marching in public. It was a bigger risk than John Mercer Langston's singular role in the mostly White Oberlin Wide Awakes. Langston was more of a figurehead, set apart from the rest; the West End Wide Awakes were a *force*. Black men had long voted in Massachusetts, first as Whigs, then moving through the Free Soilers and Know Nothings, ending up in the Republican Party. But rarely did they claim public political space as a partisan organization, mixed with White men, dressed in military uniforms. Lewis and Harriet Hayden had made their names in secrecy, in private meetings in their fortified home. Now the movement was in the streets, announcing its political agency in public. And Boston, though not quite Baltimore, still had plenty of Democratic rowdies who could make Wide Awaking a risky proposition for a Black man.

The press grasped the revolutionary implications right away. The first reports of Black Wide Awakes were mostly positive. Even the Democratic-leaning *Boston Courier* attempted a (still very racist) compliment, claiming that because of the "peculiar taste for parade, ceremonials, processions, and fuss and feathers generally" of "the African race," the "colored Wide Awakes" made a particularly grand marching corps. While "there was some wincing among the less advanced Republicans" about marching with a Black company, the *Courier* claimed, White party members were reminded that the West Boston Wide Awakes could bring "FOUR HUNDRED COLORED VOTES" along with them. The abolitionist *Liberator* was thrilled by the idea of Black Wide Awakes, taking the club as proof of "declining spirit of colorphobia" in Massachusetts. The *Liberator*'s editor, William Lloyd Garrison, attended a rally of Wide Awakes, marching through Boston to the tune of the song "Ain't You Glad You Joined the Republicans?" Even the stiff and uncompromising Garrison found it "hard not to tap one's feet to the jaunty rhythms."[60]

More revolutionary than the rise of a single Black Wide Awake club was its inclusion in marches that fall. By October 17 a rally of eight to ten thousand included the West Boston Wide Awakes, now numbering closer to two hundred marchers. They were joined by thirty-eight men from the Black Militia of Portland, Maine, captained by Henry Daniels, a powerfully built African American chef. The clubs marched under banners sewn by "the colored daughters of the West End." And, most important, all of these Black Wide Awakes mixed in a sea of thousands of White Republican club members.[61]

Not everyone was tapping their feet. The Democratic and southern press were predictably inflamed. The West End Wide Awakes started marching just nine days after the New York Hotel brawl. To their opponents, Black Wide Awakes were a worst-case scenario, just another step toward the final invasion of the South. Within a few weeks of Election Day, three fears—southern Wide Awakes, fighting Wide Awakes, and Black Wide Awakes—filled the newspapers. It was a perfect October surprise.

Initial reports from northern Democrats were simply angry, venting about White Massachusetts Republicans like John A. Andrew parading with "the escort of a band of filthy negroes." Others attacked the White Wide Awake clubs for being willing to march behind the Black companies in parade order. "The chief object," the *Lancaster Intelligencer* accused, "seems to be to give the negro the supremacy over the white man." "We doubt if it is possible for the

"SEE THEM ON THEIR WINDING WAY."

MOHAWK WIDE AWAKES AND BAND

Parade, In honor of the Republican Victories, November, 1860.

Compared to the usual chaos of mob-driven public politics, Wide Awake rallies like this one in Mohawk, New York, show the clubs' particular love of military discipline, snazzy uniforms, and marching bands (often of questionable musical talent).

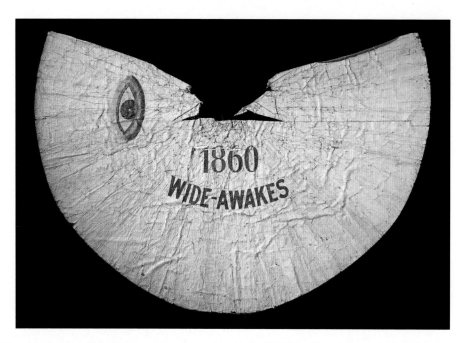

After decades in a New Hampshire attic, George P. Holt's Wide Awake cape remains one of the best-preserved objects from 1860, though its initial bright-white background and violet lettering have faded considerably.

Hartford in the 1860s was among the most prosperous cities in America, featuring a bustling Main Street lined with church spires and populated with the kind of go-ahead young clerks who would invent the Wide Awakes.

Left: Edgar S. Yergason, creator of the first Wide Awake cape in 1860, joined the Twenty-Second Connecticut Volunteers during the Civil War. That means he looked even younger than in this picture when he kicked off the most consequential partisan organization in U.S. history.

Below: Though Yergason treated his first cambric cape as a relic and preserved it well into the twentieth century, it has since been lost.

Above: A photograph shows twelve of the thirty-six Wide Awakes known as the "Hartford Originals." Among them, Henry T. Sperry can be seen standing on the far left, and James S. Chalker stands in the middle, fifth to the right, holding an officer's lantern.

Right: Within a few months of formation, the Hartford Wide Awakes found themselves so inundated with inquiries about forming companies that they printed up fill-in-the-blank membership forms, part of the club's franchising out of the movement across the country.

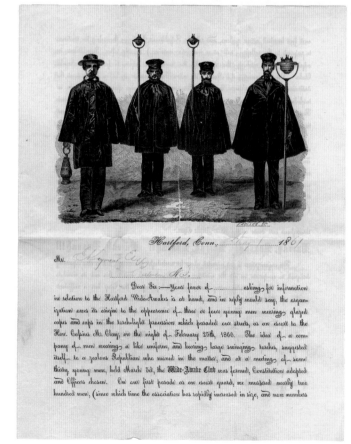

Hartford, Conn., _____ 1861

Mr. _____
_____ N.J.

Dear Sir:—Your favor of _____ asking for information in relation to the Hartford Wide-Awakes is at hand, and in reply would say, the organization owes its origin to the appearance of three or four young men wearing glazed capes and caps in the torchlight procession which paraded our streets, as an escort to the Hon. Cassius M. Clay, on the night of February 25th, 1860. The idea of a company of men wearing a like uniform, and bearing large swinging torches, suggested itself to a zealous Republican who moved in the matter, and at a meeting of some thirty young men, held March 3d, the Wide-Awake Club was formed, Constitution adopted and Officers chosen. On our first parade as an escort guard, we mustered nearly two hundred men, (since which time the association has rapidly increased in size, and now numbers

Walt Whitman, who often wore a white wideawake hat of the kind the club was (in part) named for, was closely associated with the working-class, mid-Atlantic men who toyed with democracy, populism, and nativism across the 1850s.

Although swiveling torches existed before 1860, the Wide Awakes popularized the design and would be associated with the style for the rest of the nineteenth century.

Abraham Lincoln visits Hartford: 1860

This 1947 drawing imagines the fertile moment when Abraham Lincoln first glimpsed the Wide Awakes. If anything, this depiction may exaggerate the order and organization of the club, which was then just two days old.

Großes Bankett der Wide-Awakes von New-Jersey und den New-Englandstaaten, veranstaltet in der City Hall zu Hartford, Conn., am 27. Juli 1860.

The Hartford Wide Awakes built a friendly relationship and sense of fraternal competition with the Wide Awakes of Newark, New Jersey, hosting them for a midsummer banquet.

This depiction of an 1862 Democratic march captures the wild cacophony of typical nineteenth-century processions, as opposed to the strict, often silent order that the martial Wide Awakes debuted. It also shows the New York Hotel in the background (famously attacked by the Wide Awakes in 1860) where Democratic and southern guests crowded the balconies to salute their preferred party and candidate.

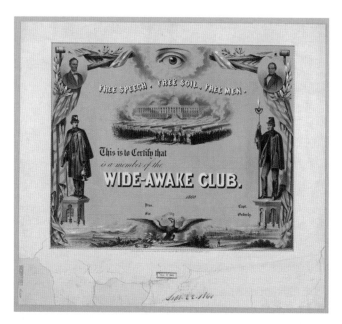

This membership certificate, printed in large numbers in Manhattan, affirmed Wide Awake Republicans' commitment to "Free Speech, Free Soil, Free Men," with "Free Speech" meaningfully listed first. Among the symbols included—the open eye, broken shackles, Lincoln, Hannibal Hamlin, locomotives, and others—perhaps the most prescient is the huge crowd attending an inauguration before the U.S. Capitol, hinting at the Wide Awakes' growing consideration of re-forming into an army of inauguration.

This *Harper's Weekly* print shows the inside of the famous Republican Wigwam assembled in Chicago. Perhaps most noticeable is the significant presence of women, during a convention where Chicago's female population became notorious as engaged and vocal Republicans.

This colorful Wide Awake banner captures the particular energy of the clubs around the Belfast and Bangor areas in Maine.

Chatham and East Chatham, New York, fielded a strong Wide Awake contingent, including one of the only known female companies, drawn from East Chatham's prominent young Republican ladies, and costumed in sand-colored capes with "ABE" spelled out in vibrant letters.

George Beza Woodward of Derry, New Hampshire, holds the more modern, swiveling torch favored by the Wide Awakes in his posed photograph in uniform.

Enos Christman, like Lewis Hayden, was a slightly older and better traveled Wide Awake. At thirty-one years old, he had already worked as a California gold prospector and a newspaperman when he helped organize a Westchester, Pennsylvania, Wide Awake company.

A young, unknown Iowa Wide Awake affects the stern stare the clubs made famous.

Lewis Hayden escaped slavery and established himself as a daring leader of Boston's African American community, before helping to form the West Boston Wide Awakes at the peak of the 1860 campaign. From there, Hayden played a key role in organizing the famous Massachusetts Fifty-Fourth Regiment, borrowing what he learned from Wide Awaking in 1860.

Left: A French cartoonist did his best to capture the strange, sometimes ominous appeal of the Wide Awakes. European observers, a London newspaper noted, "frequently complain that they cannot comprehend the character and drift of the suddenly created and often oddly named organizations to which the political contests of the United States give birth." *Right:* Democratic campaign clubs in 1860 never matched the coordination or martial order of Wide Awake clubs, as seen in this French cartoonist's rendering of a slightly messy-looking Douglas Club.

Lincoln's association with the Wide Awakes was such that this Currier & Ives cartoon shows him costumed in cape and cap, and armed with a fence pole, guarding the White House from his three rival candidates and the current president—all of whom were drawn as bumbling and ridiculous compared to the poised and bold-looking young Lincoln.

A PROCESSION, PROBABLY IN THE 1858 CAMPAIGN, HALTED IN FRONT OF LINCOLN'S SPRINGFIELD HOME

Abraham Lincoln is the tall figure in white at the right of the doorway

Above: The mass rally in Springfield, Illinois, on August 8, 1860, drew together scores of Wide Awake companies from across several states, and this photograph even includes a number of likely club members— wearing caps and capes— visible in the crowds surrounding Lincoln's home.

Right: The sheet music for this jaunty "Wide Awake Quick Step" seems to have no real connection to the Wide Awakes (and no words), but rather represents one of many industries eager to cash in on the Wide Awake trend, with sales in mind.

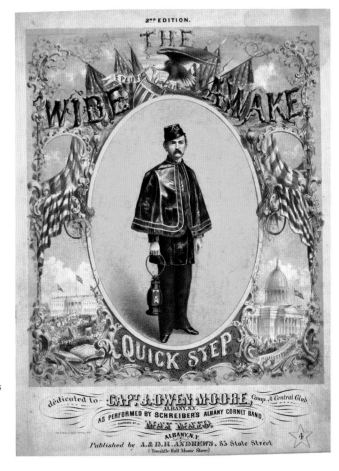

EXPULSION OF NEGROES AND ABOLITIONISTS FROM TREMONT TEMPLE, BOSTON, MASSACHUSETTS, ON DECEMBER 3, 1860.—[See Page 787.]

Harper's Weekly tried to capture the chaotic scene in Boston's Tremont Temple on December 3, when "unionist" crowds attacked abolitionist leaders like Frederick Douglass and Lewis Hayden, blaming the movement for Lincoln's recent election and fears of secession and war.

THE LEXINGTON OF 1861.

The Massachusetts Volunteers fighting their way through the Streets of Baltimore, on their march to the defence of the National Capital, April 19th, 1861. Hurrah for the Glorious 6th.

The so-called Pratt Street riot represented the first bloodshed of the Civil War, as gangs of anti–Wide Awake National Volunteers set upon Union troops from Massachusetts.

Left: Over the rest of the nineteenth century and well into the twentieth, former Wide Awakes held reunions and rallies, marching and lobbying for the Republican Party. Because most Wide Awakes were so young, they were able to stay active for many years after the movement itself had ended.

Below: And yet, as time passed, the once vibrant, exciting, even intimidating movement came to resemble the "old fogies" they had once denounced. By 1914, the New Hampshire cape owner George P. Holt looked like something from a long-gone era when he donned his uniform again.

Though the Wide Awakes are mostly forgotten, Civil War buffs, historians, and reenactors have kept the movement's memory alive, sometimes even designing tattoos like this one on film producer Shane Seley's shoulder.

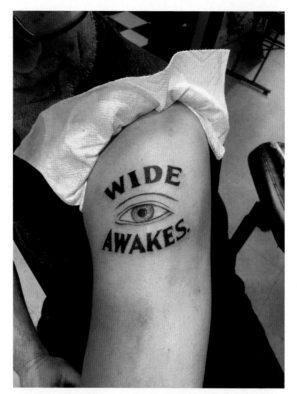

During the 2020 election, the Civic Arts organization For Freedoms made an effort to bring back the Wide Awakes, hoping to capture the movement's grassroots energy, although with an entirely different, twenty-first-century vibe.

southern states to remain in the union," the *Rock Island Argus* concluded. "Can anything be more disgusting?" the *Quad City Times* asked; "Is there any lower depth to which a party can crawl?"[62]

As news spread farther south, the real events in Boston (revolutionary as they were) started to meld with exaggerated fake news. The hysterical *Dallas Herald* was sure that the editor Horace Greeley was raising money to equip "one thousand darkies" with Wide Awake uniforms. The *Jackson Semi-Weekly Mississippian* informed its readers that "in many parts of the North, the Wide Awakes are composed mainly of Negroes." There were between 144 and 250 Black Wide Awakes, in a movement with between 100,000 and 500,000 total members. But the presence of any meant a conspiracy of all.[63]

Finally, the news entered an even more confusing phase. In unlikely corners of the lower North, broadsides and handbills started to appear advertising "Negro Wide Awake Clubs and Committees of Vigilance." Some demanded "NEGRO EQUALITY," others advocated "POLITICAL INCENDIARISM," still more called on Black citizens to "act at the Polls as a vigilance committee." Many were signed "Osawatomie," in reference to John Brown's Kansas raiders. They were clearly false flags, spread by Democrats in Pittsburgh, Cincinnati, Wheeling, Rock Island, and Brooklyn. Wheeling's Wide Awake-aligned newspaper warned that the handbills were a ridiculous fraud, designed "to bring odium on the Republican cause." The *Chicago Tribune* scoffed that the campaign "is a forgery. We have no doubt of this." Obviously, in the last month of the campaign, Democrats in doubtful regions were weaponizing news of African American Wide Awakes to scare Whites away from the Republican Party.[64]

The predictable White response should not distract from just how daring Lewis Hayden's West Boston Wide Awakes were. Wide Awaking as a Black man took more than donning a cape or lighting a torch. It meant marching with, associating with, and ultimately trusting huge crowds of young White men in uniforms, in the dark, with torches. All election long, African American political thinkers—Frederick Douglass, the editors of the *Anglo-African*, H. Ford Douglas—had warned not to trust White Republicans. Some of those Republicans had proclaimed themselves "the party of White men," others said far worse. It is some indication of the power of the campaign that Black men who were painfully aware of the realities of race in America would feel compelled to join in this movement as it burned hottest in October 1860.[65]

For Lewis Hayden, it must have taken almost unimaginable political muscle, harder than shooting his revolver at federal marshals. In a strange coincidence, the challenge was compounded by the Wide Awakes' constant invoking of the late Kentucky senator Henry Clay. The clubs often cited Clay to indicate their political moderation, respect for Southerners, and faith in old-fashioned Whig compromise. On the cover of his pamphlets, Henry T. Sperry quoted Clay's support for limiting the expansion of slavery. Abraham Lincoln considered himself a lifelong "disciple of Henry Clay." But Clay was the very same master who, back in Lexington in the 1830s, enslaved Hayden's first wife, Esther, and his young son. It was Henry Clay who had sold Hayden's son away from him, "nobody knows where." It was Clay who had shrugged that "he had bought them, and he had sold them." Now Lewis Hayden found himself organizing marches for a candidate and a party that claimed his personal villain as their political hero.[66]

But Hayden was an institutionalist, with faith that the Republican Party could help defend his people and his cause. It must have taken a will beyond what we can comprehend.

The awful link between Lewis Hayden and Henry Clay points to something else about the Wide Awakes. H. Ford Douglas had asked "if any man can tell me the difference between the antislavery of Abraham Lincoln" and "the antislavery of Henry Clay?" But it wasn't "the antislavery" of the Republican Party that attracted men like Hayden. If antislavery were his sole goal, he could have aligned with the abolitionist factions in Boston, or backed the Liberty Party candidate Gerrit Smith (as Frederick Douglass chose to do). It was the Wide Awakes' political style, their ability to face down mobs, and make themselves the modern inheritors of Lafayette's parade. The movement could be vague on slavery, as long as it commanded in the streets. And, unlike purer abolitionist candidates, Lincoln could *win*.[67]

Hayden's presence in the Wide Awakes revealed another key factor, something the movement hoped to conceal. Republicans had framed the election as a story of the majority asserting itself, rising up against the tiny Slave Power conspiracy. But an awakening nation could never stay that tidy. The two parties had split into four. The Big Wigwams were showing themselves to be made up of diverse and unlikely coalitions. As America got closer to Election Day, the relevant number shrank from 31 million Americans to 500,000 Wide Awakes to 2,500 Wide Awakes in the South to 1,000 National Volunteers in

Washington to 500 secessionists in Atlanta to 144 African American Bostonians on the West End. The future of the democracy would not be decided by
easy majorities. It depended on shaky pluralities of complex individual lives,
more complicated than the census, or the propaganda, made them seem.
Majority was a mirage.

And it was all eagerly reported, and exaggerated, in the press, magnetically
drawn to this irrepressible fracture. It was this constant splintering, not a fight
between majority and minority, that became the question of the election. The
nation split, the sections split, the parties split, states split, cities split, wards
split. Even split parties, like the remnant of the Know Nothings, were splitting anew. Which movement could split *the least?* In a nation faced with endless
division, only the Wide Awakes seemed capable of really building something
bigger, getting men who quoted Henry Clay, and men who cursed Henry Clay,
to wear the same uniforms. But it would not be enough. The democratic system
had always relied on diverse coalitions, *E Pluribus Unum.* Now, with the election just one month away, the question was who would continue to rely on this
old faith, and who would see disunion as a greater tool than Union.

CHAPTER EIGHT

The Approach of a Conquering Army

T HE LAST MONTH was a sprint. Or, really, more of a relay race. The Wide Awakes' incredible numbers, cellular structure, and rural distribution made it possible to launch hurtling excursions across huge swaths of territory. For a movement working to awaken a slumbering majority, watching strangers march through town in familiar uniforms argued a key political message: "There *is* a North." But it all exhausted those doing the marching. William Dansberry, a twenty-one-year-old New Jersey railroad guard, sent a note to Lincoln himself, documenting his "untiring" efforts as a New Brunswick Wide Awake. "I have worked my boots intirely out," Dansberry wrote to the nominee. Being "a poor hard working boy," he wondered if Lincoln would "inclose me a sufficient sum to purchace" a new pair.[1]

Republicans could not stop to buy new boots. To take a break, Carl Schurz worried, would be to leave a lifelong question: "Why did you not do this thing more?" Americans of all stripes felt certain they were careening toward some culminating point, just a few weeks away. One Brooklyn speaker announced that "30,000,000 of free people were about to choose a ruler, and we are the only free people, now on the face of the earth who had the right to shape our own destiny." The election would decide whether (some) Americans would maintain that exceptional right. Many were convinced that November 6, 1860, "would influence their fate and that of their children as no other contest ever waged before would do."[2]

On October 2, the Hartford Originals kicked off one fantastic relay that would cover the breadth of the North and touch millions of people. Julius Rathbun sold tickets amid the tinctures and nostrums at his Allyn House Drug Store; $7.75 to join in the "the most magnificent spectacle ever witnessed." Rathbun, Henry Sperry, James Chalker, two hundred Hartford Wide Awakes, a twenty-piece cornet band, and Major Braun's Drum Corps all boarded a steamer and headed south. The overnight boat ride turned into something like a big sleepover, "fun and frolic" all the way. On the evening of October 3, the Hartford boys stumbled onto Manhattan's Twenty-Third Street dock, wandering into a sea of capes, their original club multiplied by thousands, assembling for the rally the boys at 722 Broadway had been planning.[3]

The Central Committee of New York Wide Awakes loudly promoted the massive event, until the *New York Herald* worried that the October 3 rally sounded more like "the approach of a conquering army than a number of political clubs." The committee promised companies from at least a dozen states, including many southern Wide Awakes. Estimates suggested sixty thousand might arrive. A New York correspondent for the *Charleston Courier* felt that the city was being "invaded by a horde of hard looking characters from New England."[4]

It would take incredible leadership to handle the miles of marchers. For that, Grand Marshal J. H. Hobart Ward would lead, wearing a glittering golden suit and wielding a staff made from Connecticut's Charter Oak, presented by James S. Chalker himself. Ward would be attended by one hundred marchers from Maine in silver capes, each said to stand over six foot two inches. Outside their headquarters at 722 Broadway, the New York Wide Awakes constructed a twenty-six-foot-tall arch, topped with firework cannons and festooned with dangling lanterns bearing Republican slogans. Guests glaring through the New York Hotel's windows were livid. Even wilder, the parade was to include a tame buffalo from Kansas and an elk from Minnesota. Their handler promised that the huge beasts were "exceedingly tractable, and were not likely to be frightened by the glare of the torches and the fireworks." He had been training them with Roman candles.[5]

All this spectacle was to be restrained, the Central Committee insisted, by good Wide Awake order. "No derisive caricature, transparency, or device calculated to give offence, will be permitted in the pageant, and no person not in uniform will be allowed in the ranks," the committee warned. "Ribald expressions or demonstrations are unworthy the notice of Wide-Awakes."[6]

New York's chief promoter of ribald expressions decided he would cash in. P. T. Barnum promoted a "WIDE AWAKE TOUR" of his nearby museum, cobbled together from all the black, shiny items in his collection, "ALL TO BE SEEN FOR 25 CENTS." The main attraction was an enormous "WIDE-AWAKE BLACK SEA LION." But for once, he was not the center of attention. The Wide Awakes' buffalo beat Barnum's sea lion.[7]

As night fell and the companies began to march, newspaper headlines were screaming "THE WHOLE CITY ON FIRE FOR LINCOLN AND HAMLIN." Thousands tramped through Lower Manhattan, the tightness and height of the city magnifying their presence and amplifying their drumbeats. Looking up Broadway from below Houston, a *New York Times* correspondent felt that "nothing printable with leaden types and black ink could convey the impression." So many blazing torches burned so much oil that a "fuliginous canopy overhangs the procession." All along the route, "rocket batteries and Roman candles sent up glittering streams of fire, these lights casting sudden and strange tints of red, green, yellow, blue and white effulgence over the male and female faces" staring up from Manhattan's windows and rooftops. At the same moment, reporters looking west down Fourteenth Street from Union Square saw that boulevard "solidly paved with flaming torches" under another "red canopy of smoke" running to the Hudson. Big streets became a study in perspective, converging lines of crimson smoke, yellow torches, black capes, and brown boots. Surging crowds of onlookers pumped in from side streets, forming a "barricade of flesh, broadcloth and crinoline, jammed and crowded together in one inextricable mass."[8]

So many torches flickered and flared that the *New York Herald* predicted that "the metropolis will smell like a burnt oil factory for a week."[9]

Charles Dickens's New York correspondent stepped out of his hotel just before midnight. He had spent the day at a savage and seedy Democratic barbecue, watching Douglas men wrestle for greasy scraps of ox. Now he found himself immersed in something very different. Craning his head, he could see only "moving forests of torches advancing toward me from every point on the compass." Lower Manhattan was packed with "all the seething millions of

New York and its suburb cities," some in tall soldiers' shakos and crimson capes, others eerily lit from below by blue or green lanterns, still more laboring to keep up the constant bombardment of fireworks that "made the very stars wink, as if they were sneezing at the sulphorous smell." The city resounded with explosions in the heavens, hurrahs and huzzahs, cheers for Lincoln, groans for Douglas, "Tigers" for Seward, hisses for Tammany, all set to the rhythm of the ceaseless *"Champ! Champ! Champ!"* of worn-down boots on cobblestones. And yet it all unfolded in "perfect military array." No wonder, the Englishmen marveled, that "These Wideawakes are the terror of the South, and of the democrats generally."[10]

New York's ladies made up a huge percentage of these crowds. Local men, often with Democratic tendencies, turned away, but many women were thrilled by the spectacle. Large numbers seemed to have studied the parade route to select the best balcony from which to watch, wave, and holler. When thousands of young men in uniforms marched past the St. Nicholas Hotel, many of the female guests "showed their beautiful faces, like clusters of roses, at each of the 150 windows that look out on Broadway from the upper stories." Their husbands grumbled below. Ladies hurled down bouquets; others amped up their cheers to drown out the hisses. Plenty of women joined the march as well, wearing star-spangled robes or throwing yet more bouquets into the crowds. Three particularly statuesque ladies, dressed as the revolutionary goddesses of France, Italy, and America, led the company of Lafayette Wide Awakes—a French Marianne in armor, a beautiful Italian lady in chains, and an American Goddess of Liberty in red, white, and blue.[11]

John Meredith Read Jr., the aristocratic young commander whose daddy paid for his Wide Awakes' capes and whiskey, was there too. He led six hundred men down from Albany, rubbing elbows with the Hartford Originals, the 722 Broadway boys, and so many strangers. In his daily letters to his dad, Read Jr. dwelt on the incredible exhaustion of getting his Wide Awakes to Manhattan. "I had my hands full, I assure you," son wrote to father. "I was at once President, Captain, Ticket Agent, Police Officer, + general Superintendent. You have no idea the amount of labor devolving upon me—but I went through with it all and won a great many compliments." The strain was showing in Read's handwriting, deforming in his exhausted letters over that autumn. At one point, too exhausted to think straight, he scratched in his daily note, "I have worked like (a horse) (I cant find a simile) a Steam Engine in this matter . . . I have many vexations and like every one else in this world who works don't get half the credit I ought to."[12]

John Meredith Read Sr. knew firsthand what his son was up to, because the October 3 rallies spread well beyond New York. In a coordinated demonstration of Wide Awake power, the organization held simultaneous events in Philadelphia, Boston, Buffalo, Cleveland, Chicago, Wheeling, St. Louis, and elsewhere. William and Fanny Seward, still rattling around the Midwest by train, managed to appear at both Chicago's October 2 rally and Cleveland's October 5 rally, hosted by the Wide Awake mayor George B. Senter. Nothing like this had ever been attempted—newspapers, railroads, steamboats, and the Wide Awakes' clever organization made coordination possible on a national scale. Six of the nation's ten largest cities held rallies, sending perhaps fifty thousand to one hundred thousand marchers through a total population of two million city dwellers. One in every fifteen Americans lived in a locale with a Wide Awake procession over a two-day period.[13]

Philadelphia held its rally a day after New York's. Wide Awakes could strut up Broadway, clamber onto southbound trains, and march in Philly the next day. In between, the captain of the Philadelphia Invincibles told crowds that "they would have four hours sleep in the cars and that was enough for any Wide-Awake." Philadelphia's rally was held in the outlying neighborhood of Germantown, on the anniversary of the Revolutionary War battle there. And the stakes were high. Seven days later, Pennsylvania, Ohio, and Indiana would hold state elections that would provide a window into how the presidential election would go. So Aleck McClure and his allies dragged ten thousand to thirteen thousand marchers to Germantown. They organized a carnival atmosphere, complete with campaign swag, refreshments, and "lung-testing and strength and weight telling machines." It was all a clever trap. While Philadelphians sipped lemonade or enjoyed the games, Republican operatives moved through the crowds, methodically "talking, canvassing, bargaining." It was one final drive at the "counting noses" that Lincoln had asked of McClure.[14]

Pennsylvania Republicans brought Frank Blair as the keynote speaker, hoping the brusque Southerner could convince the Lower North that voting Republican was the "patriotic" thing to do. It was Democrats, Blair snarled, who were radicals, "tearing down established principles" because "they knew the power was passing out of their hands." Some of his fellow Southerners were talking about secession, Blair admitted. But he threatened that Union men in the South would drive disunionists into the Gulf of Mexico with no more American soil than they could "carry under their dirty finger nails." Halfway through his talk, a noisy company of Wide Awakes arrived at the grounds. Blair paused, joking that it was useless to try to shout over Wide Awakes, who always "carried everything before them." He had seen the power of the movement firsthand, and was beginning to envision a force that could do more than march. "The Southern newspapers appeared to think that the Wide-Awakes were organized to do some fighting," Blair explained. Perhaps these Wide Awakes might "have to go to Washington to see old Abe inaugurated."[15]

What had begun as Democratic disinformation about a Wide Awake inauguration force was becoming a real possibility among combative Republicans.

Lucius E. Chittenden took the stage in Germantown too. The young Republican state senator was down from Vermont, where he grew up as local royalty in a county named for his ancestors. His Democratic enemies in Chittenden County liked to mock him as a naive princeling, and hoped that "when he gets older and wiser he will cease to make an ass of himself." And he looked the part; an 1860 picture shows Chittenden with chubby, ill-shaven cheeks, hair hanging over his ears, and an expression of bleary confusion in his eyes, like a big man on campus just graduated into the real world. But he had been giving strong speeches at Wide Awake rallies, joking that the trick to converting Democrats was "to get them sober first." In Jersey City, Chittenden shared a stage with William Darrah Kelley Jr. That looming, hard-fisted Philly abolitionist liked Chittenden's style and invited him to speak at the Germantown rally. Kelley promised to send the young orator back to Vermont afterward.[16]

Reminiscing thirty-one years later, Chittenden still regretted "trusting myself the friendly contact of Philadelphia politicians."[17]

Chittenden gave "a cracker" of a speech to ten thousand Wide Awakes at Germantown. Afterward, Will Kelley and Aleck McClure cornered him, informing him that "they had decided that Col. Frank Blair and myself were a matched pair of speakers." They had scheduled the two for a barnstorming trip across Pennsylvania, two lectures a day, until the state election. Lucius stammered that "this was rather a cool proceeding." He had never met Colonel Blair, and he had business back in Vermont.[18]

Kelley and McClure leaned in over Chittenden. Kelley was six foot three, with prominent scars on his face and a gravelly voice "like an eloquent graveyard." McClure was a solid brick of a man with deep, Mephistophelian eyes. Chittenden gulped. "They swept my objections away like cobwebs; declared that we 'Vermonters did not know the first principles of running a campaign.' " They had to make the arrangements first, "and then capture the speakers." Did Chittenden want "to disappoint fifty thousand Republicans, disengage the plans of the committee, and perhaps endanger the election"?[19]

"I surrendered," Chittenden sighed decades later. He "telegraphed home some of the details of my capture, and that I did not anticipate an early escape out of the hands into which I had fallen." He was introduced to Frank Blair and a few zealous young Republicans, who kept referring to him as a "poor, unsophisticated Vermonter." Then they "carried us far into the dark regions of a Democratic country."[20]

"Where we traveled, what places we visited, I never inquired," Chittenden recalled. The next few days were a blurry montage of speeches and train rides, "mass-meetings, torch-light processions, Wide-awakes in uniform, shouting, singing political songs, and hurrahing for the ticket." One night he slept standing up, on a steamboat packed to the handrails with Wide Awakes in crinkling capes. Another evening, a worn-down Chittenden tried to back out of an early-morning event the next day, pleading "exhaustion, loss of voice, general dilapidation and worthlessness." But the local Republican congressional candidate snarled that "I must go and show myself, if I had to be carried on a stretcher, or he would be accused of intentionally deceiving and disappointing five thousand people in a rural community." The candidate sent a company of Wide Awakes to drag Chittenden out of his hotel bed at seven the next morning.[21]

In his memories, Chittenden believed that his kidnapping lasted "two or three weeks." But really it was just five days—between the Wide Awakes' October 4 Germantown rally and the October 9 state election. That it felt much longer is no surprise. Finally McClure returned Chittenden to the Girard House Hotel in Philadelphia for election night. "We were a used-up pair of campaigners. We had lost our voices; could not speak above a whisper, and were in desperate need of rest." Somehow, Frank Blair zoomed off to another doubtful state. Chittenden wobbled around the election-night headquarters. When he heard that Republicans had won Pennsylvania, Ohio, and Indiana, he felt it "settled the presidential contest." Having learned the good news,

Chittenden "quietly elbowed my way through the crowd to my hotel" and went to sleep.[22]

It had been just one week since the Hartford Originals boarded their steamboat south. In the intervening seven days, Wide Awake Republicans had orchestrated a stomping, pyrotechnic, handkerchief-waving, Buffalo-marching, boot-ruining series of spectacles, running from northern Vermont down to the Mason-Dixon Line, from the biggest city in the western hemisphere to Keokuk, Iowa. They had mobilized the movement's founders, the boys of 722 Broadway, aristocrats like John Meredith Read Jr., novices like Lucius Crittenden, and some of the nation's most prominent figures, from William Seward to P. T. Barnum.

If the movement's primary purpose had been not the election of Abraham Lincoln per se, but the ability to command the public square in the face of decades of mob rule, the Wide Awakes had already won. What had been risky to say in a Hartford street in February was now a deafening clamor across much of the North in October. As the Central Committee of New York Wide Awakes constructed their gigantic firework-blasting arch on the east side of Broadway, Hiram Cranston of the New York Hotel had stationed guards in front of his "severely conservative" establishment. He gave strict orders to keep guests inside, and the doors barred, during the parade.[23]

While the outcome of November 6, and the response from the South, remained unclear, the *New York Tribune* knew what was undeniable by mid-October. "The most imposing, influential, and potent political organization which ever existed in this country is the Wide-Awakes," the *Tribune* declared, "They have been the salient characteristic of the campaign. They have thrown into the canvass an incalculable amount of enthusiasm. They are the terror of the Democracy and its allies."[24]

Or, as Charles "Ducksy" O'Neill wrote to his girlfriend, Carrie, of his last-minute Wide Awaking in Connecticut: "Hurrah for old Abe. We are going to win, true as you live." He had searched for someone in New Haven who thought differently for a friendly wager. But "I cannot make any bets," he sighed. "There is no one to bet with."[25]

AND YET HERE was James Sanks Brisbin, scrambling for the safety of the Wheeling Bridge, white hat askew, fear in his eyes, and rowdies on his heels.

A black wall of Wide Awakes offered him protection if he could just reach them. What looked like a coming consensus in the North could scarcely be uttered on the far side of the Ohio. The Wide Awakes were icons north of that line, and targets south of it. In the final days of the campaign, the movement itself provided material proof of the unbridgeable split in the center of American politics, a disunion beginning before any votes were cast.[26]

James Sanks Brisbin had been lecturing the same small-town Pennsylvania rallies as Lucius Chittenden that October. But Brisbin was not "captured"; there was something in his nature that propelled him hungrily into such fights. And he was a perfect Wide Awake. Twenty-three years old, with hooded bug eyes, a twitchy black mustache, and the long, slicked hair of a radical, he was a Protestant White working-class antislavery dreamer who talked of arcane conspiracies. He had faith in newspapers, militias, and the Republican Party. He had been a "colonel" in Boalsburg, Pennsylvania's militia, in the hilly region where the Pennsylvania State University would be located. Brisbin edited Centre County's populist Republican newspaper—the *Bellefonte Centre Democrat*—which often devolved into personal attacks on local rivals (". . . but Smithy, why did you not pitch into the arguments . . ."). Brisbin referred to himself as "an Abolitionist." He wrote to his future wife, "You know I hate foreigners." He wore a white hat. He checked every box.[27]

And he had been barnstorming. Madly traversing the state in the days before the October election, Brisbin spoke in Philadelphia one night, outside Pittsburgh soon after, stopping in Blairsville and Lockport and Latrobe along the way—all to ensure that "the people of the north are thoroughly awake." He had voted Democratic in the 1856 election, but felt that the Slave Power had captured that party, writing to his father: "Democracy in 1860 means something more than it did in 1856." His chief issue was "the exercise of our constitutional rights—liberty of conscience, speech and press." At Altoona, he attended a talk by Democratic vice presidential nominee Herschel V. Johnson. Brisbin loudly scoffed when Johnson claimed that the South had the same freedom of speech as the North. Soon he was heckling from the stands, buffeting and questioning until the candidate fell back to the assertion that a northern man could enjoy free speech in the South, so long as he didn't mention slavery.[28]

"Even this I knew to be false," Brisbin wrote to his dad, "and subsequent events have proved the correctness of my views."[29]

When news spread that the Wheeling Wide Awakes were being attacked in the streets, Brisbin eagerly volunteered to speak at an excursion of northern Wide Awakes to what was then the largest city in Virginia's western reaches. The native-born mill workers and German Turner clubs who made up Wheeling's three Wide Awake companies were having a rough fall, facing about as much violence, they said, as "any place that we know of, except Baltimore.' " Wide Awaking within Virginia, the undisputed core of southern civilization and recent site of the John Brown raid, was especially controversial. But the clubs had kept at it. Often, they headed up to Pittsburgh to march in more peaceful streets. Now they needed Pennsylvania's help commanding the streets of their own pretty, prosperous river town.[30]

The excursion set out on a dreary, wet Tuesday, October 30, exactly one week before the presidential election, led by a smiling, squint-eyed, mustachioed Mexican War veteran, General James S. Negley. Though the Wheeling Wide Awakes tried to cancel the rally on account of the rain, Negley insisted. He told Brisbin that the Pittsburgh papers had already sent announcements of the excursion to the *New York Tribune*. As with Chittenden's capture, as with the formation of rural Wide Awake companies, as with the Hartford Originals, the papers were a goad, making the news as much as reporting it. "To turn back now," Negley told Brisbin, "would be to show the white feathers before the whole country North and South."[31]

With drums beating and colors flying, the Pennsylvania Wide Awakes marched across Wheeling's famous suspension bridge and into town. It was still pouring, but huge crowds turned out, some waving handkerchiefs, but many more jeering and cussing. As soon as the Wide Awakes got settled in Wheeling's crenellated Gothic castle of an auditorium, they were surrounded. Called to the rostrum, Brisbin did his best. Remembering his debate with Herschel Johnson, he "carefully refrained from mentioning the subject of slavery." But even this "modest and moderate" case for Lincoln did not calm the crowds outside. Soon Brisbin was passed a note, informing him of the growing threat outside. The worthies seated behind him on stage murmured frantically among themselves.

Brisbin slipped out through a side door into a carriage, leaving the remaining Wide Awakes to fight their way back to the bridge. Heading out, one hundred and eighty Wide Awakes pushed into the jostling and howling crowd, clumped tightly together, inching toward the bridge. Bricks and stones began to sail down on them. "Many of our men," a reporter for Brisbin's *Centre Democrat* wrote, "were knocked down, cut, bruised and otherwise hurt. One only, we believe, was shot." Wide Awakes drew revolvers from under their capes and trained them jerkily on the crowds. General Negley kept his men tight, skillfully countermarching them as they had drilled so many times in northern streets. Whenever a Wide Awake broke ranks, thrashing a rowdy with fists or torch-staff, Negley ordered them back into the column.[32]

All the while, wrote the *Democrat*'s reporter afterward, "we could not help thinking of John Brown," his corpse dangling from that Virginia gallows.[33]

Finally they reached the bridge. General Negley got his Wide Awakes most of the way across the span, then wheeled around to stop the mobs from following them. Pistols drawn, hammers cocked, they steeled themselves to "rake the bridge" with gunfire if the Virginians pursued them across.

Wheeling was not just a random small city in the Upper South. Everything about the town depended on the artful union of disparate elements. It was as far north as the South got; closer to the capitals of Pennsylvania, Ohio, Indiana, and even Michigan than to its own government in Richmond. It was technically a slave city, though home to more abolitionists than enslaved people. And that grand bridge was a prominent icon of America's Union. One of the first significant federal infrastructure projects, begun back in 1811, was a national road running all the way to Illinois, with the Wheeling bridge as a symbol of the whole achievement. If there was ever a faith in uniting the divided nation across section and party, relying on the bold promise of nineteenth-century progress, it was that edifice of mottled stone and taut wire.[34]

Now Wide Awakes stared through gun sights across a national landmark. On one side stood a howling mob, on the other their paramilitary partisan force. In between, James Sanks Brisbin was sprinting toward safety, white hat flapping.[35]

Negley's men did not fire on Brisbin as he scrambled into their ranks, panting and bleeding and missing a clump of hair. Brisbin believed the Wide Awakes would have "killed a great many" had the Virginians followed him. But the crowd stopped at the bridge's iron gates, respecting that boundary, for now. Negley turned his men around and marched back toward Pennsylvania.[36]

After the Wide Awakes made it back, the *Centre Democrat* reported the drama in Wheeling under the title "A TRIP DOWN SOUTH," writing, "The last week of the contest for Lincoln, we got a taste of Southern Democracy." And

Brisbin wrote to tell his father of his adventure. He would come home to vote for Lincoln the next Tuesday, but after his recent experiences, Brisbin doubted whether "the people of the South will submit to his election."[37]

Few other papers mentioned the affair, because the same thing just kept happening that last week. Elsewhere in western Virginia, a mob of college students set upon nineteen Wide Awake marchers, throwing stones, waving bowie knives, and hollering for "Bell, Breckenridge, and Wm. L. Yancey." "Our Wide Awake friends," the *Pittsburgh Gazette* bragged, "gallantly stood their ground," producing pistols and shooting several students. In New York, the Ninth Ward Wide Awakes of the West Village fought a running battle with a Democratic fire company, chasing each other up and down Thirteenth Street, Wide Awakes waving torches, firemen swinging axes. The biggest fight unfolded in Maryland. Much like the events in Wheeling, 250 Wide Awakes found themselves surrounded by threatening crowds in Baltimore's Front Street Theatre. But this time, their besiegers broke into the theater, the same hall where the Democratic convention had split that summer. Furious rowdies swarmed the building. Retreating from the hordes, Baltimore Wide Awakes drew up on the stage, defending the approaches while attackers ran wild in the aisles. Local ladies backing the Constitutional Unionists arrived with baskets of rotten eggs and "served up an odoriferous omelette" on the Wide Awakes' green capes. Eventually Baltimore's police escorted the Wide Awakes out of the theater and down Pratt Street one by one.[38]

Republicans saw the Baltimore theater fight as further proof of the assault on free speech, with newspapers screaming "Wide Awakes! How Do You Like That?" In response, the *Buffalo Morning Express* frothed, Americans must vote for Lincoln, to affirm "that we live in a State where a man, if he sees fit, can wear an oil cloth cape and carry a torch to light Republicanism on to victory, and not suffer at the hands of a mob maddened by the curse of Slavery."[39]

"If he sees fit." Of course, no one had *wanted* to march around in oilcloth capes prior to 1860. It was not some ancient right needing defense. Instead, the Wide Awakes represented a provocation whose suppression proved its importance. On the other side, radical Southerners argued an equally circular logic. The Wide Awakes were a force organized to stop secession, and therefore, the South must secede. The feuds of the 1850s were spiraling in that last week before the vote.

Most Americans were not chasing each other around with axes, or throwing rotten eggs, or shooting loudmouth college kids. Most supported neither disunion nor coercion. But they were reading about it, every day, as the election drew closer. And many, as James Brisbin had written to his father, were already looking past next Tuesday's vote. It was widely assumed that Lincoln would win. Ducksy couldn't find anyone to bet against. The tougher question was what the fire-eaters would do upon learning of a Republican victory.

George N. Sanders offered a warning. Sanders was a well-connected Kentucky Democrat, living in New York, with a long record as a proponent of the Young America movement, stretching back to the 1830s. With one foot in each section, Sanders tried to make northern voters see just how dire the conversation had gotten in the South. It simply did not matter what the party platform said on slavery extension or if Abraham Lincoln was a kindly moderate, Sanders wrote in a published letter. The Republican candidate hardly mattered at all. "Mr. Lincoln, possibly, may not commit any aggressive act upon the South if he shall be elected. He may even disappoint his party, and form a conservative Cabinet," Sanders declared. "The Gulf States will have acted long before Mr. Lincoln's inauguration. . . . The South looks to your military and militant Wide Awakes, to your banners, your speeches, your press, and your votes, and not to what Mr. Lincoln may say or do after his election." The Wide Awakes embodied a force more significant than the actions of that rail-splitter in Illinois. "The only voice that can or ought to have weight with the South is the vote of the North."[40]

For Sanders, and for many other southern observers, the Wide Awakes served as a tangible symbol of their darkest fears. In the absence of proof that Lincoln was anything other than a careful moderate, the Wide Awakes themselves provided evidence of a northern army of coercion. In many southern newspapers, "Wide Awakes" became a metonym for everyone they feared in the North. The movement embodied a Yankee nemesis, replacing the section of relatives, trading partners, and countrymen that Southerners had long shared the Union with. Many southern voices expressed the same conspiratorial thinking heard among Republicans fighting the Slave Power, or Know Nothings ranting about the pope. But the difference, from the southern perspective, was that the Wide Awakes were poised to win the presidency. Such a loss would confirm everything the fire-eaters feared.

Radical southern papers began using the Wide Awakes as a tool to shatter faith in the democratic process, even before the voting began. Some claimed that Stephen Douglas had joined the companies. Such disinformation worked to subvert long-standing affection for the Democratic Party. When Douglas promised to oppose disunion in a speech at Norfolk, Virginia—a position so standard that most associated it with Andrew Jackson—radicals accused him of being a secret Wide Awake. He was, the *Nashville Union* asserted, plotting coercion as part of the "Lincoln Douglas Forces Organizing for the Black Republican Inauguration." Going further, Georgia's *Milledgeville Federal Union* claimed that the Wide Awakes were undermining the entire electoral system. Lincoln might win, but would be only "the President of the fanatics and the Wide Awakes," not "the choice of a majority of the people." The Wide Awakes were really an election-stealing force, the *Union* alleged, preparing to surround polling places, intimidate Democrats, and seize ballots. The election would only be "a humbug and a mockery, and is no expression of the wishes of a majority of the people." With militant Wide Awakes in control of the northern polls, "Lincoln can get just as many votes as is necessary; it is as easy for them to give ten thousand majority as one." The only remaining question was not whether the Wide Awakes would steal the election but "what is the best for us to do, under all these circumstances."[41]

Southern Unionists pushed back, arguing everything from patriotism to rule of law to the South's dependence on northern bacon. But all this moderation sounded flat in the face of romantic radicals who were already on the barricades, pointing to the Wide Awakes marching their way. The *Nashville Patriot*'s editors shrilly challenged: " 'Come on, Mr Lincoln! come on with your half million," ready to battle "white and black Wide-Awakes." The striking clubs made it easy for these fire-eaters to visualize the coming invasion. "Secede now," the *New Orleans Daily Delta* demanded; "We shall have four months start" against the inaugural army of "the half million of Wide-Awakes who lately made a demonstration in the streets of NY, and whose parade is pictured by all the illustrated papers." A heady mix of fear and arrogance fired this talk. The Deep South was a political minority, but it was an economic powerhouse. "We are defeated in the Union," the *Montgomery Advertiser* smirked, "but out of it we are still masters of the world." The Republicans might have "a half million Wide Awakes prepared to invade," but the South had something more powerful in the eyes of the world. "We have cotton."[42]

Many sensed that, with the vote just days away, disunion was already begin-ning. George N. Sanders warned Northerners that "we are now in the throes of dissolution." His friends in New York had no sense of "the ease with which this gigantic republic can be disintegrated." William Tecumseh Sherman agreed, from Louisiana. The Ohioan had always felt that the paltry federal edifice was "the only thing in America that has even the semblance of a govern-ment. These state governments are ridiculous pretenses of a government, liable to explode at the call of any mob." Secession would be so easy. Three days before the election, Sherman noticed that "people here now talk as though disunion was a fixed thing."[43]

Ellen Ellington, a youthful Mississippi poet, paused with trepidation in her composition "The Sixth of November, 1860." "The day is fast approaching which will, to a great extent, decide the destinies of a mighty nation," she warned. Dark clouds—the same metaphor so many others had chosen—suddenly over-whelmed the sunny land. Looking in one direction, she sensed the flash of lightning coming from South Carolina. In the other, she could almost hear "the deep-toned tramp of the 'Wide Awakes,' " a solemn chorus registering "the pent-up thunders of the North."[44]

But the northern majority seemed deaf to the threat. Northern Democratic papers—either better in touch with the South, or hoping to scare undecided voters—denounced their section's deafness. "It seems hard to convince the people of the North that there is actual danger," the *Lancaster Intelligencer* vented. The Wide Awake campaign had distracted Northerners, even as it terrified Southerners. The *New York Herald* was certain that "the inflammable materials are there, the train of gunpower is laid, and it only requires that the match of the incendiary, the torch of the Wide Awake, be applied, in order to set the whole South in one blaze."[45]

James Sanks Brisbin's *Centre Democrat* scoffed at such threats. It was pure humbug, the old boy-who-cried-wolf southern trick, "the stock in trade of a class of politicians who wish to frighten the people into submission to their slave propaganda schemes." The best way to end this habit of threatening disunion at every election was to finally call the Slave Power's bluff. Elect Lincoln. It was one of the ironies of history that many Northerners were finally ready to disregard southern threats at the same moment that many South-erners were ready to follow through. In a nice inversion of Stephen Douglas's purported "Don't care" policy on slavery, the Wide Awake editors of the *Centre*

Democrat scoffed: "Who believes that kind of talk, or who cares?" For generations, fear of disunion had motivated White Americans more than hatred of slavery. But the 1860 campaign had altered the relationship between fear and care.[46]

There was one thing all could agree on. A letter writer in the Catskills was sick of "nothing but political discussions ringing in your ears. Wide Awakes, Half Asleeps, Little Giants, Bell Ringers, Torch Lights, &c. appear to be the absorbing topics." The saloons were packed with boys in capes, drinking whiskey and rum and arguing. "I am afraid in some cases their dear mothers don't know they're out." But the campaign was almost over. Soon they will "settle down after the excitement and become good men and women again."[47]

"Without a doubt," the writer sighed, "all will be exceedingly glad when the great political campaign is over."[48]

CHAPTER NINE

I Think That Settles It

E LECTION DAY BEGAN early, even before Wide Awakes started going door-to-door. It got moving deep in the November night, with the clatter and hum of steam-powered printing presses, as America's newspapers manufactured the tickets that would decide the election. The government did not provide ballots in those days. It was parties' job to print them, and get them into voters' hands. So they turned to America's four thousand newspaper presses, 95 percent of which had explicit party affiliations. During election season papers published ballots—that essential tool of democracy—at the top left corner of their editions. Partisan presses made more tickets, to be cut and stacked and handed out at polling places.[1]

Some of the nation's presses were silent as the sun came up on November 6. They sat in muddy river bottoms, their cast-iron frames entwined by grasses, their odd architecture home to minnows and tadpoles. They had been thrown there over the years for printing newspapers critical of slavery. Elijah Lovejoy's press sat in the Mississippi, Cassius Clay's in the Kentucky, James G. Birney's in the Ohio; others were submerged in the Kansas River, the Patapsco, the Potomac. And where a newspaper had been drowned, there were no ballots for antislavery candidates. It is often said that Abraham Lincoln was "not on the ballot" in much of the South in 1860, but really, there was no such thing as "*the* ballot." The machinery of free speech was also the mechanism of democracy.[2]

With ballots printed and distributed by the parties, not the government, Election Day presented a logistical challenge as well as a political one. Someone had to do all the "little dirty jobs necessary to make an interesting election," explained a newspaper in the Catskills. The Wide Awakes could do this work. Their structure made it easy to dispatch members to newspaper offices and polling places, or break into specialized units to oversee the many strange tasks that this makeshift democracy required. Republicans had lost the 1856 presidential election, they believed, because the new party acted like "a sort of mob, unorganized." In 1860 they had the best organized political movement in American history. In the 1850s newspapers had warned voters to "BE WIDE AWAKE against all sorts of devices to deceive you on Election Day." Now that vigilance had evolved into a coordinated movement, devoted to protecting embattled public speech.[3]

The movement had been preparing for this day since its birth. Henry T. Sperry's pamphlets explained that the companies must do "all the minutiae of political work"—escort Republican voters to the polls, knock on doors, and saturate polling places with "distributors, checkers, challengers and especially patrol-men." It was in this context that Sperry wrote, "Wherever the fight is hottest, there is their post of duty, and there the Wide-Awakes are found." Election Day was not a dry government process but a public confrontation, and the Wide Awakes had formed to help Republicans fight back.[4]

Despite elder Republicans' fears that the youthful clubs mostly cared about the "fun and frolic" of rallies, the Wide Awakes had built an impressive ground game. In the spring elections in Connecticut, they helped escort would-be Republicans to cast ballots safely at Democratic-controlled polling places. They sent fifty men in plainclothes to each of Hartford's voting districts. The Waterbury club left behind a plan of battle for Election Day, a dignified book designating which Wide Awakes should be stationed on which street corners. Looking at its careful calligraphy, you'd hardly believe that it came from a democracy on the verge of killing itself.[5]

In early-fall state elections, the Wide Awakes leaned into the vigilant tone of the era. In Maine's September vote, companies made sure that "every suspicious person was challenged peremptorily." Captains sent "men of pluck and muscle" to confront illegal voters or pursue them into neighborhoods to learn their real names. Milder club members knocked on doors or stuck their heads into saloons and workplaces, calling Republicans to vote. One Portland Wide

Awake captain offered fifty-dollar bounties to anyone who "captured" an illegal voter. Fraudulent voting was rampant in this era, but so were baseless accusations aimed at naturalized immigrant voters. Defending free speech quickly veered into suppressing rival voices.[6]

As November approached, rumors of fraud flew back and forth. Elections had grown uglier across the 1850s, especially with the rise of violent Know Nothings. No one expected the 1860 vote to be peaceful. Critics in Brooklyn accused local Wide Awakes of scheming with the police to challenge every third voter in Democratic wards, to slow down voting. Across the river, Manhattan's Central Wide Awakes offered *one-hundred-dollar* bounties for catching an illegal vote, goading: "Policemen! Wide-Awakes! Sharp-eyed Republicans! You can make your Winter's coal easily by catching an illegal voter To-Morrow!" This astounding sum suggests how rare catching, and keeping, an illegal voter actually was. New York City was a Democratic bastion in a Republican-leaning state, and Wide Awakes seemed to be plotting a slow, annoying game of defense in the metropolitan region.[7]

In the last day before the vote, northern editors lectured young Wide Awakes on their duties. The companies had been "showy and satisfactory holiday soldiers" during the campaign, the *Cincinnati Commercial* admitted. But as November 6 approached, the *Berkshire County Eagle* reminded Williams College's Wide Awake students, "we have dryer work to do." Horace Greeley's *New York Tribune* banged that drum the hardest. The torchlight parades had been fun, but really, they were beside the point. "In plain English, the prime object of these Clubs is to secure a majority of the Electoral votes for Lincoln." Anything else was a waste. Instead of plotting victory marches, the Wide Awakes should put away their capes, divide into squads, and "work at the polls from early dawn to set of sun."[8]

These condescending lectures would not have been aimed at a movement made up of older men. But of course some really were enjoying their role as "holiday soldiers." In Hartford, Eddie Yergason was having a grand time. In the last few days before the election, he wrote to his mom about the Hartford Originals' status as "envited guests" at rallies, parties, and "monstrous suppers." Yergason always had a sweet tooth, and delighted in the cakes with Lincoln's name in sweet red icing on them presented to the company. He also made note of the ladies who baked them, bragging: "They think every thing of the Original Wide Awakes." But Yergason was still nineteen years old. Like perhaps a quarter of Wide Awakes, he would be too young to vote.[9]

By dawn on November 6, the ballot printing was done, and newspapers were churning out Election Day content. Many had little to report yet, and spent the morning arguing about the Wide Awakes. One Iowa paper happily waved "Good bye, Wide Awakes—you have fooled away considerable time this year." Others, like the Republican *Chicago Tribune*, advocated the movement's usual blend of forbearance and menace. In the face of a Democratic mayor and police allegedly conspiring to give the election to Douglas, Chicago Wide Awakes were told, "Let nothing short of violence and outrage tempt you to strike; but if strike you must, hit hard!"[10]

In their headquarters, company captains were giving final pep talks as they divided into specialized squads. In big cities, there would be "workies" to hand out ballots, "challengers" to oppose and intimidate rivals, and "look-outs" to watch the ballot box all day, monitoring for fraud. Wide Awake captains would dispatch men as needed, moving crews to the rougher polling places. Runners would sprint from headquarters to printing offices to polling places, resupplying ballots. Speeches were made, often heavy on the rhetoric of awakening with the dawn. Those who drank made a celebratory toast, or three, but others were strictly temperance organizations. Finally they marched out, capeless, into the rising sun. The morning was clear and bracing across much of the North, its streets scoured by days of heavy rain.[11]

Frederick Douglass woke strangely conflicted on Election Day. He could vote in New York State, as a Black man with at least $250 to his name. But he could not bring himself to give a ballot to a man as lukewarm on slavery as Abraham Lincoln. Douglass would cast his vote for the abolitionist Gerrit Smith. Yet at the same time he *wanted* the Republicans to win, hoping "for the triumph of that party over all the odds and ends of slavery combined against it." He felt more certain of the historic significance of the moment than of his own waffling vote. "Since the organization of Government," Douglass was sure, "there has been no election so exciting and interesting as this."[12]

Stepping out of his Gramercy Park mansion, George Templeton Strong would have agreed with Douglass, at least on the import of the election. "Think I will vote the Republican ticket," he wrote in his diary. The manly and orderly Wide Awake parades had convinced him that the North must assert itself. Voting early, he joined the masses coursing downtown to await returns around Printing House Square, where New York's newspapers had their offices. As he walked, he considered possible outcomes—"Perhaps for the disintegration of the country, perhaps for another proof that the North is timid and merce-nary, perhaps for demonstration that Southern bluster is worthless. We cannot tell yet what historical lesson the event of Nov 6, 1860, will teach, but the lesson cannot fail to be weighty."[13]

It didn't take specialized squads of Wide Awakes to drag out most voters that day. The polls drew a higher turnout of eligible voters—81.2 percent—than any other presidential election in American history, before or since, save the slightly bigger 1876 race. Angry, contested campaigns win greater participa-tion, and no election ever loomed larger over the American people. Wide Awake strongholds like Illinois, Indiana, New York, and Wisconsin all enjoyed monster turnouts, but in a heated nation and a four-way race, participation was also unusually high across swaths of Georgia, Mississippi, and Louisiana. Turnout was lowest in those places where the results felt obvious, like Repub-lican northern Vermont or Democratic southern Florida. Either way, the record numbers prove that few voters felt like the outcome was predetermined.

Even as the polls were opening in eastern districts, predawn Springfield was getting to work. A crew of forty local Wide Awakes set out from the state-house square, dragging a huge Mexican War cannon with them. It was likely the same behemoth that ruined Anna Ridgely's prayer meetings. Sweating and grunting in the dark, they pushed the artillery piece up a high bluff overlooking the slumbering town. The sun was slowly rising on what would be the biggest day in Springfield's short history. At the order of the young barber who led the company, the Wide Awakes fired a deafening salute to Lincoln. All across the tidy state capital, church bells, firecrackers, and brass bands answered back, eager to start the day.[14]

Abraham Lincoln was already awake and drinking coffee when the Wide Awakes' cannon split the morning's calm. He finished his cup, pocketed an apple for lunch, and headed out to vote. The Republican nominee had carefully altered his ballot, slicing off his own name and those of his party's presiden-tial electors in a show of modesty common among candidates. After voting, he loped off to his campaign office in the garish state capitol for one last excruci-ating day of waiting. Crowds gathered around his lanky shoulders to watch the candidate wait. Lincoln's friends tried to shoo them off, but the nominee kept encouraging well-wishers, happy for the company. Mostly he maintained a calm veneer, but a reporter from the *St. Louis Democrat* noted a "nervous twitch on his countenance" whenever the messenger from the telegraphic offices came with updates, betraying an internal anxiety "that no coolness from without could repress."[15]

As the polls closed and news started to flood in, Lincoln relocated to Springfield's telegraph office. There, results came in by dribs and drabs that evening, a county here, a district there, read aloud by the telegraph operator. It was all fractured and unsystematic, driven by rumor and inside knowledge. Like much of American life in 1860, the system was both radically connected and oddly disjointed. It was possible for all four main candidates to be receiving breaking, game-changing, entirely contradictory news at the same time. The Illinois senator Lyman Trumbull paced the room, muttering "We've got 'em, we've got 'em." Anxious voices in the crowd wondered, "Why don't we have something from New York?" Rumors came up from Alton, Illinois, that the town that murdered Elijah Lovejoy had given a majority to the Republicans. Owen Lovejoy was already partying there. Lincoln grew more confident as the night darkened and the crowds grew, wondering aloud, "What has Frank Blair's constituency done?" in Missouri. Finally, the crooked, gossipy Pennsylvania politico Simon Cameron sent word from the east. Philly and Pittsburgh were Lincoln's, perhaps a seventy-thousand-vote majority for the Republicans in that crucial state. Soon after, the elite Manhattan Republican Simeon Draper, who had been in 722 Broadway when the Wide Awakes beat the New York Hotel guests, telegraphed. The Democrats had won the city, but by an insufficient margin to hold off the upstate avalanche of Republicans. New York was theirs, by fifty thousand votes.[16]

"I think that settles it," president-elect Lincoln said, calmly.[17]

"It is utterly impossible to describe the scene," gasped a reporter in the telegraph office with Lincoln. A shout went up, burbling and cracking and overlapping voices "yelling like demons." Outside, a *Whoop, whoop, hurrah!* resonated as Springfield "went off like one immense cannon," its streets filling with "10,000 crazy people" making as much noise as they could. Springfield's Republican ladies had prepared a collation of treats for Lincoln to enjoy as he waited, and their cries cut through the deeper male bellows in the room, "a hundred feminine voices" congratulating the president-elect and gathering around to shake his big hand. At about the same time in Milwaukee, Carl Schurz watched a Republican hall explode in wild cheering as they learned of the New York victory, with hats "flying to the ceiling, against the walls, and to the floor as if they were worth nothing at all." On the other side of the North, a sustained ten-minute scream alerted all of New Haven to Lincoln's win. "Heigh ho! hurrah! hurrah! hurrah!" cheered Emily Hawley Gillespie, of Iowa, in her nightly diary entry. George Templeton Strong, on the other hand, inscribed a flaccid "Lincoln elected. Hooray."[18]

Back in Springfield, Lincoln shook hands happily, and headed home alone a little after one thirty A.M. But much of Springfield stayed up. "Everybody, by common consent, was voted a Wide-Awake," wrote the St. Louis reporter, staying out and partaking in a night of wild revelry.[19]

Wide Awake–related violence began right away, even before the full results were known. In Kingston, New York, a Wide Awake club smashed the windows of the Democratic newspapers' printing office, and the homes of anyone in town who had illuminated their windows for a recent "Little Giant parade" for Stephen Douglas. "Not a whole pane of glass" was left intact. So much for free speech. At the same time, in Manhattan, a huge procession of Wide Awakes started to march down Broadway, six abreast and cheering. Their march quickly devolved into mayhem as they were attacked by armed and bitter Democrats. Six hundred fighting men clogged a chunk of lower Manhattan, the battle ending only when Wide Awakes left many Democrats "most unmercifully pummeled."[20]

Washington saw the worst of it. The town's streets filled with feverish crowds on election night, "alive with people," the *Evening Star* recorded, "scurrying in hot haste from one hotel to another," some celebrating, some cursing, fights breaking out here and there. Around midnight, the shadowy National Volunteers movement assembled. Just about the time the Kingston Wide Awakes were smashing up Democratic windows, the National Volunteers set upon the Wide Awakes' three-story Wigwam. The steely Lewis Clephane and four other Wide Awakes were inside, smoking and celebrating. As the National Volunteers broke down the door, the Wide Awakes snuck quietly to the second floor. They could hear the mob breaking windows, tearing capes, and smashing the club's printing press below them. When the enraged Southern Democrats started for the second floor, Clephane's crew retreated to the third floor, and finally climbed an attic ladder onto the building's roof. The handful of Wide Awakes stood there in the windy November night, each clutching a loose brick for self-defense, listening as the rioters sacked their headquarters. Voices below were yelling, "Fire the Building!" But the wooden structure—and Lewis Clephane—survived yet another attack. A handful of well-liked police officers arrived and gently convinced the crowds to disperse.[21]

Clephane and the Washington Wide Awakes climbed down, stepping gingerly through three stories of smashed glass, floorboards piled with thrown stones, bent window frames, bullet-hole-pocked walls, and tattered Wide Awake capes flung about like black confetti. Yet another printing press sat in ruins; its little metal type scattered around the first floor. But unlike the presses at the bottom of the Ohio or Mississippi, Clephane's had accomplished its mission first. The sun rose over a trashed Wigwam, but in a capital with a Republican president-elect.[22]

The results, as they became known, were both bigger and smaller than anticipated. The Republicans had won the largest number of votes ever cast for a candidate: 1,865,000 for Lincoln. And yet that meant that he had only 39.8 percent of the popular vote, winning a plurality in a four -way race. It was significantly better than Stephen Douglas's 29.5 percent, and swamped out Breckenridge's 18 percent and Bell's 12 percent. And it was true that three of the last four presidents had failed to win full majorities of the popular vote. Still, Lincoln would be entering the White House with the second smallest percentage of the popular vote of any American president ever.[23]

And this was from a party that had claimed to speak for the majority. It turned out that opposing minority rule was easier than building a majority themselves. The Republicans, to be fair, did win the majority of votes in the majority section, taking 55 percent of northern ballots. But more voters, nation-wide, didn't want Lincoln to be president than did. They failed, however, in that first task of politics, the systematic organization of hatreds. They hated each other too much to unite against Lincoln, and lacked a movement like the Wide Awakes to cloak a diverse coalition in a single campaign. And the Republicans' big talk about majority rule looks even more ridiculous in view of the fact that just 7 percent of the total population of the United States voted for Lincoln, in an unequal and restricted democracy where only 15 percent of the population of America voted at all.[24]

Still, the victory of even a moderate antislavery man was revolutionary. After decades in which antislavery candidates struggled to win at any level, after untold numbers had been mobbed, expelled, or murdered, the American people had, in Frederick Douglass's words, elected, "if not an Abolitionist, at least a man with an *anti-slavery reputation* to the Presidency of the United States." Even a tough critic like Douglass was pleasantly shocked. "For fifty years the country has taken the law from the lips of an exacting, haughty and imperious slave oligarchy," he wrote. "The masters of slaves have been masters of the Republic." All that changed with a single campaign. Lincoln's election had "broken their power. It has taught the North its strength, and shown the South its weakness."[25]

On the ground, the Republicans' local victories confirmed Douglass's interpretation, and affirmed the choices the party had made. The six-year-old party's growth was incredible, up half a million votes from 1856, expanding particularly in places like Pennsylvania, Indiana, Illinois, and California. Lincoln won every northern state, except for ultra-Democratic corners of New Jersey, which split its vote. The party managed the feat of simultaneously growing among ex–Know Nothings in the eastern Lower North and winning huge support among Germans in the Midwest. Even in states the Republicans had no chance of winning, like Maryland, Lincoln did ten times better than Fremont had in 1856. Missouri Republicans recorded zero votes in 1856, jumping to seventeen thousand (10 percent of the electorate) in 1860.[26]

Digging into the data from 1860, historians and political scientists have found the core of Republicans' strength among farmers and skilled laborers, and have detected little connection between wealth and partisan preference. Scholars have found that younger voters strongly preferred Lincoln, though, especially in the western states. It is easy to see that the Republicans' strategic choices—nominating a young, moderate Lower North man—paid off. Lincoln did less well in those far northern spots where the Wide Awakes were less active (and where Seward would have been preferred). But in regions where the Wide Awakes fought hardest—central Illinois, central Pennsylvania, southeastern Wisconsin, across Indiana—the Republicans showed their greatest gains.[27]

Besides, the electoral college decided things, and the Republicans won that handily. Lincoln took 59 percent of the electoral vote, compared to Breckenridge's 24, Bell's 13, and Douglas's 4. It was a bigger electoral win than James Buchanan's, four years earlier. It is ironic that the Republicans, opposed to the Three-Fifths Clause and other antidemocratic structures, made it to the White House because of the electoral college. And yet even if all the anti-Republican movements had united under one banner, they still would have lost the electoral vote. It was not just Democratic fracture but also the Republicans' campaign that determined this outcome. At the same time, the Republicans' dominant showing in congressional races—winning

55 percent of the Senate and 60 percent of the House—helped confirm this narrative of Republican sweep.[28]

It would be facile to claim that Lincoln won *because* of the Wide Awakes. It is true that his most decisive victories took place exactly where that movement was strongest. But to make a causal case would be lazy history. To ask "What would have happened if the Wide Awakes had not existed?" is useless, because they *did* exist. And however they may have shaped the actual number of votes, the Wide Awakes certainly characterized the outcome, determining how Americans interpreted what had just happened. In its postelection assessment, Horace Greeley's *New York Tribune* (somewhat wrongly) listed Democratic division as the first element of Republican success, and cited the Wide Awakes as the second decisive factor. Their organization, mobilization of young voters, work at the polls, and most importantly their symbolic power defined the proceedings. Greeley wrote that the Wide Awakes were "not merely auditors" of the unfolding campaign, a colorful illustration of the politics of the day. Their material, physical, and rhetorical presence "embodied" the campaign more than any policy plank.[29]

Whether or not the Wide Awakes caused Lincoln's election, they certainly flavored Americans' interpretations of the outcome. It's possible to imagine a nation that, seeing no popular vote majority and a 39 to 29 to 18 to 12 percent split, would interpret the results as a sign that no one could claim a mandate. Another electorate, facing such numbers, might prepare for four more years of petty feuding and executive inactivity. In a parliamentary democracy, this four-way split would have looked like a normal election, inviting creative coalition building. And yet most Americans saw the vote as decisive, for two reasons. The first was the growing awareness that some southern voters would accept nothing other than total victory, viewing a legitimate loss as a humiliating submission. The second was that, as George N. Sanders had explained, many Americans looked to the "militant Wide Awakes," not "to what Mr. Lincoln may say or do." The Wide Awakes had shaped impressions of Republicans far beyond Lincoln's individual agency. The movement had insisted that the election would be a revolutionary awakening, a turning point after which "none but Republicans will be born in the United States after the year of 1860." Regardless of how the actual numbers broke down, or the fact that 60 percent of voters rejected the Republicans, Americans believed the Wide Awakes' rhetoric. The campaign had drowned out its candidate.[30]

Observers were split on what the election had decided. For some, it meant that the days of huzzahing were done. Overseas correspondents were packing up, glad to have finished covering the headache-inducing race. British readers found it hard to follow the proliferation of "oddly named organizations to which the political contests of the United States give birth." "Happily," a London reporter wrote about the Wide Awakes, "the very motive of the organization disbands it on the day of election," ready to say good-bye to what he believed to be a temporary campaign club.[31]

In New Haven, Charles "Ducksy" O'Neill agreed. Writing to Carrie on the night of the election, he hung up his cape. "Lincoln is elected," Ducksy exalted. "The country is safe." Happy and tired, he wrote that he would discourage any further Wide Awaking or celebratory excursions, unless, of course, they planned to visit Carrie's hometown of New London. The campaign fun was over. "I tell you," he wrote Carrie, "I had some good times, but after all there is something wanting. That is you."[32]

Lincoln himself compared an American election to a painfully infected boil, musing that both "cause a great deal of pain before they come to a head, but after the trouble is over the body is in better health than before." This typically folksy bit of wisdom misjudged a contested election's ability to fester.[33]

Some felt that the election had only begun the real conflict. Down in Charleston on Election Day, Mary Boykin Chesnut sat on a packed train. A man with a telegraph loudly exclaimed, "That settles the hash," and informed the riders of Lincoln's victory. Anxious voices took over the train car. "Everybody was talking at the same time," Chesnut wrote. One voice could be heard over the rest, fretting: "I suppose they will Brown us all." It was a claim disunionists had been pushing all year. Edmund Ruffin, a ghoulish Virginia planter with long, wispy white hair, had been mailing pikes to southern state legislatures, as a reminder of John Brown's raid and "a sample of the favors designed for us by our Northern breathren." When he learned of the Republican victory, Ruffin saw it as a confirmation of his dreams of disunion. "It is good news for me," he wrote in his diary.[34]

The day after that, another irrepressible hothead also saw the election as a starting pistol. James Sanks Brisbin wrote to his father, on November 8, that he was putting the finishing touches on a new speech, and packing his bags.

"I will start for Virginia tomorrow," Brisbin announced.[35]

PART THREE

The Transmogrification of the Wide Awakes

CHAPTER TEN

Permit Me to Suggest a Plan

S OME DAPPER GOON had Frederick Douglass by the hair. Another tried to wrench a wooden chair from his hands. Sleeves rolled up, powerful forearms tensing, Douglass grappled manfully for the chair's wooden spindles. Fellow abolitionists dove in on his side, the ferocious Lewis Hayden likely among them. Hoarse voices in the audience were yelling in Douglass's direction: "*Put him out! Down him! Put a rope round his neck!*"[1]

At Wheeling, rowdies had surrounded the theater. In Baltimore they had swarmed the aisles, but Wide Awakes kept them off the stage. In Boston, weeks after the election that was supposed to have settled everything, there were no Wide Awakes in sight. Lewis Hayden had gathered the American Anti-Slavery Society to mark the one-year anniversary of John Brown's execution and consider "the Great Question of the Age, 'How Can American Slavery Be Abolished?' " But infuriated by the growing national crisis, proslavery "unionists" stormed the hall and seized the stage, proposing to save the nation by mobbing down abolition.[2]

The thugs in Boston were an unusual lot, a noticeably well-dressed crew of Beacon Street aristocrats, Harvard students, and conservative Constitutional Unionists. Their leader, a loudmouthed wool manufacturer named Richard S. Fay, had fifty thousand dollars to his name and a working knowledge of committee rules. Even as his buddies pulled hair, Fay commandeered the podium and introduced a series of antiabolitionist resolutions. "Resolved: That the people of this city have submitted too long in allowing irresponsible persons and political demagogues to hold public meetings," Fay snarled. "They have become a nuisance, which, in self-defense, we are determined shall hence forward be summarily abated." When some abolitionists in the crowd made a good-faith effort to reason with the invaders, arguing that surely "every man is entitled to express his own opinion," mobs hooted, "*No! No!*"[3]

Frederick Douglass was more blunt. One of America's most experienced speakers, used to being heckled and Jim Crowed, he was nonetheless surprised by the vehemence of this mob. He could only lob sentence fragments over the chaos of Boston accents arguing over whether he should be silenced: "This is one of the most impudent, (*order! order!*) barefaced, (*knock him down! sit down!*) outrageous attacks on free speech (*stop him! you shall hear him!*)—I can make myself heard—(*great confusion*) that I have ever witnessed in Boston or else-where." But Douglas understood who had sent these noisy goons. "I know your masters"—he pointed a shaking finger at the rioters—"I have served the same master that you are serving. You are serving the slaveholders."[4]

After three hours of warring speeches, scrums for the podium, and wres-tling over chairs, the police forced everyone out, including the abolitionists who had booked the hall for a private event. As the "unionists" left, they could be heard calling, "Three cheers for South Carolina!"[5]

Catching word of the unfolding mayhem, the German revolutionary refugee Karl Henzein rushed to the scene. He was too late. The Tremont Temple was dark, its massive front doors padlocked, Boston's streets deserted. Henzein began to consider what had gone wrong. Hadn't the Republicans just won an election on this issue? He quickly took two actions. First, he organized an armed bodyguard of Forty-Eighters to defend abolitionists in Boston—fifty Germans with rifles who knew how to use them. Second, he published a scathing assault in his radical weekly *Der Pioneer*, translated and reprinted with gusto in the *Liberator*.[6]

The Republicans had won promising that Lincoln "would restore freedom of speech and of the press." But with secession simmering in the South, and fearful unionists backsliding in the North, Henzein was worried less about "freedom at the South, but of the preservation of freedom at the North!" He wondered if the nation could make it to Lincoln's March 4 inauguration without backing down. And where were the Republicans, that force of ten thousand men who had marched through downtown Boston for free speech a month earlier? "Where," Henzein demanded to know, "are your Wide Awakes, when the defense of free speech against the brutality of slavery is at stake? Where are your Wide Awakes, when the issue is to crush out the mobocracy that is rampant before your eyes? Where are your organizations, your orators, your leaders, your principles, your promises?" Maybe H. Ford Douglas—who was at the Tremont that night—was right. Maybe the whole Republican campaign had been no more than a bunch of White men patting themselves on the back for their cardboard bravery.[7]

"One day," Henzein predicted, the history books would read, "After the election of Lincoln, there were in the North American Republic only two parties,—the traitors and the cowards."[8]

WHERE WERE THE Wide Awakes after the election? It was a question many were debating. For that matter, *what* were the Wide Awakes? Were they a force devoted to defending free speech, "wherever the fight is hottest," an obligation that would last as long as there were rowdies wielding the ideal of union like a cudgel? Or were they a campaign club, organized to "secure a majority of the Electoral votes for Lincoln," whose job was done? Were they temporary or permanent? Political or paramilitary? All along, some farsighted orators had pushed the Wide Awakes to think this through. Outside Elizabeth Cady Stanton's torch-illuminated house, Susan B. Anthony hoped that they would "keep *Wide awake*" once Lincoln had won. Carl Schurz had said the same. Dejected Democrats certainly had asked it too. The campaign had given the movement a clear narrative for itself, but after the election everything splintered. Some thought the movement had accomplished its mission, and should disband; others argued that the North needed Wide Awakes more than ever. They could not go back to sleep now. Especially as war clouds gathered, the militant, organized, devoted Wide Awakes were exactly what the North required.[9]

Many were asking themselves, that dismal early winter of 1860: What happens to rhetorical militarism when real war threatens? But no one was quite sure where politics ended and war began.

Immediately after the November 6 election, most Wide Awakes celebrated as if 1860 had been a normal campaign. Across the North—especially in those corners that had enjoyed the fun, peaceful Wide Awake summer—companies planned grand jollifications. Henry Sperry sent appeals to the "Wide Awakes Ladies of Hartford." He instructed them to throw the Hartford Originals a party. Never the most progressive club, the Originals took an awfully entitled tone, declaring themselves "confident you will gladly cooperate in the celebration." Hartford's Republican ladies should cook "plain substantial food, such as boiled meats, sandwiches, pies, cakes and the like." They could even attend, in a separate gallery. Other companies were a little more considerate. Out in Independence, Iowa, Wide Awakes ladies cooked up a celebratory feast of six hundred chickens, seventy turkeys, seven roast hogs, and a whole cow, not to mention biscuits, pies, puddings, and dozens of cakes dotted with frosted raisins. Wide Awakes, in their capes, served as waiters for the ladies and fifteen hundred other locals.[10]

While Iowans were frosting raisins, the college students at Mount Holyoke Female Seminary decided to celebrate in style. Procuring lanterns and declaring themselves Wide Awakes, they led a celebratory march around campus, 250 young women parading up and down the floors of their school's buildings by torchlight. About 30 of their classmates who favored Douglas scowled from the sidelines. The campus resounded with laughter and shouting that evening, with students drinking lemonade, waving torches, and marching under a banner reading: "PRESIDENT—ABRAHAM LINCOLN. Behind a homely exterior, we recognize inner beauty."[11]

The usual speechifiers were out too, patting the Wide Awakes on the back. Senator Henry Wilson told a Boston crowd (two weeks before the Tremont Temple fight), "We stand with the Slave Power beneath our feet." The Slave Power had infected and destroyed the Whig, American, and Democratic Parties, but with the Wide Awakes' help, Republicans would ensure "that power never rises again; it can never more sway the destinies of the Government of the United States." Charles Sumner told a crowd of Wide Awakes, on the steps of Ralph Waldo Emerson's house in Concord, "Every four years we choose a new President, but it rarely happens that we choose a new government."[12]

That same sense of moment powered ominous rumors. Some were so silly that they could not be taken seriously. Tennessee readers learned that New York City was in the midst of a Wide Awake revolution. New Yorkers were informed that ex-governor Henry Wise of Virginia had seized Washington, and also that he had been murdered. In those early days of secession, the hotheaded and

North-adjacent Governor Wise was made a symbol of all disunionists. George Templeton Strong proposed that he be "publicly spanked on the steps of the Capitol."[13]

Behind all the hysteria lay the darker truth. Within days of Lincoln's election, South Carolina's senators had resigned their posts in Washington. Others were planning a secession convention for December, and free Blacks were ordered to leave the state. The South Carolina legislature had agreed to raise a force of ten thousand fighting men. In Louisiana, politicians set aside five hundred thousand dollars for weapons, while Georgian legislators authorized spending one million dollars for defense. In Washington, James Buchanan was still in office until March 4, and the government had taken no steps against any states (nor did Lincoln propose to). But disunion was clearly under way. "We are generally reconciling ourselves," George Templeton Strong wrote, "to the prospect of secession by South Carolina, Georgia, Alabama, little Florida, and perhaps Mississippi too." The Virginia-born secretary of war John B. Floyd even began to move federal arsenals from northern locations into the South, stockpiling weapons for a future fight against the government he had sworn an oath to defend.[14]

Americans, already obsessed with predicting the future, debated what was coming. A New York–based correspondent for the *Charleston Daily Courier* gleefully informed Carolinians that the crisis had ruined the Republicans' jollifications. Instead, everyone was walking around, searchingly asking each other: "What will the South really do?" John Meredith Read Jr., so self-impressed during the campaign, now wrote to his dad, wondering, "How do you fancy this is to result?" Strong predicted war in one diary entry, a peaceful resolution the next, sighing that "one's opinions change fast in revolutionary times." Traveling through the Upper Midwest, Ulysses S. Grant found that locals expected him to have special insights as a military man. Whenever he stopped at some rural Minnesota tavern, Grant would "sit till a late hour discussing the probabilities of the future." His conclusion: war was coming, probably a ninety-day affair.[15]

As the weather cooled, many noted a sullen tone in the North. The strident African American magazine the *Anglo-African* moaned, "Ominous quiet is this. It is but the breathless stillness preceding a storm big with violence, ruin and outrage, which will perhaps very soon break with terrible fury on their heads."[16]

"Are we in the position," the paper wondered, "to hope for anything but disaster?"[17]

This was the tone that roused unionist mobs in Boston and elsewhere, blaming abolitionists and Republicans for pushing the Deep South too far. Carl Schurz sensed "a compromise epidemic in the country." Frederick Douglass mocked the way "one rebellious frown of South Carolina has muzzled the mouths of all our large cities, and filled the air with whines for compromise." Conciliationists in the North considered what they might do to placate the fire-eaters. Of course, no amount of mobbing would achieve that. A letter writer in Charleston laughed at the Yankee's eleventh-hour hope that things could be made right. "All is too late, too late," he wrote. "The people of the North are beginning to see, when seeing is no good. They *would* not believe the people of the South were in earnest, and now they are astounded to find that they were not half as 'wide awake' as they thought."[18]

Northern Democrats specifically blamed the Wide Awake movement, especially as the panic hurt business. The *Wayne County Herald* sarcastically summarized the mood: "Secession, suspension, banks bursting, money shaving, business stopping, poor men begging, women starving and babies crying. Hoorah for Lincoln. So what if the Union is on the eve of dissolution, states withdrawing, Minute Men arming, and Civil War threatening." Instead, "Bring on the Wide Awakes! Let us go on with the jubilee!" In Pennsylvania, Democrats specifically blamed "the thousands of dollars distributed by Col. McClure." All those Wide Awake rallies, all those lectures. "Is it what you bargained for when you gave a heavy majority for Lincoln?"[19]

The overwhelming sense, even as events hurtled out of control, was that neither Democrats nor Republicans were done with the campaign of 1860. So while secessionists convened, Northerners debated, diarists scribbled, and unionists pulled hair, some of the more aggressive members of the Wide Awakes conceived an urgent new use for their movement. As usual for the Wide Awakes, what happened next was led not by the top men in the Republican Party but by scattered, irrepressible on-the-ground twentysomethings who moved before anyone told them to. Interestingly, the most aggressive Wide Awakes surfaced not among radical abolitionists in stereotypically extreme spots like Boston or Oberlin, but among moderate Pennsylvanians and Missourians on the very edge of the North.

The first question was whether the Wide Awakes should disband at all. Campaign companies were nothing new in American democracy, but they usually died the day after the election. "It is fortunate," explained the *New York Herald*, that most partisan clubs "carry within them the germs of dissolution." Usually made up of distractable youths and self-interested office seekers, they fell apart as soon as the campaign fun was over. And in the weeks after the November 6, the Wide Awakes seemed to be following this course. But then, in an unprecedented step—thrilling to some, galling to others—the clubs kept meeting. And in typical Wide Awake fashion, they sustained a noisy conversation in the nation's newspapers about whether they should continue to exist, given the crisis.[20]

On November 16 Charles Sumner stepped out of the house where he was staying in Providence, Rhode Island, to find a huge gathering of uniformed Wide Awakes. He was surprised, but Sumner always half expected to be serenaded by adoring fans. "I had supposed that with our great triumph," he told the clubs, "you would naturally retire to your homes, like soldiers when peace has come." But here they were. Sumner—whose brutal beating in the Senate chamber had made him the very avatar of aggrieved Republicans' war on Slave Power suppression—thanked the Providence Wide Awakes for proving "that here at the North are men ready, if the exigency requires, to leap forward in defense of Northern rights." Other Wide Awake clubs actually formed after the election, in key spots like Georgetown, on the fringes of Washington, D.C. The Union Wide Awakes of New York City ordered new uniforms. A New York–based correspondent warned Charleston readers: "As you are, perhaps, aware, the Wide Awake organization is *not* to be discontinued. . . . What the Wide Awakes will do is a vexed question."[21]

Just then, James Sanks Brisbin popped up in Virginia. Brisbin simply could not stay out of trouble that autumn—his brand of half-aggressive, half-naive speechifying typified the Wide Awakes' posture in the crisis. In the wake of Lincoln's election, Brisbin immediately decided to head south again. He wrote his father that he was "curious to learn how far the Virginians might be trusted." Hoping to make the case for free speech and "hit the dogma of State Rights a lick," he left Pennsylvania with no Wide Awake escort, clutching a draft of a new speech titled "The State of the Nation."[22]

But he was back within a week, with a harrowing story. All the way south he had daydreamed about "how glad the people would be to hear from one of the dominant party and learn how mild and loving we meant to be in the administration of the government toward our Southern brethren." This from a newspaperman, who nonetheless sounds cartoonishly unaware of the tensions in the nation as he whistled his way into a restive South. "Imagine then my surprise," Brisbin wrote his father, when in every central Virginia town where he tried to speak, he was met with a stream of " 'You get out of this' and 'We want none of your lip' or 'Damn you and your President.' " Men threatened to tar and feather him. Lawyers sought warrants for his arrest as an incendiary. Virginians, it seemed to this meddlesome Pennsylvanian, "are mad not in the everyday expression of that term but raving stark mad." Catching word of his agitations, Virginia's moderate governor John Letcher, who opposed disunion, took action. Brisbin received an official letter from Letcher while near Warrenton, accusing him of "inciting the people of Virginia and stirring up discord in the state." This wounded Brisbin, who felt that "it was the people who were inciting me and stirring up discord in my breast."[23]

The governor, however, "had troops and I had none."[24]

Or did he? Instead of leaving the state, Brisbin headed over the mountains to Wheeling, connecting with Wide Awakes there who had saved him a few weeks before. When he told the Wheeling companies about his expulsion, Wide Awake "General" Jacob Hornbrook allegedly told Brisbin that his two hundred men would protect him, even from the governor. Hornbrook promised (or so Brisbin claimed) that the Wheeling Wide Awakes were willing to "maintain free speech" by marching under Brisbin's command "against the enemies of the Union." Brisbin declined, fleeing Virginia for the second time in three weeks. But he wasn't done. When he got back to the *Centre Democrat*'s offices, Brisbin wrote a long letter to Governor Letcher. The guy just couldn't help himself. His note to Letcher included a long lecture on the evils of disunion, and informed the governor that "two hundred of your Virginians loyal men have tendered me their command in the event of disunion."[25]

It was not exactly a threat—Brisbin seemed to think his Wide Awake army could help Letcher—but the governor read it as one. Letcher shot back an immediate response. In the midst of this "fear ful and alarming" crisis, the governor wrote, "you send me a letter" full of insults to the South. Letcher claimed that if Pennsylvania wanted to defuse tensions, it should enforce the Fugitive Slave Law. Clearly enraged, the governor concluded: "You say that two hundred Virginians have agreed to place themselves under your command in the event of disunion. . . . Sir you have no right to come into Virginia to raise troops for any purpose what ever." Doing so, he underlined, "will be taken at your peril." If Brisbin was so intent on marching Wide Awakes against a southern state, "raise your troops at home and present them to the sons of the South 'as food for gunpowder.' We have other and better uses for our Virginians."[26]

Before sending this to Brisbin, Governor Letcher gave a copy to the *Richmond Enquirer*, well aware of how it would spread. It was just the kind of extreme news the press loved, reported in dozens of articles from as far away as Minnesota and Louisiana. Most chuckled at Brisbin, dismissing him as a troublemaker whose goal was "being written down as an ass." Brisbin's local Democratic rival in Bellefonte, W. C. MacMannis, published a letter joking that he would raise *one thousand men* in Pennsylvania to put down Brisbin's two hundred Wide Awakes. The whole affair elicited the kind of laughter that only concealed fear can bring out. Even the usually pro–Wide Awake *Wheeling Intelligencer* weighed in, attacking Brisbin as "the same chap who spoke at Washington Hall on the eve of the Presidential election, and is, for his years, about as big a humbug as exists out of the United States Congress." Instead of defending the Pennsylvanian, Wheeling's Republican paper—perhaps eager to distance themselves from his belligerence—begged Governor Letcher to "take no more notice of the stuff such fellows as Brisbin may write to you; for if you do you will soon be no better than Wise."[27]

All this made Brisbin madder. He scribbled another letter to Letcher, also widely published. "Recently when I went to your state I was rudely treated," he sputtered. "I know you are surrounded by flatterers and disunionists and no citizen of the north is allowed now to speak in your state." But Brisbin demanded to be taken seriously. First, in response to Letcher's talk about enforcing the Fugitive Slave Act, Brisbin shot back, "No Governor we cannot make Slave Catchers of our Pennsylvanians even to please the south and if the Union depends upon that then it must go."[28]

Then he turned to the idea of a coming civil war, for which he was being mocked. "Your letter convinces me that there is indeed an irrepressible conflict between slavery and freedom." Maybe it was time, Brisbin prophesied, "to fight-it-out and let the stronger party prevail." This was a tragedy; "poor old Virginia" would bear the brunt, "her fair fields being made the scene of contending armies her cities and towns laid in ashes and her soil drenched with her best blood." Brisbin was trying to help avert that, and he was furious at being mocked in the press and bullied by the governor.[29] "You need not have threatened me Governor with what you would do if I came into the South," Brisbin warned. If he ever came back, "it will be at the head of northern troops and in that event I advise you to keep out of the way."[30]

James Sanks Brisbin was a troublemaker, profoundly naive, and perhaps a genuine fool, but in others ways he was prescient. Leading a force of Wide Awakes as foot soldiers against secession was not nearly as absurd as it sounded to some in the last few days of November 1860.

Then came the Tremont Temple debacle on December 3, reported in nearly every northern state. Republicans again saw themselves not as jolly victors but as embattled victims of a widening conspiracy—disunionists to their South, and mobbers in their midst. And South Carolina's secession convention was due to meet on December 10. Wide Awakes nationwide were discussing their options. On December 6, a Chicago company on the North Side announced that they would reorganize "on a permanent political basis." New York's clubs declared the same thing, using the same language of permanence. Simeon Draper—the head of the New York State Republican committee who had tele-graphed Lincoln the news that he had won New York, and had been at 722 Broadway during the New York hotel brawl—publicly asked the Wide Awakes to continue meeting. He recommended that they all host lectures by Professor Amasa McCoy, who was traveling the state giving "a plea" to Wide Awake companies to become permanent clubs. On December 8 a Washington paper reported that "efforts are being made" nationwide to make the Wide Awakes "a permanent political body."[31]

The idea of permanent Wide Awake companies drove Democrats mad. Many believed that the movement had already ruined the 1860 campaign, undermined the election, and pushed Southerners to threaten disunion. Their only consolation was that the election was over. And now companies were talking about continuing *forever*? A Missouri paper half joked, half whined, "We never heard that the committee was to remain in power until the end of the world." Responding to the announcements of new meetings in Buffalo, Democrats there complained that the Republicans were "reviving obnoxious associations" at a time when "they certainly can do no good." Democrats picked up on the sense that no one in the movement really knew what the Wide Awakes would be used for. Celebrants? Bodyguards? Invaders? The movement was taking on "proportions which its progenitors never deemed it would assume," a writer to the *New York Herald* warned.[32]

Privately, some Wide Awakes saw a new purpose for what had been campaign clubs. President-elect Lincoln started getting letters in December proposing various schemes. One came from Major David Hunter, a veteran with strong antislavery views stationed at Fort Leavenworth, Kansas. He warned Lincoln that the regular army could not be trusted against a secessionist conspiracy. "Would it not be well," Hunter wrote, "to have a hundred thousand Wide Awakes, wend their way quietly to Washington?" They could bring their capes and caps, and "by a coup-de-main we could arm them in Washington."[33]

A few days later another note appeared, this one from George P. Bissell, the same white-hatted marshal who had noticed the Talcott boys during that first Wide Awake parade for Cassius Clay back in February. He was once again waving the Wide Awakes to the front. Bissell warned the president-elect that he was receiving letters from Republicans in Washington "which give a very dark picture," and was writing "to offer you my services." "If you say the word," Bissell promised Lincoln, "I will be there with from twenty to one thousand men, or one hundred, (any reasonable number) organized & armed." Lincoln would not even have to publicly admit this plan; Bissell just needed "a hint" to dispatch "a true delegation of Hartford Wide Awakes, not in uniform but ready for duty."[34]

Throughout the campaign, Wide Awakes had insisted that they were merely a political organization, with "no warlike intention whatever." Now, with war in the air, many were looking to the clubs as a readymade force. Seward had allegedly speculated, on the stump in La Crosse, that the companies "would be found mighty convenient" in the event of a Slave Power revolution. If southern Minutemen were spotted heading to Washington, a Utah journalist proposed, a northern counterforce could probably be built "on the foundation already laid by the wide-awakes."[35]

But veterans with actual military experience rolled their eyes as politicos treated campaign clubs like tin soldiers. The deluded David Hunter might imagine a hundred thousand Wide Awakes secretly wending their way to Washington, but when had the Wide Awakes ever gone anywhere quietly? Who would keep them in ham sandwiches along the way? William Tecumseh Sherman was a bit more realistic. It was feeling more and more as if "a long, confused and disorganized Civil War" was coming, and "we shall see," he wondered, "whether the Wide-awakes will fight as well as carry cheap lamps." "Zig-zagging through the streets" was not the same as facing combat. It took more than young men in uniforms to assemble an army.[36]

Yet the men who spent the campaign waving cheap lamps were taking concrete steps. Each public escalation of the conflict—Brisbin's public feuds, the Tremont Temple fight, the secretary of war's traitorous handling of Federal arsenals, the very real disunion movement burbling up in South Carolina—pushed Wide Awakes to think of new possibilities for their club. And again, mild old Pennsylvania was at the fore. All of Pittsburgh's fifteen Wide Awake clubs gathered for a mass meeting in Witkins Hall. There they took an unusual step—disbanding as a partisan force and immediately reforming as a militia under Pennsylvania law. General James S. Negley—the same mustachioed, squinting veteran whose Wide Awakes saved James Sanks Brisbin at Wheeling—would lead them. And, interestingly, the Pittsburgh Wide Awake militia promised to "drop all political significance."[37]

It was a bold step. All through 1860, the Wide Awakes had insisted that they were political but not military. Now, suddenly, they were military but not political. Of course, essentially every man in those fifteen Pittsburgh companies had just campaigned for Lincoln's election. And Pennsylvania already had plenty of militias—what was the added benefit of turning Wide Awakes into another, if not the knowledge that their companies contained irrepressible Republicans who were eager for a fight? Dropping "political significance" was harder than it sounded.

Picking up on the newly militant tone coming from his old friend General Negley, James Sanks Brisbin weighed in, again, printing frothing pleas to mobilize. "Call meetings at once; organize yourselves into military companies . . . these are dark hours and we must prepare for the worst" his *Centre Democrat* trumpeted. To those companies that had already disbanded, Brisbin commanded that it was time to "hunt up your lamps boys." Quickly moving past the torchlit rhetoric of the campaign, the *Democrat* insisted that "if the worst comes to worst throw them away and take muskets in your hands." Soon it would be time to make "the earth shake to the tread of *three millions* of armed Wide-Awakes." Well versed in the movement's code words, Brisbin's paper called on the movement to "Do your duty."[38]

If any man was ready—even eager—to do his duty in December 1860, it was Carl Schurz. He had seen the 1848 revolutions. He had seen the 1860 Wide Awakes. He had even, some believed, seen the future. And he had never stopped campaigning. Carl and Margarethe's finances were a mess, and he was forced to travel the country giving for-profit talks almost immediately after the 1860 election. As he traveled, people kept asking Schurz what was coming. It happened so often that one sarcastic Democrat in Milwaukee joked: "In ancient times people consulted oracles in times of trouble." Now Wide Awakes, facing disunion, shouted, "Let Carl Schurz be sent for" instead.[39]

Schurz worked across November and December to keep Republicans from backsliding. He immediately felt the chill as Northerners debated "what might be done to avert the awful calamity." Even Republican politicians like William Seward or Cassius Clay were considering compromises that might keep the South in the Union. This, Schurz thundered, would be fatal to American democracy. They must not turn election results into "a matter of bargain and compromise between the majority and the minority." He kept in regular touch with Wide Awakes as he traveled and speechified. And as December dawned, South Carolina debated, and unionists attacked abolitionists, Schurz felt northern spines stiffening again. The ugliness at the Tremont Temple, in particular, "served to bring on a reaction," pushing many in the North to consider whether they wanted to fall back under the sway of the "the slave-drivers whip."[40]

Soon Schurz was writing to powerful Republicans, hatching plans. To the New York governor Edwin Morgan he advised that the state should send its militias to Washington for the inauguration, suggesting that "it is absolutely necessary that we should have a sufficient force of well armed militia—and wide awake companies on the ground." Morgan had marched at the head of Wide Awake processions—what did he think of the idea of turning them into fighters? Then Schurz wrote to Lincoln himself, whom he knew and deeply admired. "I have seen something of revolutionary movements," he wrote the president-elect. "Permit me to suggest a plan."[41]

Schurz's plan, it must be noted, was terrible. He suggested massing northern state militias on the borders of Maryland, Virginia, and Kentucky—unseceded states in good standing, home to furious debates over what to do in the event of the Deep South's disunion. "A thing like this," he believed, "would completely overawe the border-states," and "have a wonderfully soothing effect upon the bellicose humor of the border-state-fire eaters." It's striking that Schurz could use "overawe" and "soothing" in the same sentence, equivalent to James Sanks Brisbin's delusion that the people of Virginia would be "glad" to hear from the "mild and loving" Republicans to their north. Both men demonstrated that same combination of foresight and blindness characteristic of Wide Awake favorites.[42]

In fact, Schurz's plot would come across as exactly the coercion Southerners feared, assisting the very fire-eaters he claimed to oppose. Lincoln knew better. He based his strategy on keeping the border states in the Union at all costs, reputedly saying "I hope to have God on my side, but I must have Kentucky."

But Schurz showed more clarity when it came to the Wide Awakes themselves. He wrote to Lincoln about the whispering campaign among their friends, who often "speak of the Wide-Awakes going down to Washington." Schurz knew the Wide Awakes as well as anyone, and he was certain that the companies, without weapons and training, "are worth nothing." Schurz, like Sherman, saw the clear distinction between a political club and a military force.[43]

Christmas Eve found Schurz alone in a Boston hotel, missing his wife and musing, as usual, about the future. He was lonesome, he was worried, but he was also energized. Northerners were finally debating standing up for themselves, challenging the old southern assumption that Yankees "have no desire to fight." At their head was a president-elect who "stands like a stone wall." "It would not surprise me," Schurz wrote of Lincoln, "if his administration were to determine the future development of the Republic."[44]

Schurz's letters to his Margarethe exude a manic energy, an almost messianic sense that a long-predicted moment was finally here. "I often regret," he wrote, that he was too young to take the lead in the revolutions in 1848. But his new nation seemed to be waking up to the Revolution of 1861, and he was finally situated to play a key role. Again and again, Schurz repeated, "We are living at a great time."[45]

NO ONE IN the North knew what to do with the Wide Awakes, but some in the South saw their obvious utility.

Most Southerners, in November 1860, had no immediate plans to leave the United States. The great scholar of disunion, William W. Freehling, has estimated that upward of 70 percent of all Southerners were not ready to secede and preferred to wait and see what happened next. The *New Orleans Bee* issued a famous one-word bit of advice—"Wait"—in response to Lincoln's election. Even die-hard defenders of slavery did not all favor secession. After all, abolitionists like Frederick Douglass and Elizur Wright believed that disunion "would be highly beneficial to the cause of liberty," disentangling the Slave Power from the U.S. government, making fleeing slavery easier, and returning fugitives harder. And on a more basic level, most White Southerners *liked* the United States and held strong bonds of affection and memory. There's a reason so many politicians cried when they left Congress for the last time. In November 1860, secession was not the irrepressible course.[46]

But an agitated minority believed that, after decades of threats, this was their moment. Most radical disunionists hailed from a tiny class of Deep South aristocrats, made rich from stolen labor growing cotton, rice, and sugar. They lived in elite White islands amid huge numbers of enslaved people, sometimes upward of 80 percent of the local population. But this minority of a minority had succeeded before. They had broken the Democratic Party back in May, not by proposing a more popular candidate than Stephen A. Douglas but by flatly refusing the will of the majority. The same playbook could work here too.

The Wide Awakes could be a useful crowbar to pry their states from the Union. Though few southern Whites were eager to secede, most fumed when they thought of the campaign just past. Many hated the Wide Awakes and the Republican leadership that encouraged the movement. Secessionists would have to play on emotions stirred up by the campaign and keep the Wide Awakes in the public's mind. The notion of permanent clubs served that purpose. But they had to hurry. William Tecumseh Sherman observed, just before leaving Louisiana himself, that "there is an evident purpose, a dark design, not to allow time for thought and reflections. These southern leaders understand the character of their people and want action before the spirit subsides."[47]

Many people advocating secession never mentioned the Wide Awakes. But a large and prominent number did, invoking the movement as a kind of shorthand, a useful gesture toward everything that was driving them out of the United States. The words instantly conjured images of aggressive, militaristic, permanent, partisan midnight militias. The clubs provided a far more potent symbol than the moderate and mostly quiet president-elect Lincoln. In the months after the election, the term *Wide Awakes* appeared nearly as often in southern newspapers as in actual reports of the clubs' activities in the northern press. Often it was used as an epithet for all Northerners, evaporating from a solid organization into a toxic miasma looming over the whole North. And because the clubs were so visually striking and distinctive, they were an especially easy threat to conjure. Everything that made the Wide Awakes an iconic campaign force also made them an effective bogeyman.

As soon as news of the election spread, disunionists mobilized to make their case. Again and again, they worked to remind audiences of the Wide Awakes. By November 14 the *Alabama State Sentinel* warned about "thousands of well trained 'Wide Awakes,' well armed with Sharps rifles, encouraged by Federal power, and supported by Federal money," on a mission to "deprive us of our property." Just as Charles Sumner was telling Wide Awakes in Rhode Island to be ready to "leap forward in defense of Northern rights," Senator Laurence Keitt said in South Carolina, specifically referencing Sumner and the Wide Awakes, that "there were Southern cowhides enough" for them all. But stepping beyond bluster, Keitt told crowds that it was time to "take your destinies in your own hands and shatter this accursed union."[48]

To get over Southerners' reluctance to secede immediately, many disunionists argued that the choice had already been made. Secession was inevitable—"a fetus in the womb of Time," as a New Orleans paper called it. They argued that the North had broken the Union, first by passing "personal liberty laws" against the Fugitive Slave Act, then by organizing "Modern Huns"—the Wide Awakes—to invade the South. Georgia's legislature introduced language blaming "many thousand northern men, organized under the name of 'Wide Awakes' " for destroying any obligation Southerners should feel toward "a Northern sectional majority." In Virginia, George Mason's radical grandson James Murray Mason made this case. The shared ideal of Union that his founding ancestor helped create no longer linked the states; that compact had been severed by Lincoln, his Republican allies, and "the rabble that fill the ranks of the Wide Awakes organization." Mason's claim was printed in the same issue of the *Richmond Enquirer* that spread news of James Sanks Brisbin's invasion plans.[49]

The claim that Republicans had already broken the Union of states, and were preparing for worse, made it into the U.S. Senate by December. There, the combative Texas senator Louis Wigfall invoked the Wide Awakes too. Wigfall, a well-born South Carolinian, had cut a swath across the South, drinking and fighting. With his full, dark beard, leering eyebrows, and aggressive politics, Wigfall was like a black-hatted villain from an old Western. In a senatorial harangue, he informed the Republican side of the chamber that for Texas to stay in the Union, the North "must abolish abolition societies, stop abolition newspapers, and stop the clamor now raging in their midst." Amid growing laughter from the other side of the aisle, the red-faced Wigfall blamed the North for the fires in Texas that summer, poisoning wells with strychnine, and organizing "a Praetorian guard" of Wide Awakes who "like that of Rome in its decline might one day put up the Empire at auction." Decrying "Praetorian guards" and "Modern Huns," disunionists were clearly drawing from a classical grab bag of decline-and-fall rhetoric. Those "politico-Military, John Brown Wide-awake Praetorians," Wigfall cursed, were not even disbanding. "The Senator from New York had bidden to maintain their organization after the election, to insure the fruits of their victory." Wigfall pointed at William H. Seward, accusing him of preparing half a million "Wide-awake Praetorians" to "sweep the country in which I live with fire and sword."[50]

Seward objected that he had never recommended the Wide Awakes continue after the election. But it had been widely reported that he had said just that, in a La Crosse, Wisconsin, speech in September. He may not have—newspapers were often wrong—but it seems equally likely that he did, caught up in his own heated campaign oratory. Either way, Wigfall harrumphed, no one doubted that "the Wide Awakes still continued their organization in menace to the South."[51]

The next day, December 13, 1860, seven southern senators and twenty-three congressmen publicly called for the secession of South Carolina. And four days later the secession convention met in the Palmetto State. Disunion was likely— South Carolinians had already adjourned their federal courts and were harassing federal postmasters—but now it was time to actually vote. The men selected to do that voting could not have been less representative. Of the 169 men present, 90 percent were slave owners, and 41 percent enslaved more than fifty people, making them wildly, disproportionately wealthy. After voting unanimously to secede from the Union, they drafted a Secession Ordinance that drew heavily from the Declaration of Independence, minus its references to human equality or the consent of the governed.[52]

Even among the unanimous secessionists in South Carolina's convention, the Wide Awakes served as a rhetorical tool. A debate emerged, deep in the night of December 20, as to whether to secede right away, or wait until the next morning. Edward McCrady, a former U.S. attorney turned lukewarm secessionist, warned his fellows, "I think we are acting in too much haste." It would be wiser, strategically, to ratify "in broad daylight, under the blue sky, where all our fellow-citizens could witness it." Moving in the middle of the night seemed conspiratorial. "We do not wish to march," McCrady argued, "as the Wide Awakes of the North, by torchlight." Though he was mostly using the Wide Awakes as a device to make an unrelated point, it is telling that the movement served as a cautionary example of the political system South Carolina was leaving behind.[53]

South Carolina opened the door, and over the next month more states took what one Mississippian schoolteacher called "a leap in the dark, flying from ills which perhaps we have—to more dreadful ones we know not of." There was no consensus, though. Generally, elite White Lower South Democrats living in areas with large populations of enslaved people were most eager to secede. Poorer upland populations with few enslaved people, former Whigs and Know Nothings, older people, and those in the Upper South held back. Some of them invoked the Wide Awakes as a reason *not* to leave. Former Whig Ben Hill of Georgia made this case in Georgia's notorious secession debates. Hill argued that Georgia should stay in the Union, rely on the checks and balances in the Constitution, and watch what Lincoln actually did in office. Hecklers interrupted his earnest attempt, shouting "How long will you wait?" to which Hill reasonably suggested: "Until the experiment is tried." This was the "spirit subsiding" that Sherman foresaw as the enemy of secession. Another heckler shouted, "The 'Wide Awakes' will be there." "Very well," Hill shrugged, "if we are afraid of the 'Wide Awakes' we had better surrender without further debate. The 'Wide Awakes' will be there if we secede, and if they are to be dreaded, our only remedy is to *hide*. No, my friends, we are not afraid of anybody."[54]

Hill's arguments aside, the momentum for a fast secession gripped many. Those who kept the animosities of the 1860 campaign in the public mind were most successful. Mississippi followed South Carolina out of the Union on January 9 (a Jackson newspaper warning "Wide-Awake Invasion Anticipated" that very morning). Florida seceded on January 10, Alabama on the eleventh,

Georgia on the nineteenth, Louisiana on the twenty-sixth, and Texas on February 1. These states immediately began preparations for some kind of fight. John Dimitry—who had marched in a uniformed Southern Democratic "offset" to the Wide Awakes—noted that just-seceded New Orleans began to feel like "a garrison city" almost overnight. "No words were quite so commonly heard on the streets as 'drilling,' 'organizing,' 'election of officers,' the 'convention,' 'secession!' "[55]

The case was harder to make in the Upper South, but those who tried to drive secession also made flagrant use of the Wide Awake threat, waving the black cape. As predicted, the frenzied ex-governor Henry A. Wise led the way. When Virginia convened a long-running secession convention in February, Wise cited entirely imaginary Wide Awake plots. He repeatedly claimed that a force of Wide Awake marines was on its way to seize Norfolk Navy Yard, with plans to ransack tidewater Virginia. Others joined in. One of the secession commissioners, sent from recently seceded Georgia to convince Virginia to join them, gave a frothing speech. Henry L. Benning made an unsubtle case that the North was plotting an "abolition war" in which "we will be completely exterminated." The Republicans' plot was to inspire a bloody slave revolt, then send in Wide Awakes "in thousands, and we will be overpowered and our men will be compelled to wander like vagabonds all over the earth; and as for our women, the horrors of their state we cannot contemplate in imagination."

It all came back to the threat of majority rule, Benning argued, an evil he invoked fifteen times in his speech. There was already "a permanent majority" of Wide Awake Republicans in the North, and they planned to establish a ruling Black majority in the South. Only secession could prevent "the fate which Abolition will bring upon the white race."[56]

Such lurid predictions failed to scare the Upper South into immediate disunion: secession votes failed in Virginia, North Carolina, Arkansas, and Missouri. Confirming Sherman's hunch, Virginia's extremely drawn-out debates yielded a (temporary) decision to stay in the Union, whereas the Deep South's midnight conventions won secession right away. But nothing could stop Henry A. Wise from ranting that the choice was between disunion or being "cut to pieces by the Wide Awakes."[57]

Probably no one seceded *because of* the Wide Awakes alone. The movement was not the core of the issue, but it was a succinct embodiment of everything secessionists wanted to leave. Across the South, the Wide Awakes proved to be a powerful symbol, even at a time when the North could not agree whether the movement should still exist at all. But belligerents on both sides saw the same use of the Wide Awake movement, invoked as a "permanent political" presence. In the months after the November election, agitators chose to prolong the campaign. Southern secessionists sought to keep fears of the clubs alive, while some Northerners looked to their campaign companies as a makeshift fighting force. By keeping the fierce momentum of a political campaign going, well after its official purpose of influencing voters passed, agitators on both sides smashed through the normal boundaries of political practice. The Wide Awakes had already tested the hazy distinction between political and military metaphors; now they questioned the crucial line between cause and effect, campaign and administration.[58]

Democracy had been invented to mitigate the conflict at the heart of public life. Now it was becoming an avenue for sustaining electoral conflict indefinitely. Maybe there really was a plan, as Missouri Democrats complained, to keep the Wide Awakes going "until the end of the world."[59]

CHAPTER ELEVEN

Our Most Determined and Reckless Followers

Rumor had it that Lum Cooper was flying South Carolina's secessionist flag outside his home on the edge of Capitol Hill. He said it was his neighbor's. Papers reported that he was stockpiling weapons, but he said those were his neighbor's too. He had been quoted predicting that God would not let Lincoln "survive his victory more than three months." Coworkers even heard him say he would shoot the president-elect himself, "if nobody else would do it." But old Lum denied this, threatening that no man who spread this falsehood "would dare to face him."[1]

A few things were more certain. Lum—short for Columbus—was a Washington Democrat, small and talkative and belligerent, a man whose boss described him as having "a great deal to say, and very little judgement." Columbus was a known collector of cushy government jobs, simultaneously earning thousands as a district canal commissioner, a mayoral employee, and a Capitol lamplighter. That last gig mixed him in with a group of questionable Washington roughnecks, just hired as extra security to protect the U.S. Capitol.[2]

One other thing was certain: Columbus Cooper was a member of the shadowy National Volunteers Democratic militia. Not to worry, his employer at the Capitol assured the congressional committee investigating "Alleged Hostile Organization Against the Government Within the District of Columbia." The National Volunteers were no threat. They were merely meeting, training, and possibly arming, in Washington and Baltimore, "pretty much because of the Wide-Awake movement." Lum told his boss that he trained with the National Volunteers, to be prepared in case the Wide Awakes came down to Lincoln's inauguration "to cut up any shines."[3]

Lum Cooper wasn't the only shady character entrusted with the security of the capital. Vague rumors were flying in Washington as the nation tumbled toward Lincoln's March 4 inauguration. Washington's authorities seemed woefully—perhaps willfully—unprepared. The entire city employed one hundred police officers; the huge Capitol complex had just twenty-nine more. When congressmen asked the Democratic mayor James G. Berrit about his intelligence sources on coming plots, he shrugged that he had "looked into the newspapers." The commissioner in charge of the Capitol police told the committee that he did not "apprehend the least danger at all," though his statements about his force were disconcerting. "They are all men of good character," he swore, ". . . except one man." The exception was a known Democratic gang member, who was "always a terrible fellow for fighting." Yet that "terrible fellow" had promised to "behave himself." When congressmen asked about another troublesome officer, the commissioner blurted, "Was there anything about him?" as if learning of another fire to put out. And the National Volunteers' threats to fight for secession, if Maryland and Virginia left the Union, he dismissed with a carefree "It did not make the slightest impression whatever upon my mind."[4]

While Washington's Democratic leadership may have been drowsy, the National Volunteers were wide awake. There were, reportedly, hundreds of Volunteers in Washington and thousands in Baltimore. Most National Volunteers came from the southern and northern Democratic Party's campaign clubs, and before that the street gangs that had spent the 1850s fighting Know Nothings. A reporter who snuck into one of their midnight meetings found that "the principal business in hand when we entered was cussing." Yet he also noted (sounding like James Brisbin's description of Virginians as "stark raving mad") that "the 'Volunteers' were undoubtedly mad—crazy mad—darned mad." Ever since Lincoln's election, a National Volunteer told the congressional committee, the chief topic of conversation was how "the inauguration of Mr. Lincoln could be defeated." Dr. Cornelius Boyle, a well-connected Washington physician and the National Volunteers' senior officer, proudly read aloud the group's recent resolutions during the congressional inquiry. Dr. Boyle produced a paper and recited the club's promise to "stand by and defend the south" in the event of coercion. If Maryland and Virginia chose to secede, Dr. Boyle promised, "we will act."[5]

Nearly all the National Volunteers who testified mentioned the Wide Awakes. Dr. Boyle's resolution began with a preamble warning that any attempts to make the capital safer were really a Republican plot "to place arms, at the public expense, in the hands of Wide-awakes of this city." "These sympathizers with John Brown," Dr. Boyle had written, would then "make similar assaults upon life and property." National Volunteers agreed that their chief purpose was fighting "black republican Wide-awake mobs" if they came south to inaugurate Lincoln. A more temperate Baltimore Volunteer proposed that "Mr. Lincoln will not be interrupted as a citizen alone, but with an armed body of men he would be." This followed the same circular logic as some Southerners' threats to secede so that the Wide Awakes could not coerce them not to secede. Here men were plotting violence against the president-elect, yet if he arrived with protection, *that* would be cause for violence.[6]

Toward the end of the inquiry, the exasperated Massachusetts Republican representative Henry L. Dawes (who had marched with the Williams College Wide Awakes) had had enough. To Dawes, it was clear that the National Volunteers were operating "under the guise of an organization to prevent the Wide-awakes coming here," but really using these fears as "a cloak" to plot an assault on the capital or Baltimore's Fort McHenry.[7]

And yet the Wide Awakes may have offered that cloak to their rivals. Again and again, the committee asked the same question. As they put it to Dr. Boyle: Were the National Volunteers "a political or military company?" He said they were "military," but without weapons. The mayor said they were political, with no military intent. One former National Volunteer, J. Tyler Powell, told Congress that the groups started as a political organization among peaceable Democrats, but "merged into a military association." Powell noisily left the club, affirming in the papers that "*political military organizations* are antagonistic to the true principles of a republican government." It was the Wide Awakes, the previous February, who had opened this whole question of the shady boundaries between the two.[8]

So much had changed since that February. It seemed like every dangerous tendency from back then had accelerated, and the dreary Washington winter of 1861 burned hot under its artificial calm. Fanny Seward's brother Fred wrote to her that the capital felt "ludicrously intense." Locals scrutinized every new face arriving in the small city. Shady forces were conspiring, and the authorities were doing nothing. In the White House, the outgoing James Buchanan believed the federal government was helpless to stop secession. It was only the resignation of his most traitorous cabinet members, like John B. Floyd, that allowed a few decent ministers to slip into key positions. Northerners excoriated him. George Templeton Strong considered Buchanan worse than the secessionists, because he seemed to be aiding disunion without any purpose, "by mere want of moral force." A Wide Awake schoolgirl called the president an "imbecile Grandpapa" in her letters.[9]

Washington is a city built on compromises. Compromise between North and South, between freedom and slavery, between political parties, between glittering hotels and seedy boardinghouses. Even its streets are a compromise, a numbered and lettered grid overlaid with broad state avenues at random angles, and an entire dimension of back alleys behind everything. Compromise had been the engine of government for fifty years. But each compromise delayed a conflict (and favored unfreedom). Now, in the winter of 1861, what had once been handled with discrete compromise was considered a zero-sum showdown. Someone would win D.C.; someone would lose it. But would the victors come marching down its avenues, or sneaking through its alleyways?

One day in January, a man sauntered into the Senate's refreshment room wearing a black Wide Awake cape. Three Marylanders angrily confronted him, and as senators looked on over their coffee cups, the Wide Awake drew a revolver from under his cape and threatened to blow "out the brains of any one assaulting him." Politicians hurried to resolve this standoff—the soon-to-secede Virginian R. M. T. Hunter somehow calmed everyone—but many were shaken. It was one thing for senators to bully each other, part of the strange code of the Capitol. It was worse when a *representative* came into the senate and caned Charles Sumner, presumptuous as well as violent. But now men off the street, Wide Awakes no less, were strolling into the Capitol and waving pistols? A newspaper wondered "how many such scenes will occur between now and the 4th of March." How many would end peacefully?[10]

Even more men concealed pistols than usual. Colt's new 1860 army revolvers were selling briskly. What else was concealed, rumored, or plotted? The Wide Awake campaign of 1860 had turned on a debate over public politics, but now the question inverted from open political speech to private military preparation.[11]

Into this environment of danger and intrigue strolled the 1860 campaign's most hapless speechifier, that "poor, unsophisticated Vermonter," Lucius E. Chittenden. After his capture by Philadelphia politicians, and his forced march across Pennsylvania orating to Wide Awake clubs, the scion returned to Chittenden county to wait for his reward. He was certain that his campaign service merited a choice job in the new administration. Maybe customs collector at some port, for two thousand dollars a year? But "October, November, December passed" with no word from Mr. Lincoln. Finally, late on February 2, Chittenden received a hurried telegraph from Vermont's governor. He was "to lay aside all business" and get on the next train to Washington. Someone would explain his mission on the way. Captured again, Chittenden climbed aboard another mystery train.[12]

On the southbound ride, Chittenden learned that he had been selected to help represent Vermont in a hastily assembled Peace Conference, called by James Brisbin's adversary, the Virginia governor John Letcher. It did not pay two thousand dollars a year, but perhaps it was a sign of trust. Perhaps select leaders, assembled outside of a violent Congress and a toxic campaign system, might calm the republic. Perhaps Chittenden's chest swelled a little from the appointment, worthy of the squire of Chittenden County. He arrived in Washington, washed his face at the Willard Hotel, and took a carriage up to the Capitol to meet Vermont's long-serving Senator Solomon Foot to discuss his crucial new position.[13]

"It is a fraud, a trick, a deception, a device of traitors and conspirators to cheat the North and to gain time to ripen their conspiracy," a visibly enraged Senator Foot practically shouted into Chittenden's face. The Peace Conference would fail, only distracting a guileless North while secessionists prepared for war. "At home they do not believe we are living here in a nest of traitors," Foot sputtered, his eyes bulging. Chittenden's campaigning had earned him the worst job in America.[14]

"You do not mean, senator, that we are on the eve of rebellion—that there is danger?" asked another delegate. *Of course* there was danger, Foot exploded.

Forces were preparing to attack the Capitol, to assassinate Lincoln. The whole city was crawling with "roughs and adventurers . . . traitors, conspirators, rebels, leagued together for the destruction of the Union." "They will probably insult you," Foot predicted. "Northern men now carry arms who never carried them before." "Senator!" a shocked Chittenden broke in, "Do you advise us to prepare for street fights? to carry pistols?" To which the old politico gave a classic Washington answer: "I advise nothing. I am merely putting you upon your guard. . . . After you have been here a few days you will judge for yourself whether it will be wise for you to carry arms."[15]

Foot was basically right about the Peace Conference. Chittenden joined in the meetings, sitting with the enervated old establishment while men outside were plotting rebellion. The notion that unelected worthies could head off the crisis missed just how unrestrainably different America's mass democracy had become from the old republic run by dispersed, compromising elites. Some Upper Midwest states refused to send anyone to participate in the conference; a Michigan newspaper summarized: "We have fed the whiners with sugar plums for too long." Carl Schurz, invited to Washington by John Fox Potter to stiffen Republican spines, dismissed the meetings as "the last pathetic gasp of the policy of compromise." At least the Peace Conference achieved one thing, according to Schurz, allowing Republicans to "gain time" while waiting for Lincoln to arrive. Senator Foot had told Chittenden it would "gain time" for the secessionists. If they agreed on something, it was that no one was prepared for what was coming.[16]

Chittenden, with time to kill, wandered Washington, meeting with anyone who had insights or predictions. A few days before congress counted the states' electoral votes from the 1860 election, he visited Winfield Scott, the commanding general of the U.S. Army. "Old Fuss and Feathers" was a gruff septuagenarian, six foot five and well over three hundred pounds, his massive shoulders fringed with epaulets, his broad chest tinkling with medals earned from a lifetime fighting Americans wars. Among those, it must be remembered, was his commanding role in the ethnic cleansing of southeastern Native American nations known as the Trail of Tears. But in 1861 the Virginian had pledged to defend the Union. When Lucius met with him to share his concerns about the electoral count, the old general bellowed, "A Chittenden of Vermont!" and reminisced about fighting alongside his ancestors on the Canadian front of the War of 1812. He also sought to reassure Chittenden about Washington's security. The Capitol Police might include men like Lum Cooper, but the army was ready. Anyone who interfered with the counting of the electoral votes on February 13, Scott blustered, would "be lashed to the muzzle of a twelve-pounder and fired out of a window of the Capitol. I would manure the hills of Arlington with fragments of his body. . . . It is my duty to suppress insurrection—*my duty!*"[17]

Scott was right about the counting of the electoral votes. The congressional inquiry found that most threats now focused on the inauguration, when Lincoln (and perhaps an army of Wide Awakes) would actually be in town. Nonetheless, Winfield Scott showed that at least one official was taking his job seriously. Surrounding the Capitol grounds with uniformed and plainclothed soldiers, General Scott banned most noncongressmen from entering the complex and stashed weapons in anterooms throughout. Crowds surrounded the massive structure, trying to talk their way in and sometimes cursing the officers, but Scott's men held. Congress counted the electoral votes, the decisive 59 percent Republican majority, the hard work of so many Wide Awakes a few months before. In fact, Lincoln's Southern Democratic opponent in the race, John C. Breckenridge, officiated over the proceedings as vice president, doing his duty even if it meant counting in his rival.[18]

Many breathed a sigh of relief. But most Americans believed that counting electoral votes was a formality, rarely a tense scene in American history. The real drama was still coming, with Lincoln's inauguration three weeks away.

As if to prove the point, angry mobs filled Washington's broad boulevards that evening, cursing Lincoln and Scott and cheering for Jefferson Davis. They occupied Pennsylvania Avenue, the very boulevard that Lincoln was supposed to ride down to accept his presidency. Lucius Chittenden watched from the windows of the Willard Hotel, observing that "reputable people kept in-doors" that night. The Republican Party had conquered the formal electoral system, but thugs still mobbed democracy in the streets.[19]

The fundamental question lingered: Was a partisan paramilitary force coming to Washington? Though it was never the movement's official policy, Americans had long believed the Wide Awakes were formed as an army of inauguration. The idea started among Democrats, with the *New York Herald* suggesting that "it is the opinion of many Southerners" that the Wide Awakes were really "designed to act as a kind of life guard to Abraham Lincoln at his inauguration at Washington." This misinformation played perfectly into southern fears of coercion: the Wide Awakes were not organized to march in Hartford but to come seize a southern city. As Democrats repeated this idea, and as more creditable threats against Lincoln's life emerged, Wide Awakes themselves embraced it. Even the Hartford Originals believed that they were "entitled to the honor of escorting the President to the Capitol next March." The club was linked, in the minds of many, with Lincoln's safety. Henry Wilson, speaking to Wide Awakes in Keene, New Hampshire, paraphrased an old song from the English Civil War, chanting, "And shall Abe Lincoln die, and shall Abe Lincoln die / Then a half million Wide Awakes will know the reason why."[20]

Lincoln's victory turned a campaign boast into the kind of possibility that politicos like to kick around. Were the Wide Awakes coming? The movement's loose structure meant that no one really could say. By January, the *New York Herald* was claiming that the club of "beardless boys" was re-forming into "a secret society, with the known, though not publicly avowed, design of sustaining the President elect by force of arms." This is how disinformation makes its own reality. Subsequent reports in Democratic papers had one thousand, then five thousand, then seven thousand Wide Awakes drilling in Philadelphia warehouses. None of these numbers can be believed, but some clubs were mobilizing. Multiple New York state companies had announced excursions for the inauguration; others were booking steamboats to Washington. The D.C. Wide Awakes' secretary printed notices in national newspapers, promising to help find lodgings for companies attending the inauguration. The veteran New York politician James Watson Webb wrote to Lincoln, offering five thousand New York Wide Awakes to Washington as inauguration security. But the question remains: Were these excursions of a political club eager to celebrate its victory? Or a show of force by paramilitaries looking for a fight?[21]

And would their presence do more harm than good? For the first time, vocal Republicans started asking the Wide Awakes to go away. During the 1860 campaign, few Republican leaders—even sleepy ones—bothered to push back against the movement. There seemed to be little downside to the corps of excited and inexpensive young men swamping the North. But now many figures, a correspondent for the Republican *Chicago Tribune* warned, "entertain serious apprehensions" that if the Wide Awakes attended the inauguration with their usual "defiance and insolent swagger . . . a collision with some

Southern Minute Men will be inevitable." Mobs in Washington and Baltimore were "prepared to resent any insults." Even a small conflict in a crowded street or hotel lobby might "precipitate a revolution beyond the power of man to avert."[22]

A meeting of the Philadelphia Invincibles club showcased the debate. All acknowledged the threat to Lincoln, particularly when crossing through Maryland. Many grumbled—justly—that Washington was not a foreign capital but the center of the federal government that they had just swept in the 1860 elections, fair and square. Why should a Slave Power minority dictate terms? But one vocal Invincible said that he would only go to Washington as an individual. Lincoln would be president of the United States, "and not of the Republican party, and hence the Republicans would do wrong to go to Washington in their organized capacity. If they did go, it would only be giving force to the argument of the South that Mr. Lincoln was the President of a party." The campaign was over, its organizations temporary. At last some Wide Awakes were considering the consequences of their actions.[23]

No one was weighing those consequences more carefully than the president-elect. Though Abraham Lincoln is mostly remembered for what he said and what he did as a president, in this tense period his most important contribution may be what he did not say or do. He was, after all, daily receiving reports of his upcoming assassination. Pinkerton detectives learned of plots in Baltimore to mob his train car and stab him hundreds of times. Consider how easily Lincoln could have called up tens of thousands of Wide Awakes to leap to his defense, how many club members between Springfield and Washington would have happily escorted the man they had elected to the Capitol. Less confident leaders would have looked to the companies as a bulwark in a time of real danger. But, caught between those who wished him harm and those who promised to defend him, Lincoln demonstrated great care.[24]

Mostly, he kept his mouth shut. After his November victory he sent a thank-you note to Henry Sperry of the Hartford Originals, "acknowledging the great services of the Wide Awakes during the campaign," but phrased his note as if that service were now complete. In response to David Hunter's scheme for a hundred thousand Wide Awakes to secretly infiltrate Washington, Lincoln coolly responded that "the most we can do now is to watch events." Lincoln deftly handled Wide Awakes as a historic movement, a campaign club that had done valuable work, whose moment had passed.[25]

If Lincoln kept his distance from irrepressible Wide Awakes, it was because he saw a bigger prize. His chief goal was to build the strongest possible coalition against the secessionist minority. As soon as states began to secede, they had lost their ability to use "Union" against Republicans. Lincoln saw a historic opportunity to pick up this discarded weapon, aligning the love of the Union with criticism of the Slave Power. This would be a real majority, bigger than the 39 percent who voted Republican in 1860. "I would save the Union," the president famously wrote the following year, as a thesis statement for his time in office. Many of his admirers compared the Republican president-elect, surprisingly, to that Democratic forefather Andrew Jackson, famous for facing down South Carolinian threats in the Nullification Crisis decades earlier. "I hear the men all around, Little Giants and Wide Awakes alike saying 'I hope Lincoln will prove to be another Jackson,'" a New York Republican wrote him. It was a rare chance to seize the political middle that Republicans had long coveted, to keep the Upper South from seceding, and welcome northern Democrats to his fight.[26]

Nothing could undermine this big unionist coalition more than a partisan, paramilitary force of Wide Awakes flooding into Washington, picking fights, and reminding Southerners and Democrats of exactly what had made them so furious back in October. No one would benefit less from the permanent campaign than its winner.

So Lincoln took a strategic risk in those months, valuing the possible benefit of building a broad Union coalition over the possible downside of riding into a Washington or Baltimore ambush without a Wide Awake bodyguard. This was the kind of quiet political bravery that defined Lincoln's administration from the very start.

He was not alone. Many of the "leading minds of the party" had given up on the idea of a Wide Awake inauguration. In Buffalo, "Conservative Republicans" were telling their Wide Awakes not to plan an excursion. In Pennsylvania, governor-elect Andrew Curtin asked the companies to attend no inaugurations, neither his own nor Lincoln's. William Seward, who had taken both sides of the issue, spent the winter telling the Wide Awakes to "lay aside the emblems of your political associations, at least for a time, and to return to your industrial pursuits and social enjoyments." Leave "the theatre of public duty at the National Capital" to professionals, like himself. His new traveling buddy, the young Charles Francis Adams Jr., wrote that Seward's chief worry was that the Upper South leaders would perceive "some invasion of their constitutional rights" and join their southern sisters in secession. A Wide Awake inauguration would be a gift to men like Governor Wise.[27]

And so, when Lincoln set off on his thirteen-day train ride to the inauguration, his handlers were wary of Wide Awakes along the way. They had planned a grand, winding odyssey, like Seward's summer excursion, a nineteen-hundred-mile voyage that would take him through almost every major northern city, looping across the Midwest and up into New York, before swooping down through New Jersey, Pennsylvania, Maryland, and into Washington. The *New York Tribune* printed the words of the excursion's organizer, William S. Wood. Mr. Lincoln "desires it to be made known that the anticipated Wide-Awake demonstrations" in cities along the way would "be unacceptable to the party." Strong warnings appeared across the press, calling Wide Awake rallies "objectionable." Lincoln's hometown paper "slyly intimates that Wide Awake demonstrations will not be suited to Mr. Lincoln's present notion of things, and requests such organizations to leave the black cape and stinking laps at home," summarized the *Daily Missouri Republican*. The same press that had heated Wide Awake fires were now ordering them to simmer down.[28]

Lincoln's handlers tried to put the same word out on the ground. Louis D. Rosette—the secretary for the Springfield Wide Awakes who coordinated the August 8 rally—had planned to attend the inauguration in Washington with his company. But Lincoln's secretary John Hay (who knew every young person in Springfield) told the local Wide Awakes company not to come. "Owing to the difficulties with the South," Rosette wrote his sister Ann, "it is thought by Mr. Lincoln and his friends that it is not advisable for our Military Co. to go with him." Still, expecting a patronage job in the new administration, Rosette planned to tag along as an individual, writing, "If we go it will be as citizens."[29]

Outside of Springfield, Wide Awakes were not so obliging. Members turned out in the thousands along Lincoln's route—to see the man they had marched for, to shake his hand, or at least to ruin his sleep. Many wiped four months' dust off of their black capes and crowded the train depots as Lincoln passed through. In Buffalo, John Meredith Read Jr. escorted the Lincoln family through town, making small talk about his father with Mary Todd and befriending Lincoln's hulking bodyguard, Ward Lamon. In New York, 150 Wide Awakes and a forty-piece band played all night outside the hotel where

Lincoln was staying. A German club from Hoboken made it into the hallway outside his suite and sang serenades at his closed door.[30]

Unlimbering his powerful sense of humor, Lincoln courted the Wide Awakes with the same jokey, familiar style that Seward had debuted on his earlier train trip. At Philadelphia, he spoke outside his train to a huge crowd, asking if a Wide Awake who had written to him was in attendance. This club member had apparently "toiled for me night and day through the whole contest. He organized the first battalion of Wide-Awakes, spent all his money, spoiled all his clothes with oil, damaged his constitution, and wore out a new pair of boots. As I understand his letter he didn't sleep a wink from June till November. His name is SMITH—JOHN SMITH—is he here? Can any one point to me that watchful Wide-Awake?" The crowds laughed, seeing exactly what people so liked about the man. Perhaps William Dansberry, the Wide Awake from just across the Delaware who really had written to Lincoln about having "worked my boots intirely out," was in the crowd.[31]

But buried in his jokey yarn, Lincoln made a clear point. The Wide Awakes were a creature of the 1860 campaign, busy from "June till November." That contest was now complete.

The one thing Lincoln did not do, at any of these moments, was ask Wide Awakes to come with him. When fears of an assassination attempt in Baltimore peaked, Lincoln snuck into Washington in a private car with just two bodyguards. He told almost no one, including the large assembly of Wide Awakes who gathered to receive him at the Baltimore train station. Lewis Clephane, Washington's Wide Awakes, hundreds of police officers, and plenty of troublemakers were all left waiting on the platform. The whole outing had been a feint, designed to drag the very public Wide Awakes away from Washington while Lincoln nonchalantly disembarked in the capital.[32]

Lincoln was famously secreted into Washington wearing a plaid Scotch cap and a pea jacket, and newspapers soon joked that this should be the Wide Awakes' new outfit. "The old oil-cloth capes and caps should be laid up in among the archieves of the nation as a memento of the folly of 1860," Democrats snarked. Capes and caps were part of history now.[33]

But the president-elect wasn't the only one sneaking into the city. Even if the Republican establishment begged Wide Awakes to "leave the black capes and stinking laps at home," men still wanted to defend their president. Lucius Chittenden noticed them filtering in over the weeks leading to the inauguration. "Another type of American now became common in the streets of Washington," he noted, "the young stalwart Republicans from all sections of the North and West who had been influential in the election of Mr. Lincoln and who had come to give their personal attention to his inauguration." Soon the southern "roughs and adventurers" Senator Foot had warned Chittenden about grew quieter. Gustav Koerner arrived in Washington, happy to see "thousands of young men had come for the sole purpose of protecting Mr. Lincoln against violence or assassination, all well-armed."[34]

Lewis Clephane took the lead. The head of the Washington Wide Awakes had graduated from printing *Uncle Tom's Cabin,* to protecting Charles Sumner, to hiding on his Wigwam's roof, to organizing inaugural security. Clephane sat down with Winfield Scott to lobby the general to hold a public inauguration. Years later, he remembered sitting across from the great uniformed bulk of the man as they debated. Wriggling in his chair against his "rotundity," Scott pulled a batch of letters out from within his old-fashioned uniform. The letters were all gruesome death threats, aimed at Lincoln. "Old Fuss and Feathers" thought a private event would be the safest option. But the whole point of the Wide Awake election had been to publicly affirm anti–Slave Power speech. Lincoln must be seen and must be heard, Clephane countered. General Scott agreed, with stipulations.[35]

First and foremost, Scott decreed, "There were to be no Wide Awakes in the procession." Clearly, this question of a Wide Awake inauguration was a priority to the Virginian veteran. He told others that, if not for his efforts, "an Army of Wide Awakes would have been marched southward long ago." Scott's other main stipulations—no banners, and placing sharpshooters on the highest rooftops along Pennsylvania Avenue and artillery at every cross street—made good sense. Scott began to plan the event, taking full responsibility for Lincoln's safety. If any disunionists "even venture to raise a finger," the old general promised, "I shall blow them to hell."[36]

March 4 dawned nasty, but soon a beaming sun brightened the day. Looking down from atop Pennsylvania Avenue's rooftops, sharpshooters leaning on long rifles enjoyed the sights of a Washington spring emerging from that terrible winter. The streets were busy but orderly. Large crowds milled about, yet businesses were closed, including saloons, a rarity in the boozy capital. Most soldiers stayed out of sight, but cavalry and artillery units waited on the numbered side streets. A formation of the army's sappers and miners escorted

President Buchanan from the executive mansion, stopping at the Willard Hotel for Abraham and Mary Todd Lincoln. Along with the real soldiers and District of Columbia militia cavalry came ten Wide Awakes in shimmering black capes and caps. Just enough to make a statement, a ceremonial gesture but not a full provocation.[37]

Yet many more club members joined the crowds. Five hundred men from Washington's Republican association and Georgetown's new Wide Awake company were present. None wore a uniform, but each had a silver eagle pin on his lapel, a sign of their membership. J. H. Hobart Ward and 250 more New York Wide Awakes were in attendance, also uncaped but bearing white satin Wide Awake badges. A Cleveland correspondent noticed that "large numbers of strangers" concealed the distinctive Wide Awake cap covers in their pockets. Clephane and Ward marched down the route as official marshals, while hundreds of plainclothed club members milled about the thirty thousand assembled spectators. The *New York Times* was certainly struck by "large bodies of Wide-Awakes" in the crowd, but noted how careful they were not to make any "offensive demonstration of their presence."[38]

After months of false claims, detractors had finally succeeded in turning the Wide Awakes into the secret movement they feared.

James S. Chalker was there, his ferocious eyebrows, stern face, and short, solid frame planted along the parade route. Overheated newspapers had once promised that the captain of the Originals would chaperone Lincoln to the Capitol himself, but that was no longer possible. "We did not go down and act as his escort," Julius Rathbun later sighed. But Chalker was there in the ranks. Perhaps he was thinking of the evening, 364 days before, when he and a few dozen friends guided the lanky Illinoisian's carriage through the streets of Hartford. Since then, the novel club he led had ballooned into American democracy's most prominent campaign organization, then melted back into the crowds.[39]

"When Abraham rose and came forward," wrote Dwight Wilder, a young Massachusetts Republican who had campaigned with the Wide Awakes, "and rang out the words, 'Fellow-citizens of the *United States*,' he loomed and grew, and was ugly no longer." Chief Justice Roger Taney, the proslavery author of the *Dred Scott* decision, swore Lincoln in. Wilder recalled that watching his candidate take the oath of office seemed to lighten a tension that had been building all winter. "I breather freer and gladder than for months," Wilder wrote. "The man looked a man, and acted a man and a President."[40]

Lincoln's speech has made history, his voice strong and clear and high, the first great address of his presidency. It is remembered mostly for generosity. Lincoln did not call down hellfire on rebellion; he preached, "We are not enemies, but friends" and honored "the bonds of affection" that held the Union together. And yet, for a lengthy chunk of the middle, the new president centered majority rule as "the only true sovereign of a free people." "Unanimity is impossible," the new president acknowledged, but minority rule inevitably led to "divide and ruin." The Slave Power was seceding, but soon they too would bicker, and a minority of that Confederacy would secede again, and so on, and so on. The same would happen in every political community if secession were permitted. In a Union of states, in states made up of districts, in coalitions made up of individuals, refusing to accept the will of the majority would lead to endless division. "The central idea of secession is the essence of anarchy," Lincoln argued. Majority meant order. Lincoln hit the themes of his campaign, simultaneously settled and ongoing.[41]

As the new president finished up, men along Pennsylvania Avenue pulled Wide Awake cap covers from their pockets and put them on, "thus demonstrating" observed the *Cleveland Daily Leader*, "the fact that they are here in large force."[42]

The rest of the day, remarked a surprised schoolteacher, passed "without bloodshed." No army invaded the capital. Winfield Scott did not blow anyone to hell. A president had shown himself and proudly argued that majority rule and public order upheld each other. Rather than a prescription for chaos, democracy guaranteed peace in Lincoln's view, strengthening a Union held together by the "mystic chords of memory." Politics was not a zero-sum game of "who hates who," but a self-reinforcing compact. Secession looked so small in contrast.[43]

Yet this all came from a man who had essentially sat out the campaign that never seemed to end. Southerners were noticeably absent in Lincoln's Washington. Few showed themselves at his inaugural ball. A *New York Herald* correspondent claimed that among the two thousand partygoers, "the nasal twang of the strong-willed Puritan was heard on every side," in a hall packed with stumpers, office seekers, and Wide Awakes. Most seemed to have come down from the North and Northwest, uneasy in the new southern setting, unsure of "new responsibilities and dangers which they could not comprehend."[44]

Word radiated out from there. Across the North, Wide Awake companies organized yet another round of jollifications. Tantalizingly, a group of slaves in Florida refused to work on March 4. The land had a new Republican president. If the rumors were true, an army of freedom would be heading south.[45]

Others were less optimistic. "This is the first time in our history," grumbled a correspondent who went by "Pen," writing for the Democratic *Indiana State Sentinel*, "that a President of the United States was inaugurated, surrounded by armed soldiers, with loaded pieces and fixed bayonets. I hope never to see such a sight again." It was the Wide Awakes who had gotten this ball rolling, Pen wrote; now he watched a "mob of Wide Awakes" occupying the Senate galleries, hooting and cursing, "grossly insulting" Stephen Douglas and others. "This is the first time in the history of our country that the Senate has been menaced by a mob," Pen claimed. Of course that was nonsense—the Capitol had seen so much outlandish violence over the years. But something had certainly changed. Now, instead of a slave-owning minority doing the bullying, it was that "true sovereign of a free people," majority rule, shouting down from the galleries.[46]

COOLER HEADS WON out for the inauguration, but the same couldn't be said in St. Louis. President Lincoln, General Scott, and all their deliberate caution were eight hundred miles to the East. In the city of bluffs along the Mississippi, Wide Awakes were concealing more than campaign caps.

Walking the damp, coal-smoke-shrouded streets that winter, Missourians could just barely hear the tread of boots from inside Winkelmeyer's brewery, or by Filley's stove factory, or near Yaeger's Beer Garden. Listening closely, they could pick up German voices singing songs to the "Vater-land," toasting with Staehlin's lager, mixed in with Yankee accents bleating the hurrahs and huzzahs of the bygone campaign. In some places, boot prints trailed sawdust into the snow, tracked out from warehouse floors that had been strewn with the stuff to dampen the sound of military drilling. In others spots "little black piles of powder" were noticeable, spilled from the barrels of gunpowder being moved around by men who had recently been Wide Awakes.[47]

Yet these forces were not technically Wide Awakes anymore. The spiraling events of the secession winter had driven the clubs into something new. If any city in America might "precipitate a revolution beyond the power of man to avert," it was not Washington but St. Louis.[48]

The town had always been a bit of an island, planted on the western edge of the settled nation, a city-state unto itself. Its diverse populations—Old South, go-ahead Yankee, transplanted German, free African American, and French Creole—all believed it belonged to them. And on the hot summer nights of an earlier era, with the whole town out on the levee, or perched on cool stone steps in front of brick houses, it almost worked. But since the election, St. Louis had become tense and sullen. Nowhere in the country was more split. Missouri was the only state where each of the four candidates in the 1860 election won double digits of the popular vote—which meant that each side had enough supporters to raise a fighting force, if it came to that. Missouri had not seceded, but an upcoming secession convention could decide much for the whole nation. Among the state's prizes were St. Louis itself, key points for navigating the Mississippi River and thus the West, and a federal arsenal in St. Louis with enough guns and ammunition to equip the largest army in the land.[49]

No one was sunbathing on the levee now. Even though Lincoln had won the city, with 41 percent of the vote, his supporters felt pressured to keep their mouths shut. It was considered provocative to publicly make pro-Union state-ments, to fly the American flag, or even to hum the "Star Spangled Banner." The secessionist minority rarely felt the same compunctions. Instead they were "noisy, intolerant, and undisturbed," in the furious recollection of the Wide Awake organizer James Peckham. Many of the old southern families who had run the city, and were losing votes year by year, saw this as their last chance to wrest power from the German immigrants and Yankee merchants who were turning St. Louis into another Chicago. Aggressive youths in the Democratic Minutemen militias armed and plotted. At their head was Basil Duke, a provocative twenty-two-year-old Kentuckian with a face of a boxer dog. Duke was looking for a way to "precipitate the collision we desired." Missouri's governor, Claiborne Jackson, appeared eager to help. He had campaigned as a Union-loving Democrat, but now he was making noises about vague plans to "stand by the South."[50]

The forces squaring off over St. Louis were not from the radical fringes so often blamed for the crisis. Governor Jackson and his men were Douglas

Democrats. Stephen Douglas had won Missouri, his only complete electoral college victory, while the more extreme Southern Democratic wing finished an embarrassing fourth in St. Louis. On the other side, Republicans rallied around Frank Blair, and he was no radical. The son of a southern dynasty of former enslavers, Blair stood out as among the most bigoted voices of the Republican Party. What transpired in St. Louis was not a war brought by the extremes but a wrenching fracture in the middle. As in the campaign, what distinguished these men was not their political ideology but their behavior, their willingness to break norms and escalate conflicts.[51]

Not content to wait for Basil Duke to provoke some collision, St. Louis's Republicans acted first. And they had a potential tool at their disposal. Hardened by the campaign's frequent clashes, the local Wide Awake companies were full of Yankees and Germans who knew how to swing a torch-staff. But to be most useful, they would have to undergo a strange metamorphosis. Calling a mass meeting in Washington Hall on January 11, Frank Blair launched what a Democratic local paper dismissed as "the transmogrification from Wide Awakes to Union men." After speeches mocking secessionists as sore losers who "hate democracy," the Wide Awakes of St. Louis formally disbanded. In their place, the companies immediately re-formed as a "Central Union Organization," sometimes calling their clubs "Union Safety Clubs" or the "Union Home Guard." They publicly invited "all sincere Union men" to join, regardless of party.[52]

This was a nice gesture, but fooled no one. Frank Blair and the Republicans were weaponizing their political club. Democrats scoffed at the Wide Awakes "doffing their glazed caps and capes, and wrapping themselves up in the star-spangled banner." Even the hot-headed James Peckham admitted that "very few but the Republicans seemed to take any interest in it." Most members of the clubs had marched with the Wide Awakes, and the press often forgot that it was supposed to call the organization by a new name. Officers of the Union companies were mostly ex–Wide Awake officers. In their postwar reminiscences, Union-club leaders dropped the facade and simply referred to them as "Wide Awakes."[53]

Frank Blair was trying to have it both ways. Changing the organization's name was an effort to simultaneously step away from the partisan divisions of the campaign while still laying the groundwork for a fighting force of Wide Awake Republicans. It's hard to say if the Union clubs ever *stopped* being Wide

Awakes, or if they actually realized the ultimate goal the movement had always flirted with. Either way, the clubs initially recruited eight hundred members, and started to grow into the thousands from there.[54]

"There were men enough, but no guns," reflected James Peckham. Missouri's governor was inching toward secession, and that massive federal arsenal was controlled by a North Carolinian who was said to be plotting to give over "everything" to disunionists. Turning over those sixty thousand muskets to the Missouri State Militia would be the equivalent of building an army of treason in the middle of the Mississippi watershed. Union men could no longer afford, by early 1861, to keep quiet and hope things would turn out all right. Frank Blair told a gathering of Republican leaders assembled at the Connecticut-born mayor's office that "talk was useless" (sounding quite like John Brown). "Nothing could be done to avert war," Blair warned. It was time to arm.[55]

But arming the former Wide Awake clubs, James Peckham warned, "must be done secretly as there were Secesh detectives following, like shadows, every movement of the leading Republicans." Union men quietly visited Woodward's hardware store and bought all sixty Sharps rifles in stock. Mayor Oliver Filley's brother, Giles Filley, started training men with them in his stove factory. Illinois's Republican governor snuck more rifles into town in crates marked as stove-factory supplies. German brewers moved weapons around, hidden in empty beer barrels. Galusha Anderson, a good-humored, square-jawed young Baptist minister and active Wide Awake, helped organize perhaps the greatest coup. Announcing an art exhibit—an odd choice in a city on the brink—Union men imported crate upon crate of fragile "art supplies" from the east. When Republicans pried open these boxes in hidden warehouses, they found neat rows of shiny new muskets. Ex–Wide Awakes produced worn copies of William J. Hardee's *Rifle and Light Infantry Tactics* and began to train with actual rifles instead of the torches.[56]

The premonition that Wide Awakes would soon shoulder muskets had come true. Just as the movement was eventually forced into secrecy by its opponents, the previously unarmed club was now an equipped paramilitary force. The Wide Awakes' rivals ultimately helped it become exactly what they had accused it of being all along.

A singular character was now seen training with the clubs: the U.S. Army captain Nathaniel Lyon. Slim and straight, with an angular face, reddish whiskers, and a piercing blue stare, he gave the impression of a man without any impediments slowing him down, with a personality that argued its points through "straight marches to your reason." Two Colt revolvers on his slender hips were equally direct. The Connecticut-born Lyon was originally a Democrat, but service in the U.S. Army in Kansas turned him into an uncompromising antislavery man. Now stationed with the army in St. Louis, Lyon quickly choose sides. He befriended many of the Wide Awakes, especially Frank Blair, and started joining their covert training sessions. Lyon seemed to inspire strong passions from everyone in town. Minutemen cursed him, but James Peckham's reflections vibrate with the kind of nineteenth-century male love that mixed grandiose rhetoric and cryptic sexuality. "Noble champion of the right!" he said of Lyon, "Hero of bewildered humanity!" Peckham wrote that Lyon's finely made head displayed "every phrenological organ well defined." He also liked his eyes.[57]

With the gruff Frank Blair and the forthright Nathaniel Lyon training their men, the Union clubs were coalescing into a force of thousands. The Minutemen militias were smaller, but they were also armed and training. St. Louis shivered with tension. Everyone was watching that main asset, the federal arsenal. Spies circulated in streets around its nicely manicured lawn, unofficial sentries lurked with revolvers in their pockets. Nathaniel Lyon rented out vacant buildings around the arsenal, stationing sharpshooters in empty rooms. On a random night in February, a fire alarm supposedly spooked several German Union club members who, "mistaking it for a signal to muster arms," rushed into the streets with rifles. The story might be false, spread by the anti-Republican *Daily Missouri Republican*. The paper's editors saw the incident as a sign that Wide Awakes were preparing "to do a large amount of shooting, stabbing and ripping open of stomachs." Rumors circulated among unionists as well, like claims that secessionists were posting messages around town in tiny, color-coded slips of paper, indicating when to attack.[58]

The two camps were also working to leverage whatever government power they could. Democratic Missouri lawmakers accused the Republican mayor of a plot to use the city's riot laws "to call out his Wide Awake friends to shoot down Democrats and Americans." Frank Blair called on his old family's connections, writing to Winfield Scott, Simon Cameron, and even Lincoln himself. On the other side, Governor Jackson seized control of St. Louis's police force, giving it over to a police board featuring Basil Duke. Purely out of spite, the new board banned Black St. Louisans from meeting publicly or in houses of worship without permission, and closed German saloons, opera houses, and restaurants on Sundays.[59]

This is how politics becomes warfare—winning elections, then using the state power to position forces, equip fighters, and punish enemies. There was no single clear line to be crossed. It happened naturally as men on both sides embraced the logic of the permanent campaign. Nearly everyone arming and training on one side had been Republicans a few months before; everyone on the other came from one of the parties opposing Lincoln. In Washington, fossils like Winfield Scott and crusaders for Union like Abraham Lincoln had worked to ensure a peaceful inauguration. But in St. Louis, no one paused. What had been a race for votes was now a race for weapons, high ground, and government power. And many of those training still had shiny black capes in their closets.

Then, on March 1, Missouri's secession convention dismissed the idea of leaving the Union, 70 to 23. Those who hoped to join the Southern Confederacy realized they could not vote their way out of the Union. But if they sparked a fight, giving Missourians the sense that they were being coerced, that might do the trick. With this in mind, as Lincoln's inauguration preparations were finalized on March 3, 1861, Basil Duke set a trap.

Duke had long felt that the older members of his southern community were holding back secession. But he saw his Wide Awake opponents as an asset. If Union clubs charged into the streets at every firebell, how might they react to an actual provocation? With that, he assembled fifty or sixty of his "most determined and reckless followers" to the grand, porticoed Berthold mansion. There he explained his plot to offer a public "challenge to the Wide Awakes," and armed his Minutemen with rifles, pistols, and shotguns. They assembled two secession flags, but unaware of what the official flag of the Confederacy would look like, they emblazoned "every conceivable thing that was suggestive of a Southern meaning" on the fabric. The Minute Men hoisted them high in the St. Louis sky and waited for the Wide Awakes to take the bait.[60]

Duke's men also secretly positioned a cannon inside the mansion's front vestibule, loaded with musket balls and ten-penny nails, half hoping to use it against Wide Awakes forcing their way through the front door. The once public 1860 campaign was melting into a game of secret weapons and booby-trapped front doors.[61]

Soon Duke's followers heard the drums converging on the plaza, as Union clubs poured forth to surround the mansion. Italian food sellers and confused donkeys got caught up in the melee. Men waved rifles and pistols and wrestled and threatened, hollering in southern accents and German curses. The makeshift secession flags flapped in the breeze overhead. Wide Awakes, Duke recalled, "made several abortive rushes" to seize the mansion's front porch, unaware of what lurked behind that door. Thankfully for all involved, they were forced back to street level repeatedly by the Minutemen. There was "some rough and tumble fighting" in the streets. Authorities rushed in to mediate, though Duke felt that the state militia "would have cheerfully sided with us had the Wide Awakes and the mob attacked." Soon Duke was pulled into negotiations with Mayor Filley about the flags. The Minuteman made a both-sides argument: If others could fly the U.S. flag, why couldn't he fly a Confederate one?[62]

Duke's trap failed. The Union clubs cursed and wrestled some more, and then went home. They did not force their way into the house and give Duke "the opportunity we had hoped for." Lincoln's inaugural day did not dawn with news of a political massacre out west. But the rival factions—with their origins in Republican Wide Awakes and Douglas Democratic Minutemen—were "now to all intents and purposes transformed into military bodies," in the words of Galusha Anderson. And all had eyes on that federal arsenal. It was only a matter of time before they would collide.[63]

ST. LOUIS AND WASHINGTON were outliers. Most in the North still convinced themselves that the crisis might end peacefully. With Lincoln safely inaugurated, many Wide Awakes turned to the seasonal labor of lobbying for cushy government jobs. Ignoring the Confederate government, the armies equipping, and the cannons trained on federal forts, Republicans honored the old American tradition of bickering over patronage.

Frederick Douglass famously joked that "after each election one host of incompetent kin folks takes the place of another," but more than nepotism was at play. In a big, noisy, exhausting campaign culture, this "spoils system" offered some reward for the incredible unpaid labor done on the parties' behalf. Patronage fueled democracy on the ground. And no campaign was bigger, noisier, or more exhausting than 1860. Washington flooded with fellows in worn boots, clutching letters testifying to their efforts the previous October. Newspapers joked that Lincoln now needed Wide Awakes to protect him from office seekers, not assassins. Yet many of those office seekers had been Wide Awakes too. Typical newspaper columns in spring 1861 announced something along the lines of "We learn that Captain X of Wide Awake company Y got Z federal position." Lewis Clephane got a good job. So did J. H. Hobart Ward. John Meredith Read Jr. schemed with his father, leaving an embarrassingly craven record. "I have worked harder than any other man in this section of the country + I have given money more liberally," Read Jr. insisted. "I ought not let this opportunity slip—otherwise when the Wide Awake Movement is over I shall pass out of the minds of people and be forgotten."[64]

Democrats, typically, fumed about jobs going to such "unwashed Jacobinical Bohemians as Carl Schurz" and "scullions from rural Wide Awake clubs." Lincoln's appointees, a Raleigh paper grumped, were made up of sleazy ex–Wide Awakes: "the greasy, hirsute, half-savage Western barbarian, the skulking, mousy, thievish New Englanders, or the New York 'dead rabbit.' " But unlike with past presidencies, many unseceded southern states talked as if Lincoln's administration were a foreign occupier. When a U.S. mail position in Virginia went to a Washington Wide Awake, Richmond papers snarled that "Wide Awake Black Republican pro-consuls" were colonizing the South using tactics borrowed from the Roman, British, and Ottoman Empires.[65]

While shortsighted Republicans squabbled over appointments, secessionists still considered how to "precipitate" a clash that might pry the rest of the South loose. "The Wide Awakes and the fire-eaters are getting hungry," the *New York Herald* observed, "the first for the spoils, the latter for blood."[66]

The solution was sitting right in the middle of Charleston Harbor. Fort Sumter was an obvious embodiment of the U.S. government that South Carolina had supposedly left behind. If the new Confederacy wanted to include the Upper and Middle South, they would need some galling act of federal coercion to rally their fellow Southerners. Lincoln would not oblige, merely resupplying the eighty-five U.S. soldiers at Fort Sumter peacefully. On April 9, Jeff Davis's cabinet elected to strike first, despite warnings from some members that the move would "strike a hornets nest." On April 12, 1861, the Confederate general P. G. T. Beauregard gave the orders to fire on the United States.[67]

Forty-three Confederate guns bombarded the little island fortress. They shot three thousand rounds, though they killed no one. The clearest casualty

was the U.S. flag. In St. Louis, Basil Duke's ersatz Confederate banner fluttered untouched over the Berthold mansion. In Washington, Lum Cooper's
Palmetto flag waved unimpeded over his Capitol Hill home. But on Fort
Sumter, the thundering Confederate shelling finally knocked down the pole
that flew the Stars and Stripes. After thirty-six hours of shelling, the U.S.
Major John Anderson had to surrender the fort. Oddly, the Confederate he
surrendered to was none other than Texas senator Louis Wigfall, last seen
frothing in the U.S. Senate about "Wide-awake Praetorians."[68]

News shot out, north, south, and west. On Illinois's St. Louis outskirts,
Gustav Koerner felt that "it was almost a relief to the Union men when the
news arrived of the bombardment of Fort Sumter." The irrepressible conflict
was finally here. Radicals on all sides felt vindicated. Enterprising reporters
for the *New York Herald* hustled to the lobby of the New York Hotel, where
they found a scene of "considerable excitement," as southern guests "conversed
with great vehemence" in the lobby and dining rooms.[69]

In Washington, a correspondent who went by "LEO" reported back to
Charleston. Watching the hubbub and future-predicting and position-
jockeying that followed Fort Sumter, LEO made the obvious comparison:
"The country rushes into war with the same spirit and zeal and recklessness
with which it has been accustomed to enter into Presidential elections. There
is not much difference in the principle which governed the one and that which
rules the other." The previous year had eroded the line between the two.[70]

CHAPTER TWELVE

"I Would Rather Be a Soldier Than a Wide Awake"

W HERE ARE THE WIDE-AWAKES?" screamed headlines in Democratic papers across the North.[1]

It started in the *Boston Courier*, but showed up in papers from Greensburgh, Pennsylvania, to East Saginaw, Michigan. The same pointed tirade began: "Night after night last Fall our streets blazed with the torches, and resounded with the shouts of men and boys, who kept military time and wore glazed caps." Democrats "warned them time and again of the sad and disastrous consequences which must follow from their insanity. We begged of them by every consideration of patriotism and humanity to desist from a course that must inevitably result in ruin to the country. But the Wide-Awakes would not listen. Lanterns, and capes, and flags multiplied in our streets, Banners floated, and drums were beaten, and in a while, the deed was done. And now, Gentleman Wide-Awakes, how do you like it?"[2]

"War is now begun," the *Courier* snapped. But where were those "half-million of Wide-Awakes who were ready to overrun the South?" "We insist," furious Democratic editors agreed, that after all that militaristic spectacle and boastful play-acting, "they shall do the fighting."[3]

The "I told you so"s kept coming. John David Billings, a mechanic in Canton, Massachusetts, had marched with the Wide Awakes the previous fall. Now Democrats in his shop kept telling him, "I hope you fellows are satisfied now" and "I hope you and every other Black Republican will be made to go and fight for the niggers." Years later, when Billings wrote the bestselling war memoir *Hardtack and Coffee*, this was how he explained the beginning of the conflict.[4]

It is commonly said that the attack on Fort Sumter united the North, but often that sense of unity comes from postwar reminiscences. When Sumter fell, even many outraged northern Democrats could not help but interpret the frightening news through the prism of the 1860 campaign. They had predicted all of this last November. There was no other cause for the war "but the election," chided the *Detroit Free Press*, "which has brought upon us our present misfortunes."[5]

At the same time, many Republicans who had spent the campaign drilling were now eager to leap into action. Wide Awakes formed the North's advance guard, first to fight. George Kimball, a Boston Wide Awake, felt that Fort Sumter merely fit into a larger pattern. He was an abolitionist, convinced that the conflict had been brewing since the first enslaved Africans arrived in 1619. But it was the behavior of Boston's Democratic ruffians during the campaign that rankled him the most. He had been hit in the eye with a brick at a rally in Bowdoin Square the previous fall. "That brick was to me as much a *casus belli* as was the firing upon Fort Sumter." His Wide Awake company kept meeting all winter and spring, expecting to be called upon to fight the Slave Power locally or further afield. Kimball claimed (exaggerating a bit) that "ninety-nine per cent of the men" who served as Wide Awakes were eager in the spring of 1861 "to march forth as soldiers."[6]

But even as they did, the meaning of their movement changed. Actual warfare complicated their rhetorical militarism, making the Wide Awakes of 1860 prescient, useful, and irrelevant. The war was the first step toward forgetting the Wide Awakes.

In general, the North did turn out together in patriotic anger, shocked that their countrymen had fired upon the federal government. Frederick Douglass noted that all the weaselly talk of "concession" and "compromise" fell away. Instead, "the dead North is alive, and its divided people united. Never was a change so sudden, so universal, and so portentous. The whole North, East and West is in arms. Drums are beating, men are enlisting, companies forming, regiments marching, banners are flying, and money is pouring into the national treasury to put an end to the slave-holding rebellion." South Carolina's aggression was certainly a gift to abolitionists. The feisty *Anglo-African* went further, demanding that "We want Nat Turner—not speeches; Denmark Vesey—not resolutions; John Brown—not meetings."[7]

But meetings were the first step. Indignation meetings and Union meetings and recruitment meetings, packed not just with the abolitionist fringe but with the kind of "Don't care" Northerners who had finally been roused awake. Among those attending such meetings were non-Republicans like Ulysses S. Grant and William Tecumseh Sherman, men in the political middle whose futures would be determined by what happened next. They watched as a Republican plurality grew into a Union majority, aided by Lincoln's careful maneuvering and the Confederacy's reckless provocations. The long scramble for Union had placed that political weapon tightly in Lincoln's hands.

George Kimball, the Boston Wide Awake with the brick-bloodied eye, was proud to witness the mobilization of his often passive region. "No one had ever before dreamed that the proverbially cold-blooded Northerners could be stirred to such depths," he wrote, watching as "prayer meetings turned into war meetings; stores were changing into recruiting stations; workshops became rallying places." Carl Schurz's conscientious Yankees were now filled with zeal, far beyond the partisan spectacle the Wide Awakes had stirred. To Schurz, the shift was thrilling. Riding south toward Washington by train, he trumpeted: "What a change! Every railroad station filled with an excited crowd hurrahing for the Union and Lincoln!" Depots buzzed with young men hurrying home to enlist.[8]

"All the world," Schurz wrote, "wants to march."[9]

Then he shifted, typically, to himself, bemoaning, "And I cannot. I almost regret being a foreign minister." His recent appointment as minister to Spain by Lincoln suddenly looked less glittering, now that his second shot at revolution was brewing in America. Schurz packed two pistols he had used in Germany's 1848 revolutions and headed to D.C. Hopefully they would fare better against the Slave Power than they had against the Prussian autocracy.[10]

It was in Washington that eager recruits were needed most direly. The placement of the federal capital sixty miles into southern territory now looked awfully foolish. As Virginia and Maryland teetered, the national government might suddenly find itself outside the nation it led. Secessionist forces were organizing to the north, in Baltimore and Rockville and other southern-leaning Maryland towns in between. Whatever confused mix of party allegiances the population between Pennsylvania and Washington held, it was certainly hostile to Republicans. And despite months of warnings, Washington was lightly defended. Winfield Scott joked that Fort Washington itself was protected by a "single old soldier," and he was only reliable when sober. The whole complex could be taken "with a single bottle of whiskey."[11]

Here the much-despised "spoils system" saved the republic. Washington lacked trained soldiers, but it was packed with patronage-seekers come to beg Lincoln for jobs. Wide Awakes and other fighting Republicans had been flocking to the capital for months, first to defend the inauguration and then to cash in. So when Fort Sumter fell, the vulnerable city's hotels and boardinghouses crawled with just the men needed to defend it.

One of those men had witnessed the birth of the Wide Awakes. Cassius M. Clay, speaker at the first Wide Awake march on February 25, 1860, was in Washington in April 1861 to collect his spoils. The Kentucky abolitionist had been granted the post of minister to Russia, as a reward for a hard-fought campaign. The dashing, slick-haired Cash Clay visited government officials just after Sumter was shelled, noticing a barely concealed panic. Even Winfield Scott seemed worried. Meeting with Secretary of War Simon Cameron, Clay asked if he could help defend Washington somehow. Cameron said he knew of no precedent for a sitting foreign minister serving as a military volunteer. Clay arched a dark eyebrow and—as if the line between politics and warfare wasn't already tattered enough—responded, "Then, let's make a little history."[12]

Clay sought out Senator James H. Lane of Kansas, a veteran of that state's bloody antislavery fighting. Jim Lane was gaunt and haunted and crazy-eyed, with a closet full of scandals (both murder and sex) and a mouth full of tobacco. Carl Schurz had recently seen him furiously eyeing Virginia through a telescope, muttering, "We have got to whip these scoundrels to hell." He was, in his own words, "a-howling for blood." But Clay admired Lane as a fellow fighter, writing that the two "had all along been at war with the Slave-power." While most of Washington was paralyzed, he said, "we were ready to move steadily in defense."[13]

Clay and Lane agreed to organize battalions of trustworthy (i.e., Republican) fighting men. General Lane set up his forces in the East Room of the Executive Mansion. Clay chose Washington's real nerve center, the marbled, mirrored, chandeliered halls of the Willard Hotel. Working out of a bedroom there, he assembled the Cassius M. Clay Battalion. In a southern town, in a hotel packed with strangers and spies, Clay wore "a fine pair of Colt's revolvers" and his "accustomed Bowie knife" at all times. He chased away some suspicious lurkers at gunpoint, warning "these are war-times, and I am not to be trifled with." But mostly he recruited for his battalion. Drinking cup after cup of coffee, Clay set up code words, procured high-tech breech-loading carbines, and held meetings in the Willard's dancing hall. Though many in the Lincoln administration chuckled behind his back at his immense self-regard— he could be seen swaggering around the Willard now wearing *three* pistols, a saber, and a bowie knife—the force Clay assembled says much about how the war came.[14]

Some called Clay's battalion "the Strangers' Guard." In a city with few local Republicans, the men who volunteered for the battalion were mostly outsiders. But they were hardly strangers; many of the most famous Republicans in the country joined as rank and file. Congressman John Fox "Bowie Knife" Potter volunteered as a private. So did Galusha Grow, who would be elected Speaker of the House in a few months. Senator David Wilmot—who fifteen years earlier had introduced the famous proviso attempting to halt the westward expansion of slavery—signed up too. Seward's "coarse, genial, humorous" drinking buddy James W. Nye was chosen as commanding major. It was an oddly martial post for a beloved man described as an "irrepressibly funny character" and "a fat Cupid."[15]

But most striking were the Wide Awakes. The Hartford Originals captain James S. Chalker joined Clay's battalion. During the first march escorting Cassius Clay through Hartford back in February 1860, Chalker had leaped into the fight to wrest back torches from "dirty-mouthed" Democrats. Now he shouldered a carbine and patrolled the dark streets of the capital. Years later, his wife proudly displayed Chalker's membership form, which honored his service "when the destruction of the Capitol of our country was threatened by the traitorous designs of the so called SOUTHERN CONFEDERACY." Silas B. Dutcher, the president of the New York Wide Awakes Central Committee, joined the battalion as well. Dutcher had led the Manhattan Wide Awakes through the fight with the New York Hotel and organized the massive October 3 rallies. Now he was out on patrol. Amasa McCoy, the professor who had been traveling New York state calling for a permanent Wide Awake movement, joined his fellow club members. And Lewis Clephane, who led the Washington Wide Awakes, printed *Uncle Tom's Cabin* and, faced with as many Washington rowdies as any other man, enlisted as well.[16]

Together they collected their carbines, learned Clay's passwords, and patrolled the town day and night during those tense weeks after Fort Sumter. Clay's battalion checked in on key locations and potential troublemakers, intimidating the sons of the South attending Columbian College (now George Washington University). In its enlistees' recollections it was always nighttime in those weeks, the dark district besieged from outside and abandoned within, a landscape of glittering hotels and echoing federal buildings, plotting conspirators and paralyzed civil servants, with blooming magnolias and dogwoods perfuming the ominous nights. Clay's battalion never fired a shot, but it provided a source of confidence when the capital was uniquely vulnerable. And they affirmed the Wide Awakes' centrality as politics became war. Clephane later claimed that—of the millions who would volunteer to fight for the Union—the Cassius M. Clay Battalion came first.[17]

IF WASHINGTON REMAINED eerily quiet, Baltimore was becoming a battle-field. Events unfolded quickly after the firing on Fort Sumter. On April 15 Lincoln called on loyal states to provide seventy-five thousand militiamen to suppress the rebellion. On April 17, Virginia seceded, denouncing Lincoln's call-up as "coercion." And all those Northern boys, enlisting by the thousands, began heading south.

But the men riding down the Eastern Seaboard would have to pass through a complicated Baltimore bottleneck. Trains in 1861 could not chug through the city itself. Passengers would have to disembark on one side of town and ride horse-drawn streetcars a mile to another train station, before boarding new trains to Washington. It meant that the military might of the Lincoln administration could not rattle quietly through, but would have to get out and cross the roughest city in the nation.

This put Maryland in a bind. Secession was hotly debated. Some vocal leaders in Baltimore and the Eastern Shore pushed the idea, but western Maryland was politically more like loyal Pennsylvania. There were a lot of Whigs turned Know Nothings turned Constitutional Unionists who were not eager to leave the Union. Nonetheless, many Marylanders detested playing any role in "coercing" Virginia and other southern states. It was a worldview, police marshal Jacob Frey would explain, "hardly comprehended by the New Yorker or New Englander" but fundamental to White Marylanders. They were

Southerners after all, and residents of a Mid-Atlantic region used to negotiating extremes. Baltimore's notoriously complex and violent politics amped everything up. Crowds of Southern Democrats filled the streets each day after Fort Sumter, promising to "repel, if need be, any invader who may come to establish a military despotism over us." Those National Volunteer clubs—organized "pretty much because of the Wide-Awake movement"—held a mass late-night rally to denounce Lincoln's call for troops and to give notice that they were, in the words of one speaker, "No longer willing to submit."[18]

As northern volunteers started to move through town, Baltimore's mayor sensed "a deep and pervading impression of impending evil." On April 18, militias from Pennsylvania made their way through the inner harbor. They traveled without uniform or rifles, and crowds mostly just booed. The next day, as Massachusetts's Sixth Regiment rumbled into town, it was clear things were about to get uglier. The Massachusetts troops were uniformed, wearing gray greatcoats with built-in capes around their shoulders, looking like a bunch of Wide Awakes. And they had rifles. As they prepared to traverse Baltimore, the hound-eyed, droopy-mustached Colonel Edward F. Jones ordered the boys from Middlesex County to load their rifles and fix their bayonets. They were to ignore stones or bricks thrown their way. But if fired upon, the Sixth Regiment should shoot back. "Drop any man," Colonel Jones instructed, "whom you might see aiming at you and be sure you drop him."[19]

Already huge crowds were gathering in the path between the stations, filling the busy downtown section with "a perfect babel of noise and excited people on the verge of a riot." The growing throngs went by many names—National Volunteers, Minutemen, states' rights men, Southern Democrats, Bloody Eights, and Baltimore's other Democratic clubs and gangs—but were united in their goal of stopping the federal troops. Along the route between the train stations, people started to barricade the avenues and destroy the streetcar rails. Ransacking construction sites and wharfs, they tore up tracks and built obstructions for the Massachusetts troops. They piled mountains of sand, felled telegraph poles, and dragged a huge ship's anchor into the middle of the street. The Massachusetts' Sixth would have to walk.[20]

As the militia set out on foot, in uniform, with glinting rifles and fixed bayonets, the crowds roiled. Shopkeepers closed their stores. Men and boys sprinted back and forth, hollering updates and hunting for weapons. Most were unarmed, simply a huge mass of angry men, women, boys, and girls blocking the path across town. Decades of political compromise and evasion, maneuver and negotiation, came down to this: the unavoidable presence of some Americans in the way of others. It was exactly the kind of fight the Wide Awakes had found hard to win—a march from point A to point B through a hostile crowd. But now the marchers had guns, and their harassers seemed willing to tear down their own city to stop them. A tense drama hung over it all. Would the mob overwhelm the forces of order? Would angry crowds tolerate the presence of people whose politics they hated? Would military men be able to restrain themselves, now that they held rifles instead of torches?

As the Massachusetts men rushed, double-time, down Pratt Street, the crowds began to escalate from cursing and hissing to throwing bottles and bricks. Soon Baltimoreans produced pickaxes and began to tear up cobblestones, hurling them at the heads of the militia as they passed. The soldiers were clearly trying to avoid a confrontation, as was Baltimore's mayor, George William Brown, a pencil-necked professor and library lover who showed unexpected bravery that day. Mayor Brown marched with the Sixth Regiment, waving his umbrella between the troops and his furious constituents. At one point he even yanked a loaded rifle out of a rioter's hands. He shouted advice to the Massachusetts men, telling them that their frantic rush was panicking the crowds, begging them to slow down and exude some calm. But the thickening hail of bricks and stones, and the random crack of gunfire, made even Mayor Brown see the danger. "You must defend yourself," he shouted over the racket. Now shots were coming from both sides. The soldiers were moving so quickly that they could not really aim, shooting into a mass of their fellow citizens. Even as both sides opened fire, the streets were still packed with onlookers, taunters, Confederate flag wavers, people struggling to get closer to the action or to flee from it.[21]

The fighting was hottest around Pratt and Light Streets, nearly the same parade route where six months earlier Baltimore's Wide Awakes had fought their way into and back out of the Front Street Theatre. And that theater had been the site where the Democratic Party split at its convention six months before that. This half-mile radius of downtown Baltimore could tell the full story of a single year's escalation, from a splintering party system to a militarized political movement to soldiers shooting into crowds.[22]

The presence of Massachusetts' Sixth Regiment was the catalyst that ignited an explosive reaction that had been building in Baltimore for decades. In City

Hall, Baltimore's leaders hollered and threatened, promising to cut off each other's noses and ears. (False) reports came back that Mayor Brown himself was shooting at the troops. Everyone in town had to pick a side. At the head of the mob were Baltimore's First Families—elite, native-born, southern-leaning Democratic merchants who had made up the National Volunteers. Later analysis of 159 known rioters showed that most were "gentlemen of property and standing," three quarters were American-born, and they averaged $9,878 in property. As with so many other fights, the mobbers in nineteenth-century America were not the impoverished Irish immigrants seen in nasty political cartoons, or even of Baltimore's many, many gangs. They were its "merchants and all the best citizens."[23]

Baltimore's large Know Nothing population broke the other way, attacking the Democratic mobs, breaking up the barricades the Massachusetts Sixth had to climb over, yanking down Confederate flags, and beating men firing salutes to South Carolina. Most local Germans picked the same side, fighting largely for the Union. Every demographic experienced a wrenching split. Baltimore's free Black community mostly sided with the Union, but teams of African American laborers and ship-builders helped construct the barricades at the behest of their elite Democratic employers. Even Baltimore's Jewish community was out and fighting among itself. Some identified with the secessionist merchants (and later joined the Confederate Army), even as proslavery Democrats tried to tar and feather the bombastic abolitionist rabbi David Einhorn. The former Prussian officer Leopold Blumenberg organized German Jewish unionist militias. It was a mess, all the diversity of America's most complex city at war with itself.[24]

Finally the troops made it to Camden train station. Some were still taking potshots at random Baltimoreans, shaking with anger, as their trains rattled out of town. When they could take a count, they found that four Massachusetts men had been killed—two shot, one felled by hurled stones, another beaten to the death by the raging mob. Thirty-six more were wounded. And twelve citizens of Baltimore were dead.

The bombardment of Fort Sumter had injured no one. The Pratt Street riot was the first bloodshed of the war. The fact that—in the words of an outraged western Maryland paper—it "originated with the leading men of the National Volunteers," themselves originating out of fear of the Wide Awakes, tells much about the spiraling paranoia that brought the war. Also, those first sixteen Civil

War deaths (of the hundreds of thousands to come) were caused not by distant cannons or snipers or dysentery but by American citizens beating each other to death with fists, crushing skulls with cobblestones, or firing wildly into crowds. It shows the link back to the political chaos that had been escalating since the 1830s. What happened on Pratt Street was not just the start of something; it was also a culmination of the antebellum politics of mobbing that preceded it.[25]

After the Massachusetts Sixth left Baltimore, the city declared "armed neutrality." Simmering violence broke out between Southern Democrats on one side and Know Nothings and German unionists on the other. A fifteen-thousand-man militia—the outgrowth of the National Volunteers—swore to "defend" their city. Union troops found ways around Baltimore for a while. Finally Lincoln declared martial law, retook the city, and arrested many (some say too many) of those involved. Maryland held its secession convention, organized by a canny unionist governor in the loyal town of Frederick, which voted 53 to 13 against secession. The mobs in Baltimore, noisy and deadly as they had been, were just another minority trying to overrule the public politics of a majority by force. Maryland would stay in the Union.[26]

THE ASSAULT ON Pratt Street riled an already wide-awake nation. Late spring 1861 was like a dark repeat of the Wide Awake summer of 1860—a giddy mass enthusiasm mobilizing the rural North, without much reflection on what it all would mean. Clarke Harrington, a fifteen-year-old Wide Awake in East Hampton, Massachusetts, felt that the attack on his state's militiamen made the boys his age delirious, frenzied, "crazy to enlist." It was like "an "electric shock" to his drowsy region; he ran away to fight soon after. George Kimball was "intensely excited by the news of the cowardly attack." Awoken by Democratic mobs the previous autumn, by summer George was a soldier. Over the next few years he would fight at Second Bull Run, Antietam, Fredericksburg, Gettysburg, the Wilderness, Spotsylvania, and Petersburg. He survived the war, but what began with a brick to the eye led to a bullet to the knee and another in his groin before it was all done.[27]

This "frenzy" was not limited to New England. Union volunteers quickly exceeded Lincoln's call for seventy-five thousand. Some states, especially in the West, ended up with far more than their requested federal quota. Twice as many Illinoisians offered to fight as the War Department asked for.[28]

"Can you or any one else give information concerning the Wide Awakes?" an older letter writer from Fall River, Massachusetts, asked. "Is it not time for a re-organization of the company? . . . Brother Wide Awakes, let us up and be doing; let us put down the treason." But young people were way ahead of him. The Wide Awakes of 1860 were fast becoming the volunteers of 1861. Of course they could never make up most of the Union forces, totaling around 2.6 million over the conflict. Neither is it possible to offer concrete numbers; we just don't know how many Wide Awakes there were. But every bit of anecdotal evidence suggests that Wide Awake members surged forward in 1861, making up a huge proportion of Union army volunteers. They had the right politics. They averaged the right age—twenty-four years old on available rosters, same as the average Union soldier. And they had been marching, drilling, and huzzahing for a year now.

Over the Civil War, roughly half of military-aged northern men served at one time or another. But among the Wide Awakes, it is rare to find a club member who saw no service. It seems fair to guess that around three in four Wide Awakes made the leap from faux militarism to the real thing. In at least six northern states, recruiting offices even saw whole companies of Wide Awakes showing up together to volunteer.[29]

Wide Awake leaders directed the march. Across the North, men who had commanded Wide Awake companies volunteered as officers. In response to that annoying Democratic question—"Where Are the Wide Awakes?"—the *Berkshire County Eagle* shot back with pride, "We can answer briefly. The captain of the Wide Awakes is the Captain of the Allen Guard, and has been in Boston this week offering his services," along with three of his Wide Awake lieutenants and a majority of the company. The *Eagle* had spent the campaign reporting on the Wide Awakes of Williams College, the first outside of Connecticut. Now those college boys were becoming soldiers.[30] Much of the North showed the same trend. The captain of the Pontiac, Illinois, Wide Awakes was the first man in his town to volunteer. Same with the Wide Awake captain of Newark, Ohio. And Three Rivers, Michigan. And Ottawa, Illinois. The kind of guys who became Wide Awake captains also made natural officers.[31]

Not everyone agreed that leading a company of costumed Republicans was suitable qualification for military leadership. One grumbling private in New York's Twenty-Seventh Volunteers snarkily observed that leading a Wide Awake club was the only experience his lieutenant had, "so of course he knew all about war."[32]

The Hartford Originals demonstrated the Wide Awakes' eagerness to enlist. Years later, the druggist Julius Rathbun would assert the "semi-military feature of the clubs, with obedience to the word of command, was of immense benefit to the tens of thousands of young Wide Awakes, from all parts of the north, who enlisted for the defense of the old flag." Rathbun himself rose to rank of major. The Wide Awake secretary Henry T. Sperry, the hat-waving promoter George P. Bissell, the torch designer Silliman Ives, and the newspaperman Joseph Hawley all fought. Many were eager to play a role in the conflict they had been rehearsing. Hawley, the editor of the antislavery *Hartford Press*, enlisted immediately and rejoiced to his wife, Harriet: "You cannot imagine how wonderfully I am absorbed in my work."[33]

Close to seven in ten of the Originals' officers served during the war. Most enlisted early, in April or May 1861.[34] Of the five Talcott boys who started the whole movement, four fought in the war. One rose to the rank of captain, another served as a surgeon, and a third died fighting in Louisiana. Daniel Francis, one of the five who had sewn a Wide Awake cape on February 25, 1860, was among the first volunteers in Connecticut. The ladies who stayed in the same boardinghouse as the bearded, bedroom-eyed Francis (though on another floor) raised funds and sent him off with a Colt revolver.[35]

And Eddie Yergason? He intended to volunteer right away, but when his mother caught word she wrote a stern letter, telling him not to "do anything rashly." "Your constitution," she declared, "is not strong enough for that Southern climate." Warning of yellow fever, she claimed "it is a bad season of the year for troops to go South I think you better sell goods a while longer." Her request—"Appreciate your Mother's feelings, no one on the broad earth cares for you as much as your mom"—worked for a while. Edgar Yergason stayed home until 1862, then he enlisted in Connecticut's Twenty-Second Regiment. A photograph shows him as a skinny wraith with piercing dark eyes, wearing a greatcoat with a built-in cape around its shoulders. Yergason survived the war, but his mother was right: everyone who died in his regiment was felled by disease.[36]

Across the North, Wide Awakes turned into soldiers. George P. Holt, owner of that bright-white cape recently discovered in a New Hampshire attic, enlisted right after Lincoln's proclamation, served under New York's flamboyant General Daniel Sickles, and was wounded four times. Louis D. Rosette, who coordinated the massive Wide Awake rally in Springfield in August, was also ready to fight. The day after Fort Sumter he wrote to Lincoln's secretary John Nicolay, "In case the President needs assistance we hope he will first call on Illinois—for we have fought for him once & now will do it again." Charles "Ducksy" O'Neill also enlisted soon after Fort Sumter and served for three years. In 1864 he mustered out to finally marry Caroline Bartholomew.[37]

And James Sanks Brisbin enlisted right away. Brisbin's premonition about Virginia's "fair fields being made the scene of contending armies" proved accurate. He was wounded at First Bull Run, outside Manassas, in a chaotic rout. It was just ten months after he had warned Governor Letcher that if he ever returned to the state, "it will be at the head of northern troops and in that event I advise you to keep out of the way." Brisbin proved to be better as a soldier than as a politician. He rose steadily through the ranks as a respected cavalry officer, seeing combat all over the Confederacy and winning a brigadier general's star. He was still as vigorous, and as reckless, as ever. Over the course of the war Brisbin was shot in the arm, shot in the leg, injured by artillery fire, crushed under a horse, and slashed by a saber. Typical of a man skilled at making enemies, that saber slash came from a fellow Union officer. But Brisbin survived to keep on fighting and speaking.[38]

Good Wide Awakes did not always make good soldiers. Politics was not really warfare, in the end. John Meredith Read Jr. learned this the hard way. Governor Edwin Morgan made him New York's adjutant general, the state's highest ranking militia officer, hoping Read's logistical skill with the Wide Awakes would help ready New York's forces. In response, Read Jr. took the train to New York City and got fitted for a three-hundred-dollar uniform, telling his father that the price was worth it, "taking into consideration the State of the National Affairs."[39]

But as war simmered that spring, Read Jr.'s letters took on that same put-upon-ness of the Wide Awake campaign. He wrote cryptically of coming disaster. Then he disappeared. In his place, letters started arriving at John Meredith Read Sr.'s Philadelphia home from his daughter-in-law, Delphine. "Dellie" often wrote ingratiating notes to Read Sr. when her husband was most frantic. Now these letters warned, "My husband is a little *run down*." Suspiciously, her missives arrived on stationery from western New York resorts, even as she claimed the couple was visiting Fire Island. "I have not been allowed (by my Husband) to write to tell you how he was for fear of worrying you," Dellie informed her father-in-law, but Read Jr. was clearly having some kind of a breakdown. "Don't say any thing to my husband about my having written about his health he is so very sensitive," she wrote, but begged, "Do write letters—*as his mind must be amused*." Finally Read Jr. resigned his post as adjutant general, telling Governor Morgan that he needed "relaxation." Retiring his three-hundred-dollar uniform, Read Jr. spent the remainder of the war years working on a biography of Henry Hudson.[40]

John Meredith Read Jr.'s story demonstrated a point the long, hard war would come to prove: there was little connection between zeal in the 1860 election and success in actual warfare. In fact, many of the Wide Awakes' favorite figures proved to be mediocre generals. Former Speaker of the House Nathaniel P. Banks had been a hero of the early Connecticut Wide Awakes, but as a Union general he flubbed campaign after campaign, dragging many Hartford Wide Awakes with him into a never-ending mess in deepest Louisiana. "Cash" Clay, despite the many pistols clanking on his belt, also turned out to be a pretty poor general. Brigadier General J. H. Hobart Ward fought as an able leader through much of the war, until he was removed for drunkenness.[41] His Wide Awakes had been drinking the night of the New York Hotel fight too. Even Carl Schurz, so eager to enter the fray that he resigned his role as minister to Spain, fought a mediocre war. His experiences from the 1848 revolution made him no better than anyone else—not that this stopped the incorrigible Schurz from showering Lincoln with hectoring, annoying letters.

Really, the best Union generals came not from the ranks of Republicans eager for a fight in 1860 but from doubtful moderates like Ulysses S. Grant and William Tecumseh Sherman, who grew along with Lincoln into the men who won the war.

Others were eager to fight but long denied. From the very first days of the war, African Americans volunteered to defend the Union. As early as April 17, 1861, Pittsburgh's Black militia, the Hannibal Guards, offered their services. They were rejected by General James S. Negley, the same Wide Awake commander who saved James Sanks Brisbin at the Wheeling bridge. Likewise, while Cassius M. Clay and General Jim Lane were assembling their battalions,

Washington's Black community offered to form a force. Jacob Dobson, a famous African American explorer who worked in the Senate, sent a letter to Secretary of War Simon Cameron: "I desire to inform you that I know of some three hundred of reliable colored free citizens of this city, who desire to enter the service for the defense of the City," he wrote. Cameron rejected the idea.[42]

Many Whites insisted, much as they had during the 1860 campaign, that African Americans had no place in the conflict. When Cincinnati's African American community organized a "Home Guard" and began to drill, they were threatened by a mob and told by the police: "We want you damned niggers to keep out of this; this is a white man's war." Nearly the same thing happened in Manhattan. Frank Blair's brother Montgomery told Massachusetts governor John A. Andrew to "drop the nigger" when he discussed the conflict.[43]

Governor Andrew would drop nothing. Nor would his good friend, Lewis Hayden. In May 1861, Hayden held a mass meeting of the Home Guard of 125 Black Bostonians. They assembled on the same strip of Cambridge Street where African American families ran clothing, shoe, and furniture stores, where the Haydens' famous house sat and where Black Wide Awakes had marched. We do not know most of the Home Guards' names, but with the same leadership, the same neighborhood, and roughly the same number of men, it seems likely that many were former Wide Awakes. In 1863 Lincoln's Emancipation Proclamation finally allowed African American men to fight for the Union. The most prominent force they rose, Massachusetts' famous Fifty-Fourth Regiment, drew from Black communities from across the North. But its core was built on the West Boston Wide Awakes of 1860.[44]

One man connects the dots among all these organizations. Mark Réné DeMortie was dapper and doe-eyed, but his genteel demeanor belied a lifetime in the fight. DeMortie was born a slave in a mixed French Haitian clan in Norfolk, Virginia. Freed on his twenty-first birthday, he quickly began to smuggle slaves to Philadelphia and New Bedford. In Boston he befriended Hayden, who sent funds down to help DeMortie free twenty-two men and women. When he learned that he was a wanted man in Virginia, while staying in Boston, DeMortie bought himself a pistol and swore to shoot any slave hunters who came looking for him, reasoning "that it would be better to be tried in Massachusetts for murder than to be tried in Virginia for running away slaves."[45]

DeMortie increased his fight across the 1850s. Using his well-known shoe store as a base, he knocked on doors, canvassing for the Republican Party. He turned out for marches of the Massasoit Guards. Then, in October 1860, he joined his friend Hayden's West Boston Wide Awake company, elegant clothes and fine muttonchops concealed under a black cape and cap. DeMortie marched through Boston's streets in uniform, hoping to "arouse an enthusiasm" for "our much beloved Abraham Lincoln." Six months after Wide Awaking, DeMortie lectured to Black Boston's Home Guard right after Fort Sumter. And when the Massachusetts Fifty-Fourth finally marched south, DeMortie joined as sutler (a vendor who accompanied soldiers and provided supplies). Even in the midst of the raging fighting, DeMortie objected that Black Union troops received roughly half the pay of White soldiers. He organized a boycott, providing thousands of dollars on credit at his own expense, until they won better pay.[46]

From slave to wanted man, from Republican canvasser to militia member to Wide Awake to army sutler to civil rights activist, DeMortie climbed the escalating steps of activism across the decades. Historians have long pointed to Boston's Black community in the 1850s as the template for the Massachusetts Fifty-Fourth, but missed the key Wide Awake stepping stone in between. The same men organized each, but every new organization represented an evolution into public, aggressive, militaristic, and integrated activism. After the war, African Americans' military service (tested in Boston's streets) formed the bedrock of the successful argument for Black voting rights, enshrined in the Fifteenth Amendment. Politics led to warfare, and warfare back to politics.

Nearly two hundred thousand Black men served in the war. George E. Stephens, who wrote those blistering editorials in the *Anglo-African*, fought in the Massachusetts Fifty-Fourth. H. Ford Douglas, that cutting critic of Lincoln, became the first Black officer to command his own unit. Henry Daniels of the Portland club was too old to fight, but joined up as a cook. And John Mercer Langston, the first Black Wide Awake, busily recruited fighters out in Oberlin. Many prominent White Wide Awakes—including James Sanks Brisbin, Edgar Yergason, and Silliman Ives—ended up commanding Black forces as well. Major General David Hunter, who had suggested to Lincoln that "a hundred thousand Wide Awakes, wend their way quietly to Washington," famously issued a preemptive (and rejected) emancipation proclamation, and led the Massachusetts' Fifty-Fourth in some of their most remarkable battles.[47]

Being a Wide Awake was, for many, a conduit to military service. And yet becoming soldiers unmade the movement. Enlistment covered their tracks, part of the reason the Wide Awakes have largely been forgotten. In a nation coming out of the chaotic 1850s, Wide Awake militarism made sense. It was so different from the American reality—orderly in a mob democracy, romantically international in a society of banal shopkeepers, and vigilant in a world haunted by arcane conspiracies. But with the war militarizing society, who would want to play dress-up as a soldier?

Wide Awaking after 1861 seemed hokey. Millions of Americans had "seen the elephant," as they put it, living actual military life, facing the trauma of combat, coming home as veterans, or struggling on the home front as militarism stole away their loved ones. "Wide Awake torch light processions are not exactly the thing now," one Pennsylvanian explained delicately. Being a Wide Awake, after Fort Sumter, meant stepping into that next identity as Union soldiers, like graduating high school seniors defined by what they were leaving behind.[48]

In 1864, the former Wide Awake and Wisconsin infantryman Dolphus Damuth wrote to his sister Maria, reflecting on the coming presidential election and the change in his life since he had marched by torchlight for Lincoln four years before. "It don't seem but a short time since I carried a lamp," Dolph wrote. Now he was "carrying a gun." "You know that most of them have enlisted," he wrote of his fellow Wide Awakes. "I find by experience that thear is quite a difference" between the two identities; but, Dolph wrote Maria, "I would rather be a Soldier than a Wide Awake."[49]

Dolph grew out of Wide Awaking, but not out of the tribal partisanship that underlay it. When he learned that his brother John had been hanging around the local Democratic club back in Wisconsin, Dolph wrote to him: "I would shoot my own brother as soon as I would a Snake if I should see him in the ranks of such a god forsaken set of trators. It makes me mad to think of it."[50]

Democrats felt the same way. Many served in the Union army, many fought and died, a good number converted to Republicanism over the course of the war. But others avoided service, undermined the war effort, or even rioted against the draft. As they did so, loyal and disloyal Democrats kept pointing back to the Wide Awakes as culprits. The popular song "Two Years Ago" by "A Drafted Wide Awake" laid it all out:

> I was a glorious Wide-Awake, all marching in row;
> And wore a shiny oil cloth cape, About two years ago.
> Our torches flared with turpentine, And filled the streets with smoke;
> And we were sure, whate'er might come; Secession was a joke.[51]

After bemoaning the war that killed two of his brothers, this (entirely fictional) ex–Wide Awake sings:

> Just now I saw my torch and cape, which once made such a show;
> They are not now what once they seemed, About two years ago.
> I thought I carried freedom's light in that smoky, flaming band;
> I've learned I bore *destruction's* 'torch'—That *wedge* has split the land.
> Oh if I then had only dreamed, the things that now I know,
> I ne'er had been a Wide-Awake, about two years ago.[52]

The song is ridiculous, ignoring the culpability of slavery, the Democratic Party, and the rebels who had actually seceded and killed U.S. soldiers. But it did acknowledge the way the weird club of 1860 had remade society. The Wide Awakes disappeared as their utility evaporated, but they flavored the rest of northern society as they went.

As Wide Awakes melted into the core of the Union army, many believed that their time in the club was "a good and useful training . . . in military drill, in developing the spirit of comradeship, in evolving manly qualities and patriotic enthusiasm." Or perhaps it was not that the Wide Awakes had become the Union army, but the army had become Wide Awakes. Before the fighting, James Sanks Brisbin's *Centre Democrat* called on all loyal Northerners to rally to fight for the Union, hurrahing: "From Maine to Oregon let the earth shake to the tread of *three millions* of armed Wide-Awakes." The New Hampshire Wide Awake Benjamin F. Thompson put it similarly, reflecting years later on how the issues of the 1860 campaign would be resolved only when "2,000,000 of Wide Awakes went marching over the southland."[53]

On the evening of March 10, 1860, when the Originals first starting drilling in Hartford's streets, they assembled a package of symbols into a movement.

By May 1861 nearly that same package was in use, not by an aggressive partisan faction but by the armed representatives of the U.S. government. Union forces spent May organizing companies, electing officers, choosing uniforms, and learning drills, just as the Wide Awakes had done a year before. They began to shout a Union cheer—"Huzzah! Huzzah! Huzzah!"—not too far from Henry T. Sperry's Wide Awake chant. Behavior that had once been singular, strange, and factional was now happening in each state. The North, once slowest to rise, was wide awake.

Even as tempers warmed, "miserable cold weather" soaked much of the North that spring. Volunteers shivered in damp and slapdash militia camps. Then someone had what the *Buffalo Commercial Advertiser* called "A Good Idea." Northern closets were packed with old oilcloth Wide Awake capes. Resourceful ex–Wide Awakes had been using them as tarps on fishing vessels, or cutting them up to make covers for schoolbooks. But now thousands of boys would be heading south in a drizzly spring, and those old capes "will be found very serviceable" for guard duty in rough weather. Republican newspapers launched a campaign, coordinated with committees of local ladies, to collect old Wide Awake capes and donate them to military camps. The relics of 1860, the mayor of Bucyrus, Ohio, explained, are "of no value here," but might be useful to the soldiers of 1861.[54]

It was a pretty bad idea. Sure, the troops were getting wet, but they were also preparing to prosecute a complex Civil War, which could only be won when the other side was convinced to stop fighting. Parading through the South dressed like Wide Awakes would not help that happen. Nor could the Union army ask loyal Democratic volunteers to risk their lives while wearing Wide Awake capes. It was so typical of the expiring movement: an idea that seemed natural within one political bubble, but would be outrageously provoking to others. Reporters found that soldiers in one Wisconsin army camp were "decidedly opposed to wearing second hand wide-awake capes, because of old associations," while in Iowa they chuckled "about the propriety of said capes going down South."[55]

Not everyone hated the idea. At least one Rochester, New York, volunteer— John Boultwood Edson—wrote to his parents asking them to track down a Wide Awake cape for him. His barracks were "a pretty hard looking place," and the young machinist thought his father could visit his old workplace at Woodbury's steam engine shop to "try some of the boys & see if he could not get me a Wide-Awake cape." Edson repeated the idea in several letters. George W. Benedict of Pennsylvania's Thirteenth Regiment did get his hands on a cape, which he wore while on guard duty in the rain. Both implied that others sported Wide Awake capes too. But few of the hundreds of thousands of Wide Awake capes out there reached Union soldiers.[56]

In the end, they didn't need to. The federal government bought waterproof capes in huge numbers: 1,158,733 ponchos and 1,753,401 waterproof blankets. Many men spent much of the next four years in the rain looking very much like Wide Awakes. What started with five hand-sewn cambric capes in the waterproof section of Talcott & Post's textile store was now the style, not of a stray and forgotten movement but of the irrepressible army marching south.[57]

During the freewheeling Wide Awake summer of 1860, an eager sixteen-year-old in Iowa had predicted that "three-fourths of the rising generation will be Republicans." Four years later, when it came time for the Union army to vote for president, the Iowan was proved nearly exactly right. Seventy-eight percent of soldiers voted for Lincoln. Somewhere along the way, a club became a movement became an army.[58]

THE SAME RAIN pattered on St. Louis on the morning of May 10. Despite the weather, this was the day, the chosen moment when Captain Nathaniel Lyon, Frank Blair, and eight thousand Wide Awake soldiers were finally making their move. After months of mounting tensions, covert drilling in breweries, and arming at art shows, spying and angling and plotting, it was finally time. Glowering Colonel Blair set out at the head of his regiment. Most were "Turners," members of German immigrants' "Turnverein" gymnastic associations, "sinewy, muscular fellows" strengthened by years of lifting weights, climbing ropes, tumbling, and sparring. Over the last year they had traded in their tight white calisthenics outfits for flowing black Wide Awake capes, and were now marching in soldiers' great coats. Blair's "Turners" were joined by native-born fighters, Yankee merchants, and western "trappers and hunters," all united by the systematic organization of hatreds. At the head of other soggy detachments rode Nathaniel Lyon—that oddly intense son of Connecticut—and prominent German Forty-Eighters.[59]

It was a typical Wide Awake force—Upper South and Lower Saxony, New England abolitionists, border-state conservatives, and continental radicals—marching out in momentary unity against a shared enemy.

On this damp morning, that enemy was a force mustering on the far side of a city. A four-day-old tent city called "Camp Jackson" had popped up in a wooded valley on the western fringes of St. Louis. It was named for Missouri's slippery Democratic governor, Claiborne Fox Jackson. Though he insisted he was merely a defender of states' rights, Governor Jackson was coyly inching toward secession. After Fort Sumter, when Lincoln called for loyal states to send militiamen to defend the Union, the governor wrote back, calling the president's proclamation "inhuman and diabolical." Instead, he ordered a muster of Missouri volunteer militias in St. Louis, attracting eight hundred militiamen. Almost all were Southern Democrats with vague plans for disunion. The Governor passed a law banning other militias not under his control, and dispatched Basil Duke—that boxer-faced young Minuteman eager for a fight—to beg weapons from Jeff Davis.[60]

The men drilling and arming, drinking and singing at Camp Jackson swore they were Union-loving Missourians preparing to defend their state from outside coercion. But if any of them believed that, joked the amiable Wide Awake preacher Galusha Anderson, "they must have been unusually stupid."[61]

While Governor Jackson was leveraging his authority to roll Missouri out of the Union, Frank Blair Jr. was using all his inherited connections to push the doubtful state into Lincoln's camp. Blair may have been an unsavory character—racist, crude, and mercenary—but he had been plotting this since at least the rally outside Philadelphia, last October, when he publicly suggested that the Wide Awakes be "organized to do some fighting." And he had a lot of friends to help him organize. He was busily writing to President Lincoln, to General Scott, to Secretary of War Cameron, to Pennsylvania governor Curtin, and to the old men who had run the country and knew his father, lining up federal authority behind his Wide Awakes.[62]

Blair soon won permission to withdraw five thousand guns from the federal arsenal to arm his Union Home Guard. The Democratic press cursed and frothed: "The organization of the Wide-Awakes was bad enough," but at least they did not hold federal rifles. Then Blair shipped much of the rest of that arsenal out of state, for safekeeping in loyal Illinois. Finally Lincoln struck a quiet, clever blow, permitting Captain Nathaniel Lyon to organize a ten-thousand-man "U.S. Reserve" force. These soldiers were now officially federal troops. It allowed them to get around Governor Jackson's control of all state militias, and set up a large number of U.S. soldiers in the city without bringing in a single man from outside. The "states' rights" crowd could not complain, as they had in Baltimore, about Massachusetts soldiers in Maryland streets. The idea was unusual, wrote General Winfield Scott, but "it is revolutionary times, and therefore I do not object to the irregularity of this."[63]

Lincoln's maneuver was, to Galusha Anderson, "fitting and beautiful." But it was all pretty confusing. Both sides in St. Louis were engaged in a crazy leapfrogging of authority, turning political clubs into paramilitaries into soldiers. The names of their organizations kept changing. Over a few short years, Turners became Republicans became Wide Awakes, who became Union Guards, who became U.S. Reserves. Democrats and Bell Men became Minutemen, who became Missouri Volunteer Militia (and would soon become Confederates). It was not too different from what would happen in Boston's Black community, how vigilance committees morphed into Massasoit Guards, then West Boston Wide Awakes, and eventually the Massachusetts Fifty-Fourth Regiment. The porous boundaries between politics and war made it possible to inch ever closer.[64]

In later years, Americans would talk about the "coming" of the Civil War, as if that war were an animate force. But at the time Americans came to the war, in little hops from club to club until those clubs became armies. And the Wide Awakes represented the pivot. What had been private and sometimes secret organizations in the 1850s (the vigilance committees, the German Turners, the Massasoit Guards, the Know Nothings) became, after the Wide Awakes of 1860, public political organizations with access to government power and the legitimate use of force. If there was any line between politics and war, it was obscured under their shiny black capes.

By early May the unionists had some ten thousand armed men in St. Louis, but the governor's militia at Camp Jackson had only eight hundred. Why the disparity? Perhaps because the latter lacked clarity—were they mustering to defend their state, or make it secede? Were they unconditional secessionists, or conditional unionists? Drawn from northern Democrats, Southern Democrats, and Constitutional Unionists, with hazy motivations and a clearly dishonest governor, it was a hard force to rally. Camp Jackson attracted many of the sons of St. Louis's old southern elite, but it just wasn't clear what they were there for. Galusha Anderson joked, of one commander who swore he was not pushing secession, that "this very loyal man a little later went straight into the rebel army." On the other hand, the forces of Frank Blair and Nathaniel Lyon had clarity of purpose, a big pool of motivated and aggrieved German immigrants, and a Wide Awake inheritance that stressed simple martial order as both a style and a dogma.[65]

Then Basil Duke came back from the Confederate capital in Montgomery, Alabama, finally precipitating the fight he had long hoped for. Jefferson Davis made the Missouri secessionists a little gift: two cannons, two siege mortars, and a bunch of ammunition, all stolen from the federal arsenal. He sent them up to Camp Jackson on a steamer, the *J. C. Swon*. But St. Louis was still the gossipy river city it had always been. People talked. The deckhands on the *Swon* suspected what was in those heavy crates, supposedly containing marble. Word got back to Nathaniel Lyon, and then half of St. Louis, and much of Illinois. Lyon started sniffing around Camp Jackson's defenses, allegedly dressed in ladies' clothes (this trope is so common in many stories from this era that it should never be entirely believed). Rumor and recon flowed back and forth. As the Confederate cannons arrived, the city "ran wild with fantasies, monstrous and awful," in the always purple prose of James Peckham.[66]

Captain Lyon called a meeting with Frank Blair and a number of leaders of the Union Home Guards, former Wide Awake commanders, and German community representatives. As a huge storm raged outside, Lyon paced and shouted, blue eyes flashing, insisting that it was time to strike. Others argued that the governor's actions were totally legal—he had the authority to call a militia muster—and the Union men had no legitimate reason to attack. But Captain Lyon and Frank Blair were certain: "We must take Camp Jackson, and we must take it at once."[67]

Everyone seemed to know. Basil Duke got word of the attack and headed to Jefferson City to warn the governor. Gustav Koerner, the German émigré who built a Wide Awake force in southern Illinois, heard too. He started to coordinate with the unionists in St. Louis, promising that he could deliver Illinois troops from Alton in two hours if need be. Koerner was worried, after the Pratt Street riot in Baltimore, about a mob uprising seizing the armory. He visited St. Louis and found Nathaniel Lyon deep in preparation. The captain was "earnest and energetic," but gave off a sense that "there was very little military air about him." There was something frantic and jerky in his manner. William Tecumseh Sherman, who was living in St. Louis at this point, noticed it too. When he visited Lyon, the captain was handing out ammunition himself, "running about with his hair in the wind, his pockets full of papers, wild and irregular." At his disposal were thousands of men with rifles. Some had been training quietly since January, but most had been declared soldiers by Washington overnight.[68]

Then they were out. The forces that had been evolving for nearly a year assembled on the sodden morning of May 10. Six months before, Wide Awakes had filled these streets. Then they had disappeared after the election. Ever since, the people of St. Louis had heard mounting rumors of forces arming, drilling, and plotting. They heard hurrahing from warehouses. Now there were eight thousand fighters in the streets, Republicans almost to a man. They held newly acquired muskets, but almost none wore uniforms. The volunteer fever in the east had made it impossible to obtain military garb. It was like an inversion of the Wide Awake model of uniforms but no guns. This was the start of something new. And clearly, no one was prepared. As they trod west across St. Louis, some marching as far as twelve miles in the rain, the men formed sloppy columns, clumping, breaking up, toy soldiers awkwardly become real. By about three fifteen P.M., their eight thousand fighters surrounded the eight hundred at Camp Jackson. The militia surrendered sullenly.[69]

At this moment Captain Lyon—still exuding the twitchy vibe Sherman and Koerner had noted—got himself kicked by a horse. With their leader knocked out, the forces were now tasked with marching back across St. Louis, escorting eight hundred captives.[70]

Anyone who had been watching American public life could have predicted what would happen next. But no one seemed to. As in Baltimore, as in so many other locales, bystanders flooded the streets. The American love of big public spectacle, the public's tendency to turn out en masse to watch, or serenade, or harass, drew them with magnetic force. Capturing the militia was the easy part. Maintaining order while marching through the streets of a nineteenth-century American city would be the challenge. And considering that the captives were the first sons of St. Louis, and their captors a bunch of "Black Republicans" and "Damned Dutchmen," the mood would not be friendly.[71]

William Tecumseh Sherman—a veteran military man who really should have known better—had brought his seven-year-old son Willie to watch.

Another fifteen-year-old boy—Philip Dangerfield Stephenson—left school to join the crowds heckling the soldiers as they marched back through town. Philip noted how the Union lines kept clumping and breaking apart again, and the anxious way so many of the soldiers pointed their rifles into the crowds as they wheeled around. A familiar hysteria began to grow. Galusha Anderson was in the same crowd, confronted by angry men cursing his Republican sermons, shouting, "This is the result of just such preaching as yours!" The mob began to climb those familiar stairs of escalation, seen over and over again with increasing fervor since the 1830s. Bottles began to fly. Then rocks. Then bricks. Finally bullets. Anderson saw more and more men with pistols and shotguns, pushing past kids like Willie Sherman. Onlookers snarled anti-German slurs at the blank-faced soldiers, Anderson wrote. "Throngs of angry men and women pressed up close to them, gesticulating and heaping upon them opprobrious, stinging epithets." A well-dressed lady marched up to the troops and spat in the face of a German soldier, who chased her around at bayonet point until his sergeant pulled him back into the column.[72]

The Wide Awakes' greatest fiction—that militarism alone could bring order out of this chaos, that stoic marching could silence howling mobs, that hastily organized young men driven by shared hatred could become soldiers—was evaporating. In its place, Anderson wrote, "Human nature at last gave way."[73]

It's futile to try to narrate, step-by-step, how exactly it played out. No one present that day witnessed all the steps in order. Surely someone fired first, but nobody knew who it was back then, and we can't know now. Many agreed that they heard a racket up at the front of the long messy column. Was that *shooting* in the distance, a volley barely audible above the racket? Young Philip Stephenson said he saw youths throwing clods of mud at Union troops, who responded by firing over the boys' heads. A German newspaperman commanding one column of troops said he could see fifteen to twenty men with revolvers begin to shoot from a construction site. "Shots came from the building, from the trees, and from the camp fences," he recalled. Soldiers started aiming into the crowds. One managed to accidentally shoot his own captain in the leg. William Tecumseh Sherman watched a sergeant knock down a drunk man. The man got up, put his hat back on, then drew a small pistol and started to shoot into the column. James Peckham may have seen the same drunk man, and watched in horror as he reached out and fired one, two, three, four rounds into the mass of soldiers, before he was "thrust through with a bayonet." The shooting picked up now. Sherman "saw men and women running in all directions." Realizing what a mistake it had been to bring Willie, Sherman grabbed his son, and the two of them tumbled down an embankment. They could hear "the balls cutting the leaves over our heads" as he shielded his son. When the soldiers stopped to reload, Sherman hustled them away to safety.[74]

Thirty were killed, twenty-eight of them civilians, including three women, and seventy-five more wounded. Worse than Pratt Street, worse than John Brown's raid or anything in Kansas, or any fighting among Americans in decades. The Union side mostly celebrated. Ulysses S. Grant happened to be outside the Berthold mansion at Fifth and Pine, to watch as Basil Duke's boys finally lowered their makeshift Confederate flags. He noted the way the seizure of the camp, and the shooting into the crowds, made the unionists "rampant, aggressive, and, if you will, intolerant." Nathaniel Lyon sure was. After he recovered from his horse kick, the captain issued a statement blaming the "innocent men, women, and children" for getting themselves shot. "It is no fault of the troops," he spat, that a raucous mob let curiosity overcome them. Even though the violence sparked days of rioting, it was seen as a bold blow for the Union. Northern newspapers cheered, and Captain Lyon became a hero, winning the "admiration of loyal people all over the country." Lincoln sent praise. Watching from Illinois, Gustav Koerner smirked that the deaths might help teach the mobs "that the secession business was more dangerous than they thought it was."[75]

This was about right. Union forces proved willing to be dangerous for once. In marching on Camp Jackson, Lyon and Blair took an initiative that few on their side had been willing to hazard. All along, those opposed to the Slave Power had bristled with grievance, a humiliated sense that their opponents were always willing to go further, be bolder, more likely to throw rocks, or cane senators, or fire on federal forts. Now the rhetorical fighting men in Congress, and performative fighting men of the Wide Awakes, had turned into actual fighters—albeit jumpy and ill-trained ones. Camp Jackson was like an answer to Pratt Street. In Baltimore, the mobs had been at fault, and a quarter of those killed were Union soldiers. But in St. Louis, the soldiers were responsible for most of the violence. Over 90 percent of those killed were civilians in the crowd. It would still take months before the Union and Confederate armies would meet on grand battlefields, in something that looked like the Civil War many of us learned about in school. But its final evolution—out of the street-level politics and neighborhood mobbing of the antebellum era, into columns of men with rifles—had taken place in St. Louis's streets.

All along this process, Americans debated the line between free expression and political violence, asking over and over where the boundary between competition and war lay. In St. Louis after Camp Jackson, they could finally see it, if only in hindsight. Louis D. Rosette—secretary of the Springfield Wide Awakes—witnessed the fight and wrote to his brother afterward: "It looks quite like war in St. Louis now." A local twelve-year-old boy agreed. He happened upon a dead body outside his house, and watched as a servant tried to scrub blood off the sidewalk. "The sight to me was indescribably horrible," he recalled. "My father said this was civil war." A nation used to political instability, but which had mostly glimpsed warfare from afar, could finally tell the difference up close.[76]

The Wide Awakes of 1860 had become, with so much goading, the dangerous military presence their enemies had always accused them of being. The ranks of the first volunteer forces assembling across the North swelled with the same men—James S. Chalker and James Sanks Brisbin and Henry T. Sperry and Ducksy O'Neill and so many others. They had changed in the process, transmogrifying from a political club with militarist symbols into a military organization with political biases.

After the shooting at Camp Jackson, a Washington newspaper offered a eulogy for the strange club: "They went into the meetings, pacific, political associations; they came out of them, formidable military bodies, already well drilled and fitted by the long practice of the Presidential campaign to act as an efficient organization against armed treason." On one side of their winding story, their birth was witnessed by Cassius Clay and Abraham Lincoln; on the other side their ultimate destination was observed by Ulysses S. Grant and William Tecumseh Sherman. The Wide Awakes were gone, and the Civil War was here.[77]

CODA

"Power Must Follow"

E VEN IN 1889, the Hartford Originals were still synchronizing their uniforms. Twenty-eight years after Abraham Lincoln took his oath of office—watched over by rooftop snipers and plainclothes Wide Awakes—the middle-aged club members rode south to Washington again. This time they were honored guests, on a pilgrimage to shake hands with incoming Republican president Benjamin Harrison. Of course they would need matching outfits. But instead of black capes, they ordered all members to wear dark suits, dark derby hats, white silk lapel badges, white gloves, and white ties, and carry a white cane.[1]

The boys who marched like antebellum paramilitaries reassembled as spiffy Gilded Age gentlemen.

The 1889 reunion was merely the grandest the Hartford Originals held in those years. Immediately after the Civil War, most had gone their separate ways. But middle-age nostalgia brought them back together for nearly every presidential election between 1880 and 1908. Henry Sperry, Julius Rathbun, George Bissell, and hundreds of others turned out to laugh about old times over salmon hollandaise and imperial punch. The insurance millionaire Henry P. Hitchcock—who had first suggested the name Wide Awakes—organized the reunions and kept the scrapbooks. Even outside Hartford, even into the twentieth century, reporters found that the command "Wideawakes, attention!" still brought a "happy gleam" to the eyes of "old gray heads of today who were boys 48 years ago."[2]

Among the amiable fellows chatting over punch stood one noticeably slender, sharp-faced, finely dressed gentleman. Photographs show Edgar

Yergason in a dark three-piece suit and derby hat, wearing a gold watch chain and a little mustache. Instead of a "happy gleam," Yergason eyes the camera with keen appraisal. That sharp eye helped Yergason rise from obscure clerk to famous decorator. Soon after shaking President Harrison's hand on that reunion excursion, Yergason was back in the White House, redecorating it in a grand, sunny Colonial Revival style. Considered "one of the most picturesque cosmopolitans" by turn-of-the-century society papers, "Colonel Yergason" liked to tell banquet guests that when he was a boy, he "started the Wide-Awake Clubs."[3]

As the fiery young predictors of 1860 became doughty preservers of a gauzy memory of the conflict, Yergason complained that "no one seems to know the facts" about his Wide Awakes. So he invited visitors to his grand Asylum Hill mansion, where he had assembled one of the country's great Civil War collections. There he displayed his original hand-stitched cambric cape, and the spiffier enameled-cloth version that he wore for most of the campaign of 1860, as well as the coat, shirt, shoes, suspenders, and backpack he wore in the Union army. And, at the stunning center of Yergason's collection, a six-foot American flag that had hung behind Abraham Lincoln in his Ford's Theatre box on April 14, 1865. When John Wilkes Booth shot the president, Lincoln is said to have fallen back, clutching at that very flag. After acquiring the relic in the 1870s, Yergason could tell the story of the Civil War in textiles, from his cambric Wide Awake capes to a wool soldier's coat to the silk flag that fluttered over the martyred president.[4]

But by the end of the century, shimmering black and Union army blue evoked a bygone past. The present belonged in Yergason's closet, not his collection—in that dark suit, derby hat, white gloves, and white tie he wore to the White House. And when ex–Wide Awakes assembled, it was no longer in the boardinghouses and barrooms of 1860 but in the Senate chambers, boardrooms, and first-class railroad cars that ruled a new civilization, headquartered somewhere between Hartford, Chicago, and Washington.

"The seed which we then planted has taken root," the battle-scarred Lewis Clephane told another Wide Awake reunion celebrating the 1889 Harrison inauguration. "We are to-day enjoying its fruit as the great Republican Party." Other Republicans called the once grassroot movement "the Grand Old Party," a term that came into use in 1874. That same year, the cartoonist Thomas Nast selected the lumbering elephant as the organization's symbol. It all captured a moment when—with the South devastated and the West unsettled—northern Republicans built the sprawling empire later historians would call the "Yankee Leviathan." If before the Civil War most of the wealthiest states were in the South, by 1890 the Northeast and Midwest held every one of the forty-eight most developed counties in America, while all of the "least developed" were in the former Confederacy. Politics was still a hard-fought slog, but at the top of the heap there was usually a man from Ohio or New York (often a bearded Republican Union army vet) in the White House. Such men held that post for all but four of the fifty years after 1860, a longer reign even than the Virginians of the early republic.[5]

And many of them had been on intimate terms with the Wide Awakes in 1860. Over the rest of the nineteenth century, five of the nine presidents had ties to the movement. Lincoln was present at their debut, Grant trained companies in Galena, Hayes and Garfield spoke at torchlit rallies, and Benjamin Harrison was reported to have been a member. Further down the ladder, friends of the movement like Carl Schurz and Henry Wilson became secretary of the interior and vice president, respectively, while former members found office as secretary of the treasury, senators from Connecticut, New York, and Ohio, and governors of Illinois and Ohio. John Mercer Langston, that first Black Wide Awake, fought for Reconstruction as a congressman representing Virginia. John Meredith Read Jr. served as an ambassador. Lewis Clephane ran the Washington postal service, as well as banks and railroads. And James Sanks Brisbin went west, fighting in Indian Wars and penning *The Beef Bonanza*, a bestseller on ranching that inspired many to take up western cattle farming, including Theodore Roosevelt.[6]

More broadly, the dawning trends the Wide Awakes "embodied" in 1860 became the national ethos over the next generation. America after the war was more martial, a country formerly committed to temporary citizen soldiers now filled with colonels and war memorials. It was more majoritarian—not actually representative, but rhetorically committed to the power of the ballot box. Over time, this devotion to majority contorted into a Gilded Age hostility toward any "special interest"—a bias formed against the Slave Power but used to silence Black, Indigenous, Chinese, labor, and women's suffrage voices. The national culture was also generally more excited by associations, clubs, and fraternal orders, better at marketing and advertising and branding, more in love with the power of organization, and more awed by spectacle and bigness.

These were all tendencies that the Wide Awakes of 1860 pointed toward. Of course, the few hundred thousand Wide Awakes did not remake all of American society, but they were the advance guard, scouting terrain over which the culture would march.[7]

The movement's legacy was clearest in how Americans fought for power. In a trend started by the Wide Awakes, and supercharged by the war, diverse political campaigners chose torchlit militarism as their preferred device across the rest of the nineteenth century. Uniformed young men marched for free trade and for high tariffs, for White supremacy and for Black voting rights, for Chinese exclusion, for prohibition. Fireworks companies mass-produced campaign outfits, selling the same capes and kepis, knight's tunics and Prussian *pickehaubes*, to all sides. What had been revolutionary militarism for the Wide Awakes became a routine element of status quo politics. By 1890 one suffragist complained that it was hard to make reasoned arguments to men who expected politics to mean only "brass bands and huzzahs."[8]

That militarism influenced politics at all levels. The most powerful interest group in late nineteenth-century America was the Grand Army of the Republic, a Union veterans' organization with strong Republican sympathies. Five presidents and half a million White and Black vets were members (many of them once Wide Awakes). They marched and lobbied for generous Union pensions, until such handouts made up nearly one third of all federal expenditures. Militarism also suffused southern politics, including numerous African American political clubs calling themselves "Wide Awakes" during Reconstruction. More virulently, White supremacist Democrats formed rifle clubs, Red Shirts, White Leagues, and other companies using uniforms, army drums, militaristic drilling, and open violence to stamp out Black voting rights. When Republican congressmen argued for suppressing uniformed groups at southern elections, one Mississippi representative (and ex–Confederate brigadier general) asked if Congress would have sicced the army on the "quasi-military organization of 'the Wide-Awakes' in 1860" who started it all.[9]

The genie was out of the bottle, cracked by the Wide Awakes, and shattered by the war.

But even as northern Republicans ascended to power, the causes that the Wide Awakes had marched for seemed to dissipate. The movement had a kind of Doppler effect: separate concerns about slavery, free speech, public order, majority rule, and militarism had bunched together as the war hurtled closer, then scattered as it rattled off into memory. At Wide Awake reunions, the speeches mostly focused on the Gilded Age fixation with economic growth. *Hartford Courant* articles covering the Originals' many reunions have a palpable air of boredom about them. They even began to meet in that reserve of Hartford's political establishment, the Young Men's Republican Club rooms. The Originals exemplify how a once heated youth movement became a comfortable association of old buddies, how insurgency became hegemony.

Free speech was the Wide Awake cause that fell the hardest. Though it lay at the core of their campaign in 1860, even during the war years many Wide Awakes abandoned the principle when it didn't suit them. Republican mobs targeted Democratic "Copperheads" who criticized the Lincoln administration in at least a hundred attacks across the North, many led by Union soldiers. Men who had recently marched for free speech used their new power to "send a strong signal to the untrustworthy people among us!"—sometimes wearing Wide Awake uniforms. Copperhead printing presses joined old abolitionist apparatuses at the bottom of riverbeds.[10]

After the war, some prominent Wide Awakes helped suppress the public speech of the growing labor movement, participating in the hundreds of attacks on strikers across the rest of the century. General James S. Negley, who had defended James Sanks Brisbin's right to speak in Wheeling, led the militia against railroad strikers in bloody fighting in Pittsburgh in 1877. This approach to public political assembly was by no means unique to Republicans, but it does make the Wide Awakes' fight for free speech in 1860 look less like a principle and more like a tactic.[11]

And the populism that helped electrify the movement in 1860 lost its utility as well, once the Republicans no longer battled the Slave Power aristocracy. By the end of the Gilded Age it was hard to seriously claim that Republicans were the party of the mechanics and mudsills. John Meredith Read Jr. captured this drift into elitism perfectly. He spent the years after the war as a U.S. ambassador in Europe, preferring to live in a land "where the differences of class & breeding are still visible." Read Jr. complained that "the sons of rich men" were the truly oppressed in America. Historians have long puzzled over how the free-labor Republicans of 1860 morphed into the ultraconservatives of the 1890s, but the Wide Awakes show that the seeds of militaristic, nativist tribalism had been there all along.[12]

Concern for African American rights wobbled as well. Part of the trouble was the runaway success of the Wide Awakes' one coherent goal—halting the spread of slavery—which ended with complete emancipation. Almost no one saw that coming in 1860. Without opposition to the expansion of slavery to unite their diverse coalition, Republicans agreed on little else about race. The radical wing of the party—led by many of the fighting men who so inspired the Wide Awakes—helped build Reconstruction. But in a political system driven by "the systematic organization of hatreds," anger at the South lost its punch among many White Republican Northerners by the mid-1870s. Freedpeople suffered.

The African American leaders who organized Wide Awake clubs saw this painfully. Lewis Hayden, finding less support for integration in Boston, shifted his phenomenal organizational energies toward the African American fraternal order of the Prince Hall Free Masons. And while John Mercer Langston became the first African American to represent Virginia in Congress, he managed to hold that seat for just six months. Fraud and voter suppression would make Langston the last Black congressman from the state for a century.[13]

Even the militarism that clad much of American society started to look more and more like a costume. By the 1880s and 1890s, the Grand Army of the Republic lost its fighting edge, becoming an influential club for an older generation of middle-class, middle-aged, middle-American veterans to enjoy. George Kimball—the Wide Awake whose war began with a Boston brick to the eye—considered how the veterans of the GAR seemed in the 1880s. "I often wonder, as I look upon the young men of today, how we appear to them? Do they sometimes place us back, in imagination, and see us as we once were? Do they ever picture to their minds the long processions of men in blue, as they marched away with steady tread, ready to do or die, at the call of our country?" When the next generation of militarists appeared in the 1890s, the so-called war lovers like Theodore Roosevelt and Henry Cabot Lodge, their eagerness for combat looked dissonant to men who had wrapped themselves in militaristic garb for decades.[14]

The falling away of all these causes underlines the incredible achievement of the Wide Awakes and Lincoln's campaign, the era-defining success of getting all these diverse camps to march together as one host, if only for a time.

The demographic revolution of 1860 lasted longer. What Seward had color-fully called "the effort of the country to turn over" to its north side had staying power. In time, this looked less like a democratic love of majority rule and more like self-interest, the banal efforts of privileged northeastern and midwestern rural Protestants to hold on to power in the face of calls for reform from western, southern, urban, and immigrant populations. "Who hates who" outlived free speech by decades.[15]

But this "Yankee Leviathan" could not both run the county *and* claim the outsider verve that had made the Wide Awakes so thrilling. The problems of the late nineteenth and early twentieth centuries would look not like the conspiracies that had mobilized so many in 1860 but like what Louis Brandeis would call "the curse of bigness," epitomized in the Grand Old Party itself. Perhaps this helps explain why the story of the Wide Awakes has gone unwritten. Northern hegemony seemed so ubiquitous, and the halls of power were packed with former club members, shaking presidents' hands and redec-orating the White House. Henry P. Hitchcock sighed to reporters in 1908 that he had little left to say about the Wide Awakes, "because the story has so often been told." The movement looked like a fun fraternity from their youth, with little application to the present.[16]

Meanwhile, the defeated Confederacy nursed a Lost Cause narrative that, powered by searing defeat, lives on to this day. Sometimes history is written not so much by the comfortable victors as by the entitled and aggrieved.

When the country finally "turned over" again, a lifetime later, Franklin Delano Roosevelt built a New Deal coalition—the mightiest since Lincoln's Republicans—powered by grievance toward the very northeastern Republi-cans whose grandfathers had been Wide Awakes. FDR's winning campaign in 1932 relied on many of the demographic groups—southern Democrats, urban voters, immigrants, and non-Protestants—that the Wide Awakes had battled back in 1860. It was least popular in places like Connecticut, New Hampshire, Vermont, and Pennsylvania, old Republican strongholds with Wide Awake capes in their attics.

The country is "turning over" again in our lifetime. The northern stretches of the nation that crowed so loudly about majority rule in 1860 now lose congressional seats in every census. Three fifths of Americans lived in the Northeast and Midwest as late as 1920, yet the 2020 census found that as many live in the South as in the Northeast and Midwest combined. A majority live in the southern half of the country, a civilizational change too often overlooked. Elections today often turn on a handful of those Sun Belt states. The combined electoral college votes of California, Texas, and Florida carry nearly as much weight today as New York, Pennsylvania, and Ohio did in 1860. In America, as William Tecumseh Sherman wrote, where majority goes, "Power must follow."[17]

The longest-lasting Wide Awake innovation is the thing we still do in every campaign: try to convincingly link concrete symbols to abstract causes, the way the movement used militaristic uniforms to unite against the Slave Power. A walk through the Smithsonian's political history collections tells this story. The cape and torch discovered in that New Hampshire attic are now at home among rail-splitters' axes and full dinner pails, peace signs and MAGA hats. Elephants and donkeys (not to mention Black Panthers and prohibitionists' camels) stare down from the shelves. The very words we use to talk about politics rely on metaphor: *campaigning* and *running*, *dark horses* and *favorite sons*, *hardball* and *hatchet jobs*, *big shots* and *big leagues* and *big cheeses* and *big sticks*. They all attempt a symbolic borrowing, a matching game in the unsteady relationship between ideas and things.[18]

And no metaphor has more power than violence. We know this in our own politics: the menacing and mobilizing vibrations of a rifle scope's crosshairs over a rival candidate, or Kevlar vests and homemade shields at protests, or an AR-15 pin on a congressperson's lapel. We debate the distinction between meaning something literally and seriously. Were President Donald Trump's twenty calls to "fight" in his January 6, 2021, speech before the attack on the Capitol tactical or "aspirational"? The Wide Awakes of 1860 played this matching game too. Their choice of military symbols, just before America's central military conflict, has no equal in the Smithsonian's vaults.[19]

As with so many metaphors, the symbols the Hartford Originals chose were not premeditated. It happened, as Henry Hitchcock later explained, "quite by accident." Perhaps this improvisation is why it was so hard to tell whether the Wide Awakes were wearing costumes or battle gear, preparing for a vote or a fight. They didn't know either. After the election, the clubs engaged in another tentative borrowing, repurposing a campaign organization to do a military job, first to defend Lincoln, then to fight secession. The story of the Wide Awakes is the story of improvisation, a movement of tailors fashioning a striking outfit for a special occasion. They literally looked around a fabric shop and found the symbols that would launch an army.[20]

The Kentucky Cassandra George N. Sanders warned New Yorkers, on the eve of the 1860 election, "The South looks to your military and militant Wide Awakes, to your banners, your speeches, your press, and your votes, and not to what Mr. Lincoln may say or do after his election." Political campaigns are designed to be publicly consumable, as articulate as the finest orator. That's what the young men who organized the Wide Awakes understood, from the evening George Bissell ordered the Talcott boys to the front of the march, from the moment the New Haven company put their bloodied marchers onstage. Their democracy was itself a public performance. The era's hatred of conspiracies grew from fear that the real action was taking place off that stage, not in the public eye where it belonged. Democrats called the Wide Awake movement a "dumb show," but really it was quite the opposite. What seemed unintelligible, or superficial, or just plain silly, mattered deeply in the end.

For much of the last century or so, this all looked like a lot of hullabaloo. But citizens living in a stable political system, inexperienced with the hazy line between politics and violence, could not see what was right in front of them. Today, Americans have been jolted awake by a furious energy, latent in our democracy. It helps make the Wide Awakes more comprehensible than they were just a few election cycles ago. Their story only seemed strange in contrast to the American exceptionalism that taught us that political violence can't happen here. Among the many uncanny elements of their movement, the most recognizable to us today may be the conception of American democracy as a noisy, confrontational, symbolic performance, just on the verge of a fight.

What the Wide Awakes wanted mattered less than how they tried to show it. Those skinny nineteen-year-olds drilling for war proved to be better forecasters of what was coming than all the august orators or party platforms.

We look back on all of this through a century and a half of mostly viewing political spectacle as hoopla, just a matter of elephants and donkeys and confetti and balloons. People often dismiss performative politics as empty, a collection of stock gestures going nowhere, the work of self-interested politicians or high-priced consultants. But our own era reminds us of the power of spectacle and bluff, costume and prop. They can be intellectually richer, and better indicators of what is to come, than forms of political expression we traditionally consider more substantive. Perhaps one of the central lessons of recent American politics is that, while the chattering classes parse phrases, and conspiracists hunt for hidden meanings, the key plotlines take place right out in the open.

It is a burning imperative we share with Americans of 1860–61, but which most intervening generations of Americans could not understand: take the show seriously.

The Wide Awakes knew this. The young Republicans of 1860 expressed it most clearly, not in their capes, or their drilling, but in the most universal and self-evident symbol they chose, a signal of both their own alertness and their awareness that they were being watched. Their open eye stared, rapt, at the same spectacle that transfixes us today.

ACKNOWLEDGMENTS

How do you thank everyone who contributed to a project that has lasted nearly your entire professional life? I started after the Wide Awakes as a twenty-three-year-old, just getting up the confidence to call myself a "historian" out loud. Seventeen years later I'm still chasing them, even as I become one of the old fogies the movement mocked. Over those years, I've accumulated huge debts. First, to those who preserved the resources upon which this story was built. Then, for those who offered up their own knowledge and guidance. And finally, to the kind souls who buoyed this project along the way, keeping my balloon afloat by simply asking polite questions, listening to me talk Wide Awakes even as the term risked becoming a jumble of syllables in my mouth.

Everyone who asked me some version of "How are those Wide Awakes treating you today?" over the last seventeen years has contributed to this project.

The University of Virginia, back in 2007, set me on off this long hunt. Michael F. Holt showed early curiosity and confidence, with frequent reminders of what junior researchers could uncover, and an unparalleled ability to make this well-trod era feel fresh. Gary W. Gallagher provided interest and faith and rigor and humor. Elizabeth R. Varon has been a sage guide, combining endless commitment, pinpoint questions, and broad historical analysis. Fellow students Brent Cebul, Will Kurtz, and Mike Caires asked key questions at a formative time.

This book started as an article in the *Journal of American History*, where Ed Linenthal threw me an academic lifeline when I most needed one. I'll always be grateful.

The Smithsonian's National Museum of American History picked up where UVA left off. I'll always maintain that I got the job because the curator Larry Bird got a kick out of a funny anecdote about a Wide Awake street fight I shared with him. I have to thank the whole institution for bringing together political historians like Larry, Harry Rubenstein, Lisa Kathleen

Graddy, Claire Jerry, and Barbara Clark Smith. Friends and colleagues, especially Tim Winkle, Peter Manseau, and Ellen Feingold, contributed the kind
of curiosity and encouragement that makes it possible to complete long projects. Eric Hintz, at the Lemelson Center for the Study of Invention and
Innovation, did essential scholarship on Hartford, and made the debatable
decision of letting me into the museum to begin with. Many other staff
members (Roberta Walsdorf, Bennie Bunton, and Valeska Hilbig among
them) kept the institution going, found ways to machete through the wilds of
federal bureaucracy, and get this work out to the public.

This book draws from evidence accumulated in historical societies,
archives, and museums across the country—at least twenty-seven institutions
in two dozen states. I want to thank all the librarians, archivists, curators,
and various specialists who not only met my specific Wide Awake needs, but
built and maintained institutions that preserve what would otherwise be lost.
First among them, the wonderful little Milford Historical Society and its
wide-awake curator Charlie Annand, not to mention Mark Genovesi and
Heather Flynn, who rediscovered George P. Holt's cape there. The Connecticut Museum of History and Culture provided much additional evidence and
support, especially Tasha Caswell and Natalie Belanger.

If UVA trained me, the Smithsonian supported me, and many historical
societies fed me evidence, a small crew of scholars and enthusiasts showed an
appetite for this story. First among them is Ted Widmer, whom I cannot
thank enough for his kindness, his talent, and his inspiring work. Alexis
Coe, Kanisorn Wongsrichanalai, Jonathan White, Adam Goodheart, and
Meg Groeling offered guidance, resources, ideas, and role models. Shane
Seley of Wide Awake Films was just a blast of energy and ideas, along with
Brian Rose and Michael Mavretic. Eric Gottesman and Hank Willis Thomas
of For Freedoms showed me how twenty-first-century the Wide Awakes
story could be. A number of avid collectors made it clear how many people
out there just love the Wide Awakes.

Bloomsbury Publishing and Calligraph Literary Agency made seventeen
years of digging into something that could speak to the world. Ben Hyman
has been—again—wise, clear-thinking, broad-minded, and sure-footed,
capable of seeing both a story's widest connotations and most nuanced subt-
lies. At Calligraph, Katherine Flynn's sound judgment and easy confidence
has again helped me turn a hunch into a real live book. At Bloomsbury,

Barbara Darko, Morgan Jones, and Rose Mahorter brought an additional arsenal of insight, curiosity, and know-how.

Revisiting the Wide Awakes in the 2020s felt like playing in a cover band of myself, reprising an earlier rendition. It drew out, in sharp relief, what had changed since 2007, and what has stayed the same. My parents and siblings helped from the beginning and still do. Ed Grinspan is still my most thorough and rewarding reader. But the newer additions, first Keiana, and later Solomon, revised and deepened the experience along the way. Keiana planted the seed (maybe yet to come?) of a graphic novel version of the Wide Awakes' story. And Solomon padded into my study, early in the morning, to ask about the Wide Awake engravings and make up silly songs about them. It's been a good seventeen years, and I'm thankful for all of it.

IMAGE PLATE CREDITS

Page One:
—Mohawk Wide Awake rally: Heritage Auctions / HA.com

Page Two:
—George P. Holt's cape: Collections of the Division of Political History, National Museum of American History, Smithsonian Institution
—Hartford in the 1860s: Connecticut Museum of Culture and History, 1960.93.20

Page Three:
—Edgar S. Yergason: Connecticut Museum of Culture and History, Ms 96829
—Cambric cape: Connecticut Museum of Culture and History, Ms 13264

Page Four:
—Hartford Originals: Connecticut Museum of Culture and History, Julius G. Rathbun, "The 'Wide Awakes': The Great Political Organization of 1860," *Connecticut Quarterly* 1, no. 4 (October–December 1895), 332, F91.C8
—Fill-in-the-blank membership form: Connecticut Museum of Culture and History, Ms 13264

Page Five:
—Walt Whitman: Library of Congress Prints and Photographs Division, LC-USZ62-82781
—Swiveling torch: Collections of the Division of Political History, National Museum of American History, Smithsonian Institution

Page Six:
—Abraham Lincoln first glimpsed: Connecticut Museum of Culture and History, 1980.93.36

—Wide Awakes of Newark, New Jersey: Connecticut Museum of Culture and History, 1972.36.22

Page Seven:
—Typical nineteenth-century processions: Getty Images via DEA / BIBLIO-TECA AMBROSIANA

Page Eight:
—Membership certificate: Library of Congress Prints and Photographs Division, LC-DIG-pga-06782
—*Harper's Weekly* print: Collections of the Division of Political History, National Museum of American History, Smithsonian Institution

Page Nine:
—Wide Awake banner: Courtesy of the Equator Collection, Washington, D.C.
—Chatham Wide Awake contingent: Permanent Collection, Columbia County Historical Society, NY

Page Ten:
—George Beza Woodward: Library of Congress Prints and Photographs Division, LC-DIG-ppmsca-71615
—Enos Christman: Courtesy of the Collection of Jonathan W. White

Page Eleven:
—Unknown Iowa Wide Awake: Floyd and Marion Rinhart Papers, SPEC. RARE.CMS.0360, Rare Books and Manuscripts Library, Ohio State University
—Lewis Hayden: Courtesy of the Ohio History Connection, MSS116AV BOX48 02MA 066

Page Twelve:
—French Cartoon: Collections of the Division of Political History, National Museum of American History, Smithsonian Institution
—Douglas Club: Collections of the Division of Political History, National Museum of American History, Smithsonian Institution

—Lincoln's association with the Wide Awakes: Library of Congress, Rare Book and Special Collections Division, Alfred Whital Stern Collection of Lincolniana

Page Thirteen:
—Mass rally in Springfield, Illinois: Library of Congress Prints and Photographs Division, LC-USZ62-13682
—Sheet music: Collections of the Division of Political History, National Museum of American History, Smithsonian Institution

Page Fourteen:
—Chaotic scene in Boston's Tremont Temple: Library of Congress Prints and Photographs Division, LC-USZ62-13682
—Pratt Street riot: Library of Congress Prints and Photographs Division, LC-DIG-pga-09285

Page Fifteen:
—Former Wide Awakes held reunions and rallies: Connecticut Museum of Culture and History, Ms 13264
—Cape owner George P. Holt: Milford Historical Society

Page Sixteen:
—The movement's memory: Courtesy of Shane Seley
—For Freedoms: Courtesy of For Freedoms

NOTES

EPIGRAPH

Walt Whitman, "To the States, to Identify the 16th, 17th, or 18th Presidentiad," *Leaves of Grass* (Boston: Thayer and Eldridge, 1860), 400–401.

PREFACE: WE SHALL ALL BE WIDE-AWAKES

1. James Sanks Brisbin to Ezra Brisbin, November 1, 1860, James Sanks Brisbin Papers, Montana Historical Society Library and Archives, Helena (hereafter Brisbin Papers), 17; "A Trip Down South," *Bellefonte (PA) Centre Democrat*, November 15, 1860; "Notwithstanding the Rain," *Wheeling (VA) Intelligencer*, November 3, 1860; "The Lincoln Man," *Wheeling (VA) Intelligencer*, November 6, 1860; and "In Our Telegraphic Columns," *Wheeling (VA) Intelligencer*, November 23, 1860.
2. Brisbin to Brisbin, 9–10.
3. Brisbin to Brisbin, 17.
4. Brisbin to Brisbin, 16; and "Trip Down South."
5. Brisbin to Brisbin, 18.
6. Brisbin to Brisbin, 20; and Emory L. Kemp and Beverly B. Fluty, *The Wheeling Suspension Bridge: A Pictorial History* (Charleston, WV: Pictorial Histories, 1999).
7. Brisbin to Brisbin, 20–22; and "Trip Down South."
8. Brisbin to Brisbin, 15; Preston Bailhache, quoted in Jeremy Prichard, "In Lincoln's Shadow: The Civil War in Springfield, Illinois" (PhD diss., University of Kansas, 2014); "Read and Tremble!" *Chicago Tribune*, November 24, 1860, reprinted from *New Orleans Courier*; "Wide Awakes," *Los Angeles Daily News*, November 14, 1860; and "Political Riot at Troy," *Troy (NY) Times*, October 16, 1860.
9. "The Wide Awakes," *New York Tribune*, October 31, 1860.
10. "The Wide-Awakes on Saturday Evening," *Wisconsin State Journal* (Madison), June 11, 1860.
11. The exact number of Wide Awakes will always remain a mystery. We have only a few club rosters, and though newspapers often published the names of companies' elected officers, they usually neglected the full rank and file. Even the *New York Herald* shrugged, at the height of the campaign, "As to the number of

the Wide Awakes, we cannot form, just now, even an approximate idea." In my 2009 *Journal of American History* article, I guessed that there were about one hundred thousand members, based on the rough average of one hundred members per club, and roughly one thousand clubs in the nation. Fifteen additional years of research leads me to believe the number was probably much larger. The safest answer is that there were more than one hundred thousand Wide Awakes, but fewer than five hundred thousand.

Yet the national conception in 1860 was that the Wide Awakes had five hundred thousand members. The nation's most widely circulated newspaper, the *New York Herald*, made this claim on September 19, 1860, and over the next few months, it became the number cited in the *Nashville Union*, the *Chicago Tribune*, the *Daily Nashville Patriot*, the *New Orleans Daily Delta*, the *Lancaster Intelligencer*, the *Philadelphia Public Ledger*, the *Charleston Daily Courier*, and many other newspapers, North and South, Republican, Democratic, and Constitutional Union. Multiple senators (Henry Wilson, Alfred Iverson Sr., and Louis Wigfall) were quoted citing "half a million," and it appeared in reports as far away as London. When the Hartford Wide Awakes house organ, the *Hartford Courant*, offered a postelection accounting, they based their numbers on the idea of half a million Wide Awakes. James Sanks Brisbin, writing in the *Bellefonte (PA) Centre Democrat*, gathered "carefully prepared statistics" to suggest there were four hundred thousand members. In American memory, five hundred thousand calcified as the correct number of members in later accounts by Julius Rathbun, Gustav Koerner, and Benjamin F. Thompson.

But this number is too high. Lincoln only won 1.8 million votes total; it's impossible that nearly a third of his voters were Wide Awakes. Often, at Wide Awake rallies, the ratio of spectators to actual members was something like ten to one. There were thirty-one million people in the nation; it's hard to believe that one out of every sixty-two was a Wide Awake. On top of this, though the Wide Awakes kept rosters and membership rolls, and the Hartford Originals *tried* to keep track of the movement, the very idea of membership is a hazy one. How many of the men who marched in one procession were consistent members, and how many participated for one night, joining a crowd, and then quit? And what to do with the many other Republican clubs: Railsplitters and Zouaves and Young Men's Republican Organizations? At bottom, no statistics from this era, certainly not the self-serving exaggerations printed in newspapers, should be trusted. As with every other estimate of crowd size in this book, the notion of a half-million Wide Awake army must be viewed as a rough indication of the immense scale and importance of the club, rather than a literal count of total members.

Nonetheless, five hundred thousand is the number that stuck. And in a nation that was at once unprecedentedly connected, and shockingly diffuse, the myth of half a million Wide Awakes mattered more than the actual number. Everyone could hear that number; no one could really count. The belief that there were half a million Wide Awakes tells us as much about the nation in 1860 as an accurate head count would. *New York Herald*, September 10, 1860; Jon Grinspan, " 'Young Men for War': The Wide Awakes and Lincoln's 1860 Presidential Campaign," *Journal of American History* 96 (September 2009): 357–78; *New York Herald*, September 19, 1860; *Nashville Union*, September 22, 1860; *Chicago Tribune*, October 4, 1860; *Daily Nashville Patriot*, October 17, 1860; *New Orleans Daily Delta*, October 23, 1860; *Lancaster (PA) Intelligencer*, November 6, 1860; *Philadelphia Public Ledger*, December 13, 1860; *Charleston (SC) Daily Courier*, May 8, 1861; Benjamin F. Thompson, "The Wide Awakes of 1860," *Magazine of History with Notes and Queries* 10 (November 1909): 293–96; "Senator Iverson of Georgia," *Baltimore Sun*, December 28, 1860; "Louis Wigfall," *Philadelphia Public Ledger*, December 13, 1860; *Hartford Courant*, December 13, 1860; *Bellefont (PA) Centre Democrat*, October 4, 1860; *London Standard*, November 19, 1860; Julius G. Rathbun, "The 'Wide Awakes': The Great Political Organization of 1860," *Connecticut Quarterly* 1 (October 1895): 327–35; and *Memoirs of Gustav Koerner, 1809–1896: Life-Sketches Written at the Suggestion of His Children* (Cedar Rapids, IA: Torch Press, 1909), 2:98.

12. Whether there truly were 500,000 Wide Awakes—or closer to 100,000—their scale dwarfs many comparable organizations from recent times. The Proud Boys maintain seventy-two chapters nationwide in 2023. In 2017 it was estimated that they had 6,000 members nationwide, and in 2020 their (entirely unreliable) leader claimed 20,000 members. Looking back further, the Black Panthers cast a wide cultural shadow, but counted no more than 5,000 members, in thirty-four to forty chapters, at their peak in 1969. Deeper in American history, other organizations that recruited members, maintained distinctive uniforms and iconography, and worked to advance political and cultural causes rivaled the Wide Awakes' size. Estimates for the Second Ku Klux Klan (1915–44) range from 2 to 4 million members in 1925. In a nation of about 115 million people, this places membership at roughly the same proportion, or a bit bigger, than the supposed 500,000 Wide Awakes in a nation of 31 million. The American Protective League, which emerged during World War I, boasted 250,000 members— roughly the likely size of the Wide Awakes, but in a nation with three times the population. The Union League clubs that helped African Americans vote and defend themselves during Reconstruction claimed 300,000 members across the

South, organized in three thousand leagues. The Know Nothing movement of the 1850s probably looms largest. The numbers here are the haziest, but it is believed that shadowy organization may have had around 1 million adherents, and between 600,000 and 800,000 voters for their American Party in the 1855–56 congressional and presidential elections. This in a nation of perhaps 27 million people. The Know Nothings had the advantage of appeal in all sections of the nation, whereas the Wide Awakes won no members below the Upper South.

All of which is to say that in the history of American mass political movements, the Wide Awakes rank among the very largest, certainly compared to the more recent organizations.

Cassie Miller and Rachel Rivas, "The Year in Hate and Extremism 2022," Southern Poverty Law Center, Montgomery, Alabama, accessed June 20, 2023, https://www.splcenter.org/year-hate-extremism-2022; "Proud Boys: Organizational Overview," Mapping Militant Project, Stanford University Center for International Security and Cooperation, accessed June 20, 2023, https://cisac.fsi.stanford.edu/mappingmilitants/profiles/proud-boys; Michael X. Delli Carpini, "Black Panther Party, 1966–1982," in *The Encyclopedia of Third Parties in America*, ed. Immanuel Ness and James Ciment (Armonk, NY: Sharpe Reference, 2000), 194; Linda Gordon, *The Second Coming of the Ku Klux Klan and the American Political Tradition* (New York: Liveright, 2017); Adam Hochschild, "The Proud Boys and the Long-Lived Anxieties of American Men," *New York Times*, September 18, 2022; Michael Fitzgerald, *The Union League Movement in the Deep South* (Baton Rouge: Louisiana State University Press, 2000), 12–13; Craig Phelan, *Grand Master Workman: Terence Powderly and the Knights of Labor* (New York: Praeger, 2000); and Tyler Anbinder, *Nativism and Slavery: The Northern Know Nothings and the Politics of the 1850s* (New York: Oxford University Press, 1992), 43.

13. "Wide Awakes," *Janesville (WI) Daily Gazette*, May 24, 1860; and "The Canvas," *New York Tribune*, November 8, 1860.

14. "Wide Awakes and Minute Men," *San Francisco Bulletin*, November 6, 1860; and "Armed Wide Awakes," *Wayne County (PA) Herald*, July 19, 1860, citing *New York Express*.

15. Carl von Clausewitz, *On War (Vom Krieg)*, ed. Peter Pater (Princeton, NJ: Princeton University Press, 1984), 87.

16. This is not a slight to some otherwise great works, including David M. Potter, *The Impending Crisis, 1848–1861*, ed. Donald Fehrenbacher (New York: Harper & Row, 1976), 435; Osborn Hamiline Oldroyal, *Lincoln's Campaign; or, The Political Revolution of 1860* (Chicago: Laird & Lee, 1896), 103–7; and Ernest A.

McKay, *The Civil War and New York City* (Syracuse, NY: Syracuse University Press, 1990), 20.

17. Grinspan, " 'Young Men for War.' "

18. Matt Dellinger, "A Civil War Movement Reawakens," *New York Times*, September 16, 2020; Ben Domenech and Fox News Staff, "Ben Domenech Explains Why It Is Time to Ask: Are You Woke or Are You Wide Awake?" *Fox News*, August 2, 2021, https://www.foxnews.com/media/ben-domenech -woke-wide-awake; and Victoria Benzine, "How the Wide Awakes Revived a Nineteenth Century Movement in the Name of Joy," *Brooklyn Magazine*, October 18, 2021.

19. In the intervening years after 2007, a crew of talented historians have made clever use of the Wide Awakes as illuminating leitmotifs in books on 1860–61, producing some of the very best writing about the era, including Douglas Egerton, *Year of Meteors: Stephen Douglas, Abraham Lincoln, and the Election That Brought the Civil War* (New York: Bloomsbury, 2010); Adam Goodheart, *1861: The Civil War Awakening* (New York: Alfred A. Knopf, 2011); and Edward L. Widmer, *Lincoln on the Verge: Thirteen Days to Washington* (New York: Simon & Schuster, 2020).

20. "Wide Awakes," *New York Tribune*.

CHAPTER ONE: DON'T CARE

1. There are varying accounts of the founding of the Wide Awakes. One centers on Edgar S. Yergason's designing of the Wide Awakes' cape, a second on the creation of their torches, a third on Lincoln's reputed role inspiring the movement, and a fourth on the fight the future Hartford Captain James S. Chalker got into the night of their formation. The latter two are entirely false—Chalker was not one of the first Wide Awakes in the Clay march, nor did he attend their initial meeting. Lincoln arrived in town after two Wide Awake events had transpired. The torch-invention bears more merit, but the Wide Awakes' torch design was not the most salient, distinctive, or exciting aspect of the movement in 1860. Yergason's cape was, and his account serves as the best place to begin their story.

   In addition Yergason proved to be a consistently reliable source. Yergason told similar versions of his story in 1888, 1909, and 1916, maintaining key details across decades. He was widely reputed to have a "keen memory," especially for physical attributes, and his records as a collector of Civil War objects have been widely cited. His version coheres with other accounts, including Henry T. Sperry's writings from 1860 and Julius Rathbun's 1895 history of the movement.

Henry P. Hitchcock, acting as the caretaker of the Hartford Original's memory, affirmatively included it in his scrapbook of the club's press clippings, which he then passed on to Yergason at his death. Edgar S. Yergason, letter to the editor, *Hartford Courant*, January 30, 1909, in Henry P. Hitchcock, Wide Awake Scrapbook (MS13264-25), Hartford Wide Awakes Records and Memorabilia (MS13264), Connecticut Historical Society, Hartford (hereafter Wide Awakes Records). See also "Personal Statement by Edgar S. Yergason," December 23, 1908, Yergason Family Papers, box 1, Connecticut Historical Society, Hartford (hereafter Yergason Papers); "The Old 'Wide Awakes,' " *Washington Press*, December 16, 1888; "Edgar S. Yergason's Collection of Relics," *Hartford Courant*, February 27, 1916; Keith MacKay, "The White House Interiors of Caroline Harrison and Edgar Yergason, 1890–1892" (master's thesis, Corcoran College of Art and Design, 2009), 11; and Julius G. Rathbun, "The 'Wide Awakes': The Great Political Organization of 1860," *Connecticut Quarterly* 1 (October 1895): 328.

For Talcott & Post's store, see Edgar S. Yergason to Charlotte Yergason, March 4, 1860, Yergason Papers, box 1; "Talcott & Post," *Hartford Courant*, January 18, 1860; "A Mammoth Sale!" *Hartford Courant*, December 19, 1859; and "Talcott & Post, Best Woven Hoop Skirts," *Hartford Courant*, February 15, 1860. For Cassius Clay's speech, see "Touro Hall," *Hartford Courant*, February 25, 1860; and "Border Ruffianism Revived by the Democracy," *Hartford Courant*, February 27, 1860.

2. MacKay, "White House Interiors"; "Make Your Home Beautiful, Failing This—I'll Do It For You," advertisements for E. S. Yergason Interior Decoration and Furnishings, Yergason Papers, box 3; and "Seen and Heard in the Cafes," *New-Yorker* 1, no. 9 (May 1, 1901).

3. David Ross Locke, *Divers Views, Opinions and Prophecies of Yoors Trooly, Petroleum V. Nasby* (Cincinnati: R. W. Carroll, 1867), 241.

4. Adam Goodheart, *1861: The Civil War Awakening* (New York: Alfred A. Knopf, 2011), 97; and William Cullen Bryant to Frances Bryant, November 29, 1860, in *The Letters of William Cullen Bryant*, ed. William Cullen Bryant II and Thomas G. Voss (New York: Fordham University Press, 1984), 4: Letter 1183.

5. Peter Kolchin, *American Slavery, 1619–1865* (New York: Hill and Wang, 1993), 82–83.

6. Ralph Waldo Emerson, "Natural Religion," February 3, 1861, in *The Later Lectures of Ralph Waldo Emerson, 1843–1871*, ed. Ronald A. Bosco and Joel Myerson (Athens: University of Georgia Press, 2001), 2:186.

7. Elizur Wright, *An Eye Opener for the Wide Awakes* (Boston: Thayer & Eldridge, 1860), 52; *The Life and Writings of Frederick Douglass: Pre–Civil War Decade,*

1850–1860, ed. Philip Sheldon Foner (New York: International, 1950), 505; James L. Huston, *Calculating the Value of the Union: Slavery, Property Rights, and the Economic Origins of the Civil War* (Chapel Hill: University of North Carolina Press, 2003); and B. D. Humes et al., "Representation of the Antebellum South in the House of Representatives: Measuring the Impact of the Three-Fifths Clause," in *Party, Process, and Political Change in Congress: New Perspectives on the History of Congress*, ed. D. W. Brady and M. D. McKubbins (Stanford, CA: Stanford University Press, 2002), 1:455; and Goodheart, *1861*, 7.

8. Campbell Gibson and Kay Jung, *Historical Census Statistics on Population Totals, 1790 to 1990*, Working Paper 56 (Washington, D.C.: U.S. Census Bureau, 2002), 22.

9. "I don't believe that the present excitement in politics is anything more than the signs of the passage of power from southern politicians to northern and western politicians," Sherman wrote elsewhere. William Tecumseh Sherman to George Mason Graham, September 20, 1860, in *William T. Sherman as a College President*, ed. Walter L. Fleming (Cleveland: Arthur Clark, 1912), 286; and William Tecumseh Sherman to Ellen Boyle Ewing, July 10, 1860, in *Home Letters of General Sherman*, ed. M. A. DeWolfe Howe (New York: Charles Scribner's Sons, 1909), 179.

10. William W. Freehling, *Secessionists at Bay, 1776–1854*, vol. 1 of *The Road to Disunion* (New York: Oxford University Press, 1990), 39; and Frank Towers, *The Urban South and the Coming of the Civil War* (Charlottesville: University of Virginia Press, 2004), 32–33, see also 16–33.

11. Joanne Freeman, *The Field of Blood: Violence in Congress and the Road to Civil War* (New York: Farrar, Straus and Giroux), 240; and Drew Gilpin Faust, *John Henry Hammond and the Old South: A Design for Mastery* (Baton Rouge: Louisiana State University Press, 1985).

12. Elizabeth R. Varon, *Disunion! The Coming of the American Civil War, 1789–1859* (Chapel Hill: University of North Carolina Press, 2008); Gary Gallagher, *The Union War* (Cambridge, MA: Harvard University Press, 2011); Martin Van Buren to Thomas Ritchie, January 13, 1827, Papers of Martin Van Buren, ser. 5, Library of Congress; Nic Wood, " 'A Sacrifice on the Altar of Slavery': Doughface Politics and Black Disenfranchisement in Pennsylvania, 1837–1838," *Journal of the Early Republic* 31, no. 1 (Spring 2011): 99; Jane Ann Moore and William F. Moore, *Owen Lovejoy and the Coalition for Equality* (Champaign-Urbana: University of Illinois Press, 2019), 3; and Freeman, *Field of Blood*, 138.

13. Abraham Lincoln to Joshua F. Speed, August 24, 1855, in *The Life and Works of Abraham Lincoln*, ed. Marion Mills Miller (New York: Current Literature, 1907),

4:191; and Abraham Lincoln, speech at Lincoln-Douglas debate, October 15, 1858, Alton, Illinois, in *Political Debates Between Abraham Lincoln and Stephen A. Douglas* (Cleveland: O. S. Dubell, 1895), 354.

14. Without the Three-Fifths Clause, Thomas Jefferson would not have won the presidency in 1800.

15. Humes et al., "Representation of the Antebellum South in the House of Representatives," 1:455.

16. Scott Reynolds Nelson and Carol Sheriff, *A People at War: Civilians and Soldiers in America's Civil War* (New York: Oxford University Press, 2008), 4–6; and David Grimsted, *American Mobbing: Toward Civil War* (New York: Oxford University Press, 1998), 248.

17. Grimsted, *American Mobbing*, 246.

18. Grimsted, *American Mobbing*, viii; and Michael Feldberg, *The Turbulent Era: Riot and Disorder in Jacksonian America* (New York: Oxford University Press, 1980).

19. Grimsted, *American Mobbing*, 3.

20. David S. Reynolds, *Walt Whitman's America: A Cultural Biography* (New York: Vintage Books, 1996), 307; William Tecumseh Sherman to Ellen Boyle Ewing, January 5, 1861, *Home Letters*, 189; Joel Strangis, *Lewis Hayden and the War Against Slavery* (North Haven, CT: Linnet Books, 1999), 60–61, 77; and Kellie Carter Jackson, *Force and Freedom: Black Abolitionists and the Politics of Violence* (Philadelphia: University of Pennsylvania Press, 2020).

21. Dale T. Knobel, *"America for the Americans": The Nativist Movement in the United States* (New York: Twayne, 1996); Tyler Anbinder, *Nativism and Slavery: The Northern Know Nothings and the Politics of the 1850s* (New York: Oxford University Press, 1992); and Katie Oxx, *The Nativist Movement in America: Religious Conflict in the Nineteenth Century* (New York: Routledge, 2013).

22. Towers, *Urban South*, 32–33.

23. Michael F. Holt, "The Politics of Impatience: The Origins of Know Nothingism," *Journal of American History* 60, no. 2 (September 1973): 315, 318.

24. Robert M. DeWitt, *The Life, Trial and Execution of Capt. John Brown, Being a Full Account of the Attempted Insurrection at Harper's Ferry, VA* (New York: Robert M. DeWitt, 1859), 21; and H. W. Brands, *The Zealot and the Emancipator: John Brown, Abraham Lincoln, and the Struggle for American Freedom* (New York: Doubleday, 2020).

25. "Correspondent from New York," *Baltimore Sun*, November 5, 1860.

26. Charles Francis Adams Jr., *An Autobiography* (Boston: Houghton Mifflin, 1916), 43–44; and Freeman, *Field of Blood*.

27. Walt Whitman, "To the States, to Identify the 16th, 17th, or 18th Presidentiad," *Leaves of Grass* (Boston: Thayer and Eldridge, 1860), 400–401.

28. Freeman, *Field of Blood*, 136.

29. Freeman, 219.

30. Henry Adams, *The Miseducation of Henry Adams* (Boston: Houghton Mifflin, 1918), 7; and Timothy Shenk, *Realigners, Partisan Hacks, Political Visionaries, and the Struggle to Rule American Democracy* (New York: Farrar, Straus and Giroux), 170.

31. Grimsted, *American Mobbing*, 252.

32. Adams, *Miseducation*, 104; Dorothy Wickenden, *The Agitators: Three Friends Who Fought for Abolition and Women's Rights* (New York: Scribner, 2022); and Trudy Krisher, *Fanny Seward: A Life* (Syracuse, NY: Syracuse University Press, 2015), 47–50.

33. "Seward's Speech," *Chicago Tribune*, October 25, 1860.

34. William Tecumseh Sherman to Ellen Boyle Ewing, July 10, 1860, in *Home Letters*, 178; and Eric Foner, *Free Soil, Free Labor, Free Men* (New York: Oxford University Press, 1970).

35. "The Election of Mr. Banks to the Speakership," *New York Times*, February 6, 1856; Moore and Moore, *Lovejoy*, 118, 137–38; Freeman, *Field of Blood*, 210; "Letter from G. W. P.," *Liberator*, December 31, 1859; and Donald Barr Chidsey, *The Gentleman from New York: A Life of Roscoe Conkling* (New Haven, CT: Yale University Press, 1935), 11, 18.

36. *The Works of William H. Seward*, ed. George E. Baker (Boston: Houghton Mifflin, 1884), 4:56.

37. "The Mormons," *Athens (TN) Post*, April 28, 1850; "Southern Democrats," *Raleigh (NC) Times*, January 3, 1850; and "Examine Your Tickets," *Gettysburg (PA) Compiler*, October 9, 1854.

38. "Tremendous Crowd," *Pittsburgh Gazette*, March 31, 1856.

39. Yergason, letter to the editor. See also Yergason, "Personal Statement"; "Old 'Wide Awakes' "; and Rathbun, " 'Wide Awakes,' " 328.

40. Freehling, *Secessionists at Bay*, 469–70.

41. Touro Hall was also a functioning synagogue, an ironic venue considering that Puritan Connecticut had been the last state in the nation to permit Jewish congregations, only changing the state religion in 1843. Nevertheless, it had become the marquee event space in town, just a block from Talcott & Post's textile store. Ellsworth Grant and Marion H. Grant, *The City of Hartford, 1785–1984: An Illustrated History* (Hartford: Connecticut Historical Society, 1986), 62; and "Border Ruffianism Revived."

42. "Border Ruffianism Revived."

43. "Touro Hall"; Rathbun, " 'Wide Awakes,' " 327–28; George P. Bissell, *The Twenty-Fifth Regiment: Connecticut Volunteers in the War of the Rebellion* (Rockville, CT: Press of the Rockville Journal, 1913); and "The Death of Banker Bissell," *New Haven (CT) Morning Journal*, April 13, 1891.

44. Rathbun, " 'Wide Awakes,' " 328; "The Connecticut Wide-Awakes," *New York Tribune*, May 3, 1860; and John Hay and John George Nicolay, *Abraham Lincoln: A History* (New York: Century, 1890), 2:284–85, fn 1.

45. "Border Ruffianism Revived"; and J. Doyle DeWitt, *Lincoln in Hartford* (Hartford: CT Civil War Centennial Commission, 1960), 13.

46. "Border Ruffianism in Hartford!" *Hartford Courant*, November 4, 1856.

47. "Border Ruffianism Revived."

48. Yergason, letter to the editor; and Yergason, "Old 'Wide Awakes.' "

CHAPTER TWO: AMERICA'S ARMORY

1. Julius G. Rathbun, "The 'Wide Awakes': The Great Political Organization of 1860," *Connecticut Quarterly* 1 (October 1895): 329; Edgar S. Yergason, "Personal Statement of Edgar S. Yergason," December 23, 1908, Yergason Papers; "The Old 'Wide Awakes,' " *Washington Press*, December 16, 1888; and Ellsworth Grant and Marion H. Grant, *The City of Hartford, 1785–1984: An Illustrated History* (Hartford: Connecticut Historical Society, 1986), 147–48.

2. Andrew Walsh, "Hartford: A Global History," in *Confronting Urban Legacy: Rediscovering Hartford and New England's Forgotten Cities*, ed. Xiangming Chen and Nick Bacon (Lanham, MD: Lexington Books, 2013), 22; Philip Leigh, "Civil War Ordnance Bureaus," *Essential Civil War Curriculum*, accessed June 24, 2023, https://www.essentialcivilwarcurriculum.com/civil-war-ordnance-bureaus .html; and Eric S. Hintz, "Hartford," in *Places of Invention: A Companion to the Exhibition at the Smithsonian's National Museum of American History*, ed. Arthur P. Molella and Anna Karvellas (Washington, D.C.: Smithsonian Institution Scholarly Press, 2015), 110.

3. Jim Rasenberger, *Revolver: Sam Colt and the Six-Shooter that Changed America* (New York: Scribner, 2021).

4. "Mark Twain, on His Travels," *Alta California* (San Francisco), March 3, 1868; and Hintz, "Hartford," 110–16.

5. "Twain, on His Travels."

6. Somewhat like what happened with the Winchester lever-action carbine in the Wild West, the cop on the beat's .38 revolver in the twentieth century, the gangster's tommy gun in the 1920s, or the AR–15 today.

7. Hintz, "Hartford," 120–21, 128.

8. Hintz, 110.

9. "The United States—Election Matters and the Courtesies of Society," *London Morning Post*, April 17, 1860; and James L. Huston, *Calculating the Value of the Union: Slavery, Property Rights, and the Economic Origins of the Civil War* (Chapel Hill: University of North Carolina Press, 2003), 26–32; and Harvey J. Graff, *The Legacies of Literacy* (Bloomington: Indiana University Press, 1987), 343.

10. Steve Courtney, *Mark Twain's Hartford* (Charleston, SC: Arcadia, 2016), 6; and "Twain, on His Travels."

11. Phineas Taylor Barnum, *The Autobiography of P. T. Barnum* (London: Ward and Lock, 1855), 51; John Niven, *Gideon Welles: Lincoln's Secretary of the Navy* (New York: Oxford University Press, 1973); and Grant and Grant, *City of Hartford*, 25.

12. Paul E. Teed, *Joseph and Harriet Hawley's Civil War: Partnership, Ambition, and Sacrifice* (Lanham, MD: Lexington Books, 2018), 38.

13. Grant and Grant, *City of Hartford*, 25.

14. Grant and Grant, 14; Walsh, "Hartford," 28; and Grant and Grant, *City of Hartford*, 68.

15. Russell Shorto, *The Island at the Center of the World: The Epic Story of Dutch Manhattan and the Forgotten Colony That Shaped America* (New York: Alfred A. Knopf, 2005).

16. Rathbun, " 'Wide Awakes,' " 327.

17. "A Week from Today—The Republicans Are Wide Awake," *Hartford Courant*, March 6, 1860.

18. Many accounts of this first meeting of the Wide Awakes contain errors. Most notably, some claim it took place on March 5 or 6. Lincoln's secretaries John Nicolay and John Hay make this error (and a number of others) in their famous account, conveniently dating the official formation of the Wide Awakes to *after* Lincoln's appearance in town. But they cite several Hartford individuals, like Joseph Hawley, who were not present at this meeting. To add insult to injury, the Hartford Originals' secretary Henry T. Sperry lent a treasured letter from Abraham Lincoln to the club—written after the 1860 election and commending them on their "great services"—to Nicolay and Hay as they researched their book in the 1890s. The letter "was never returned," according to Julius Rathbun. The other key mistake often made is placing James S. Chalker at this meeting on March 3. Rathbun, " 'Wide Awakes,' " 328–29, 335; J. Doyle DeWitt, *Lincoln in Hartford* (Hartford: CT Civil War Centennial Commission, 1960); and "Aged Embezzler Arrested," *Chicago Inter Ocean*, October 27, 1894.

19. Lucius E. Chittenden, *Recollections of President Lincoln and His Administration* (New York: Harper and Brothers, 1891), 5–6.

20. Edgar S. Yergason, letter to the editor, *Hartford Courant*, January 30, 1909, Wide Awakes Records; "The Wide-Awakes!" *Hartford Courant*, March 3, 1860; "Rousing Wide Awake Meeting," *Hartford Evening Post*, October 22, 1884; and "Murphy McGuire" [Silliman B. Ives], "Sunbeam (Bark) of New Bedford, Mass., mastered by Thomas N. Fisher," November 1, 1868, New Bedford Whaling Museum, https://archive.org/details/odhs–618/page/n1/mode/2up.

21. Keith MacKay, "The White House Interiors of Caroline Harrison and Edgar Yergason, 1890–1892" (master's thesis, Corcoran College of Art and Design, 2009), 14.

22. "City Intelligence," *Hartford Courant*, April 20, 1861; Grant and Grant, *City of Hartford*, 15, 34; and Frank Towers, *The Urban South and the Coming of the Civil War* (Charlottesville: University of Virginia Press, 2004), 58.

23. Nathaniel Hawthorne, *The Scarlet Letter: A Romance* (London: David Bogue, 1851), 22, 27, 55; and "McGuire" [Ives], "Sunbeam."

24. Henry David Thoreau, *Walden* (Boston: Houghton Mifflin, 1854), 1:84.

25. Michael Schudson, *Discovering the News: A Society History of American Newspapers* (New York: Basic Books, 1978); William Dean Howells, *Years of My Youth* (New York: Harper and Brothers, 1916), 112, 137–38; and Mark Wahlgren Summers, *The Press Gang, 1865–1878* (Chapel Hill: University of North Carolina Press, 1994).

26. Joseph C. G. Kennedy, "Newspapers and Periodicals in the United States in 1860," *Preliminary Report of the Eight Census, 1860* (Washington, D.C.: GPO, 1862), 211; and Teed, *Hawley's Civil War*, 41, 15–16, 32.

27. William P. Fuller, "Wide-Awake!" *Hartford Courant*, March 3, 1860.

28. "Wike Awakes March Tonight," *Hartford Courant*, October 28, 1904; and John Hay and John George Nicolay, *Abraham Lincoln: A History* (New York: Century, 1890), 2:284, 284n1.

29. "Week from Today," *Hartford Courant*.

30. "A New Secret Order," *Alton (IL) Weekly Telegraph*, June 1, 1854; "The Wide Awakes," *New York Daily Herald*, June 8, 1854; "Wide Awake, or Know Nothing, Hats," *Nashville Union and American*, July 1, 1854; and "Wide Awakes," *Perrysburg (OH) Journal*, July 1, 1854.

31. Or made famous in photographs of Walt Whitman, himself toying with majoritarian northern working-class nationalism and xenophobia in the 1850s.

32. "Two Irishmen," *Buffalo Daily Republican*, July 6, 1854; "A Visit to Paris in a Wide Awake," *Lloyd's Weekly Newspaper* (London), April 29, 1855; "Shave or

Resign," *New York Tribune*, December 26, 1855; "The Jaunty Little White Hat," *Thibodaux Minera*, July 1, 1854; "Street Preaching—Riots and Assaults," *Brooklyn Daily Eagle*, September 4, 1854; and "Whiggery and the 'Know Nothings,'" *Fremont (OH) Weekly Journal*, July 21, 1854.

33. Teed, *Hawley's Civil War*, 59; and Grant and Grant, *City of Hartford*, 14.

34. MacKay, "White House Interiors," 11.

35. Teed, *Hawley's Civil War*, 40.

36. Rathbun, " 'Wide Awakes,' " 328.

37. See James S. Chalker picture in DeWitt, *Lincoln in Hartford*, 12; and "The Wide-Awakes," *Marshall County (IN) Weekly Republican*, October 4, 1860.

38. Rathbun, " 'Wide Awakes,' " 328; and Edgar S. Yergason to Charlotte Yergason, March 4, 1860, Yergason Papers.

39. Rathbun, " 'Wide Awakes,' " 328.

40. Yergason to Yergason, March 4, 1860.

41. Christopher Yergason to Edgar S. Yergason, March 25, 1860, Yergason Papers; Joseph Kett, *Rites of Passage: Adolescence in American 1790 to the Present* (New York: Basic Books, 1977), 11–13; and Anthony Rotundo, *American Manhood: Transformations in Masculinity from the Revolution to the Modern Era* (New York: Basic Books, 1993), 7, 56. For Yergason's sketches, see Critical Eye Finds, accessed January 12, 2024, https://www.criticaleyefinds.com/search?q=yergason.

42. DeWitt, *Lincoln in Hartford*, 14, 3, 5.

43. DeWitt, *Lincoln in Hartford*, 6, 7–8.

44. "Abe Lincoln at the City Hall," *Hartford Courant*, March 6, 1860; and DeWitt, *Lincoln in Hartford*, 5–6.

45. "Lincoln at the City Hall"; and DeWitt, *Lincoln in Hartford*, 11.

46. Abraham Lincoln to William H. Herndon, July 10, 1848, in *Abraham Lincoln: The Collected Works*, ed. Roy P. Basler, 8 vols. (New Brunswick, NJ: Rutgers University Press, 1953), 1:498; and Hay and Nicolay, *Abraham Lincoln*, 284–85.

CHAPTER THREE: QUIET MEN ARE DANGEROUS

1. "Inhuman Loco Foco Outrages!" *Hartford Courant*, March 31, 1860; "Wide Awake," *New Haven (CT) Palladium*, March 30, 1860; and "Democratic Outrages at New Haven," *Chicago Tribune*, April 6, 1860.

2. "Inhuman Loco"; and Julius G. Rathbun, "The 'Wide Awakes': The Great Political Organization of 1860," *Connecticut Quarterly* 1 (October 1895): 331.

3. "Democratic Outrages."

4. "Democratic Outrages"; and Andrew Walsh, "Hartford: A Global History," in *Confronting Urban Legacy: Rediscovering Hartford and New England's Forgotten*

Cities, ed. Xiangming Chen and Nick Bacon (Lanham, MD: Lexington Books, 2013), 29.

5. "Inhuman Loco"; "Wide Awake," *New Haven (CT) Palladium*; and "Democratic Outrages."

6. "Inhuman Loco."

7. *The Life and Writings of Frederick Douglass: Pre–Civil War Decade, 1850–1860*, ed. Philip Sheldon Foner (New York: International, 1950), 515.

8. "Inhuman Loco."

9. "Democratic Outrages."

10. Edgar S. Yergason to Charlotte Yergason, March 25, 1860, Yergason Papers; "The Excursion to Waterbury," *Hartford Courant*, March 17, 1860; and Rathbun, " 'Wide Awakes,' " 330.

11. Rathbun, " 'Wide Awakes,' " 330; "The Wide Awakes Held Their First Meeting Last Evening," *Hartford Courant*, March 7, 1860; "Great Republican Demonstration!" *Hartford Courant*, March 12, 1860; and Charles O'Neill to Caroline Townsend Bartholomew, July 29, 1860, O'Neill Family Papers, New York Public Library, New York (hereafter O'Neill Papers).

12. "Great Republican Demonstration!"; and Rathbun, " 'Wide Awakes,' " 330.

13. "Great Republican Demonstration!"; and Rathbun, " 'Wide Awakes,' " 330.

14. "Great Republican Demonstration!"

15. William J. Hardee, *Rifle and Light Infantry Tactics*, vol. 1 (Philadelphia: J. B. Lippincott, 1860); Henry T. Sperry, Hartford Wide Awakes membership form (MS13264-9 and MS13264-10), August 1, 1861 [misdated; must be 1860], Wide Awakes Records; and Rathbun, " 'Wide Awakes,' " 329.

16. "Excursion to Waterbury"; and Rathbun, " 'Wide Awakes,' " 330.

17. Rathbun, " 'Wide Awakes,' " 329; and Sperry, Wide Awakes membership form.

18. Sperry almost certainly was not aware of the roots of the words *hurrah* and *hooray* in a Mongol chant used in steppe warfare even deeper in the past. But perhaps what worked for Mongol cavalry now worked for Hartford's infantry. Jack Weatherford, *Genghis Khan and the Making of the Modern World* (New York: Three Rivers Press, 2004), xxiv.

19. Benjamin F. Thompson, "The Wide Awakes of 1860," *Magazine of History with Notes and Queries* 10 (November 1909), 295–96; George Kimball, *A Corporal's Story: Civil War Recollections of the Twelfth Massachusetts*, ed. Alan D. Gaff and Donald H. Gaff (Normal: University of Oklahoma Press, 2014), 5; and Charles O'Neill to Caroline Townsend Bartholomew, November 15, 1860, O'Neill Papers.

20. Marcus Cunliffe, *Soldiers and Civilians: The Martial Spirit in America, 1775–1865* (New York: Free Press, 1973), 8, 96.

21. Cunliffe, *Soldiers and Civilians*, 8, 96; Robert Walker Johannsen, *To the Halls of the Montezumas: The Mexican War in American Imagination* (New York: Oxford University Press, 1985); Mischa Honeck, "Men of Principle: Gender and the German American War for the Union," *Journal of the Civil War Era* 5, no. 1 (March 2015): 43; Meg Groeling, *First Fallen: The Life of Colonel Elmer Ellsworth, the North's First Civil War Hero* (El Dorado Hills, CA: Savas Beatie, 2021); and *The Poems of Oliver Wendell Holmes* (Boston: Houghton, Mifflin, 1849), 157.

22. Stephen Kantrowitz, *More Than Freedom: Fighting for Black Citizenship in a White Republic* (New York: Penguin, 2013), 215–16; and Margot Minardi, *Making Slavery History: Abolitionism and the Politics of Memory in Massachusetts* (New York: Oxford University Press, 2012), 157–59.

23. Perhaps one of the reasons that contemporary Americans often see later fascist and Nazi movements when they look at images of the Wide Awakes of 1860 is that they are, in fact, distant cousins. Both are offshoots, in different times and places, of this shared moment when populist, militant, revolutionary nationalism motivated diverse causes, beginning with the French Revolution's *levée en masse* and running through World War II. But in the mid-nineteenth century, these forces were still tied most closely to liberal democratic causes, and not the forces of reactionary nationalism that they became more closely associated with in the twentieth century. Mischa Honeck, *We Are the Revolutionists: German-Speaking Immigrants and American Abolitionists After 1848* (Athens: University of Georgia Press, 2011), 6; Andre M. Fleche, *The Revolution of 1861: The American Civil War in the Age of Nationalist Conflict* (Chapel Hill: University of North Carolina Press, 2012); and Enrico Dal Lago, *The Age of Lincoln and Cavour: Comparative Perspectives on 19th-Century American and Italian Nation-Building* (London: Palgrave Macmillan, 2015). For references to leaders like Garibaldi among antislavery and Republican speakers, see Charles Sumner, "Evening After the Presidential Election," speech delivered in Concord, MA, November 7, 1860, in *Charles Sumner: His Complete Works*, ed. George Frisbie Hoar (Boston: Lee and Shepard, 1900), 7: 77; and Elizur Wright, *An Eye Opener for the Wide Awakes* (Boston: Thayer & Eldridge, 1860), frontispiece. As the *Boston Evening Transcript* eventually put it, on August 27, 1860, "Garibaldi is undeniably a European 'Wide Awake.' "

24. Richard Bourne, *Garibaldi in South America: An Exploration* (London: C. Hurst, 2020), 45; Lesley J. Gordon, " 'Novices in Warfare': Elmer E. Ellsworth and

Militia Reform on the Eve of Civil War," *Journal of the Civil War Era* 11, no. 2 (June 2021): 199; and David Hackett Fischer, *Growing Old in America* (New York: Oxford University Press, 1977), 86.

25. Carl Schurz, *The Reminiscences of Carl Schurz* (New York: McClure, 1907), 2:51; Honeck, "Men of Principle," 54; William Dean Howells, *A Boy's Town: Described for Harper's Young People* (New York: Harper and Brothers, 1890), 77; and Honeck, *Revolutionists*, 21.

26. "The Connecticut Wide-Awakes," *New York Tribune*, May 3, 1860.

27. Henry T. Sperry, "The Republican Wide-Awakes of Hartford Constitution," art. 12, sec. 1, Wide Awakes Records; "Connecticut Wide-Awakes"; Thompson, "Wide Awakes of 1860," 295–96; "The Wide Awakes," *Chicago Tribune*, April 4, 1860; and "Connecticut Wide Awakes," *Poughkeepsie (NY) Journal*, May 12, 1860.

28. Anonymous, "Election Time in America," *All the Year Round*, ed. Charles Dickens, no. 103 (April 13, 1861): 67.

29. In all the commentary on the January 6, 2021, attack on the U.S. Capitol, most missed the ancient heritage of "wild" protests from deep in the British political tradition that shaped American democracy. Often these protests involved otherworldly or ridiculous costumes, horns, fur, robes, religious symbols, and so on. Even the first Ku Klux Klan, founded after the Civil War, made use of them in their early robes, often equipped with antlers. Paul A. Gilje, *The Road to Mobocracy: Popular Disorder in New York City, 1763–1834* (Chapel Hill: University of North Carolina Press in association with the Omohundru Institute of Early American History and Culture, Williamsburg, VA, 1987), 20; Jonathan Healey, *The Blazing World: A New History of Revolutionary England* (London: Borzoi Books, 2023), 13–18; and Elaine Franz Parson, *Ku Klux: The Birth of the Klan During Reconstruction* (Chapel Hill: University of North Carolina Press, 2015), 5.

30. Luna Kellie, *The Prairie Populist: The Memoirs of Luna Kellie*, ed. Jane Taylor Nelsen (Iowa City: University of Iowa Press, 1992), 110.

31. "Connecticut Wide-Awakes"; and Philadelphia Correspondent, "Pennsylvania Politics," *New York Herald*, September 26, 1860.

32. "Excursion to Waterbury"; and Rathbun, " 'Wide Awakes,' " 330; "Wide-Awakes on Hand!" *Hartford Courant*, March 13, 1860; and Republican Campaign Club Constitution, February 20, 1860, Republicans of Waterbury Campaign Club Records (MS53693), Connecticut Historical Society, Hartford.

33. "Excursion to Waterbury."

34. "Excursion to Waterbury"; and Rathbun, " 'Wide Awakes,' " 330.

35. "Excursion to Waterbury."

36. "Wide Awakes," *Chicago Tribune*; "Letter from Waterbury," *Cleveland Daily Leader*, June 7, 1860; Rathbun, " 'Wide Awakes,' " 330; and Republican Campaign Club Constitution.

37. Yergason to Yergason, March 25, 1860.

38. O'Neill to Bartholomew, July 29, 1860, and November 5, 1860, O'Neill Papers.

39. "Loco Foco Doctrine Carried Out," *Hartford Courant*, March 27, 1860.

40. "Oh, No!" *Hartford Courant*, April 2, 1860.

41. "Excursion to Waterbury"; "From Colt's Pistol Factory," *New York Tribune*, March 23, 1860; "The Times Misrepresentations," *Hartford Courant*, March 27, 1860; and "Oh, No!"

42. "Excursion to Waterbury"; "Wide Awake Rally," *Chicago Tribune*, July 8, 1860; Douglas Egerton, *Year of Meteors: Stephen Douglas, Abraham Lincoln, and the Election That Brought the Civil War* (New York: Bloomsbury, 2010), 28; "A Reckless and Perverted Sheet," *Hartford Courant*, March 8, 1860; and "A Week from Today—The Republicans Are Wide Awake," *Hartford Courant*, March 6, 1860.

43. "The Campaign in Connecticut," *New York Times*, March 23, 1860.

44. Jane Ann Moore and William F. Moore, *Owen Lovejoy and the Coalition for Equality* (Champaign-Urbana: University of Illinois Press, 2019), 20; Christopher L. Webber, *American to the Backbone: The Life of James W. C. Pennington* (New York: Pegasus Books, 2011); and Matthew Warshauer, *Connecticut in the American Civil War: Slavery, Sacrifice, and Survival* (Middletown, CT: Wesleyan University Press, 2014), 188.

45. Thomas Hamilton, in the *Weekly Anglo-African*, March 1860, quoted in James McPherson, *The Negro's Civil War: How American Blacks Felt and Acted During the War for the Union* (New York: Knopf Doubleday, 2008), 4.

46. "Presidential Election Day," *Hartford Courant*, November 6, 1860.

47. "Campaign in Connecticut"; and "The Contest of 1860," *New York Herald*, March 22, 1860.

48. "Campaign in Connecticut"; Rathbun, " 'Wide Awakes,' " 331; and Kezia Peck to Peter Peck, March 24, 1860, Peck Family Papers, Connecticut Historical Society, Hartford (hereafter Peck Papers).

49. "Campaign in Connecticut"; and "Loco Foco Doctrine"; advertisement for Smith, Gross & Company, *Hartford Courant*, March 30, 1860.

50. "The Grand Torchlight Procession!" *Hartford Courant*, March 26, 1860; "Loco Foco Doctrine"; Henry T. Sperry, "To the Republican Wide Awake Ladies, of

Hartford," 1860, Wide Awakes Records; and "The Wide Awakes of Hartford," *New York Times*, July 30, 1860.

51. Peck to Peck, March 24, 1860.

52. "The Great Political Struggle in Connecticut," *Buffalo Morning Express and Illustrated*, April 2, 1860.

53. "The Connecticut Election Today," *New York Herald*, April 2, 1860; and "The Last Call," *Hartford Courant*, April 2, 1860.

54. "City Affairs," *Hartford Courant*, April 3, 1860; "Connecticut All Right," *Hartford Courant*, April 3, 1860; and "Connecticut Wide-Awakes."

55. "How the Battle Waged," *Hartford Courant*, April 3, 1860; and "Canvassers for Campaign of 1860," Republicans of Waterbury Campaign Club Records (MS53693), Connecticut Historical Society, Hartford.

56. "Struggle in Connecticut"; "The United States—Election Matters"; and Elizabeth Dwight Cabot to Ellen Twistleton, April 16, 1860, in *Voices Without Votes: Women and Politics in Antebellum New England*, ed. Ronald J. Zboray and Mary Sarcino Zboray (Concord: University of New Hampshire Press, 2010), 204.

57. "Struggle in Connecticut."

58. "Bullying," *Hartford Courant*, April 21, 1860; and "Connecticut Wide-Awakes."

59. "The Grand Wide Awake Demonstration," *Litchfield (CT) Enquirer*, April 26, 1860; and "The New Haven *Register*," *Hartford Courant*, April 24, 1860.

60. "Contrary to All Custom and Precedent," *Bridgeport (CT) Farmer*, April 26, 1860.

CHAPTER FOUR: IF I WANT TO GO TO CHICAGO

1. Samuel Sullivan Cox, *Union—Disunion—Reunion: Three Decades of Federal Legislation, 1855–1885* (Providence, RI: J. A. Reid and R. A. Reid, 1885), 75; and Jane Ann Moore and William F. Moore, *Owen Lovejoy and the Coalition for Equality* (Champaign-Urbana: University of Illinois Press, 2019), 137–38.

2. "Gail Hamilton" [May Abigail Dodge], obituary, *Congregationalist*, April 1864; Moore and Moore, *Lovejoy*, 54; and Owen Lovejoy, "Notice of the Canada Line of Stages," *Western Citizen* (Chicago), May 24, 1843.

3. Sally Heinzel, " 'To Protect the Rights of the White Race': Illinois Republican Racial Politics in the 1860 Campaign and the Twenty-Second General Assembly," *Journal of the Illinois State Historical Society* 108, nos. 3–4 (Fall/Winter 2015): 382; and Moore and Moore, *Lovejoy*, 152–53.

4. "Lovejoy's Speech," *Cleveland Daily Leader*, April 9, 1860; LeeAnna Keith, *When It Was Grand: The Radical Republican History of the Civil War* (New York: Hill and Wang, 2020), 121; and Moore and Moore, *Lovejoy*, 137–38.

5. "Speech of Owen Lovejoy in the House of Representatives," April 5, 1860, *Congressional Globe*, 36th Cong., 1st sess., appendix, 202–7; and Charles Francis Adams Jr., *An Autobiography* (Boston: Houghton Mifflin, 1916), 44.

6. "Speech of Owen Lovejoy," 202–7; Keith, *When It Was Grand*, 121–23; and Moore and Moore, *Lovejoy*, 137–38.

7. Carl Schurz, *The Reminiscences of Carl Schurz* (New York: McClure, 1907), 2:163–67; "The Pryor and Potter Difficulty," *New York Times*, April 14, 1860; Keith, *When It Was Grand*, 121–23; and William B. Hessletime, "The Pryor-Potter Duel," *Wisconsin Magazine of History* 27, no. 4 (June 1944): 400–409.

8. "Pryor and Potter Difficulty"; and Schurz, *Reminiscences*, 2:163–67.

9. William Turner Coggeshall, *The Issue of the November Election: An Address to Young Men* (Columbus, OH: privately published, 1860), 2.

10. Douglas Egerton, *Year of Meteors: Stephen Douglas, Abraham Lincoln, and the Election That Brought the Civil War* (New York: Bloomsbury, 2010), 160; and Adams, *Autobiography*, 44; and Schurz, *Reminiscences*, 2:30.

11. Schurz, *Reminiscences*, 2:30.

12. Schurz, 2:84.

13. *Memoirs of Gustav Koerner, 1809–1896: Life-Sketches Written at the Suggestion of His Children* (Cedar Rapids, IA: Torch Press, 1909), 2:81; and Egerton, *Year of Meteors*, 51–52, 11.

14. Murat Halstead, *Three Against Lincoln: Murat Halstead Reports the Caucuses of 1860*, ed. William B. Hesseltine (Baton Rouge: Louisiana State University Press, 1960), 263–64.

15. *The Diary of George Templeton Strong, 1860–1865*, ed. Allan Nevins (New York: Macmillan, 1952), entry for May 1, 1860, 24–25.

16. Strong, *Diary*, entry for May 11, 1860, 26.

17. *Frederick Douglass: Selected Speeches and Writings*, ed. Philip Foner and Yuval Taylor, Library of Black America (Chicago: Lawrence Hill Books, 1999), 412.

18. Julius G. Rathbun, "The 'Wide Awakes': The Great Political Organization of 1860," *Connecticut Quarterly* 1 (October 1895): 331; "How the Battle Wages! Lighting of the Watch Fires! Those Glorious Wide-Awakes!!" *Hartford Courant*, July 12, 1860; and Henry T. Sperry, Hartford Wide Awakes membership form (MS13264-9 and MS13264-10), August 1, 1861 [misdated; must be 1860], Wide Awakes Records.

19. "New York Correspondence," *Cleveland Daily Leader*, April 7, 1860; "How the Battle Wages!"; "State Items," *Hartford Courant*, May 8, 1860; and "A Good Institution—Ye Wide-Awakes," *Western Reserve Chronicle* (Warren, OH), April 11, 1860.

20. Rathbun, " 'Wide Awakes,' " 331; and Sperry, Wide Awakes membership form.

21. Rathbun, " 'Wide Awakes,' " 331; "The Wide-Awake Uniforms," *Hartford Courant*, August 18, 1860; Winthrop D. Jordan et al., *The United States*, 5th ed. (Englewood Cliffs, NJ: Prentice-Hall, 1982), 317; and "The Wide-Awakes," *Chicago Tribune*, April 4, 1860.

22. "Wide Awakes!" *Hartford Courant*, May 22, 1860.

23. "Wide Awakes!"

24. "The Connecticut Wide Awakes," *Pittsfield (MA) Sun*, April 12, 1860; "Short Paragraphs," *Hartford Courant*, April 16, 1860; "Spirited Lincoln Ratification Meeting," *Berkshire County (MA) Eagle*, May 24, 1860; and "Ratification Rally," *Berkshire County (MA) Eagle*, May 31, 1860; "Wide Awakes," *Buffalo Morning Express and Illustrated*, May 14, 1860; and "Good Institution."

25. "Wide-Awakes," *Chicago Tribune*; "Democratic Outrages at New Haven," *Chicago Tribune*, April 6, 1860; and "Organize the Clubs," *Clinton (IL) Central Transcript*, April 19, 1860.

26. Paul E. Teed, *Joseph and Harriet Hawley's Civil War: Partnership, Ambition, and Sacrifice* (Lanham, MD: Lexington Books, 2018), 38; and "Correspondent at the Convention," *Lancaster (PA) Daily Evening Express*, May 15, 1860.

27. "Organize the Clubs"; "A Challenge," *Muscatine (IA) Evening Journal*, May 23, 1860; and "Wide Awakes," *Janesville (WI) Daily Gazette*, May 10 and May 24, 1860.

28. Halstead, *Three Against Lincoln*, 263–64.

29. Simon Hanscom, "Our Special Chicago Correspondent," *New York Herald*, May 19, 1860; and Michael Burlingame, *Abraham Lincoln: A Life* (Baltimore: Johns Hopkins University Press, 2013), 601–4.

30. Hanscom, "Chicago Correspondent."

31. Hanscom.

32. Hanscom.

33. "Celebration at Chicago," *Cleveland Daily Leader*, May 19, 1860,

34. Hanscom; "City Improvements," *Chicago Press and Tribune*, March 9, 1860.

35. Hanscom, "Chicago Correspondent."

36. Hanscom; Abram Jesse Dittenhoefer, *How We Elected Lincoln: Personal Recollections of Lincoln and Men of His Time* (New York: Harper & Brothers, 1916), 26–27.

37. "The Opening of Convention Week," *Chicago Tribune*, May 14, 1860; Keith, *When It Was Grand*, 123–24; and "Correspondent at the Convention."

38. *Memoirs of Koerner*, 2:79; and Schurz, *Reminiscences*, 2:174.

39. Hanscom, "Chicago Correspondent"; Schurz, *Reminiscences*, 2:179, 176; Egerton, *Year of Meteors*, 133–34; and Dittenhoefer, *How We Elected Lincoln*, 24–25.

40. "Correspondent at Chicago," *Evansville (IN) Daily Journal*, May 18, 1860; Egerton, *Year of Meteors*, 118; and "From Albany," *Lansing (MI) State Republican*, October 17, 1860.

41. Henry Wilson to John Meredith Read Sr., May 15, 1860, John Meredith Read Papers, Historical Society of Pennsylvania, Philadelphia (hereafter Read Papers); and Dittenhoefer, *How We Elected Lincoln*.

42. The Williams College Wide Awakes ultimately endorsed Lincoln with the (mean) joke: "Everything bears a good report except his mirror." "Ratification Rally"; *Douglass: Selected Speeches*, 393; and Schurz, *Reminiscences*, 2:90.

43. James Sanks Brisbin to Ezra Brisbin, November 8, 1860, Brisbin Papers, 35.

44. *Douglass: Selected Speeches*, 393; and Carl Schurz to Margarethe Schurz, February 4, 1861, in *The Intimate Letters of Carl Schurz*, ed. Joseph Schafer (New York: Da Capo Press, 1970), 242.

45. Edward L. Widmer, *Lincoln on the Verge: Thirteen Days to Washington* (New York: Simon & Schuster, 2020), 39; and Egerton, *Year of Meteors*, 143.

46. Trudy Krisher, *Fanny Seward: A Life* (Syracuse, NY: Syracuse University Press, 2015), 49–50, 51; Schurz, *Reminiscences*, 2:222; and "Popular Pulsations," *Buffalo Morning Express and Illustrated*, May 29, 1860.

47. Strong, *Diary*, entry for June 16, 1860, 33; and "Lincoln Wide Awakes," *Evansville (IN) Daily Journal*, May 21, 1860.

48. "Lincoln and Hamlin," *Cincinnati Daily Press*, May 19, 1860; "Wide Awakes," *Brooklyn Evening Star*, May 21, 1860; "Lincoln Wide Awakes"; "The Wide-Awakes," *Pomeroy (OH) Weekly Telegraph*, May 22, 1860; "Wide Awakes," *Burlington (VT) Times*, June 6, 1860; "Wide Awake Republican Club," *Burlington (IA) Hawkeye*, June 30, 1860; "Burlington," *Racine (WI) Advocate*, June 27, 1860; "Lincoln and Hamlin Club," *New York Tribune*, June 20, 1860; and "Perry Township Republican Club," *Buchanan County (IA) Guardian*, May 16, 1860.

49. "Perry Township Republican Club."

50. *Memoirs of Koerner*, 2:99; William Ernest Smith, *The Francis Preston Blair Family in Politics* (New York: Da Capo Press, 1969), 2:467, 443; and James Peckham, *Gen. Nathaniel Lyon, and Missouri in 1861: A Monograph of the Great Rebellion* (New York: American News, 1866), 8.

51. Peckham, *Gen. Lyon*, 11–12.

52. Peckham, 11–12.

53. *Memoirs of Koerner*, 2:98.

54. *Memoirs of Koerner*, 2:96.

CHAPTER FIVE: A SPONTANEOUS OUTBURST OF THE PEOPLE

1. Susan B. Anthony to Henry B. Stanton Jr. and Gerrit S. Stanton, September 27, 1860, in *Antebellum Women: Private, Public, Partisan*, ed. Carol Lasser and Stacey Robertson (Lanham, MD: Rowman & Littlefield, 2010), 203.

2. Anthony to Stanton and Stanton, 203.

3. Anthony to Stanton and Stanton, 204; and "The Ladies of Seneca Falls," *New York Tribune*, September 27, 1860.

4. "Manuscript Draft of Speech of Elizabeth Cady Stanton on Presenting a Flag from the Women of Seneca Falls to the Wide Awakes 1861 [misdated; must be 1860]," Seneca Falls Historical Society, Seneca Falls, NY; "Ladies of Seneca Falls"; "Another Grand Turnout," *Seneca County (NY) Courier*, September 13, 1860; Sally Heinzel, " 'To Protect the Rights of the White Race': Illinois Republican Racial Politics in the 1860 Campaign and the Twenty-Second General Assembly," *Journal of the Illinois State Historical Society* 108, nos. 3–4 (Fall/Winter 2015): 382; and Anthony to Stanton and Stanton, 204.

5. Anthony to Stanton and Stanton, 204.

6. Anthony to Stanton and Stanton, 204.

7. Anthony to Stanton and Stanton, 205.

8. *The Works of William H. Seward*, ed. George E. Baker (Boston: Houghton Mifflin, 1884), 84.

9. Joseph Howard Jr., "Great Demonstration of the Wide-Awakes at Hartford," *New York Times*, July 28, 1860; Benjamin F. Thompson, "The Wide Awakes of 1860," *Magazine of History with Notes and Queries* 10 (November 1909): 295–96; "The American Presidential Election," *London Morning Chronicle*, October 20, 1860; and 1856 presidential general election data from Dave Leip, "Atlas of U.S. Presidency Elections," accessed January 27, 2024, https://uselectionatlas.org /RESULTS/national.php?year=1856.

10. Henry T. Sperry, Hartford Wide Awakes membership form (MS13264-9 and MS13264-10), August 1, 1861 [misdated; must be 1860], Wide Awakes Records.

11. Howard, "Great Demonstration of the Wide-Awakes."

12. George Kimball, *A Corporal's Story: Civil War Recollections of the Twelfth Massachusetts*, ed. Alan D. Gaff and Donald H. Gaff (Normal: University of Oklahoma Press, 2014), 6; Abram Jesse Dittenhoefer, *How We Elected Lincoln: Personal*

Recollections of Lincoln and Men of His Time (New York: Harper & Brothers, 1916), 35–37; John Meredith Read Jr. to John Meredith Read Sr., letters from July 28, 1860, through February 5, 1861, Read Papers; William Dansberry to Abraham Lincoln, November 1, 1860, Abraham Lincoln Papers, ser. 1, General Correspondence, 1833–1916, Library of Congress, Washington, D.C. (hereafter Lincoln Papers); "The German Wide Awakes," *Chicago Tribune*, June 9, 1860; "Lafayette Wide Awakes," *New York Times*, September 22, 1860; "ITALIAN WIDE-AWAKES," *New York Tribune*, September 17, 1860; Hans Mattson, *Reminiscences: Story of an Emigrant* (St. Paul: D. D. Merrill, 1891), 56–58; "The People Aroused!" *Tiffin (OH) Tribune*, May 25, 1860; "Perry Township Republican Club," *Buchanan County (IA) Guardian*, May 16, 1860; "Wide Awakes," *Bradford (PA) Reporter*, May 24, 1860; "Montgomery Street Wide Awakes," *San Francisco Bulletin*, August 11, 1860; "Contra Costa Republican Club," *Contra Costa (CA) Gazette*, September 22, 1860; "Wide Awake Rally," *San Francisco Bulletin*, October 24, 1860; and "Folsom Mass Meeting," *Daily Alta California* (San Francisco), October 30, 1860.

13. "Wide Awakes," *Daily Cleveland Herald*, November 8, 1860; and "Wide Awakes, Cleveland West Side," *Daily Cleveland Herald*, May 30, 1860.

14. "The Campaign in Illinois!" *Chicago Tribune*, August 1, 1860; and "Great Demonstration in Burlington," *Burlington (WI) Gazette*, July 17, 1860.

15. "Companies of Wide Awakes," *Richmond (IN) Palladium*, July 14, 1860; *New York Tribune*, June 11, 1860; and "National Rocky Mountain Club of Brooklyn," *Brooklyn Evening Star*, June 12, 1860. J.C.M. articles appear from rallies in the *Chicago Tribune* from Pekin on July 27, Pekin again on July 30, Mackinaw on August 1, Urbana on August 1, Monticello on August 3, Tuscola on August 4, Sullivan on August 7, and Pana on August 8.

16. "A Challenge"; "A Wide Awake," letter to the editor, *Racine (WI) Journal*, August 29, 1860; and George W. Rives to Abraham Lincoln, August 2, 1860, Lincoln Papers.

17. "How the Battle Wages!" *Hartford Courant*, July 12, 1860; and "The Wide Awake Uniforms," *Hartford Courant*, August 18, 1860.

18. "Within a Month," *Wheeling (WV) Daily Intelligencer*, August 29, 1860; "Wide Awake Uniforms," *San Francisco Bulletin*, September 4, 1860; and "The Great Parade of Wide Awakes on Wednesday," *New York Times*, October 1, 1860.

19. Samuel Bruce, letter to the editor, *Bangor (ME) Daily Whig and Courier*, July 30, 1860; "Young Muscatine," letter to the editor, *Muscatine (IA) Evening Journal*, July 30, 1860; and "Wide Awake Lincoln Club," *Evansville (IN) Daily Journal*, May 22, 1860.

20. Elizur Wright, *An Eye Opener for the Wide Awakes* (Boston: Thayer & Eldridge, 1860), front cover, 7, 3, 4.

21. Wright, *Eye Opener*, 50, 7, 54.

22. "Tremendous Crowd," *Pittsburgh Gazette*, March 31, 1856; L. S. Jr., "The Progress of the Campaign," letter to the editor, *Chicago Tribune*, August 22, 1860; and Thompson, "Wide Awakes of 1860," 295–96.

23. Jane Ann Moore and William F. Moore, *Owen Lovejoy and the Coalition for Equality* (Champaign-Urbana: University of Illinois Press, 2019), 142; "The Meeting at Clyde," *Fremont (OH) Weekly Journal*, July 13, 1860; Carl Schurz to Margarethe Schurz, September 27, 1859, in *The Intimate Letters of Carl Schurz*, ed. Joseph Schafer (New York: Da Capo Press, 1970), 199; Howard, "Great Demonstration of the Wide-Awakes"; and Jon Grinspan, *The Virgin Vote: How Young Americans Made Democracy Social, Politics Personal, and Voting Popular in the Nineteenth Century* (Chapel Hill: University of North Carolina Press, 2016), 43–46.

24. Susan Sessions Rugh, " 'Awful Calamities Now upon Us': The Civil War in Fountain Green, Illinois," *Journal of the Illinois State Historical Society* 93, no. 1 (Spring 2000): 16; "Enticed by Free Gingerbread," *Daily Milwaukee News*, January 8, 1861; and "Wide Awake Demonstration," *Buchanan County (IA) Guardian*, September 18, 1860.

25. For more on the forms and limits of women's political involvement, see Elizabeth Varon, *We Mean to Be Counted: White Women and Politics in Antebellum Virginia* (Chapel Hill: University of North Carolina Press, 1998); and Ronald J. Zboray and Mary Sarcino Zboray, eds., *Voices Without Votes: Women and Politics in Antebellum New England* (Concord: University of New Hampshire Press, 2010); "Immense Gathering," *Bangor (ME) Daily Whig and Courier*, August 17, 1860; and Kezia Peck to Peter Peck, March 24, 1860, Peck Papers.

26. LeeAnna Keith, *When It Was Grand: The Radical Republican History of the Civil War* (New York: Hill and Wang, 2020), 127; and "Female Wide-Awake Club," *Baton Rouge (LA) Daily Gazette and Comet*, October 27, 1860.

27. Frank Towers, *The Urban South and the Coming of the Civil War* (Charlottesville: University of Virginia Press, 2004), 51.

28. Moore and Moore, *Lovejoy*, 140; Heinzel, " 'Rights of the White Race,' " 383; "Great Times in the Centre," *Chicago Tribune*, June 9, 1860; and Douglas Egerton, *Year of Meteors: Stephen Douglas, Abraham Lincoln, and the Election That Brought the Civil War* (New York: Bloomsbury, 2010), 16.

29. Bela A. Adams to Abraham Lincoln, October 23, 1860, Lincoln Papers; and "Good News from Jackson," *Tiffin (OH) Tribune*, August 24, 1860. George P.

Holt left behind copious (rambling) letters, poems, and postcards to the Milford
Historical Society, but his role as an enslaver is summarized in one sentence of
his memorial: "After this in 1858, he left Jersey City for Columbus, Ga., to
take entire charge of 12 male slaves, but returned in two years." The best
explanation seems to be that Holt was a bit of a nineteenth-century roustabout,
joining causes, armies, and movements, and apparently participating in slavery
without providing deep thought or reasoning for his actions. A. M. Duncklee,
Memorial to George P. Holt (Milford, NH: Milford H. & G. Society, 1916), 3,
Milford Historical Society.

30. *Frederick Douglass: Selected Speeches and Writings*, ed. Philip Foner and Yuval
Taylor, Library of Black America (Chicago: Lawrence Hill Books, 1999), 395.

31. James McPherson, *The Negro's Civil War: How American Blacks Felt and Acted
During the War for the Union* (New York: Knopf Doubleday, 2008), 5; and
Matthew Norman, "The Other Lincoln-Douglas Debate: The Race Issue in a
Comparative Context," *Journal of the Abraham Lincoln Association* 31, no. 1
(Winter 2010): 1.

32. Henry T. Sperry, "The Republican Wide-Awakes of Hartford Constitution,"
cover, Wide Awakes Records; and McPherson, *Negro's Civil War*, 5.

33. McPherson, *Negro's Civil War*, 6.

34. "Lincoln: His Supporters," *Spirit of Democracy*, October 3, 1860; and William F.
Cheek, *John Mercer Langston and the Struggle for Black Freedom, 1829–1865*
(Champaign-Urbana: University of Illinois Press, 1996), 62–70.

35. Cheek, *Langston*, 369–70; "Wide Awakes," *Crawford County (OH) Forum*,
January 18, 1861; and Cheek, *Langston*, 370.

36. Anna Ridgely, "A Girl in the Sixties: Excerpts from the Journal of Anna Ridgely,"
ed. Octavis Roberts Corneau, *Journal of the Illinois State Historical Society* 2, no. 3
(October 1929): entries for June 20, 1860, 11, and November 5, 1860, 20.

37. Ridgely, "Girl in the Sixties," entries for November 5, 1860, 20, and June 20,
1860, 11; and Carl Schurz, *The Reminiscences of Carl Schurz* (New York:
McClure, 1907), 2:193–4.

38. "The Connecticut Wide Awakes," *New York Tribune*, May 3, 1860; and "The
Wide-Awakes on Saturday Evening," *Wisconsin State Journal* (Madison),
June 11, 1860.

39. "Armed Wide Awakes," *Wayne County (PA) Herald*, July 19, 1860, quoted from
New York Express.

40. "Wide Awakes," *Detroit Free Press*, July 24, 1860; letter to the editor, *New York
Herald*, January 7, 1861; "The County Convention," *Portage (OH) Sentinel*,
August 29, 1860; "The Little Lincoln Boys," *Rock Island (IA) Argus*, September 7,

1860; "The Wide Awakes," *Lancaster (PA) Intelligencer*, August 21, 1860; and "The Pre-Emption Fizzle," *Rock Island (IA) Argus*, August 29, 1860.

41. "A New Off-Shoot of Know Nothingism," *Luzerne (PA) Union*, August 29, 1860; Paul Kleppner, *The Third Electoral System, 1853–1892: Parties, Voters, and Political Cultures* (Chapel Hill: University of North Carolina Press, 2010), 56; and "Germans, What Do You Think of It?" *Freeport (IL) Bulletin*, July 19, 1860.

42. "Wide Awakes," *Rock Island (IA) Argus*, June 13, 1860.

43. "The Wide-Awakes," *Clearfield (PA) Republican*, November 14, 1860, quoting the *Clinton (MO) Democrat*.

44. "The Chloroform Club," *New York Herald*, August 18, 1860; Heinzel, "'Rights of the White Race,'" 379; and "In Lacon," *Poughkeepsie (NY) Journal*, September 1, 1860.

45. *Memoirs of Gustav Koerner, 1809–1896: Life-Sketches Written at the Suggestion of His Children* (Cedar Rapids, IA: Torch Press, 1909), 2:100.

46. "Campaign in Illinois!"

47. Anonymous, "Election Time in America," *All the Year Round*, ed. Charles Dickens, no. 103 (April 13, 1861): 69–72.

48. "Wide Awake Club of White Haven Constitution," *Pittston (PA) Gazette*, September 13, 1860; "National Rocky Mountain Club of Brooklyn"; "The Wide-Awakes," *Pomeroy (OH) Weekly Telegraph*, May 22, 1860; "Letter to Editor by Commandant of the XXth Ward Battalion," *New York Tribune*, July 30, 1860; "A Week from Today—The Republicans Are Wide Awake," *Hartford Courant*, March 6, 1860; and "How the Battle Wages!"; and *The Diary of George Templeton Strong, 1860–1865*, ed. Allan Nevins (New York: Macmillan, 1952), entry for June 16, 1860, 36.

49. "Armed Wide Awakes," *Richmond (VA) Dispatch*, July 13, 1860; and "Armed Wide Awakes," *Wayne County (PA) Herald*, July 19, 1860, citing *New York Express*.

50. "ZADICAL," letter to the editor, *Detroit Free Press*, July 15, 1860.

51. "WIDE AWAKES, Political Associations, and Others," *Detroit Free Press*, July 15, 1860.

52. "Wide Awake Clubs vice Know Nothing Lodges," *Wayne County (PA) Herald*, August 16, 1860; and "From Pittsburgh," *Lancaster (PA) Intelligencer*, August 21, 1860.

53. Henry Adams, *The Miseducation of Henry Adams* (Boston: Houghton Mifflin, 1918), 99.

54. "Wide Awakes and Minute Men," *San Francisco Bulletin*, November 6, 1860.

CHAPTER SIX: THEY GET ME OUT WHEN I'M SLEEPY

1. Carl Schurz, *The Reminiscences of Carl Schurz* (New York: McClure, 1907), 2:149.

2. Schurz, *Reminiscences*, 2:194.

3. Schurz, 2:194.

4. Carl Schurz to Henry Meyer, November 28, 1857, in *The Intimate Letters of Carl Schurz*, ed. Joseph Schafer (New York: Da Capo Press, 1970), 180; and Carl Schurz to Margarethe Schurz, December 31, 1857, in Schafer, *Intimate Letters*, 184.

5. Schurz, *Reminiscences*, 2:194–95.

6. Schurz, 2:194; and Alexander K. McClure, *Old Time Notes of Pennsylvania* (Philadelphia: J. C. Winston, 1905), 413.

7. Schurz, *Reminiscences*, 2:193–94.

8. Schurz, 2:193.

9. Schurz.

10. Carl Schurz to Margarethe Schurz, July 17, 1860, 213; Carl Schurz to Margarethe Schurz, July 19, 1860, 214; Carl Schurz to Margarethe Schurz, July 20, 1860, 213; and Carl Schurz to Margarethe Schurz, July 23, 1860, 215–16, all in Schafer, *Intimate Letters*; and Schurz, *Reminiscences*, 2:195.

11. Schurz, *Reminiscences*, 2:200–201.

12. Galusha Anderson, *Reminiscences of St. Louis During the Civil War* (Boston: Little, Brown, 1908), 17.

13. Schurz to Meyer, November 28, 1857, 180.

14. Schurz, *Reminiscences*, 2:193.

15. William Tecumseh Sherman to Ellen Boyle Ewing, July 10, 1860, in *Home Letters of General Sherman*, ed. M. A. DeWolfe Howe (New York: Charles Scribner's Sons, 1909), 178.

16. "Wide Awakes!" *Hartford Courant*, May 22, 1860.

17. Schurz, *Reminiscences*, 2:177; and Thurlow Weed, "The Revolution in Parties," *Albany (NY) Evening Journal*, June 6, 1860.

18. "Carl Schurz Speaking in English and German," *Brooklyn Evening Star*, October 18, 1860.

19. William C. Harris, "Lincoln's Role in the 1860 Presidential Campaign," in *Exploring Lincoln: Great Historians Reappraise Our Greatest President*, ed. Harold Holzer, Craig L. Symmonds, and Frank J. Williams (New York: Fordham University Press, 2015), 14; and Abraham Lincoln to Henry Wilson, September 1, 1860, in *Lincoln, Speeches and Writings, 1850–1865*, ed. Roy P. Basler (New York: Literary Classics of the United States, 1989), 179.

20. Sidney Blumenthal, *All the Powers of Earth: The Political Life of Abraham Lincoln, 1856–1860* (New York: Simon & Schuster, 2019), 563.

21. Buffalo, New York, Lincoln Wide-Awakes to Abraham Lincoln, October 1, 1860, Chicago Wide-Awake Republican Club to Abraham Lincoln, June 1, 1860 (certificate of membership), and L. L. Hartman to Abraham Lincoln, July 17, 1860, all Lincoln Papers; Robert Allan Stevens and Bill Tharp, "Incredible Stories of Uncle Epp: Soldier, POW, Survivor, Minstrel, and Lincoln's Office Boy," *Journal of the Illinois State Historical Society* 103, no. 2 (Summer 2010): 157–59; and George W. Rives to Abraham Lincoln, August 2, 1860, Lincoln Papers.

22. "Political Carnival at Springfield," *Lima (OH) Gazette*, August 11, 1860; Louis D. Rosette to Ann Rosette, June 4 and August 24, 1860, Robert Wyatt Letters, Special Collections Department, James E. Morrow Library, Marshall University, Huntington, WV (hereafter Wyatt Letters); and J. H. Underwood to Louis D. Rosette, July 31 and August 1, 1860, in Osborn Hamiline Oldroyal, *Lincoln's Campaign; or, The Political Revolution of 1860* (Chicago: Laird & Lee, 1896), 107, 108.

23. Preston Bailhache, quoted in Jeremy Prichard, "In Lincoln's Shadow: The Civil War in Springfield, Illinois" (PhD diss., University of Kansas, 2014); "Wide Awakes," *Los Angeles Daily News*, November 14, 1860; "Rally at Lincoln's in Springfield," *Chicago Tribune*, August 10, 1860; and Rosette to Rosette, August 24, 1860.

24. Larry D. Mansch, *Abraham Lincoln, President-Elect: The Four Critical Months from Election to Inauguration* (Jefferson, NC: McFarland, 2007), 11; and George M. Brinkerhoof, interview, in *Herndon's Informant: Letters, Interviews, and Statements About Abraham Lincoln*, ed. Douglas L. Wilson and Rodney O. Davis (Urbana: University of Illinois Press, 1998), 437.

25. "The Democrats Having Threatened," *Washington Evening Star*, August 22, 1860; and "Rally at Lincoln's."

26. McClure, *Old Time Notes*, 416–19.

27. *Frederick Douglass: Selected Speeches and Writings*, ed. Philip Foner and Yuval Taylor, Library of Black America (Chicago: Lawrence Hill Books, 1999), 416; Benjamin F. Thompson, "The Wide Awakes of 1860," *Magazine of History with Notes and Queries* 10 (November 1909): 294–95; "Letter from J. S. Jr.," *Chicago Tribune*, August 22, 1860; and "Cassius M. Clay in Terre Haute!" *Wabash (IN) Express*, July 18, 1860.

28. "The Hour Has Come!" *St. Joseph (MI) Saturday Herald*, November 7, 1860; Schurz, *Reminiscences*, 2:193; McClure, *Old Time Notes*, 417, 418; and Abram

Jesse Dittenhoefer, *How We Elected Lincoln: Personal Recollections of Lincoln and Men of His Time* (New York: Harper & Brothers, 1916), 36.

29. "The Wide-Awakes," *Chicago Tribune*, April 4, 1860; "J. A. Smith and Co.," *Chicago Tribune*, May 30, 1860; and "News Items," *Hartford Courant*, December 3, 1860.

30. "News Items"; "Mirror Correspondence," *Bloomville (NY) Mirror*, December 4, 1860; Scott Derks, ed., *The Value of a Dollar: Prices and Incomes in the United States, 1860–1999*, 2nd ed. (Lakeville, CT: Grey House, 1999), 11–13; and Edgar S. Yergason to Charlotte Yergason, January 1, 1860, Yergason Papers.

31. Louis Gerteis, *Civil War St. Louis* (Lawrence: University Press of Kansas, 2001), 96; James Peckham, *Gen. Nathaniel Lyon, and Missouri in 1861: A Monograph of the Great Rebellion* (New York: American News, 1866), xiii; and Charles O'Neill to Caroline Townsend Bartholomew, July 29, 1860, and November 12, 1860, O'Neill Papers.

32. "Wide Awakes!" *Hartford Courant*, May 22, 1860.

33. Philip M. Katz, "Our Man in Paris: John Meredith Read Jr. and the Discontents of American Republicanism, 1860–1896," in *The Struggle for Equality: Essays on Sectional Conflict, the Civil War, and the Long Reconstruction*, ed. Jennifer L. Weber, Jerald Podair, and Orville Vernon Burton (Charlottesville: University of Virginia Press, 2011), 41–51; and James Ashley to John Meredith Read Sr., June 22, 1860, Read Papers.

34. For letters detailing sums exchanged, see John Meredith Read Jr. to John Meredith Read Sr., August 1, 1860; Read Sr. to Read Jr., August 9, 1860; Read Jr. to Read Sr., September 3, 1860; Read Jr. to Read Sr., October 8, 1860; Read Jr. to Read Sr., October 22, 1860; and Read Jr. to Read Sr., October 29, 1860, all in Read Papers.

35. Read Sr. to Read Jr., August 9, 1860.

36. Read Jr. to Read Sr., August 2, 1860, Read Papers.

37. Read Sr. to Read Jr., August 9, 1860.

38. *The Works of William H. Seward*, ed. George E. Baker (Boston: Houghton Mifflin, 1884), 82; and "Seward at Niagara," *New York Times*, September 5, 1860.

39. Schurz, *Reminiscences*, 2:174; and *Works of Seward*, 4:83.

40. "Governor Seward on the Wing," *New York Herald*, September 3, 1860; Charles Francis Adams Jr., *An Autobiography* (Boston: Houghton Mifflin, 1916), 61; and "Wide Awakes Are Lost in Labyrinth," *New York Herald*, September 3, 1860.

41. Adams, *Autobiography*, 61, 39, 51.

42. Fanny Seward, August 31, 1860, in "Stumping for Lincoln in 1860: Excerpts from the Diary of Fanny Seward," ed. Patricia C. Johnson, *University of*

Rochester Library Bulletin 16, no. 1 (Autumn 1960), https://rbscp.lib.rochester .edu/470#1; and Trudy Krisher, *Fanny Seward: A Life* (Syracuse, NY: Syracuse University Press, 2015), 52.

43. "Lost in Labyrinth."

44. Adams, *Autobiography*, 64–6, 63, 61, 59, 62.

45. Adams, 62.

46. "Seward," *New York Herald*, September 4, 1860; Fanny Seward, September 1, 1860, in "Stumping for Lincoln," https://rbscp.lib.rochester.edu/470#1; and "From Auburn to Niagara Falls," *New York Times*, September 5, 1860.

47. "Mr. Seward on the Stump," *New York Herald*, September 5, 1860; *Works of Seward*, 4:84; and "Seward on the Stump."

48. "Seward on the Stump."

49. Fanny Seward, September 12, 1860, in "Stumping for Lincoln," https://rbscp.lib .rochester.edu/470#1; "Seward on the Wide Awakes," *Wisconsin State Journal* (Madison), September 8, 1860; and *Works of Seward*, 4:85.

50. "The Great Political Crisis," *New York Herald*, September 8, 1860; and Fanny Seward, September 8, 1860, in "Stumping for Lincoln," https://rbscp.lib .rochester.edu/470#1.

51. Adams, *Autobiography*, 64–69.

52. *Works of Seward*, 4:85; Chicago Wide-Awake Republican Club to Abraham Lincoln, June 1, 1860 (certificate of membership), and Amos Tuck to David Davis, August 24, 1860, both Lincoln Papers; "The Opening of Convention Week," *Chicago Tribune*, May 14, 1860; "Colored Wide-Awakes," *Baltimore Sun*, October 6, 1860; Douglas Egerton, *Year of Meteors: Stephen Douglas, Abraham Lincoln, and the Election That Brought the Civil War* (New York: Bloomsbury, 2010), 183; and Gerteis, *Civil War St. Louis*, 66.

53. Adams, *Autobiography*, 65–66.

54. Adams, 69.

55. Adams, 69.

56. Adams, 69.

CHAPTER SEVEN: WIDE AWAKES! CHARGE!

1. Anonymous, "Election Time in America," *All the Year Round*, ed. Charles Dickens, no. 103 (April 13, 1861): 69; and Abram Jesse Dittenhoefer, *How We Elected Lincoln: Personal Recollections of Lincoln and Men of His Time* (New York: Harper & Brothers, 1916), 1–2.

2. "At the Lafarge Hotel," *New York Times*, October 4, 1860; and "At the New-York Hotel," *New York Times*, October 4, 1860.

3. "The Whole City on Fire for Lincoln and Hamlin," *New York Times*, October 4, 1860; and "New York Hotel, Breakfast Bill of Fare," July 1859, Buttolph Collection, New York Public Library, New York.

4. Junius Henri Browne, *The Great Metropolis: A Mirror of New York* (Hartford, CT: American, 1869), 391–92; *The Diary of George Templeton Strong, 1860–1865*, ed. Allan Nevins (New York: Macmillan, 1952), entry for October 28, 1860, 55; "The New York Hotel," *Buffalo Commercial Advertiser*, September 27, 1860; and "The Escape of Postmaster Fowler," *Buffalo Courier*, May 28, 1860.

5. "Hiram Cranston Dead," *Norfolk Virginian*, September 20, 1877; and "New York Hotel."

6. "Meeting at No 722 Broadway," *New York Tribune*, September 26, 1860; "ITALIAN WIDE-AWAKES," *New York Tribune*, September 17, 1860; and Silas B. Dutcher and Wide Awake Central Committee of the City of New York to Abraham Lincoln, January 1861, John Henry Hobart Ward Papers, Manuscripts and Archives Division, New York Public Library, New York.

7. "Meeting at No 722"; and "The Banner on the Outer Wall," *New York Herald*, July 23, 1860.

8. "New York Hotel," *Washington Evening Star*, September 26, 1860.

9. Campbell Gibson, "Population of the 100 Largest Cities and Other Urban Places in the United States, 1790 to 1990," U.S. Census Bureau, Working Paper POP-WP027, June 1998, https://www.census.gov/library/working-papers/1998/demo/POP-twps0027.html.

10. Bettie Ann Graham Diary, October 18 and 27, 1860, University of Virginia, Charlottesville; and "Wide Awake Club," *Wilmington (NC) Daily Journal*, September 17, 1860.

11. Charles Francis Adams Jr., *An Autobiography* (Boston: Houghton Mifflin, 1916), 69; and "Carolina in Gotham," *Charleston (SC) Mercury*, September 20, 1860.

12. "Stop Lying," *Chicago Tribune*, November 26, 1860; Anonymous, "Election Time in America," 68; Charles O'Neill to Caroline Townsend Bartholomew, November 15, 1860, O'Neill Papers; and "Our Readers Are Already Aware," *Wheeling (VA) Intelligencer*, October 5, 1860.

13. "Armed Wide Awakes," *Richmond (VA) Dispatch*, July 13, 1860; "Wide Awakes Permanent," *Dallas Herald*, October 31, 1860; "Our Brethren," *Montgomery (AL) Weekly Advertiser and Register*, September 12, 1860; "The Wide Awakes," *Richmond (VA) Enquirer*, September 14, 1860; "Wide Awakes Followers of

John Brown," *Nashville Union and American*, September 30, 1860; "Wide Awakes," *Dallas Daily Herald*, October 17, 1860; "The Moderate Republican," *Alexandria (VA) Gazette*, October 2, 1860; and "Erect the Guillotine," *Chicago Tribune*, October 20, 1860, quoting from *Georgia Chronicle* (Augusta).

14. "Carolina in Gotham."

15. "The 'Wide Awakes,' " *Richmond (VA) Enquirer*, September 14, 1860; and "The 'Wide Awakes,' " *Jackson Semi-Weekly Mississippian*, October 16, 1860.

16. "For the Southern Enterprise," *Greenville (SC) Southern Enterprise*, September 20, 1860; and "Governor Wise," *Richmond (VA) Enquirer*, October 12, 1860.

17. "Speech of Mr. Yancey," *Washington Evening Star*, September 22, 1860; and Eric H. Walther, "The Fire-Eaters and Seward," *Journal of the Abraham Lincoln Association* 32, no. 1 (Winter 2011): 30.

18. Walther, "Fire-Eaters," 30.

19. Dan Bouk, *Democracy's Data: The Hidden Stories in the U.S. Census and How to Read Them* (New York: MCD, 2022); Jane Ann Moore and William F. Moore, *Owen Lovejoy and the Coalition for Equality* (Champaign-Urbana: University of Illinois Press, 2019), 157; Ulysses S. Grant, *The Personal Memoirs of Ulysses S. Grant* (New York: Charles L. Webster, 1885), 1: 216; Strong, *Diary*, entry for October 22, 1860, 52; and "At the Metropolitan Hotel," *New York Times*, October 4, 1860.

20. Jonathan W. White, ed., *To Address You as My Friend: African American Letters to Lincoln* (Chapel Hill: University of North Carolina Press, 2022), 4; and *The Story of Mattie J. Jackson*, with L. S. Thompson (Lawrence, KS: Sentinel Office, 1866), 10–11.

21. Frank Towers, *The Urban South and the Coming of the Civil War* (Charlottesville: University of Virginia Press, 2004), 124.

22. Towers, *Urban South*, 143.

23. "A Rather Sensible Disunionist," *New York Times*, September 21, 1860; Towers, *Urban South*, 31; David Grimsted, *American Mobbing: Toward Civil War* (New York: Oxford University Press, 1998), 246; and James Allan Stuart MacKay, "Southern Heretics: The Republican Party in the Border South During the Civil War" (PhD diss., Carleton University, 2019).

24. "How the Battle Wages!" *Hartford Courant*, July 12, 1860; Lewis Clephane, "Birth of the Republican Party, with a Brief History of the Important Part Taken by the Original Republican Association of the National Capitol," address delivered at the Reunion of the Surviving Members of the Republican Association of 1855 to 1861, and of the Wide-Awakes, January 26, 1889 (Washington, D.C.: Gibson Bros., 1889); "Republican Meeting," *Wheeling (VA) Intelligencer*,

September 27, 1860; *Memoirs of Gustav Koerner, 1809–1896: Life-Sketches Written at the Suggestion of His Children* (Cedar Rapids, IA: Torch Press, 1909), 2:99; "Letter from a Delaware Republic," *Hartford Courant*, August 16, 1860; "The Baltimore Wide Awakes," *Cleveland Daily Leader*, November 6, 1860; MacKay, "Southern Heretics," 162; and "Baltimore Wide Awake Association Sacked," *Washington Evening Star*, October 25, 1860.

25. "Lewis Clephane: A Pioneer Washington Republican," 1919, Records of the Columbia Historical Society, Washington, D.C., 263–77; Freeman, *Field of Blood*, 256; and Clephane, "Birth."

26. Louis Clephane to Abraham Lincoln, October 27, 1860, Lincoln Papers; and "Jubilee of the Wide Awakes," *Washington Evening Star*, November 27, 1860.

27. "The Republican Procession Last Night," *Washington Evening Star*, October 13, 1860; "Wide Awake Parade," *Alexandria (VA) Gazette*, October 15, 1860; "The Republican Procession Last Night," *Washington Evening Star*, October 19, 1860; and Clephane, "Birth," 16.

28. "Republican Procession Last Night," October 19, 1860; and "Republican Procession Last Night," October 13, 1860.

29. "The 'Wide Awakes,'" *Richmond (VA) Enquirer*, September 14, 1860; "Republican Procession," October 19, 1860; Basil Duke, *The Reminiscences of General Basil W. Duke, C.S.A.* (Garden City, NY: Doubleday, Page, 1911), 37; "Wide Awakes," *Los Angeles Daily News*, November 14, 1860; and Anonymous, "Election Time in America," 67.

30. John Dimitry, "Louisiana," in *Confederate Military History: A Library of Confederate States History*, ed. Clement A. Evans (Atlanta: Confederate, 1899), 10:4–8.

31. "The Coming Struggle," *New York Herald*, September 29, 1860; and "What is Respectable Treason," *Daily Missouri Republican* (St. Louis), October 4, 1860.

32. W. A. Howard, "Alleged Hostile Organization Against the Government Within the District of Columbia," February 14, 1861, House of Representatives, 36th Cong., 2nd sess., rept. no. 79, 11–20, 81–91, 104–60; "The National Volunteers, Again," *Washington Evening Star*, January 17, 1861; and Clephane, "Birth," 16.

33. "What Is Respectable Treason," *Daily Missouri Republican* (St. Louis), October 4, 1860.

34. "Letter from New York," *Richmond (VA) Enquirer*, September 18, 1860; Anonymous, "Election Time in America," 70, 67–68; and *The Wide-Awake Songster*, ed. John Hutchinson (New York: O. Hutchinson Publisher), 1860.

35. "Meeting at No 722."

36. "Meeting at No 722"; and "First Blood of the Irrepressible Conflict," *New York Herald*, September 27, 1860.

37. "Meeting at No 722."

38. "Meeting at No 722"; and "Editor Assaulted," *Weekly Ottumwa (IA) Courier*, September 27, 1860.

39. "Meeting at No 722"; "Letter from New York"; "Reception of Mr. Douglas," *Hartford Courant*, July 17, 1860; and "Levying Money on the Police for Political Purposes," *Brooklyn Daily Eagle*, October 1, 1860.

40. "Hissing at the New York Wide-Awakes," *Brooklyn Daily Eagle*, September 26, 1860; and "Meeting at No 722."

41. "Served 'Em Right," *Long Island Farmer and Queens County (NY) Advertiser*, October 2, 1860; "First Blood of the Irrepressible Conflict"; and "An Attempt to Make Mischief," *New York Times*, September 28, 1860.

42. "Letter from Sherman Booth," *Anti-Slavery Bugle*, August 25, 1860; LeeAnna Keith, *When It Was Grand: The Radical Republican History of the Civil War* (New York: Hill and Wang, 2020), 124–25; "Republican Meeting," *Louisville (KY) Daily Courier*, August 27, 1860; "An Attempt to Muzzle Free Speech in Newburgh," *New York Tribune*, September 3, 1860; and "Unprejudiced Account of the Newburgh Outrage," *Evansville (IN) Daily Journal*, September 1, 1860.

43. "Political Riot at Troy," *New York Herald*, October 17, 1860; and "A Row at Troy," *Brooklyn Daily Eagle*, October 17, 1860.

44. "Political Riot at Troy."

45. "Meeting at No 722"; "The Way It Works," *Janesville (WI) Daily Gazette*, October 20, 1860; "More on the Newburgh Outrage," *Evansville (IN) Daily Journal*, August 27, 1860; and "Inhuman Loco."

46. Charles Godfrey Leland, *Pipps Among the Wide Awakes* (New York: Wevill & Chapin, 1860).

47. Leland, *Pipps*.

48. William Turner Coggeshall, *The Issue of the November Election: An Address to Young Men* (Columbus, OH: privately published, 1860), 2; and Henry J. Raymond to William Lowndes Yancey, November 23, 1860, in *Disunion and Slavery: A Series of Letters to Hon. W. L. Yancey of Alabama* (New York, 1861).

49. Strong, *Diary*, entries for May 11, 1860, 26; September 14, 1860, 42; and February 10, 1860, 8.

50. Strong, entry for September 14, 1860, 42.

51. Strong, entry for September 13, 1860, 41–42.

52. Strong, entry for October 22, 1860, 52.

53. Stanley J. Robboy and Anita W. Robboy, "Lewis Hayden: From Fugitive Slave to Statesman," *New England Quarterly* 46, no. 4 (December 1973): 593–94; and Joel Strangis, *Lewis Hayden and the War Against Slavery* (North Haven, CT: Linnet Books, 1999), 5–6.

54. Lewis Hayden to Sydney Howard Gay, n.d., Sydney Howard Gay Papers, Columbia University Special Collections; and Harriet Beecher Stowe, ed., *A Key to "Uncle Tom's Cabin," Presenting Original Facts and Documents upon Which the Story Is Founded* (Boston: John P. Jewett, 1853), 155.

55. Strangis, *Hayden*, 14, 21, 33–34.

56. Mary Ellen Snodgrass, *The Underground Railroad: An Encyclopedia of People, Places and Operations* (London: Routledge, 2008), 257; Strangis, *Hayden*, 77, 92, 115; and "Letter from G. W. P.," *Liberator*, December 31, 1859.

57. Adelaide M. Cromwell, *The Other Brahmins: Boston's Black Upper Class, 1750–1950* (Fayetteville: University of Arkansas Press, 1994), 43; Josh Daniels, *In Freedom's Birthplace: A Study of The Boston Negroes* (Boston: Houghton Mifflin, 1914), 454; and "Lewis Hayden; Eighteenth Grand Master of Prince Hall Grand Lodge, Boston, Mass.," 1903, photograph by William Grimshaw, print in Schomburg Center for Research in Black Culture, New York Public Library, New York.

58. Mark DeMortie, in "Some of the Incidents in the Life of Mark DeMortie," ed. G. V. Tomashevich, *Afro-Americans in New York Life and History* 3, no. 1 (1979): 61–71; Robboy and Robboy, "Lewis Hayden," 611; and William Henry Ferris, *The African Abroad: His Evolution in West Civilization* (New Haven, CT: Tuttle, Morehouse & Taylor Press, 1913), 2:710–11.

59. Ferris, *African Abroad*, 711; "Colored Wide Awakes," *Philadelphia Public Ledger*, October 6, 1860; "Monster Torchlight Procession," *Boston Transcript*, October 17, 1860; Adelaide Cromwell, "The Black Presence in the West End of Boston, 1800–1864," in *Conscious and Courage: Black and White Abolitionists in Boston* (Bloomington: Indiana University Press, 1993), 160; and Snodgrass, *Underground Railroad*, 18.

60. "Colored Wide Awakes," *Boston Courier*, October 6, 1860; "Brilliant Republican Demonstration," *Liberator*, October 19, 1860; and Douglas Egerton, *Year of Meteors: Stephen Douglas, Abraham Lincoln, and the Election That Brought the Civil War* (New York: Bloomsbury, 2010), 193.

61. "Monster Torchlight Procession"; "Brilliant Republican Demonstration"; and Henry Daniels, Portland, 1861, photograph by H. H. Wilder, Collections of the Maine Historical Society, Portland, https://www.mainememory.net/record /98698; and "Practical Illustration of Republican Tendencies," *Marysville (CA) Daily National Democrat*, November 18, 1860.

62. "The Nigger Ahead," *Lancaster (PA) Intelligencer*, October 16, 1860; "There Is Much Wincing," *Rock Island (IA) Argus*, October 22, 1860; and "Republican White Men Appealing to the Nigger," *Davenport (IA) Quad City Times*, October 15, 1860.

63. "Nigger Wide Awakes," *Dallas Herald*, October 31, 1860; and "The Free Negro North," *Jackson Semi-Weekly Mississippian*, November 2, 1860.

64. "An Infamous Trick that Did Not Succeed in Pittsburgh Will Not Succeed in Wheeling," *Wheeling (VA) Intelligencer*, October 12, 1860; "Negro Equality," *Rock Island (IA) Argus*, October 15, 1860; "Republican White Men"; and "Political Incendiarism," *Chicago Tribune*, November 5, 1860

65. "The Wide-Awakes South," *Little Rock (AR) Weekly Pantograph*, November 7, 1860.

66. Ronald C. White, *A. Lincoln: A Biography* (New York: Random House, 2009), 280; Hayden to Gay, n.d.; and Stowe, *Key to "Uncle Tom's Cabin,"* 155.

67. James McPherson, *The Negro's Civil War: How American Blacks Felt and Acted During the War for the Union* (New York: Knopf Doubleday, 2008), 5–6.

CHAPTER EIGHT: THE APPROACH OF A CONQUERING ARMY

1. "The Election of Mr. Banks to the Speakership," *New York Times*, February 6, 1856; and William Dansberry to Abraham Lincoln, November 1, 1860, Lincoln Papers.

2. Carl Schurz to Margarethe Schurz, October 2, 1860, in *The Intimate Letters of Carl Schurz*, ed. Joseph Schafer (New York: Da Capo Press, 1970), 225; and "Wide Awake Rally," *Brooklyn Evening Star*, September 14, 1860.

3. "Wide Awake Excursion," *Hartford Courant*, September 29, 1860; and "The Excursion," *Hartford Courant*, October 5, 1860.

4. "Rally," *New York Herald*, October 1, 1860; and Pink (New York correspondent), "Correspondence of the Courier," *Charleston (SC) Daily Courier*, October 6, 1860.

5. "The Great Parade of the Wide Awakes on Wednesday," *New York Times*, October 1, 1860; and "The Wide Awakes," *New York Times*, October 1, 1860.

6. "The Route of the March," *New York Times*, October 3, 1860.

7. "Wide Awakes! Wide Awakes!! Barnum's Museum," *New York Times*, October 4, 1860.

8. "Whole City on Fire for Lincoln and Hamlin," *New York Times*, October 4, 1860.

9. "The Wide Awakes," *New York Herald*, September 19, 1860.

10. Anonymous, "Election Time in America," *All the Year Round*, ed. Charles Dickens, no. 103 (April 13, 1861): 72–73.

11. "At the St. Nicholas Hotel," *New York Times*, October 4, 1860; and "The Wide Awake Demonstration," *New York Times*, October 3, 1860.

12. John Meredith Read Jr. to John Meredith Read Sr., October 5, 1860, and August 31, 1860, Read Papers.

13. "Speech of Gov. Seward," *Chicago Tribune*, October 2, 1860; and "The Grand Mass Meeting," *Cleveland Daily Leader*, October 5, 1860.

14. "The Wide-Awakes," *New York Times*, October 2, 1860; and "Another Grand Wide Awake Parade," *New York Times*, October 5, 1860.

15. "Speeches of F. P. Blair," *New York Times*, October 5, 1860.

16. "Edward Everett," *St. Albans (VT) Democrat*, October 2, 1860; "Portrait of Lucius Eugene Chittenden," Smithsonian Institution Archives, record unit 95, box 27A, image no. SIA_000095_B27A_044, Smithsonian Institution Archives, Washington, D.C.; "Our Chittenden," *Burlington (VT) Weekly Sentinel*, October 5, 1860; and Lucius E. Chittenden, *Recollections of President Lincoln and His Administration* (New York: Harper and Brothers, 1891), 8.

17. Chittenden, *Recollections*, 9–10.

18. Chittenden, 10.

19. Chittenden, 10.

20. Chittenden, 10, 15.

21. Chittenden, 10–14.

22. Chittenden, 9–12, 15.

23. "Whole City on Fire for Lincoln and Hamlin"; "At the New-York Hotel," *New York Times*, October 4, 1860; and "Letter from New York City Correspondent," *Charleston (SC) Courier*, October 2, 1860.

24. "The Wide Awakes," *New York Tribune*, October 31, 1860.

25. Charles O'Neill to Caroline Townsend Bartholomew, November 4, 1860, O'Neill Papers.

26. James Sanks Brisbin to Ezra Brisbin, November 1, 1860, Brisbin Papers, 20–21; and "A Trip Down South," *Bellefonte (PA) Centre Democrat*, November 15, 1860.

27. James Sank Brisbin, "Personal Record of James Sanks Brisbin: Colonel 1st Cavalry, Brevet Brigadier General, U.S. Army," Brisbin Papers; "Tu Sousand Folkes," *Bellefont (PA) Centre Democrat*, September 27, 1860; and James Sanks Brisbin to Jane Brisbin, July 10, 1863, Gilder Lehrman Collections, New York.

28. Brisbin to Brisbin, November 1, 1860, 3; James Sanks Brisbin to Ezra Brisbin, November 8, 1860, Brisbin Papers, 40; "What We Demand of Our Country,"

Bellefonte (PA) Centre Democrat, October 16, 1860; and Brisbin to Brisbin, November 1, 1860, 2.

29. Brisbin to Brisbin, November 1, 1860, 2.

30. "The Wide Awakes," *Wheeling (VA) Intelligencer*, November 6, 1860; "Wide Awakes," *Wheeling (VA) Intelligencer*, August 29, 1860; "Organization of a Second Wide Awake Company," *Wheeling (VA) Intelligencer*, September 7, 1860; "German Wide Awake Company," *Wheeling (VA) Intelligencer*, September 8, 1860; "German Wide Awakes Stoned Again," *Wheeling (VA) Intelligencer*, September 29, 1860; and Andre M. Fleche, *The Revolution of 1861: The American Civil War in the Age of Nationalist Conflict* (Chapel Hill: University of North Carolina Press, 2012), 32.

31. Brisbin to Brisbin, November 1, 1860, 3–4. It should be noted that the Wheeling Wide Awakes made it as clear as they could that the Pennsylvanians should not come, given the weather, and later described the event in their house organ with the irked context: "Notwithstanding the drenching rain yesterday, and the despatches, and messengers, announcing a postponement, which were sent in all directions, a large number of people came to town." "Notwithstanding the Rain," *Wheeling (VA) Intelligencer*, November 3, 1860; and Brisbin to Brisbin, November 1, 1860, 6–8.

32. The account published in the *Bellefonte (PA) Centre Democrat* generally confirms Brisbin's experience, but differs enough at key moments that it was clearly not written by Brisbin himself. Its author, perhaps Brisbin's brother and coeditor J. J. Brisbin, stayed with the Pennsylvania Wide Awakes when James Sanks Brisbin went into hiding. "Trip Down South"; and Brisbin to Brisbin, November 1, 1860, 9–15.

33. "Trip Down South."

34. Emory L. Kemp and Beverly B. Fluty, *The Wheeling Suspension Bridge: A Pictorial History* (Charleston, WV: Pictorial Histories, 1999); and Sean Patrick Duffy and Paul Rinkes, *Wheeling: Then and Now* (Charleston, SC: Arcadia, 2010).

35. Brisbin to Brisbin, November 1, 1860, 20.

36. Brisbin to Brisbin, 21–22.

37. Brisbin to Brisbin, 31; and "Trip Down South."

38. "We Have Received Quite a Lengthy Communication," *Wheeling (VA) Intelligencer*, November 1, 1860; "More About the Bethany Difficulty," *Wheeling (VA) Intelligencer*, November 22, 1860; "The Chivalry of Bethany," *Pittsburgh Gazette*, November 2, 1860; "The Attack on the Ninth Ward Wide-Awakes," *New York Tribune*, November 5, 1860; "The Wide Awake Parade in Baltimore," *Philadelphia Public Ledger*, November 3, 1860; and

"Grand Black Republican Demonstration," *Baltimore Daily Exchange*, November 2, 1860.

39. "Wide Awakes! How Do You Like That," *Buffalo Morning Express and Illustrated*, November 15, 1860.

40. George N. Sanders, "To the Republicans of New York, Who Are for the Republic," October 30, 1860, printed in *Charleston (SC) Daily Courier*, November 6, 1860.

41. "Lincoln Douglas Forces Organizing for the Black Republican Inauguration," *Nashville Union and American*, September 22, 1860; and "The Prospect Before Us—A Good Suggestion," *Wilmington (NC) Daily Journal*, October 22, 1860, printed originally in the *Milledgeville (GA) Federal Union*.

42. "Disunion," *Daily Nashville Patriot*, October 17, 1860; "The North Against Us," *New Orleans Daily Delta*, October 23, 1860; "Shall We Unite Against the Enemy!" *Richmond (VA) Enquirer*, October 19, 1860, quoting from *Montgomery (AL) Advertiser*. Tellingly, much of this coverage involved debates and extended quotations from other newspapers, as a network of southern editors weighed their options if Lincoln were to win.

43. Sanders, "To the Republicans of New York"; William Tecumseh Sherman to Ellen Boyle Ewing, November 3, 1860, in *Home Letters of General Sherman*, ed. M. A. DeWolfe Howe (New York: Charles Scribner's Sons, 1909), 188.

44. Ellen Ellington, "The Sixth of November, 1860," *Vicksburg (MS) Whig*, November 2, 1860.

45. "Fatal Incredulity," *Lancaster (PA) Intelligencer*, November 6, 1860; and "Alarming Progress of Revolution at the South," *New York Herald*, October 23, 1860.

46. "Secession," *Bellefonte (PA) Centre Democrat*, November 1, 1860.

47. "Our Durham Letter," *Windham (NY) Journal*, October 9, 1860, in Melissa Franson, "Wide Awakes, Half Asleeps, Little Giants, and Bell Ringers: Political Partisanship in the Catskills of New York During the Elections of 1860 and 1862," *New York History* 102, no. 1 (Summer 2021): 149.

48. "Our Durham Letter," 149.

CHAPTER NINE: I THINK THAT SETTLES IT

1. Michael E. McGerr, *The Decline of Popular Politics: The American North, 1865–1928* (New York: Oxford University Press, 1986), 120.

2. Kelsey Landis, "100 Years Since Lovejoy Press Lifted from River," *Alton (IL) Telegraph*, July 14, 2015; Levi Coffin, *Reminiscences of Levi Coffin* (Cincinnati: Western Tract Society, 1876), 527; and Walter William, *A History of Northwest Missouri* (Chicago: Lewis, 1915), 1:233.

3. Melissa Franson, "Wide Awakes, Half Asleeps, Little Giants, and Bell Ringers: Political Partisanship in the Catskills of New York During the Elections of 1860 and 1862," *New York History* 102, no. 1 (Summer 2021): 64; William E. Gienapp, *The Origins of the Republican Party* (New York: Oxford University Press, 1987), 415; and "Examine Your Tickets!" *Gettysburg (PA) Compiler*, October 9, 1854.

4. Henry T. Sperry, Hartford Wide Awakes membership form (MS13264-9 and MS13264-10), August 1, 1861 [misdated; must be 1860], Wide Awakes Records.

5. "The Connecticut Wide-Awakes," *New York Tribune*, May 3, 1860; "How the Battle Waged," *Hartford Courant*, April 3, 1860; and "Canvassers for Campaign of 1860," Republicans of Waterbury Campaign Club Records (MS53693), Connecticut Historical Society, Hartford.

6. "Maine Voting," *Hartford Courant*, September 17, 1860; and "The Wide Awake Movement," *Davenport (IA) Morning Democrat*, September 19, 1860.

7. "Attempts to Defraud the Union Men of Kings County," *Brooklyn Daily Eagle*, November 2, 1860; "Look Out for Trickery," *Brooklyn Evening Star*, November 3, 1860; and "One Hundred Dollars Is the Legal Reward," *New York Tribune*, November 5, 1860.

8. "Gentleman," *Cincinnati Commercial*, October 17, 1860; "Wide Awakes!" *Berkshire County (MA) Eagle*, October 18, 1860; and "The Wide Awakes," *New York Tribune*, October 31, 1860.

9. Edgar S. Yergason to Charlotte Yergason, November 4, 1860, Yergason Papers.

10. "Good Bye, Wide Awakes!" *Davenport (IA) Quad City Times*, November 6, 1860; and "Wide Awakes!" *Chicago Tribune*, November 6, 1860.

11. Joseph Howard Jr., "Great Demonstration of the Wide-Awakes at Hartford," *New York Times*, July 28, 1860; and "Wide-Awake Tactics on Election Day," *New York Tribune*, October 27, 1860.

12. *Frederick Douglass: Selected Speeches and Writings*, ed. Philip Foner and Yuval Taylor, Library of Black America (Chicago: Lawrence Hill Books, 1999), 410, 407; and James McPherson, *The Negro's Civil War: How American Blacks Felt and Acted During the War for the Union* (New York: Knopf Doubleday, 2008).

13. *The Diary of George Templeton Strong, 1860–1865*, ed. Allan Nevins (New York: Macmillan, 1952), entries for November 2, 1860, 56, and November 6, 1860, 58.

14. Larry D. Mansch, *Abraham Lincoln, President-Elect: The Four Critical Months from Election to Inauguration* (Jefferson, NC: McFarland, 2007), 50–51.

15. William Gienapp, "Who Voted for Lincoln?" in *Abraham Lincoln and the American Political Tradition*, ed. John L. Thomas (Amherst: University of Massachusetts Press, 1986), 51; Harold Holzer, *Lincoln, President-Elect: Abraham Lincoln*

and the Great Secession Winter, 1860–1861 (New York: Simon & Schuster, 2008), 31; and "Lincoln the Night of the Election," *Louisville (KY) Daily Courier*, November 10, 1860, reprinting Springfield correspondent to the *Missouri Democrat* (St. Louis), November 7, 1860.

16. "Lincoln the Night of the Election."

17. Holzer, *Lincoln, President-Elect*, 39.

18. "Lincoln the Night of the Election"; Holzer, *Lincoln, President-Elect*, 45; Carl Schurz to Margarethe Schurz, November 7, 1860, in *The Intimate Letters of Carl Schurz*, ed. Joseph Schafer (New York: Da Capo Press, 1970), 231; Edward L. Widmer, *Lincoln on the Verge : Thirteen Days to Washington* (New York: Simon & Schuster, 2020), 20; Emily Hawley Gillespie, *A Secret to Be Buried: The Diary and Life of Emily Hawley Gillespie, 1858–1888* (Iowa City: University of Iowa Press, 1989), entry for November 6, 1860, 395; and Strong, *Diary*, entry for November 7, 1860, 58.

19. "Lincoln the Night of the Election."

20. Franson, "Wide Awakes, Half Asleeps," 165; and "Impromptu Wide Awake Parade," *New York Times*, November 7, 1860.

21. "Washington City on the Night of the Election of Abraham Lincoln," *Washington Evening Star*, November 7, 1860; and "Lewis Clephane: A Pioneer Washington Republican," 1919, Records of the Columbia Historical Society, Washington, D.C., 272.

22. "Lewis Clephane," 272; and "Washington City on the Night of the Election."

23. Even losers of the popular vote like Donald Trump, George W. Bush, Benjamin Harrison, and Samuel Tilden won bigger percentages of the popular vote; only John Quincy Adams won fewer votes, back in 1824. Statistics calculated based on Gerhard Peters and John Woolley, "Presidential Elections Data," *American Presidency Project*, University of California, Santa Barbara, accessed July 12, 2023, https://www.presidency.ucsb.edu /statistics/elections/1860.

24. Peters and Woolley, "Presidential Elections Data."

25. *Douglass: Selected Speeches*, 415.

26. Gienapp, "Who Voted for Lincoln?" 65–76.

27. Gienapp, 65–76.

28. Gienapp, 65–76.

29. "The Canvas," *New York Tribune*, November 8, 1860.

30. George N. Sanders, "To the Republicans of New York, Who Are for the Republic," October 30, 1860, printed in *Charleston (SC) Daily Courier*, November 6, 1860.

31. "The Wide-Awakes," *London Daily News*, October 25, 1860; and "The Wide Awakes," *London Morning Chronicle*, October 20, 1860.

32. Charles O'Neill to Caroline Townsend Bartholomew, November 6 and November 8, 1860, O'Neill Papers.

33. Adam Goodheart, *1861: The Civil War Awakening* (New York: Alfred A. Knopf, 2011), 53.

34. Mary Boykin Chesnut, *A Diary from Dixie*, ed. Isabella D. Martin and Myrta Lockett Avary (New York: D. Appleton, 1906), entry for November 8, 1860, 1; Douglas Egerton, *Year of Meteors: Stephen Douglas, Abraham Lincoln, and the Election That Brought the Civil War* (New York: Bloomsbury, 2010), 215; and Widmer, *Lincoln on the Verge*, 27.

35. James Sanks Brisbin to Ezra Brisbin, November 8, 1860, Brisbin Papers, 42.

CHAPTER TEN: PERMIT ME TO SUGGEST A PLAN

1. Adam Goodheart, "Silencing the Fanatics," *New York Times*, December 2, 2010; and "The Recent Respectable Riot," *New York Tribune*, December 7, 1860.

2. "Tremont Temple," *Bloomsburg (PA) Star of the North*, December 5, 1860; and Goodheart, "Silencing the Fanatics."

3. Goodheart, "Silencing the Fanatics"; and *The American Annual Cyclopedia and Register of Important Events of the Year 1861* (New York: D. Appleton, 1863), 450.

4. Stephen Kantrowitz, *More Than Freedom: Fighting for Black Citizenship in a White Republic* (New York: Penguin, 2013), 269; and Goodheart, "Silencing the Fanatics."

5. Kantrowitz, *More Than Freedom*, 269.

6. Mischa Honeck, *We Are the Revolutionists: German-Speaking Immigrants and American Abolitionists After 1848* (Athens: University of Georgia Press, 2011), 151–53; and Karl Henzein, "Slavery and Mobocracy at the North," *Liberator*, December 28, 1860.

7. Henzein, "Slavery and Mobocracy."

8. Henzein.

9. Susan B. Anthony to Henry B. Stanton Jr. and Gerrit S. Stanton, September 27, 1860, in *Antebellum Women: Private, Public, Partisan*, ed. Carol Lasser and Stacey Robertson (Lanham, MD: Rowman & Littlefield, 2010), 203; and "Carl Schurz Speaking in English and German," *Brooklyn Evening Star*, October 18, 1860.

10. Henry T. Sperry, "To the Republican Wide-Awake Ladies, of Hartford," November 12, 1860, Wide Awakes Records; and "Grand Republican Jubilee!!!" *Buchanan County (IA) Guardian*, November 20, 1860.

11. "Politics in a Female Seminary," *Princeton (IN) Clarion-Leader*, November 24, 1860; and Harold Holzer, *Lincoln, President-Elect: Abraham Lincoln and the Great Secession Winter, 1860–1861* (New York: Simon & Schuster, 2008), 40.

12. "A Republican Oracle Speaks," *Burlington (VT) Weekly Sentinel*, November 16, 1860; and Charles Sumner, "Evening After the Presidential Election," speech delivered in Concord, MA, November 7, 1860, in *Charles Sumner: His Complete Works*, ed. George Frisbie Hoar (Boston: Lee and Shepard, 1900), 7:77.

13. "Absurd Rumors," *Nashville Republican Banner*, November 13, 1860; *The Diary of George Templeton Strong, 1860–1865*, ed. Allan Nevins (New York: Macmillan, 1952), entry for November 7, 1860, 60; and James Sanks Brisbin to Ezra Brisbin, November 15, 1860, Brisbin Papers, 8.

14. James Chesnut Jr., "The Legislature of South Carolina," *Charleston (SC) Mercury*, November 12, 1860; Douglas Egerton, *Year of Meteors: Stephen Douglas, Abraham Lincoln, and the Election That Brought the Civil War* (New York: Bloomsbury, 2010), 222, 228; James L. Abrahamson, *Men of Secession and War, 1859–1865* (Wilmington, DE: Scholarly Resources, 2000), 96; "Sentiment in Georgia," *New York Times*, November 12, 1860; and Strong, *Diary*, entry for November 13, 1860, 63.

15. Pink (New York correspondent), *Charleston (SC) Daily Courier*, November 14, 1860; John Meredith Read Jr. to John Meredith Read Sr., December 8, 1860, Read Papers; Strong, *Diary*, entry for January 31, 1861, 95; and Ulysses S. Grant, *The Personal Memoirs of Ulysses S. Grant* (New York: Charles L. Webster, 1885), 1:222.

16. George E. Stephens, letter to the editor, *Weekly Anglo-African*, January 15, 1861.

17. Stephens, letter to the editor.

18. Carl Schurz, *The Reminiscences of Carl Schurz*, (New York: McClure, 1907), 2:211; *Frederick Douglass: Selected Speeches and Writings*, ed. Philip Foner and Yuval Taylor, Library of Black America (Chicago: Lawrence Hill Books, 1999), 429; and "The Election for Delegates," *Charleston (SC) Courier*, December 10, 1860.

19. "Hoorah for Lincoln?" *Wayne County (PA) Herald*, December 20, 1860; and "The Effects of Lincoln's Election," *York (PA) Gazette*, December 18, 1860.

20. "Wide Awakes," *New York Herald*, September 10, 1860.

21. Charles Sumner, speech delivered in Providence, RI, November 16, 1860, in *Charles Sumner: His Complete Works*, ed. George Frisbie Hoar (Boston: Lee and Shepard, 1900), 7:82; "Georgetown," *Washington Evening Star*, November 11, 1860; "Wide Awakes and the Inauguration of Mr. Lincoln," *Liberator*, November 16,

1860; "Correspondent from New York City," *Charleston (SC) Daily Courier*, November 14, 1860.

22. James Sanks Brisbin to Ezra Brisbin, November 4, 1860, Brisbin Papers, 26; and James Sanks Brisbin to Ezra Brisbin, November 8, 1860, Brisbin Papers, 42.

23. James Sanks Brisbin to Ezra Brisbin, November 29, 1860, Brisbin Papers, 1–4.

24. Brisbin to Brisbin, 3–4.

25. James Sanks Brisbin to John Letcher, November 15, 1860, Brisbin Papers, 13.

26. John Letcher, "Letter from Gov. Letcher," *Richmond (VA) Enquirer*, November 21, 1860.

27. "In Our Telegraphic Columns," *Wheeling (VA) Intelligencer*, December 11, 1860; "Letter from Gov. Letcher"; "A Most Valiant Dogberry," *Chambersburg (PA) Valley Spirit*, November 28, 1860; and W. C. MacMannis, "An Offset to Brisbin," letter to the editor, *Richmond (VA) Enquirer*, December 12, 1860.

28. James Sanks Brisbin to John Letcher, November 25, 1860, Brisbin Papers, 26–29.

29. Brisbin to Letcher, 26–31.

30. Brisbin to Letcher, 30–31.

31. "North Side Wide Awakes Attention!" *Chicago Tribune*, December 6, 1860; Simeon Draper, "Republican State Committee and the Wide Awakes," *Buffalo Morning Express and Illustrated*, December 8, 1860; and "Efforts are being made," *National Republican*, December 8, 1860.

32. "Central Union Organization," *Daily Missouri Republican* (St. Louis), March 20, 1861; "The Wide Awakes Organization," *Buffalo Daily Republican*, December 12, 1860; and "The Inauguration of Lincoln at Washington," letter to the editor, *New York Herald*, January 7, 1861.

33. David Hunter to Abraham Lincoln, December 18, 1860, Lincoln Papers.

34. George P. Bissell to Abraham Lincoln, December 30, 1860, Lincoln Papers.

35. "Wide Awakes and Minute Men," *San Francisco Bulletin*, November 6, 1860; letter to the editor, *New York Herald*, September 20, 1860; "A Symptom of Secession," *Buffalo Weekly Express*, November 13, 1860; and "Union or Disunion," *Utah Mountaineer* (Salt Lake City), November 10, 1860.

36. William Tecumseh Sherman to Ellen Boyle Ewing, January 8, 1861, in *Home Letters of General Sherman*, ed. M. A. DeWolf Howe (New York: Charles Scribner's Sons, 1909), 190–91.

37. "Meeting to Organize," *Pittsburgh Gazette*, January 3, 1861.

38. "Ho! Wide-Awakes! Ho!" *Bellefonte (PA) Centre Democrat*, January 3, 1861.

39. "Where Is the Oracle," *Daily Milwaukee News*, November 23, 1860.

40. Schurz, *Reminiscences*, 2:207, 214, 209.

41. Carl Schurz to Edwin D. Morgan, December 21, 1860, box 11, Edwin D. Morgan Papers, New York State Library, cited in William D. Hickox, "An Uprising of the People: Military Recruitment in New York State During the Civil War" (PhD diss., University of Kansas, 2017), 64n153; and Carl Schurz to Abraham Lincoln, December 28, 1860, Lincoln Papers.

42. Schurz to Lincoln, December 28, 1860.

43. Ronald C. White, *A. Lincoln: A Biography* (New York: Random House, 2009), 449; and Schurz to Lincoln, December 28, 1860.

44. Carl Schurz to Margarethe Schurz, December 27, 1860, in *The Intimate Letters of Carl Schurz*, ed. Joseph Schafer (New York: Da Capo Press, 1970), 237.

45. Schurz to Schurz, December 27, 1860, 237; Carl Schurz to Margarethe Schurz, February 4, 1861, in Schafer, *Intimate Letters*, 242.

46. William W. Freehling, *Secessionists Triumphant*, vol. 2 of *The Road to Disunion* (New York: Oxford University Press, 2007), 345; "Wait," *New Orleans Bee*, November 8, 1860; and *Douglass: Selected Speeches*, 415.

47. William Tecumseh Sherman to Ellen Boyle Ewing, January 1861, in *Home Letters*, 188.

48. "States Rights Democracy," letter to the editor, *Alabama State Sentinel* (Montgomery), November 14, 1860; and "Compliment to the Hon. L. M. Keitt," *Charleston (SC) Mercury*, November 13, 1860.

49. "Attention! Wide Awakes!" *Chicago Tribune*, November 24, 1860, citing editorial in *New Orleans Courier*; "The Georgia Legislature," *Philadelphia Public Ledger*, November 16, 1860; and James Murray Mason, "The Right of Secession," *Richmond (VA) Enquirer*, December 11, 1860.

50. Adam Goodheart, *1861: The Civil War Awakening* (New York: Alfred A. Knopf, 2011), 71; "The Thirty-Sixth Congress," *Alexandria (VA) Gazette*, December 13, 1860; and "Thirty-Sixth Congress," *Philadelphia Public Ledger*, December 13, 1860.

51. "Thirty-Sixth Congress," *Alexandria (VA) Gazette*; and "Thirty-Sixth Congress," *Philadelphia Public Ledger*.

52. Charles B. Dew, *Apostles of Disunion: Southern Secession Commissioners and the Causes of the Civil War* (Charlottesville: University of Virginia Press, 2001), 24; Egerton, *Year of Meteors*, 228; and Harry V. Jaffa, *A New Birth of Freedom: Abraham Lincoln and the Coming of the Civil War* (New York: Rowman & Littlefield, 2000), 231.

53. "State Convention," *Charleston (SC) Courier*, December 21, 1860.

54. Caroline Seabury, *The Diary of Caroline Seabury*, ed. Suzanne L. Bunkers (Madison: University of Wisconsin Press, 1991), 60; and "Speech of the Hon. Ben. H. Hill," *North Carolina Argus* (Wadesboro), December 13, 1860.

55. "Warlike Preparations in Charleston," *Jackson Weekly Mississippian*, January 9, 1861; and John Dimitry, "Louisiana," in *Confederate Military History: A Library of Confederate States History*, ed. Clement A. Evans (Atlanta: Confederate, 1899), 10:15.

56. Henry L. Benning was the namesake of Fort Benning, Georgia, until 2023. Remarks of Henry Wise, February 16, 18, and 20, 1861, and Henry L. Benning, February 18, 1861, both in *Proceedings of the Convention of Virginia, 1861*; see Virginia Secession Convention Project, University of Richmond, Digital Scholarship Lab, https://secession.richmond.edu/.

57. Wise, remarks, April 17, 1861, *Proceedings of the Convention of Virginia*.

58. Sherman to Ewing, January 1861, 188.

59. "Central Union Organization."

CHAPTER ELEVEN: OUR MOST DETERMINED AND RECKLESS FOLLOWERS

1. W. A. Howard, "Alleged Hostile Organization Against the Government Within the District of Columbia," February 14, 1861, House of Representatives, 36th Cong., 2nd sess., rpt. no. 79, 19–20; "From Washington," *Chicago Tribune*, January 30, 1861; and "Washington City on the Night of the Election of Abraham Lincoln," *Washington Evening Star*, November 7, 1860.

2. Howard, "Alleged Hostile Organization," 19; and "From Washington."

3. Howard, "Alleged Hostile Organization," 19, 17.

4. Howard, 5, 19–20, 10; and Howard, 16, 18, 20.

5. The oath to "stand by" has weird (and purely accidental) echoes to President Donald Trump's message to the Proud Boys to "stand back and stand by" during the 2020 campaign and run-up to the January 6 attack on the U.S. Capitol. Howard, "Alleged Hostile Organization," 144, 87, 105; and "The National Volunteers, Again," *Washington Evening Star*, January 17, 1861.

6. Howard, "Alleged Hostile Organization," 119, 81, 112, 146, 31.

7. Howard, 148.

8. Howard, 104, 12, 117; and "National Volunteers, Again."

9. Trudy Krisher, *Fanny Seward: A Life* (Syracuse, NY: Syracuse University Press, 2015), 53; *The Diary of George Templeton Strong, 1860–1865*, ed. Allan Nevins (New York: Macmillan, 1952), entry for February 26, 1861, 103; and Ronald J. Zboray and Mary Sarcino Zboray, eds., *Voices Without Votes: Women and Politics in Antebellum New England* (Concord: University of New Hampshire Press, 2010), 205.

10. C. H. U., in "Correspondence of the Courier," *Zanesville (OH) Daily Courier*, January 14, 1861.

11. Jim Rasenberger, *Revolver: Sam Colt and the Six-Shooter That Changed America* (New York: Scribner, 2021), 371–73.

12. Lucius E. Chittenden, *Recollections of President Lincoln and His Administration* (New York: Harper and Brothers, 1891), 17–18.

13. Chittenden, *Recollections*, 19.

14. Chittenden, 20–21.

15. Chittenden, 20–21.

16. Adam Goodheart, *1861: The Civil War Awakening* (New York: Alfred A. Knopf, 2011), 87; Carl Schurz, *The Reminiscences of Carl Schurz* (New York: McClure, 1907), 2:212–13; and Carl Schurz to Margarethe Schurz, February 4, 1861, in *The Intimate Letters of Carl Schurz*, ed. Joseph Schafer (New York: Da Capo Press, 1970), 246.

17. Chittenden, *Recollections*, 37–38.

18. Edward L. Widmer, *Lincoln on the Verge: Thirteen Days to Washington* (New York: Simon & Schuster, 2020), 191; and Chittenden, *Recollections*, 40–48.

19. Chittenden, *Recollections*, 46.

20. "The Wide Awake Organization," *New York Herald*, September 19, 1860; Julius G. Rathbun, "The 'Wide Awakes': The Great Political Organization of 1860," *Connecticut Quarterly* 1 (October 1895): 334; and Benjamin F. Thompson, "Wide Awakes of 1860," *Magazine of History with Notes and Queries* 10 (November 1909): 295.

21. "The Inauguration of Lincoln at Washington," *New York Herald*, January 7, 1861; "Pennsylvania," *Bellefonte (PA) Centre Democrat*, April 18, 1861; "The Feeling in the Cities," *Baltimore Sun*, April 15, 1861; letter to the editor, *Richmond (VA) Enquirer*, January 25, 1861; A. C. Richards, "Rooms of the Wide Awake Association of Washington," *Washington National Republican*, January 7, 1861; "Wide Awakes and the Inauguration of Abraham Lincoln," *Liberator*, November 16, 1860; and James Watson Webb to Abraham Lincoln, February 6, 1861, Lincoln Papers.

22. "From Virginia," *Chicago Tribune*, November 16, 1860.

23. "Proposed Visit of Republicans to Washington," *Baltimore Sun*, December 28, 1860; and John Meredith Read Sr. to Charles H. T. Collis, November 7, 1860, Read Papers.

24. Widmer, *Lincoln on the Verge*, 166.

25. Rathbun, " 'Wide Awakes,' " 335; and David Hunter to Abraham Lincoln, December 18, 1860, Lincoln Papers.

26. Abraham Lincoln to Horace Greeley, "A Letter from the President," *Washington Daily National Intelligencer*, August 22, 1862; Elias B. Holmes to Abraham Lincoln, April 20, 1861, Lincoln Papers; James Sanks Brisbin to Ezra Brisbin, November 8, 1860, Brisbin Papers, 33, 27; John David Billings, *Hardtack and Coffee; or, The Unwritten Story of Army Life* (Boston: George M. Smith, 1887), 18; and Zboray and Zboray, *Voices Without Votes*, 204.

27. "The Wide Awake Organization," *Buffalo Daily Republican*, December 12, 1860; "Proposed Visit of Republicans to Washington," *Baltimore Sun*, December 28, 1860; "The Republican Victory," *New York Times*, November 24, 1860; and Charles Francis Adams Jr., *An Autobiography* (Boston: Houghton Mifflin, 1916), 73.

28. "The President Elect en Route," *New York Tribune*, February 16, 1861; "Mr. Lincoln's Route to Washington," *Baltimore Daily Exchange*, February 11, 1861; "Lincoln's Programme of Travel," *Daily Missouri Republican* (St. Louis), February 11, 1861; CENTRAL, "Lincoln's Programme of Travel," *Daily Missouri Republican* (St. Louis), February 11, 1861; and "Lincoln's Programme of Travel," *Springfield Journal*, February 9, 1861.

29. Louis D. Rosette to Ann Rosette, February 3, 1861, Wyatt Letters.

30. John Meredith Read Jr. to John Meredith Read Sr., February 5, 1861, Read Papers; and Widmer, *Lincoln on the Verge*, 347.

31. "The Him, Mr. Link-um," *Philadelphia Inquirer*, February 26, 1861; and William Dansberry to Abraham Lincoln, November 1, 1860, Lincoln Papers.

32. Widmer, *Lincoln on the Verge*, 426–29; and "The Movements of Mr. Lincoln," *Washington Evening Star*, February 25, 1861.

33. "New Dress," *Lima (OH) Times Democrat*, March 13, 1861.

34. "Lincoln's Programme of Travel"; Chittenden, *Recollections*, 81, 21; and *Memoirs of Gustav Koerner, 1809–1896: Life-Sketches Written at the Suggestion of His Children* (Cedar Rapids, IA: Torch Press, 1909), 2:117.

35. Lewis Clephane, "Birth of the Republican Party, with a Brief History of the Important Part Taken by the Original Republican Association of the National Capitol," address delivered at the Reunion of the Surviving Members of the Republican Association of 1855 to 1861, and of the Wide-Awakes, January 26, 1889 (Washington, D.C.: Gibson Bros., 1889), 18; and "Didn't Care Which," *United Journal of Labor*, May 13, 1880, 103.

36. Clephane, "Birth," 18; "Gen. Scott," *Montgomery (AL) Weekly Advertiser and Register*, May 4, 1861; and Allan Peskin, *Winfield Scott and the Profession of Arms* (Kent, OH: Kent State University Press, 2003), 237.

37. Chittenden, *Recollection*, 84–86; "The Inauguration of Abraham Lincoln," *Washington Evening Star*, March 4, 1861; and "Inauguration Day at Washington," *Daily Missouri Republican* (St. Louis), March 5, 1861.

38. "Inauguration of Abraham Lincoln"; "Washington Thronged," *New York Times*, March 4, 1861; and "Wide-Awakes About," *Cleveland Daily Leader*, March 7, 1861.

39. Rathbun, " 'Wide Awakes,' " 334.

40. Dwight Wilder, *The Life and Letters of Dwight Wilder* (Boston: Ticknor, 1868), 33.

41. Abraham Lincoln, "First Inaugural Address, Final Version," March 1861, Lincoln Papers.

42. "Wide-Awakes About."

43. Caroline Seabury, April 16, 1860, in *The Diary of Caroline Seabury, 1854–1863*, ed. Suzanne L. Bunkers (Madison: University of Wisconsin Press, 1991), 60.

44. "Inaugural Ball in Washington," *New York Herald*, March 6, 1861.

45. Jonathan W. White, ed., *To Address You as My Friend: African American Letters to Lincoln* (Chapel Hill: University of North Carolina Press, 2022), 2.

46. "Pen," *Indiana State Sentinel* (Indianapolis), March 13, 1861.

47. James Peckham, *Gen. Nathaniel Lyon, and Missouri in 1861: A Monograph of the Great Rebellion* (New York: American News, 1866), 33, 37, 79; Louis Gerteis, *Civil War St. Louis* (Lawrence: University Press of Kansas, 2001), 80; and Albert Tracy, "The Journal of Captain Albert Tracy, 1861," ed. Ray W. Irwin, entry for May 2, 1861, *Missouri Historical Review* 51, no. 1 (October 1956): 20.

48. "From Virginia," *Chicago Tribune*, November 16, 1860.

49. Gerteis, *Civil War St. Louis*, 46, 82, 87.

50. Galusha Anderson, *Reminiscences of St. Louis During the Civil War* (Boston: Little, Brown, 1908), 23; Peckham, *Gen. Lyon*, 28–29; Basil Duke, *The Reminiscences of General Basil W. Duke, C.S.A.* (Garden City, NY: Doubleday, Page, 1911), 38; and Gerteis, *Civil War St. Louis*, 79.

51. Gerteis, *Civil War St. Louis*, 79.

52. "Snubbed," *Daily Missouri Republican* (St. Louis), March 22, 1861; Peckham, *Gen. Lyon*, 33, 31.

53. "Perpetual Motion," *Daily Missouri Republican* (St. Louis), March 20, 1861; Peckham, *Gen. Lyon*, 31, 34–36; and Anderson, *Reminiscences*, 19–23.

54. Duke, *Reminiscences*, 35.

55. Peckham, *Gen. Lyon*, 36, 31–32.

56. Peckham, 36–37; Gerteis, *Civil War St. Louis*, 80; and Anderson, *Reminiscences*, 21.

57. Anderson, *Reminiscences*, 66; and Peckham, *Gen. Lyon*, 60, 140, 144, 61.

58. "The Republican Military Organization," *Daily Missouri Republican* (St. Louis), February 10, 1861; and Peckham, *Gen. Lyon*, 75–76.

59. Thomas C. Johnson, "Letter from Hon. T. C. Johnson," *Daily Missouri Republican* (St. Louis), January 19, 1861; Peckham, *Gen. Lyon*, 96; and Gerteis, *Civil War St. Louis*, 92.

60. Duke, *Reminiscences*, 39.

61. Duke, 39–40.

62. Duke, 39–42.

63. Anderson, *Reminiscences*, 20–21.

64. *Frederick Douglass: Selected Speeches and Writings*, ed. Philip Foner and Yuval Taylor, Library of Black America (Chicago: Lawrence Hill Books, 1999), 407; and John Meredith Read Jr. to John Meredith Read Sr., October 22, 1860, and September 9, 1860, Read Papers.

65. "Honest Abe Lincoln and the Spoils," *New York Herald*, March 25, 1861; "To the Office Hunters of North Carolina," *Raleigh (NC) Semi-Weekly State Journal*, April 10, 1861; and "Infernal Teachings," *Cleveland Daily Leader*, March 29, 1861, quoting from *Richmond (VA) Examiner*.

66. "Old Abe Under the Weather," *New York Herald*, April 3, 1861.

67. Donald Stoker, *The Grand Design: Strategy and the U.S. Civil War* (New York: Oxford University Press, 2010), 32.

68. Goodheart, *1861*, 184.

69. *Memoirs of Koerner*, 2:119; "Effects of the News," *New York Herald*, April 13, 1861.

70. LEO, "Correspondent from Washington," *Charleston (SC) Daily Courier*, May 8, 1861.

CHAPTER TWELVE: "I WOULD RATHER BE A SOLDIER
THAN A WIDE AWAKE"

1. "Where Are the Wide-Awakes?" *Boston Courier*, April 4, 1861.

2. "Where Are the Wide-Awakes?" *Boston Courier*; "Where Are the Wide-Awakes?" *Bedford (PA) Gazette*, April 26, 1861; and "Where Are the Wide-Awakes?" *Detroit Free Press*, April 7, 1861.

3. "Where Are the Wide-Awakes?" *Boston Courier*.

4. John David Billings, *Hardtack and Coffee; or, The Unwritten Story of Army Life* (Boston: George M. Smith, 1887), 20.

5. "Where Are the Wide-Awakes?" *Detroit Free Press*.

6. George Kimball, *A Corporal's Story: Civil War Recollections of the Twelfth Massachusetts*, ed. Alan D. Gaff and Donald H. Gaff (Normal: University of Oklahoma Press, 2014), 6–7.

7. James McPherson, *The Negro's Civil War: How American Blacks Felt and Acted During the War for the Union* (New York: Knopf Doubleday, 2008), 16; and Donald Yacovone, ed., *A Voice of Thunder: A Black Soldier's Civil War* (Champaign-Urbana: University of Illinois Press, 1998), 14.

8. Kimball, *Corporal's Story*, 8; and Carl Schurz, *The Reminiscences of Carl Schurz* (New York: McClure, 1907), 2:224.

9. Carl Schurz to Margarethe Schurz, April 17, 1861, in *The Intimate Letters of Carl Schurz*, ed. Joseph Schafer (New York: Da Capo Press, 1970), 253.

10. Schurz to Schurz, April 17, 1861; and Schurz, *Reminiscences*, 2:224.

11. W. A. Howard, "Alleged Hostile Organization Against the Government Within the District of Columbia," February 14, 1861, House of Representatives, 36th Cong., 2nd sess., rept. No. 79, 39; and Allan Peskin, *Winfield Scott and the Profession of Arms* (Kent, OH: Kent State University Press, 2003), 246.

12. John Lockwood and Charles Lockwood, *The Siege of Washington: The Untold Story of the Twelve Days That Shook the Union* (New York: Oxford University Press, 2011), 95.

13. LeeAnna Keith, *When It Was Grand : The Radical Republican History of the Civil War* (New York: Hill and Wang, 2020), 134; and Cassius Marcellus Clay, *The Life of Cassius Marcellus Clay: Memoirs, Writings, and Speeches* (Cincinnati: J. Fletcher Brennan, 1886), 1:259.

14. Clay, *Memoirs*, 259; David L. Smiley, *Lion of White Hall: The Life of Cassius M. Clay* (Madison: University of Wisconsin Press, 1962), 176; letter to the editor, *Appleton (WI) Motor*, April 25, 1861; "Notable Visitors: Cassius M. Clay," in Mr. Lincoln's White House, http://www.mrlincolnswhitehouse.org/residents -visitors/notable-visitors/notable-visitors-cassius-m-clay–1810–1903/; and William Henry Egle, *Life and Times of Andrew Gregg Curtin* (Philadelphia: Thompson, 1896), 479.

15. "The Cassius Clay Battalion," *New York Times*, April 27, 1861; and "Cassius M. Clay Battalion," *Washington National Republican*, April 29, 1861.

16. Julius G. Rathbun, "The 'Wide Awakes': The Great Political Organization of 1860," *Connecticut Quarterly* 1 (October 1895): 335; "Cassius Clay Brigade," *Appleton (WI) Motor*, April 25, 1861; "Cassius Clay Battalion"; and "Cassius M. Clay Battalion."

17. Lewis Clephane, "Birth of the Republican Party, with a Brief History of the Important Part Taken by the Original Republican Association of the National

Capitol," address delivered at the Reunion of the Surviving Members of the Republican Association of 1855 to 1861, and of the Wide-Awakes, January 26, 1889 (Washington, D.C.: Gibson Bros., 1889).

18. Jacob Frey, *Reminiscences of Baltimore* (Baltimore: Maryland Book Concern, 1893); "City Intelligence," *Baltimore Daily Exchange*, April 20, 1861; Howard, "Alleged Hostile Organization," 17–19; and "Meeting of the National Volunteers," *Baltimore Daily Exchange*, April 17, 1861.

19. Harry A. Ezratty, *Baltimore in the Civil War: The Pratt Street Riot and a City Occupied* (Charleston, SC: History Press, 2010), 40, 53.

20. Frey, *Reminiscences*, 119; and Ezratty, *Baltimore*, 56.

21. Ezratty, *Baltimore*, 60.

22. Ezratty, 61–62; and Frank Towers, *The Urban South and the Coming of the Civil War* (Charlottesville: University of Virginia Press, 2004), 170.

23. Towers, *Urban South*, 169–70.

24. Towers, 169–77.

25. "Fearful Riot in Baltimore," *Cumberland (MD) Civilian and Telegraph*, April 25, 1861.

26. Towers, *Urban South*, 166.

27. Kimball, *Corporal's Story*, 13.

28. Edward Conrad Smith, *The Borderland in the Civil War* (New York: Macmillan, 1927), 184.

29. Wide Awake, letter to the editor, *Fall River (MA) Daily Evening News*, April 16, 1861.

30. "Where Are the Wide-Awakes," *Berkshire County (MA) Eagle*, April 18, 1861; the best work on the process by which northeastern college students joined the Union Army is Kanisorn Wongrichanalai, *Northern Character: College-Educated New Englanders, Honor, Nationalism, and Leadership in the Civil War Era* (New York: Fordham University Press, 2016).

31. "Captain Henry B. Read," *The Biographical Record of Livingston County, Illinois* (Chicago: S. J. Clark, 1900), 52; Alfred E. Lee, *History of the City of Columbus, Capital of Ohio* (New York: Munnell, 1892), 2:169; Eric R. Faust, *The 11th Michigan Volunteer Infantry in the Civil War* (Jefferson, NC: McFarland, 2016), 7; and Charles M. Clark, *The History of the Thirty-Ninth Regiment, Illinois Volunteer Veteran Infantry* (Chicago: Veterans Association of the 39th Regiment, 1889), 527.

32. Adam I. P. Smith, *The American Civil War* (New York: Palgrave Macmillan, 2007), 131.

33. Rathbun, " 'Wide Awakes,' " 335; and Paul E. Teed, *Joseph and Harriet Hawley's Civil War: Partnership, Ambition, and Sacrifice* (Lanham, MD: Lexington Books, 2018), 66.

34. Officers list drawn from "The Glorious Wide Awakes!" *Hartford Courant*, June 2, 1860, cross-referenced with military service records in Ancestry.com's Library Edition.

35. First Lieutenant James L. Francis, 1st Connecticut Heavy Artillery Regiment and of Co. C, 12th Connecticut Infantry Regiment in Uniform, Photograph and Summary, Liljenquist Family Collection, Library of Congress, Washington, D.C.; and "War Feeling in Hartford!" *Hartford Courant*, April 20, 1861.

36. Edgar S. Yergason to Charlotte Yergason, April 18, 1861, and Edgar S. Yergason Diary, 1861, both in Yergason Papers.

37. A. M. Duncklee, *Memorial to George P. Holt* (Milford, NH: Milford H. & G. Society, 1916), 3, Milford Historical Society, Milford, NH; and Louis D. Rosette to John G. Nicolay, April 13, 1861, Lincoln Papers.

38. James Sank Brisbin, "Personal Record of James Sanks Brisbin: Colonel 1st Cavalry, Brevet Brigadier General, U.S. Army," Brisbin Papers.

39. John Meredith Read Jr. to John Meredith Read Sr., December 24, 1860, Read Papers.

40. Delphine Pumpelly Read to John Meredith Read Sr., July 10, 1861, and July 18, 1861, Read Papers; and Philip M. Katz, "Our Man in Paris: John Meredith Read Jr. and the Discontents of American Republicanism, 1860–1896," in *The Struggle for Equality: Essays on Sectional Conflict, the Civil War, and the Long Reconstruction*, ed. Jennifer L. Weber, Jerald Podair, and Orville Vernon Burton (Charlottesville: University of Virginia Press, 2011), 44.

41. Gordon C. Rhea, *The Battles of Spotsylvania Court House and the Road to Yellow Tavern, May 7–12, 1864* (Baton Rouge: Louisiana State University Press, 1997), 239–42.

42. McPherson, *Negro's Civil War*, 18.

43. McPherson, 22.

44. "Meeting of Colored Citizens," *Liberator*, May 3, 1861.

45. Brent Tarter, "Mark R. DeMortie, 1829–1914," in *Dictionary of Virginia Biography* (Richmond: Library of Virginia, 1998–), http://www.lva.virginia.gov/public/dvb/bio.asp?b=DeMortie_Mark_R; William Henry Ferris, *The African Abroad: or, His Evolution in West Civilization* (New Haven, CT: Tuttle, Morehouse & Taylor Press, 1913), 2:710; and Mark DeMortie, "Some of the Incidents

in the Life of Mark DeMortie," ed. G. V. Tomashevich, *Afro-Americans in New York Life and History* 3, no. 1 (1979): 61–71.

46. Tarter, "DeMortie"; Ferris, *African Abroad*, 2:710; DeMortie, "Incidents," 61–71; and Margot Minardi, *Making Slavery History: Abolitionism and the Politics of Memory in Massachusetts* (New York: Oxford University Press, 2012).

47. Yacovone, *Voice of Thunder*; Henry Daniels, Portland, photograph by H. H. Wilder, 1861, Collections of the Maine Historical Society, Portland, https://www.mainememory.net/record/98698; and William F. Cheek, *John Mercer Langston and the Struggle for Black Freedom, 1829–1865* (Champaign-Urbana: University of Illinois Press, 1996).

48. "The Coming Election," *Bedford (PA) Gazette*, May 31, 1861.

49. Dolphus Damuth to Maria Damuth, January 4, 1862, Dolphus Damuth Letters, Gilder Lehrman Collections, New York.

50. Dolphus Damuth to John Damuth, March 17, 1863, in Robert E. Bonner, *The Soldier's Pen: Firsthand Impressions of the Civil War* (New York: Hill and Wang, 2006), 127.

51. "Two Years Ago: By a Drafted Wide Awake," American Song Sheets Rare Books and Special Collections, Library of Congress, Washington, D.C.

52. The "wedge" mentioned is a reference to the railsplitter's wedge, part of the wood-chopping tools often associated with Abraham Lincoln. "Two Years Ago."

53. George E. Jepson, *The Thirteenth Massachusetts Regiment: Our Fiftieth Anniversary* (Boston, 1911), 22; "Ho! Wide Awakes! Ho!" *Bellefonte (PA) Centre Democrat*, January 1, 1861; and Benjamin F. Thompson, "The Wide Awakes of 1860," *Magazine of History with Notes and Queries* 10 (November 1909): 295.

54. "A Good Idea," *Buffalo Commercial Advertiser*, May 3, 1861; "Wide Awake Capes," *Clearfield (PA) Republican*, April 17, 1861; Thompson, "Wide Awakes of 1860"; "Wide Awake Capes," *Daily Ohio Statesman* (Columbus), May 9, 1861; "A Good Suggestion," May 13, 1861; and "Wide Awake Capes," *Bucyrus (OH) Journal*, May 10, 1861.

55. "Give the Boys Your Wide Awake Capes," *Daily Milwaukee News*, May 21, 1861; and "Anythings," *North Iowa Times* (McGregor), May 24, 1861.

56. John Boultwood Edson to Edna Wright, May 19, 1861, and John Boultwood Edson to Elijah Edson, May 24, 1861, both in "Shared & Spared: Real History from the Pen of Those Who Lived It," https://sparedshared23.com/2022/08/16/1861–63-john-b-edson-to-his-parents/; and Geo. W. Benedict, "Letter from the Junior," *Carbondale (PA) Advance*, September 20, 1862.

57. Frederick C. Gaede, "Ponchos and Waterproof Blankets During the Civil War," March 2, 2022, https://www.militaryimagesmagazine-digital.com/2022/03/02/ponchos-and-waterproof-blankets-during-the-civil-war/.

58. "Young Muscatine," letter to the editor, *Muscatine (IA) Evening Journal*, July 30, 1860; and James M. McPherson, *For Cause and Comrades: Why Men Fought in the Civil War* (New York: Oxford University Press, 1997), 146.

59. William Earl Parrish, *Frank Blair: Lincoln's Conservative* (Columbia: University of Missouri Press, 1998), 97.

60. Louis Gerteis, *Civil War St. Louis* (Lawrence: University Press of Kansas, 2001), 93.

61. Galusha Anderson, *Reminiscences of St. Louis During the Civil War* (Boston: Little, Brown, 1908), 105.

62. "Speeches of F. P. Blair," *New York Times*, October 5, 1860.

63. Gerteis, *Civil War St. Louis*, 93, 96; "A Military Election," *Daily Missouri Republican* (St. Louis), February 14, 1861; and Adam Goodheart, *1861: The Civil War Awakening* (New York: Alfred A. Knopf, 2011), 257.

64. Anderson, *Reminiscences*, 83.

65. Anderson, 94.

66. Gerteis, *Civil War St. Louis*, 112; and James Peckham, *Gen. Nathaniel Lyon, and Missouri in 1861: A Monograph of the Great Rebellion* (New York: American News, 1866), 143.

67. Peckham, *Gen. Lyon*, 137.

68. *Memoirs of Gustav Koerner, 1809–1896: Life-Sketches Written at the Suggestion of His Children* (Cedar Rapids, IA: Torch Press, 1909), 2:144; and Gerteis, *Civil War St. Louis*, 100.

69. Gerteis, *Civil War St. Louis*, 106.

70. Goodheart, *1861*, 261.

71. Gerteis, *Civil War St. Louis*, 104.

72. Gerteis, 107; Goodheart, *1861*, 262; and Anderson, *Reminiscences*, 96–97.

73. Anderson, *Reminiscences*, 97.

74. Gerteis, *Civil War St. Louis*, 108; and Peckham, *Gen. Lyon*, 154.

75. *The Personal Memoirs of Ulysses S. Grant* (New York: Charles L. Webster, 1885), 1:121; Peckham, *Gen. Lyon*, 155; "Captain Lyon," *Mattoon (IL) Gazette*, May 24, 1861; and *Memoirs of Koerner*, 2:1.

76. Louis D. Rosette to Brother (?), May 22, 1861, Wyatt Letters; Goodheart, *1861*, 263

77. "Col. Blair and Capt. Lyon," *Washington National Republican*, May 14, 1861.

CODA: "POWER MUST FOLLOW"

1. Julius G. Rathbun, "Original Hartford Wide Awakes, General Orders No. 1," February 26, 1889, Wide Awakes Records; "National Capital," *Hartford Courant*, March 4, 1889; and Kevin Murphy, *Crowbar Governor: The Life and Times of Morgan Gardner Bulkeley* (Middletown, CT: Wesleyan University Press, 2011), 113–14.

2. Wide-Awake Reunion, 1860–1890, menu and program, Rockville, CT, October 20, 1890, Wide Awakes Records; "Many Bequests to Hartford in Will of H. P. Hitchcock," *Hartford Courant*, December 5, 1917; "Hartford Republican Marching Clubs of Other Days," *Hartford Courant*, November 5, 1916; and " 'Wide Awakes' Were Organized Early Here," January 25, 1908, *Hartford Evening Post*.

3. Keith MacKay, "The White House Interiors of Caroline Harrison and Edgar Yergason, 1890–1892" (master's thesis, Corcoran College of Art and Design, 2009); and "Seen and Heard in the Cafes," *New-Yorker* 1, no. 9 (May 1, 1901).

4. Edgar S. Yergason, letter to the editor, *Hartford Courant*, January 30, 1909, Wide Awakes Records, "Edgar S. Yergason's Collection of Relics," *Hartford Courant*, February 27, 1916; Don Troiani, *Don Troiani's Civil War Infantry* (Mechanicsburg, PA: Stackpole Books, 2002), 14, 27, 49, 67; and Paul Zielbauer, "Found in Clutter, a Relic of Lincoln's Death," *New York Times*, July 5, 2001.

5. Lewis Clephane, "Birth of the Republican Party, with a Brief History of the Important Part Taken by the Original Republican Association of the National Capitol," address delivered at the Reunion of the Surviving Members of the Republican Association of 1855 to 1861, and of the Wide-Awakes, January 26, 1889 (Washington, D.C.: Gibson Bros., 1889), 8; Leo Sands, "The History of the GOP," *Washington Post*, November 9, 2022; Richard Franklin Bensel, *Yankee Leviathan: The Origins of Central State Authority, 1859–1877* (Cambridge: University of Cambridge Press, 1990); and Richard Franklin Bensel, *The Political Economy of American Industrialization, 1877–1900* (Cambridge: University of Cambridge Press, 2000), 49–52.

6. Ulysses S. Grant, *The Personal Memoirs of Ulysses S. Grant* (New York: Charles L. Webster, 1885), 1:79; "Thursday Evening Wide Awake Rally," *Delaware (OH) Gazette*, June 16, 1860; Julius G. Rathbun, "The 'Wide Awakes': The Great Political Organization of 1860," *Connecticut Quarterly* 1 (October 1895): 335; " 'Wide Awakes' Organized Early Here"; Philip M. Katz, "Our Man in Paris: John Meredith Read Jr. and the Discontents of American Republicanism,

1860–1896," in *The Struggle for Equality: Essays on Sectional Conflict, the Civil War, and the Long Reconstruction*, ed. Jennifer L. Weber, Jerald Podair, and Orville Vernon Burton (Charlottesville: University of Virginia Press, 2011), 41–51; and James Sanks Brisbin, *The Beef Bonanza: or, How to Get Rich on the Plains; Being a Description of Cattle-Growing, Sheep-Farming, Horse-Raising, and Dairying in the West* (Philadelphia: J. B. Lippincott, 1881).

7. Jon Grinspan, *The Age of Acrimony: How Americans Fought to Fix Their Politics, 1865–1915* (New York: Bloomsbury, 2021), 9–33; and Heather Cox Richardson, *West from Appomattox: The Reconstruction of America After the Civil War* (New Haven, CT: Yale University Press, 2007), 5, 66.

8. Carrie Chapman Catt to Susan B. Anthony, September 1890, in *The Life and Work of Susan B. Anthony: Including Public Addresses, Her Own Letters and Many from Her Contemporaries During Fifty Years*, ed. Ida Husted Harper (Indianapolis: Hollenbeck, 1899), 2:693.

9. Barbara Gannon, *The Won Cause: Black and White Comradeship in the Grand Army of the Republic* (Chapel Hill: University of North Carolina Press, 2011); Dora L. Costa, "Appendix A: Union Army Pensions and Civil War Records Chapter," in *The Evolution of Retirement: An American Economic History, 1880–1990* (Chicago: University of Chicago Press, 1998), 197–212; Christopher Joseph Cook, " 'As Bad as Anybody Else': The Innocents, Political Violence, and the Creole-Italian Alliance in Reconstruction New Orleans," *Journal of American Ethnic History* 40, no. 3 (Spring 2021): 70–99; and J. R. Chalmers, "Speech Against President Hayes," June 13, 1878, *Presidents from Hayes through McKinley, 1877–1901: Debating the Issues in Pro and Con Primary Documents*, ed. Amy H. Sturgis (New York: Bloomsbury, 2003), 23.

10. Stefan Lund, " 'Cowardly and Incendiary Partisans': Soldier Mobs, Loyalty, and the Democratic Press in the Civil War" (master's thesis, Corcoran Department of History, University of Virginia, May 2019); and Peter Bratt, "A Great Revolution in Feeling: The American Civil War in Niles and Grand Rapids, Michigan," *Michigan Historical Review* 31, no. 2 (Fall 2005): 43–66.

11. James McCabe, *The History of the Great Riots: Being a Full and Authentic Account of the Strikes and Riots on the Various Railroads of the United States and in the Mining Regions* (Philadelphia: Philadelphia National, 1877).

12. Katz, "Our Man in Paris," 47–51.

13. Lewis Hayden, *Masonry Among Colored Men in Massachusetts* (Boston: Prince Hall Grand Lodge, 1871); and Luis-Alejandro Dinnella-Borrego, *The Risen Phoenix: Black Politics in the Post-Civil War South* (Charlottesville: University of Virginia Press, 2016).

14. George Kimball, *A Corporal's Story: Civil War Recollections of the Twelfth Massachusetts*, ed. Alan D. Gaff and Donald H. Gaff (Normal: University of Oklahoma Press, 2014), 3; and Evan Thomas, *The War Lovers: Roosevelt, Lodge, Hearst, and the Rush to Empire, 1898* (New York: Little, Brown, 2010).

15. "Seward," *New York Herald*, September 4, 1860.

16. Jeffrey Rosen, *Louis Brandeis: American Prophet* (New Haven, CT: Yale University Press, 2016), 71; and " 'Wide Awakes' Organized Early Here."

17. William H. Frey, "Census 2020: First Results Show Historically Low Population Growth and a First-Ever Congressional Seat Loss for California," *Brookings Institution Report*, April 26, 2021, https://www.brookings.edu/articles/census-2020-data-release/#4; and William Tecumseh Sherman to Ellen Boyle Ewing, July 10, 1860, in *Home Letters of General Sherman*, ed. M. A. DeWolfe Howe (New York: Charles Scribner's Sons, 1909), 179.

18. Grant Barrett, ed., *Oxford Dictionary of American Political Slang* (New York: Oxford University Press, 2004).

19. Brian Naylor, "Read Trump's Jan. 6 Speech, a Key Part of Impeachment Trial," *NPR.com*, February 10, 2021, https://www.npr.org/2021/02/10/966396848/read-trumps-jan-6-speech-a-key-part-of-impeachment-trial.

20. " 'Wide Awakes' Organized Early Here."

INDEX

A NOTE ON THE AUTHOR

JON GRINSPAN is a curator of political history at the Smithsonian's National Museum of American History. He is the author of two other books, *The Age of Acrimony* and *The Virgin Vote*, frequently contributes to the *New York Times*, and has been featured in the *New Yorker* and the *Washington Post* and on *CBS Sunday Morning*. At the Smithsonian, he collects objects from historic and contemporary politics—attending elections, conventions, and protests—to help tell the material story of our democracy to present and future Americans. He lives in Washington, D.C.